A

Maths Links

Ray Allan
Derek Huby
Martin Williams

7

OXFORD

OXFORD
UNIVERSITY PRESS

Great Clarendon Street, Oxford OX2 6DP

Oxford University Press is a department of the University of Oxford.
It furthers the University's objective of excellence in research, scholarship, and education by publishing worldwide in

Oxford New York

Auckland Cape Town Dar es Salaam Hong Kong Karachi
Kuala Lumpur Madrid Melbourne Mexico City Nairobi
New Delhi Shanghai Taipei Toronto

With offices in

Argentina Austria Brazil Chile Czech Republic France Greece
Guatemala Hungary Italy Japan Poland Portugal Singapore
South Korea Switzerland Thailand Turkey Ukraine Vietnam

First published 2007

British Library Cataloguing in Publication Data

Data available

ISBN-13: 9780-19-915279-7
10 9 8 7 6 5 4 3 2 1

Printed in Spain by Cayfosa

Paper used in the production of this book is a natural, recyclable product made from wood grown in sustainable forests. The manufacturing process conforms to the environmental regulations to the country of origin.

Acknowledgments
The editors would like to thank: Stefanie Sullivan, Nottingham Shell Centre, for her advice with the Case Studies; Mike Heylings and Jennie Golding for their excellent reviews of this book; and Dave Capewell and Clare Plass for their contributions to the material.

p 1 Alamy; **p 7** Gerald Kooyman/Corbis UK Ltd.; **p 21** Nik Wheeler/Corbis UK Ltd.; **p 37** Graeme Purdy/iStockphoto; **p 43** iStockphoto; **p 57** Nic Hamilton/Alamy; **p 73** Bettman/Corbis UK Ltd.; **p 81** Imagebroker/Alamy; **p 95** Tammy Peluso/iStockphoto; **p 103** Alassaad/Reuters/Corbis UK Ltd.; **p 105** OUP; **p 113** iStockphoto; **p 115** Mint Photography/Alamy; **p 116** Andy Lyons/Getty Images; **p 121** Maciej Czajka/Alamy; **p 137** Stephen Rees/iStockphoto; **p 143** Rothermel/Associates/PA photos; **p 167** The Beacon Studio; **p 170** OUP; **p 175**[2] OUP; **p 179** Corbis UK Ltd.; **p 181** David Levenson/Alamy; **p 193 t & c** OUP; **p 205** Dainis Derics/iStockphoto; **p 209** Paul Ellis/AFP/Getty Images; **p 217**[2] Smith/Lonely/Getty Images; **p 219** Jon Arnold Images/Alamy; **p 225** The Print Collector/Alamy; **p 247** Ian Waldie/Getty Images; **p 265** OUP; **p 275** imagespace/Alamy; **p 277** Sandro Vannini/Corbis UK Ltd.

Figurative artworks are by:
Paul Daviz and Peter Donnelly

Contents

First page of a chapter
The first page of each chapter shows you real-life maths in context and also includes levelled Check in questions.

Lesson^2
A 'squared' lesson exists outside of the running page order and either consolidates or extends a topic.

Consolidation
The Consolidation pages offer additional practice for each lesson in the chapter.

Summary
The Summary page for each chapter contains Key Indicators, a levelled worked exam-style question and levelled past KS3 exam questions.

Case Study
The Case Studies bring maths alive through engaging real-life situations and innovative design.

1 Number

Integers and decimals

The idea of zero as a number didn't always exist. Indian mathematicians in the 9th Century were the first to use zero as a place holder. From India this idea travelled to Arabic and Chinese mathematicians, finally reaching Europe in the 13th Century.

What's the point? Mathematics is a universal language which travels around the world.

Check in

Level 2

1 Write these numbers in order from smallest to largest.
a 6, 8, 4, 7, 5 **b** 12, 10, 14, 13, 11

2 What numbers are the arrows pointing to on this number line?

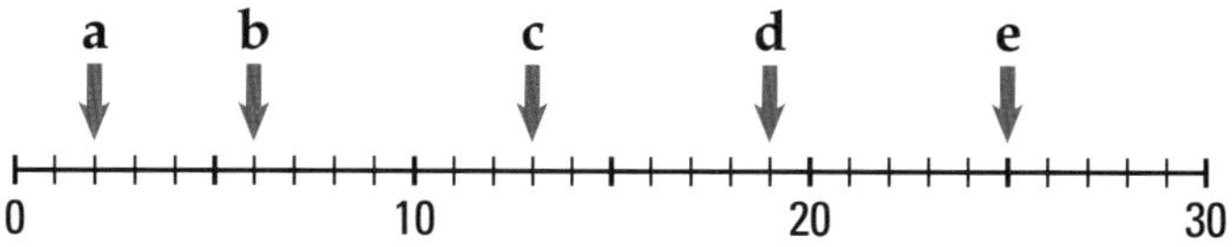

3 Copy and complete these sums without using a calculator.
a 7 + 3 = □ **b** 5 + 9 = □ **c** 8 + □ = 12 **d** □ + 6 = 10

Level 3

4 Here is a plan of an underground car park.
Each 'level' is given a number.
What level is marked by the letter '**a**'?

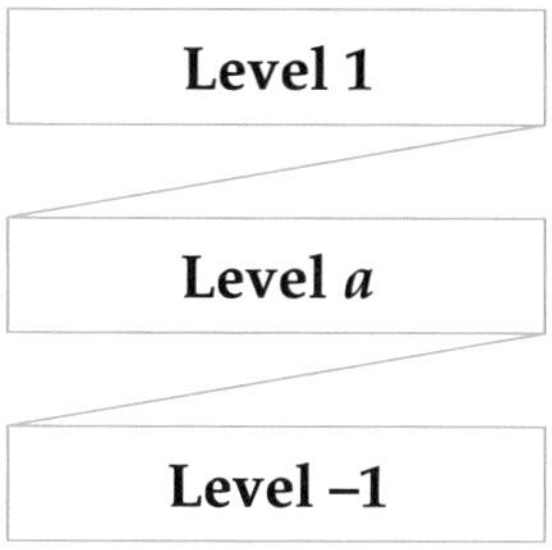

- Put numbers up to 1000 in order
- Use the symbols > and <

Keywords
Greater
Less
Order
Sorting

p. 216[2]

Rory is **sorting** these numbered cards.

10 9 11 8

He is putting the cards into **order**. He starts with the smallest number.

8	9	10	11
smallest	greater than 8	greater than 9	greater than 10

- > means **greater than.** 11 is greater than 10.
  In symbols, 11 > 10

Rory is **sorting** these numbered cards as well.

15 9 23 4

He is putting these cards into order starting with the largest number.

23	15	9	4
largest	less than 23	less than 15	less than 9

- < means **less than.** 15 is less than 23.
  In symbols, 15 < 23

example

You want to photograph this family.

Sort the family in order by height

a starting with the shortest

b starting with the tallest.

135 cm   148 cm   158 cm   172 cm   183 cm   155 cm

a 135 cm is the shortest height, so start with 135.
135   148   155   158   172   183

b 183 cm is the tallest height, so start with 183.
183   172   158   155   148   135

Exercise 1a

1 Use the **greater than** (>) and **less than** (<) symbols to complete these.

a 9 □ 5 **b** 8 □ 14 **c** 16 □ 25

d 38 □ 83 **e** 101 □ 98 **f** 210 □ 187

2 Use the three numbers in the right order to complete each sentence.

a | 9 2 5 | ____ is greater than ____ but less than ____.

b | 28 31 16 | ____ is greater than ____ but less than ____.

c | 103 86 102 | ____ is greater than ____ but less than ____.

Did you know?

It would take at least 11 days and nights to count from one to one million non-stop!

3 Write these numbers in order.
Start with the smallest number.

a 7 , 5 , 8 , 4 , 6 **b** 9 , 12 , 10 , 8 , 11

c 34 , 31 , 33 , 32 , 35 **d** 22 , 19 , 20 , 18 , 21

e 91 , 90 , 88 , 92 , 89 **f** 101 , 99 , 98 , 102 , 100

g 237 , 235 , 234 , 238 , 236 **h** 998, 1000, 996, 999, 997

i Now write out these numbers starting with the largest number.

4 Jim the postman **sorts** letters by house number before he delivers them.
Write these numbers out in order, starting with the **smallest**.

56 24 18 46 8 12 62 10

5 Jim the postman sorts these parcels by weight.
Write the weights out in order, starting with the largest.

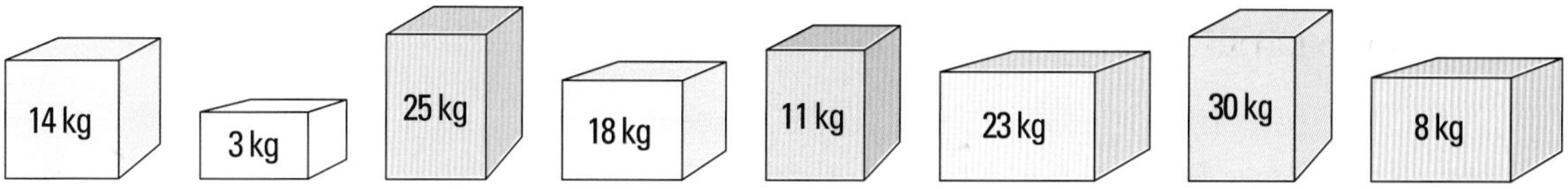

puzzle

The height of each student is written onto a card.
The cards are dropped and mixed up.

| 152 cm | 180 cm | 161 cm | 150 cm | 170 cm |

Clues: Raj is the tallest.
Kelly is 10 cm shorter than Raj.
Nita is the shortest.
James is taller than Ian.

a Use the clues to work out each student's height.

b Write out the name and height of each student in order, starting with the shortest.

1b Place value

- Know what the digits of a whole number stand for
- Know the value of each digit in a whole number

Keywords
Digit *Tens*
Hundreds *Thousands*
Place value *Units*

The number **235** can be broken up into

2 3 5

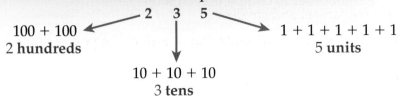

- 2 → 100 + 100, 2 **hundreds**
- 3 → 10 + 10 + 10, 3 **tens**
- 5 → 1 + 1 + 1 + 1 + 1, 5 **units**

235 is made up of:

$2 \times 100 = 200$
$3 \times 10 = 30$
$5 \times 1 = 5$
235

The number **2435** can be broken up into

2 4 3 5

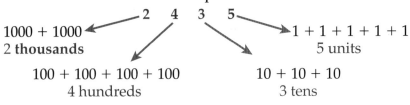

- 2 → 1000 + 1000, 2 **thousands**
- 4 → 100 + 100 + 100 + 100, 4 hundreds
- 3 → 10 + 10 + 10, 3 tens
- 5 → 1 + 1 + 1 + 1 + 1, 5 units

2435 is made up of:

$2 \times 1000 = 2000$
$4 \times 100 = 400$
$3 \times 10 = 30$
$5 \times 1 = 5$
2435

p. 108

- The place of each digit in a number is called **place value**.
  If you move the digit to a different place you change its value.

If you write the **digits** 2, 4, 3 and 5 in a different order, you get different values.

Notice how the **digit** 2 changes its value.

	Thousands 1000s	Hundreds 100s	Tens 10s	Units 1s
Five thousand four hundred and thirty **two** →	5	4	3	2
Four thousand three hundred and **twenty** five →	4	3	2	5
Three thousand **two hundred** and fifty four →	3	2	5	4
Two thousand five hundred and forty three →	2	5	4	3

example

What does the digit 8 stand for in each of these numbers?

a 148 **b** 8305 **c** 80

a 8 units
b 8 thousand
c 8 tens or eighty

Thousands	Hundreds	Tens	Units
	1	4	8
8	3	0	5
		8	0

Exercise 1b

1 Three digits are drawn onto cards.
Using all three cards make

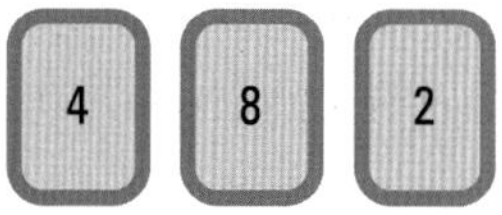

a the smallest number you can
b the largest number you can
c a number that is between the largest and smallest.

2 Split these numbers into **hundreds, tens**, and **units**. Part **a** is done for you.

a 347

3 → 100 + 100 + 100
4 → 10 + 10 + 10 + 10
7 → 1 + 1 + 1 + 1 + 1 + 1 + 1

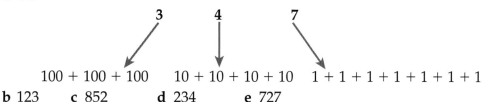

b 123 **c** 852 **d** 234 **e** 727

3 Split these numbers into **thousands**, **hundreds**, **tens**, and **units**.

a 2324

2 → 1000 + 1000
3 → 100 + 100 + 100
2 → 10 + 10
4 → 1 + 1 + 1 + 1

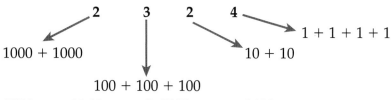

b 1354 **c** 3246 **d** 2515 **e** 2408

4 What does the red digit stand for in each number?

a 164 **b** 4927 **c** 3587
d 605 **e** 5288 **f** 1110

5 Here are the targets from a paint balling competition.

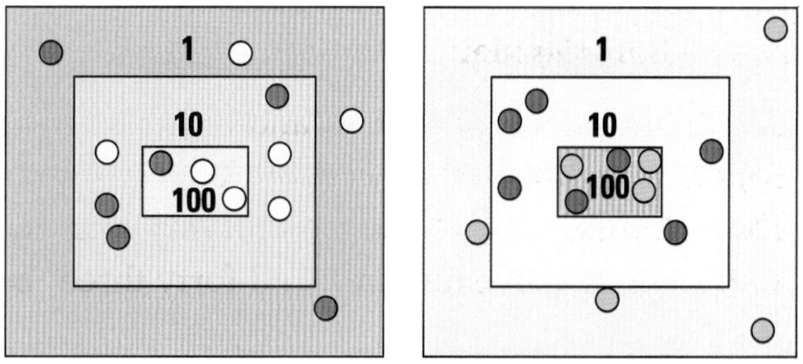

a What score did the red team get?
b What score did the yellow team get?
c What score did the blue team get?
d What score did the green team get?
e Kirsty had six shots. She says:
'I scored a ten, then a hundred, a one, another hundred, and a ten.'
What was Kirsty's total score?
f How many of Kirsty's shots missed the target?

challenge

Using all three digits see how many different numbers you can make.
Write out the numbers you make in order, smallest to largest.

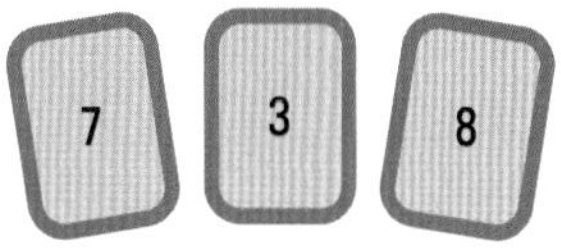

1b² Place value and decimals

- Know the meaning of a decimal point
- Know the sizes of simple decimal numbers

Keywords
Decimal
Digit
Hundredth
Place value
Tenth
Units

The arrow is pointing to a position between 2 and 3.

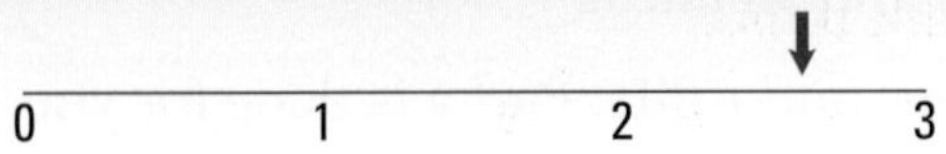

The space between 2 and 3 is divided into 10 equal parts.

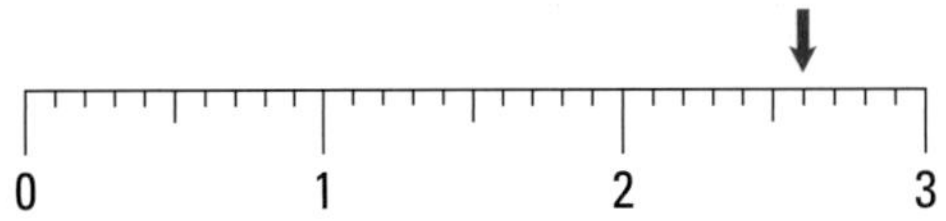

Each part is one **tenth**.
The arrow is pointing at 2.6, **2** whole units and **6** tenths.

This is a decimal number.
You say, "Two **point** six."

p. 64

- The **decimal point** separates the whole number from the decimal part.

p. 15

The number 4.2 can be broken up into

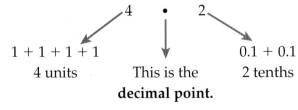

4 • 2

1 + 1 + 1 + 1 — 4 units

This is the **decimal point.**

0.1 + 0.1 — 2 tenths

The value of the 4 digit in 4.2 is 4 units.
The value of the 2 digit in 4.2 is 2 tenths.

example

What does the digit 2 stand for in each of these numbers?

a 12.1 **b** 23.5 **c** 0.2

a 2 units
b 2 tens or twenty
c 2 tenths

Tens	Units	•	Tenths
1	4	•	2
2	3	•	5
	0	•	2

If there are no units, you need to add a 0 to hold the space.

Exercise 1b²

1 What does the red digit stand for in each number?

a 6.4 **b** 4.9
c 358.7 **d** 6.0
e 28.5 **f** 123.5

2 What decimal numbers are shown on this scale?

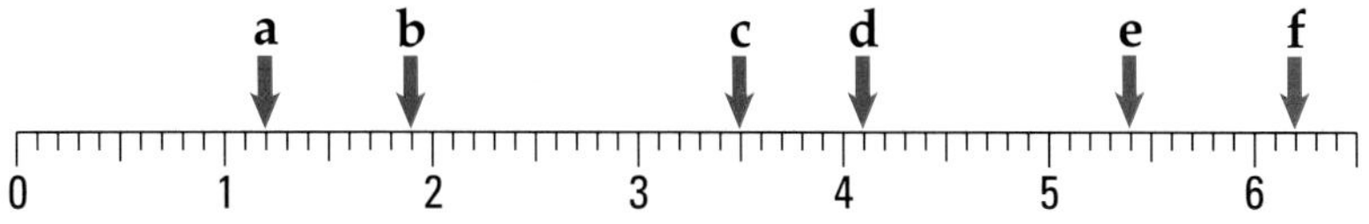

3 Use the number line to decide which is the greater decimal number. Use $<$ or $>$ in each box.

$>$ means 'is greater than'.
$<$ means 'less than'.

a 2.3 [<] 3.2 **b** 3.1 □ 2.9 **c** 5.3 □ 6.1 **d** 4.0 □ 3.8
e 3.8 □ 4.2 **f** 5.0 □ 4.9 **g** 3.0 □ 0.4 **h** 0.7 □ 0.9

4 Copy the grid.
Write the numbers as digits on the grid.

a Ten point six
b Twenty-four point three
c Sixty two point eight
d One hundred and nineteen point seven
e Six hundred and four point three

Don't forget the decimal point!

Thousands 1000s	Hundreds 100s	Tens 10s	Units 1s	•	Tenths $\frac{1}{10s}$
				•	
				•	
				•	
				•	
				•	
				•	

investigation

Money in the UK uses decimals to set apart pounds from pence.

a Which is greater £1.23 or 123 pence?
b An ice lolly costs £1.10. You have 94 × 1p coins and 3 × 5p coins. Do you have enough money to buy the ice lolly?

1c Temperature

- Use a thermometer to read the temperature
- Use positive and negative numbers for temperatures

Keywords
Celsius *Negative*
Degree *Rise*
Fall

Temperature is measured in **degrees Celsius**.
'Five degrees Celsius' is written as 5 °C.

- Numbers can go below zero.
  These are **negative**.
  -5 °C is 5 degrees below zero.

When the temperature **rises** it gets warmer.
When the temperature **falls** it gets cooler.

p. 28

You can use number lines to work with temperature.

example

The temperature was -6 °C. It rose 10 degrees.
What is the final temperature?

p. 15

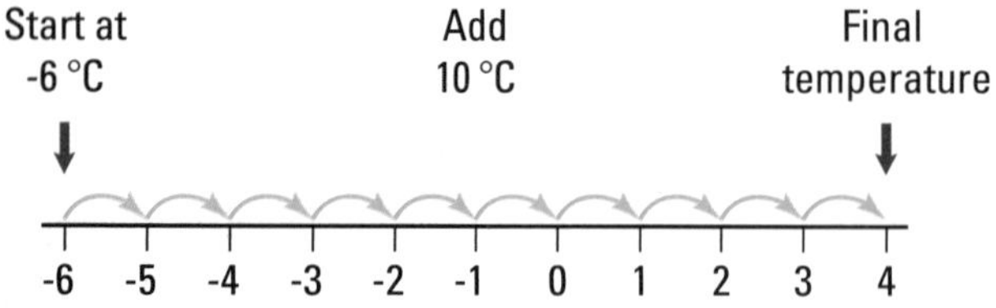

The final temperature is 4 °C.

example

The temperature was 3 °C.
An hour later it was -8 °C.
How many degrees did the temperature fall by?

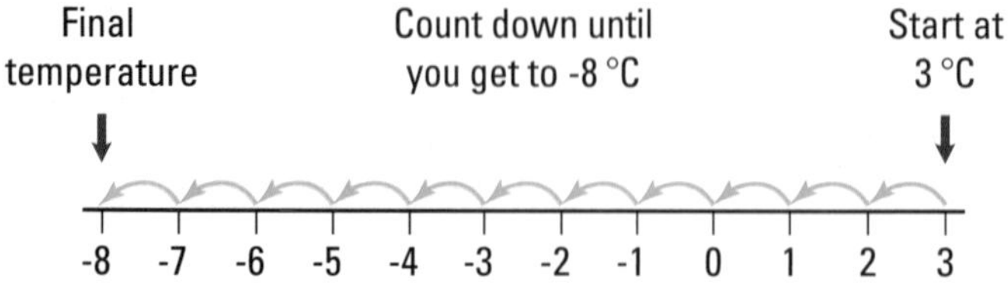

The temperature fell by 11 degrees.

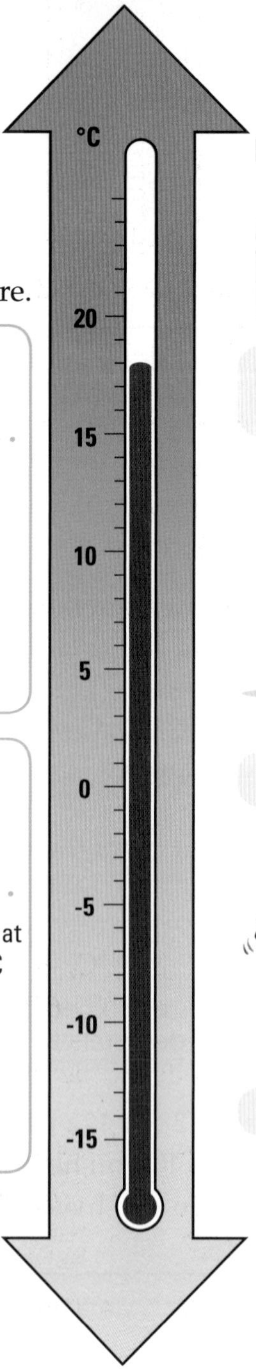

A thermometer is a number line standing up!

18 °C Your classroom is about this temperature.

Water freezes at **0 °C**.

-14 °C Very cold!

Exercise 1c

1 Write the temperatures marked on these thermometers.

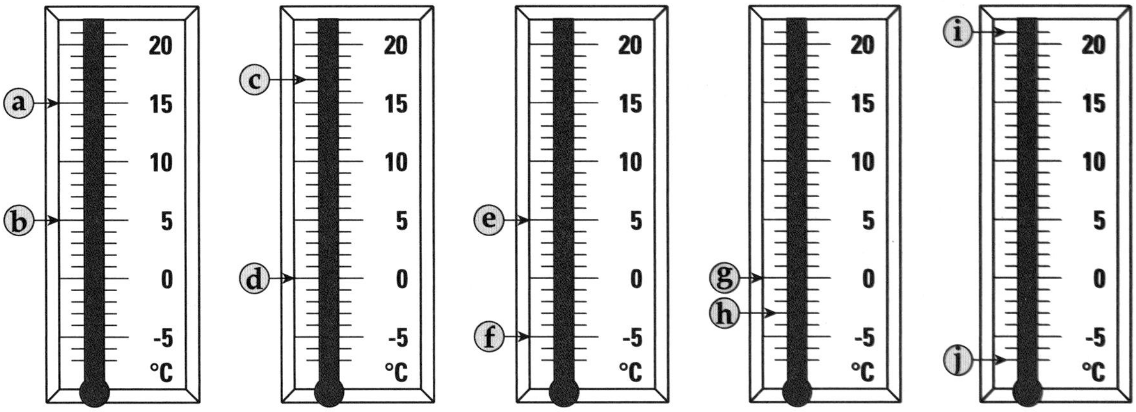

Use this number line to help you with questions **2** to **5**.

2 Find the final temperature.

a Start at -5 °C and rise by 2 °C. **b** Start at -2 °C and fall by 5 °C.
c Start at 8 °C and fall by 10 °C. **d** Start at -6 °C and rise by 6 °C.

3 What is the difference (in degrees) between these temperatures?
Does each temperature rise or fall?

a 4 °C to 9 °C **b** 11 °C to 0 °C **c** 4 °C to -4 °C
d -5 °C to 2 °C **e** -3 °C to -8 °C **f** 7 °C to -8 °C

4 Which is the colder temperature?

a -4 °C or -7 °C **b** 0 °C or -3 °C **c** -10 °C or -3 °C
d -7 °C or 6 °C **e** 0 °C or 4 °C **f** -11 °C or -14 °C

5 Put these temperatures in order. Start with the coldest.

a 3 °C, 9 °C, 0 °C **b** -2 °C, -6 °C, -5 °C **c** 4 °C, 1 °C, -6 °C
d -5 °C, 0 °C, -8 °C **e** 6 °C, -6 °C, -10 °C **f** 0 °C, 4 °C, -7 °C

Did you know?

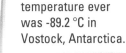

The coldest temperature ever was -89.2 °C in Vostock, Antarctica.

puzzle

Match each item with its temperature.

a cup of tea

b boiling kettle

c can of cola

d ice lolly

e you!

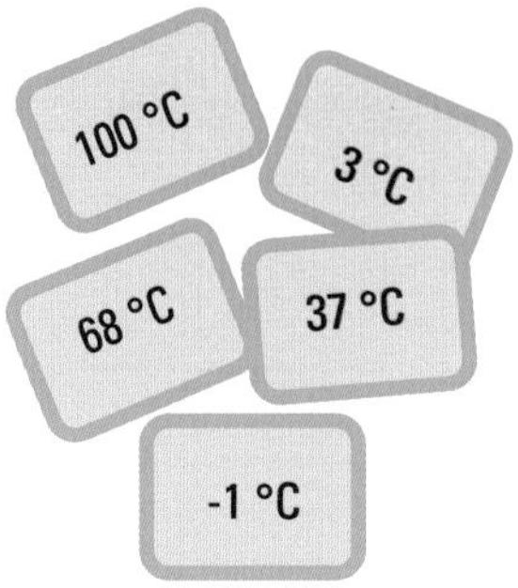

1d Mental methods of addition

- Know all the number bonds up to 20 in my head
- Add numbers up to 100 in my head

Keywords
Add *Pair*
Mental *Total*

Kia is practising her **mental addition**.
She cannot work out problems with pen and paper when …

Add 150 g of plain flour to 75 g of …

. . . she is busy with her hands

I got 25 downloads for 75p each. How much is that?

. . . she is on the move

. . . she is shopping.

Kia says adding in 10s is easy.
She has seen a pattern when you add 10 each time.
The problem here is 34 + 40.

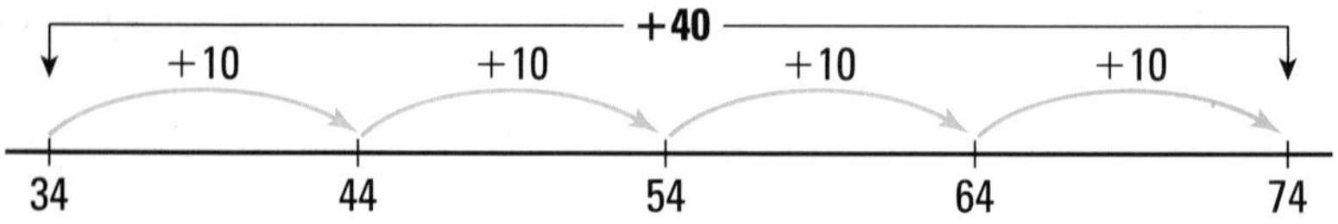

Answer: 30 + 40 = 74

example

Use mental addition to find 14 + 25.

Starting from 25, make one jump of 10.
This takes you to 35.
Then one jump of 4, brings you to 39.
14 + 25 = 39

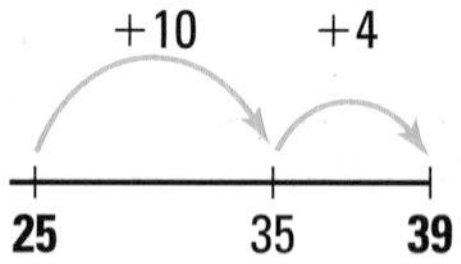

Exercise 1d

1 Write out all the number pairs that add up to 10 using these cards. You will end up with six pairs of numbers.

9 | 5 | 10 | 6 | 5 | 2 | 1 | 4 | 8 | 7 | 0 | 3

2 Write out all the number pairs that add up to 20 using these cards. You will end up with six pairs of numbers.

1 | 12 | 19 | 9 | 17 | 10 | 15 | 3 | 5 | 10 | 8 | 11

3 Add 10 to each number. Do the working out in your head.

a 8	**b** 12	**c** 16	**d** 20	**e** 33
f 57	**g** 66	**h** 84	**i** 90	**j** 108

4 Add 20 to each number. Do the working out in your head.

a 9	**b** 17	**c** 20	**d** 28	**e** 45
f 53	**g** 74	**h** 80	**i** 90	**j** 114

20 = two jumps of 10

5 What sum is shown in these mental calculations?

a

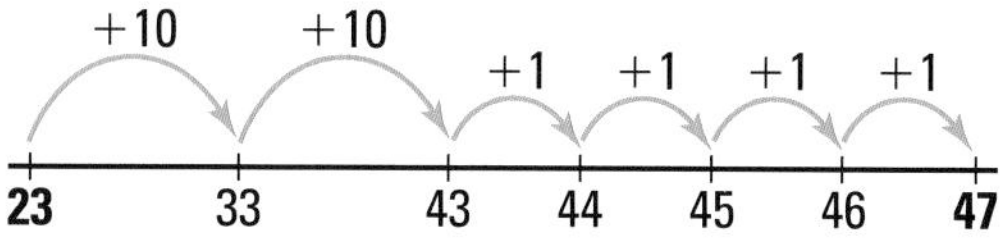

b

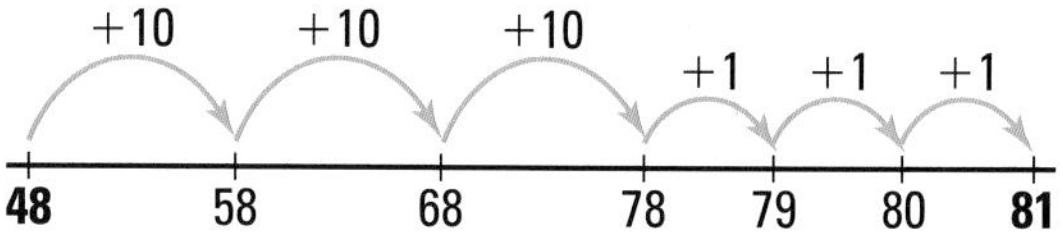

c

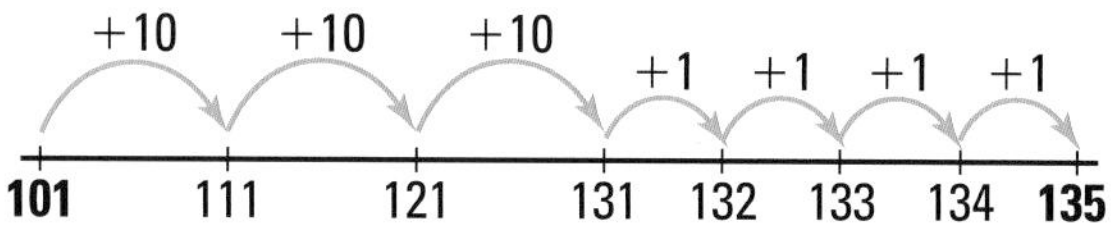

d

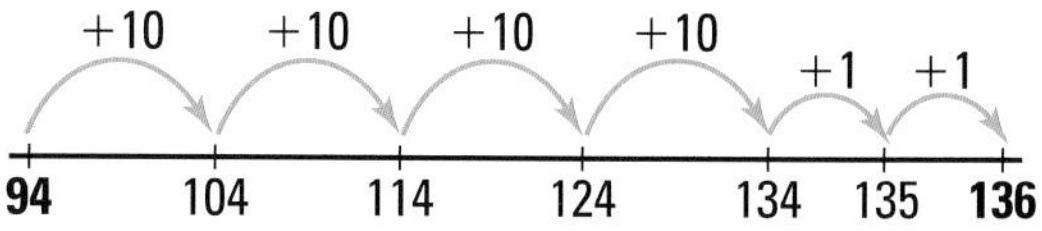

6 Work out these addition problems in your head.

a

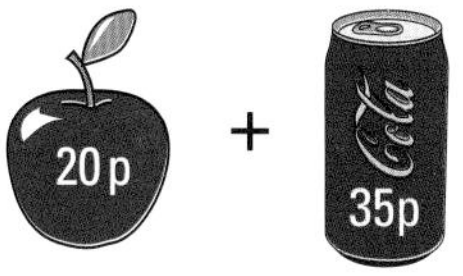

b

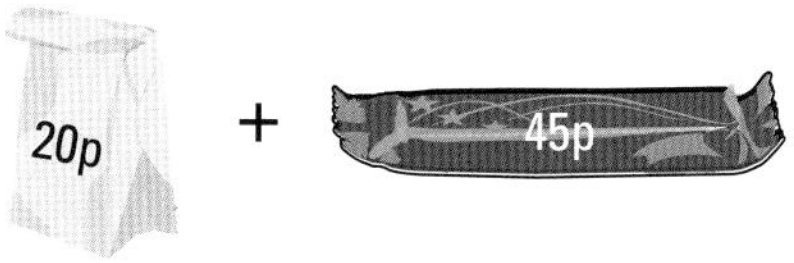

c

problem

Members of the Angling Club went fishing and caught fish of these weights (in kg).

2 + 1 + 4 + 3 + 2 + 5 + 3 + 4 + 3 + 5

Work out the **total** weight of the fish in your head.

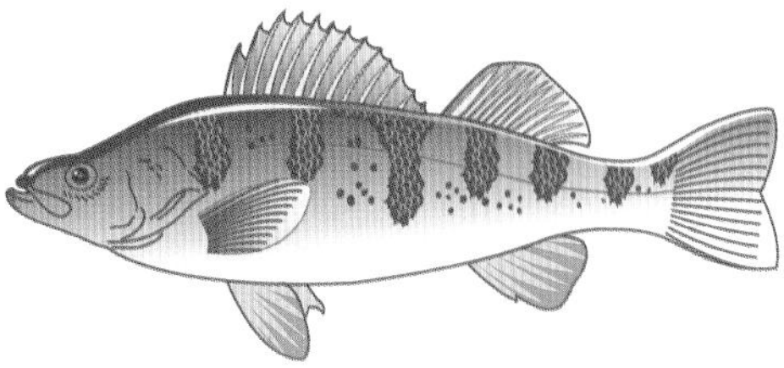

1e Mental methods of subtraction

- Use a number line to find the difference between two numbers

Keywords
Difference
Subtract

Jake is practising his mental subtraction.
He rolls three dice.
He adds to find the total score and subtracts it from 20.

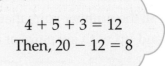

$4 + 5 + 3 = 12$
Then, $20 - 12 = 8$

In another practice Jake picks a random number and counts back in three jumps of -10.

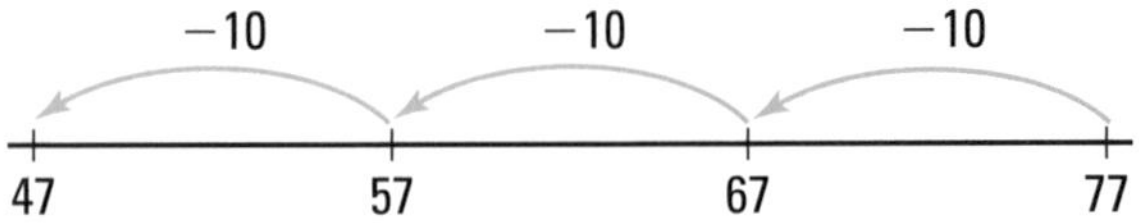

Start at 77.
Three jumps of -10 will be -30.
$77 - 30 = 47$

To subtract 10, you reduce the 10s digit by 1.
When Jake has to subtract more difficult numbers in his head, he either 'jumps back' in tens and units from the bigger number or 'jumps forward' in tens and units from the smaller number.

example

What is $57 - 25$?

Starting at 57, make two jumps of -10.
This takes you to 37.
Then one jump of -5 brings you to 32.

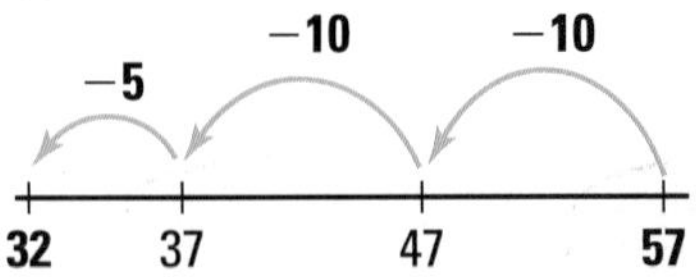

p. 228

OR

Find the **difference** between 57 and 25 by counting on.

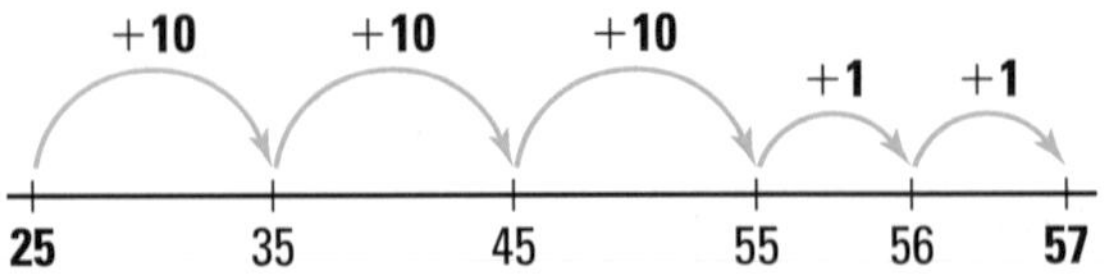

three 10s and two 1s = 32

So $57 - 25 = 32$

Exercise 1e

1 Subtract 10 from each number below.
Do the working-out in your head.

a 12	**b** 21	**c** 30	**d** 36
e 49	**f** 87	**g** 100	**h** 107

Did you know?

1 0000000000
0000000000
0000000000
0000000000
0000000000
0000000000
0000000000
0000000000
0000000000
0000000000

A googol is 1 followed by 100 zeros.

2 Work out these subtraction problems.

a 20 − 7 =	**b** 20 − 12 =
c 20 − 5 =	**d** 20 − 11 =
e 20 − 9 =	**f** 20 − 17 =

3 Add the scores from the three dice.
Subtract the total from 20 in your head.

a

b
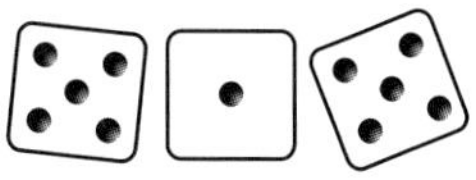

c
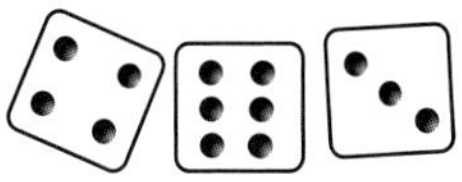

d

e

f
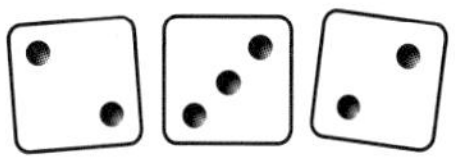

4 Subtract 30 from each number below.
Do the working-out in your head.

a 39	**b** 51	**c** 60	**d** 88
e 95	**f** 100	**g** 120	**h** 127

5 Work out these subtraction problems in your head.
Which method should you choose?

a 28 − 18 =	**b** 45 − 11 =	**c** 29 − 17 =	**d** 78 − 23 =
e 70 − 33 =	**f** 40 − 18 =	**g** 81 − 28 =	**h** 90 − 55 =

problem

Members of the Athletics Club decide that they will get fit.
They start training.
After six weeks they are weighed.
Here are four results:

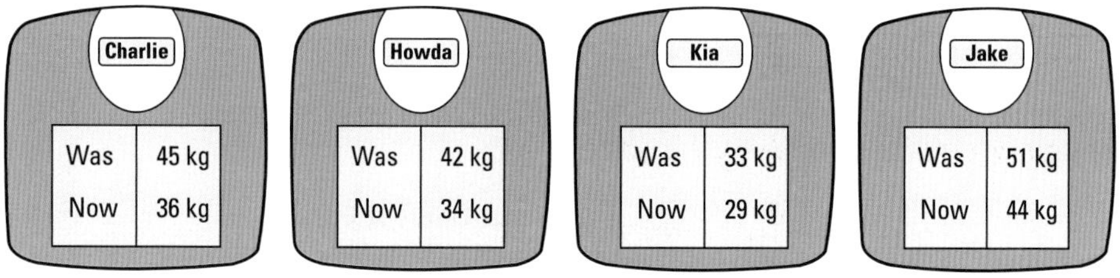

Work out each student's weight loss in your head.
Give your answers in kilograms.

1f Written methods of addition and subtraction

- Use a number line or columns to add and subtract

Keywords
Add
Columns
Equals
H T U
Subtract

You can use a number line to help with addition and subtraction problems.

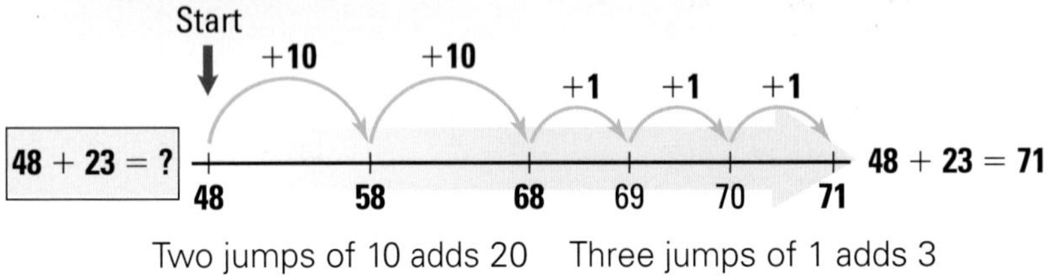

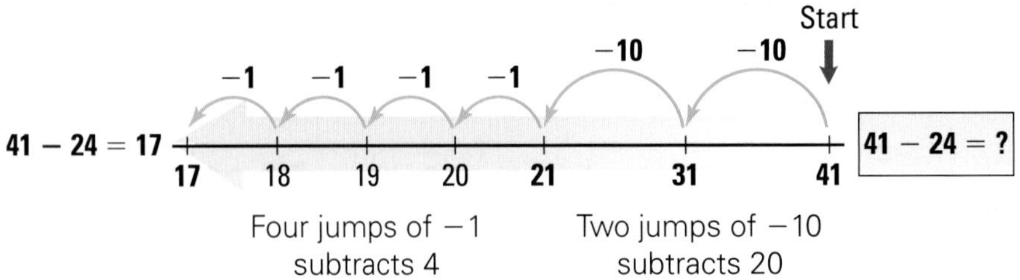

You can set out the numbers in columns to help you add and subtract.

example

Use columns to add or subtract.

a 324 + 145 **b** 548 − 235

a Set out the numbers in columns. **Hundreds, Tens and Units**

H	T	U
3	2	4
+ 1	4	5

Add the **Units**.
4 add 5 = 9

H	T	U
3	2	4
+ 1	4	5
		9

Add the **Tens** column.

Then add the Hundreds.

H	T	U
3	2	4
+ 1	4	5
4	**6**	9

324 + 145 = **469**

b Set out the numbers in columns. **Hundreds, Tens and Units**

H	T	U
5	4	8
− 2	3	5

Subtract the **Units**.
take 5 from 8 = 3

H	T	U
5	4	8
− 2	3	5
		3

Subtract the **Tens** column.

Then subtract the Hundreds.

H	T	U
5	4	8
− 2	3	5
3	**1**	3

548 − 235 = **313**

p. 230

Exercise 1f

1 Use a number line to solve these addition problems.
The first is done for you.

a 34 + 23 =

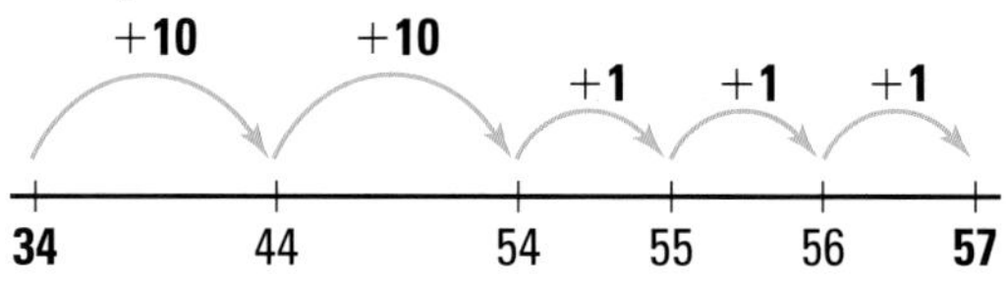

b 23 + 43 =
c 14 + 63 =
d 52 + 24 =
e 42 + 17 =

2 Use a number line to solve these subtraction problems.
The first is done for you.

a 43 − 22 =

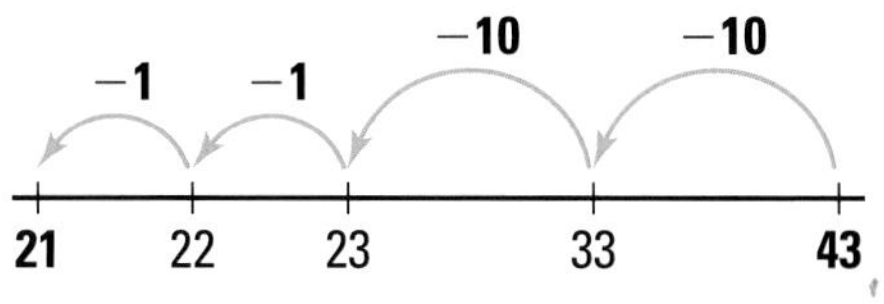

b 48 − 17 =
c 60 − 24 =
d 43 − 27 =
e 34 − 19 =

3 Copy and complete these work cards.

Addition

a 25 + 14 =	**b** 31 + 27 =	**c** 16 + 53 =
d 242 + 132 =	**e** 335 + 204 =	**f** 581 + 316 =

Subtraction

a 55 − 24 =	**b** 67 − 23 =	**c** 86 − 50 =
d 464 − 153 =	**e** 853 − 503 =	**f** 466 − 406 =

challenge

Which is greater?

a 24 + 13 or 88 − 14
b 101 + 77 or 49 + 120
c 98 − 53 or 23 + 16
d 87 − 26 or 198 − 158
e 214 + 23 or 108 + 144
f 88 + 120 or 463 − 261

1g Calculator methods

- Use a calculator to add and subtract numbers

Keywords
Calculator *Clear* *Display* *Enter* *Keys*

p. 102

Carlo is using a **calculator** to add 147 + 238.
First he makes a guess at what the answer might be in case he makes a mistake.

147 is close to 150 and 238 is close to 200.
150 + 200 = 350

This is close to 350.

Then he **enters** the problem in his calculator.

[1] [4] [7] [+] [2] [3] [8] [=] 385

Carlo starts on a second problem: 403 − 257
He presses [C] to **clear** his previous calculation.

Carlo guesses the answer will be close to: 400 − 250 = 150.
He starts entering the problem, but he makes a mistake.

[4] [0] [3] [−] [5] [2] [7] [CE] [2] [5] [7] [=] 146

Carlo makes a mistake.

Carlo presses 'Clear Entry' to cancel the error.

He then enters the correction.

p. 112

- Calculators help you to do difficult calculations quickly and check your answers.

example

Solve these problems using a calculator.

a 3450 + 1458 **b** 2489 − 1222

a Guess first

3450 is close to 3500.
1458 is close to 1500.

$$\begin{array}{r} 3500 \\ +\,1500 \\ \hline 5000 \end{array}$$

'Close to' answer: 5000

Enter the problem

[3] [4] [5] [0] [+] [1] [4] [5] [8] [=] 4908

b Guess first

2489 is close to 2500.
1222 is close to 1000.

$$\begin{array}{r} 2500 \\ -\,1000 \\ \hline 1500 \end{array}$$

'Close to' answer: 1500

Enter the problem

[2] [4] [8] [9] [−] [1] [2] [2] [2] [=] 1267

Exercise 1g

1 Use your calculator to solve these problems. Guess first.

a 1207 + 1345 — 1207 is close to ____. 1345 is close to ____.

b 3459 − 3214

c 1234 + 5678

d 3405 − 3201

2 Use a calculator to do these decimal problems.

p. 42

a 3.4 + 2.6 = **b** 5.8 + 6.3 =

c 4.3 + 2.4 = **d** 14.3 + 18.7 =

e 6.5 − 4.8 = **f** 9.0 − 6.6 =

g 16.8 − 9.8 = **h** 30.5 − 18.4 =

Enter [3] [.] [4] for 3.4.

3 Use your calculator to find the new temperatures.

p. 6

a Start at 4°C and rise by 9 degrees.

b Start at -6°C and rise by 13 degrees.

c Start at 2°C and fall by 7 degrees.

d Start at -12°C and rise by 7 degrees.

e Start at -3°C and fall by 9 degrees.

Enter [(−)] [6] [+] [1] [3] [=]

4 Use your calculator to solve these multiplication problems.

p. 156

a 11 × 11 **b** 12 × 12

c 13 × 13 **d** 14 × 14

e 15 × 15 **f** 20 × 20

Enter [1] [1] [×] [1] [1] [=]

puzzle

Key this number into your calculator: 77 345. Press the [=] key.
Turn your calculator upside down. You should see the word shell. SHELL

1.		2.				3.	
				4.			
5.							
				6.			

a Copy the crossword grid.

b Go to the first clue, **1** across.

c Complete the calculation.

d Turn your calculator upside-down.

e Copy the word onto the grid at **1** across.

f Go to the next clue and repeat these steps.

Across

1 A watering pipe 1752 + 1752 =

4 Not me; someone ____ 5000 − 1427 =

5 Not tight 20 000 + 10 000 + 5007 =

6 Not the truth 7890 − 2573 =

Down

1 Small mountain? 85 + 987 + 6642 =

2 Untidy, lazy person 11 011 − 2936 =

3 The ____ of Wight 2057 + 981 + 713 =

4 Snake-like fish 1358 − 625 =

Multiplication

- Know your multiplication tables or know how to work them out

Keywords
Multiplication tables

4 people need 3 balloons each.

3 + 3 + 3 + 3 = 12

They need 12 balloons altogether.

What if 9 people need 7 balloons each?

7 + 7 + 7 + 7 + 7 + 7 + 7 + 7 + 7

It's easier to use multiplication facts. $9 \times 7 = 63$

They need 63 balloons altogether.

p. 104

- Knowing your **multiplication tables** lets you calculate quicker.

example

Fill in the numbers missing from this multiplication table.

×	1	2	3	4	5
1	1				
2	2		6		
3					15
4	4				
5		10			

$1 \times 2 = 2$ $2 \times 2 = 4$

×	1	2	3	4	5
1	1	2	3	4	5
2	2	4	6	8	10
3	3	6	9	12	15
4	4	8	12	16	20
5	5	10	15	20	25

Exercise 1h

1 Fill in the numbers missing from each multiplication table.

a

×	1	2	3	4	5
1					5
2					
3		6			
4					
5			15		

b

×	6	7	8	9	10
6				54	
7					
8	48				
9		63			90
10					

2 Use multiplication facts to calculate each.

a 2×4 **b** 3×5 **c** 7×2 **d** 8×4 **e** 5×5

f 3×7 **g** 1×9 **h** 10×4 **i** 6×3 **j** 9×9

k 8×2 **l** 8×7 **m** 4×5 **n** 7×8 **o** 4×7

3 Each car has 4 tyres.
How many tyres do 6 cars have?

4 Each house has 10 windows.
How many windows do 8 houses have?

5 Each frame is made with 6 nails.
How many nails do you need to make 6 frames?

challenge

11 girls play for the Woodley Wolves football team.

a If each girl has one pair of boots, how many boots are there altogether?

b If each girl takes 5 practice shots on goal, how many shots were taken in all?

1a

1 Jamie caught five fish.
He measured the length of each fish:

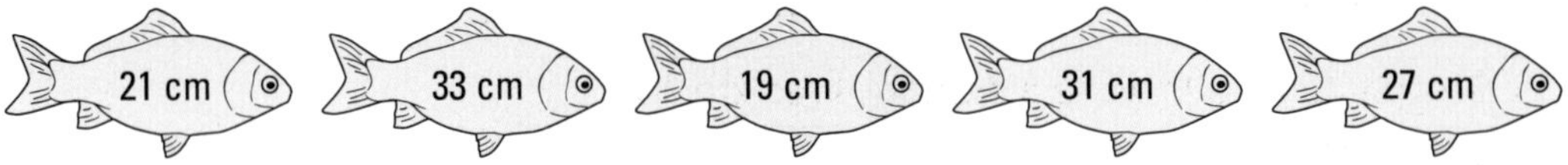

a Write out the lengths in order, starting with the largest.
Next he weighed each fish:

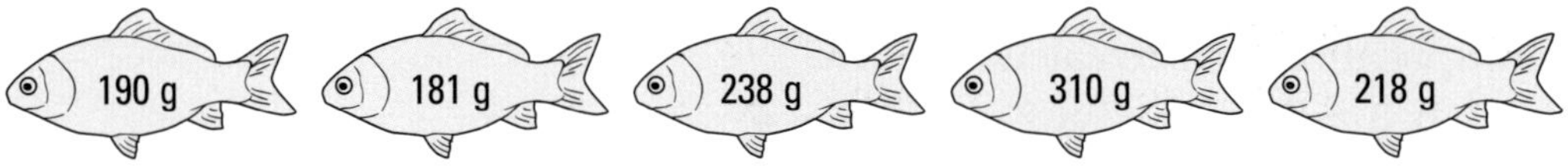

b Write out the weights in order, starting with the smallest.

1b

2 What does the red digit stand for in each number?

a 427 **b** 6009 **c** 1570
d 716 **e** 3085 **f** 5172

3 Split these numbers into 100s, 10s, and 1s. The first is done for you.

a 224 = 100 + 100 + 10 + 10 + 1 + 1 + 1 + 1
b 344 **c** 431 **d** 136 **e** 201

1b²

4 Put these decimal numbers in order, starting with the smallest.

a 5.8, 4.9, 7.2, 6.5 **b** 8.4, 3.2, 6.9, 0.9
c 2.4, 2.1, 2.0, 2.5 **d** 4.1, 3.9, 4.2, 3.8

1c

5 Use the number line to find each new temperature.

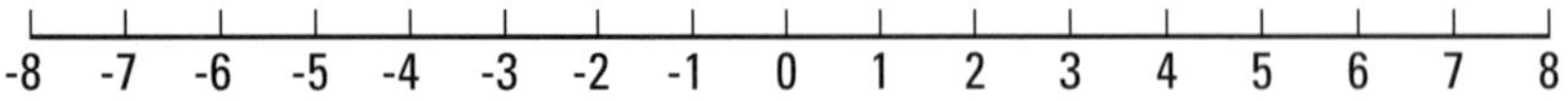

a Start at 7°C and drops by 9 degrees.
b Start at -5°C and goes up by 7 degrees.
c Start at -4°C and drops by 4 degrees.
d Start at -8°C and goes up by 5 degrees.
e Start at -5°C and goes up by 9 degrees.

6 Complete these problems using negative numbers.

a 4 − 7 = ? **b** 8 − 12 = ? **c** 10 − 12 = ? **d** 0 − 7 = ? **e** -2 − 6 = ?
f -2 + 5 = ? **g** -5 − 3 = ? **h** -10 + 6 = ? **i** -6 − 11 = ? **j** -12 + 20 = ?

1d

7 Calculate each of these.

a $54 + 16$ b $48 + 22$ c $53 + 17$

d $51 + 19$ e $65 + 39$ f $79 + 13$

8 A lorry of length 25 m is towing a trailer of length 15 m.
What is the total length?

1e

9 Calculate each of these.

a $74 - 31$ b $47 - 32$ c $54 - 12$

d $64 - 19$ e $62 - 48$ f $84 - 8$

10 At Manor Lane School there are 89 students in year 7.
How many girls are there if there are 41 boys?

1f

11 Add or subtract using columns.

a	b	c	d
H T U	H T U	H T U	H T U
4 6 4	2 1 8	4 5 2	8 1 7
+ 3 1 8	+ 3 0 2	− 1 0 6	− 2 8 0

12 Write these problems in columns and then add or subtract.

a $539 + 254$ b $107 + 448$ c $472 - 209$ d $703 - 362$

1g

13 Use your calculator to solve these problems. Guess first.

a $2438 - 1255$ 2438 is close to 2500
1255 is close to ______.

b $1470 + 3215$

c $7351 - 2222$

d $6421 + 3218$

1h

14 Use multiplication facts to calculate each of these.

a 9×8 b 7×3 c 6×5 d 10×7 e 3×8

f 8×5 g 4×6 h 7×9 i 3×4 j 7×1

k 6×2 l 8×3 m 2×9 n 4×4 o 9×7

1 Summary

Key indicators
- Read, write and order positive whole numbers **Level 3**
- Recognise negative whole numbers in context **Level 3**

Level 3

1 Three numbers and a number line are shown.

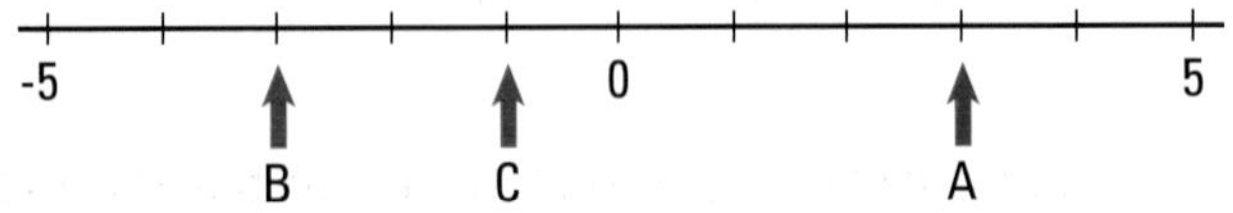

a Write down the number at A, B and C.
b List your answers in order of size, smallest first.

Amber's answer ✔

Amber first numbers the whole line.

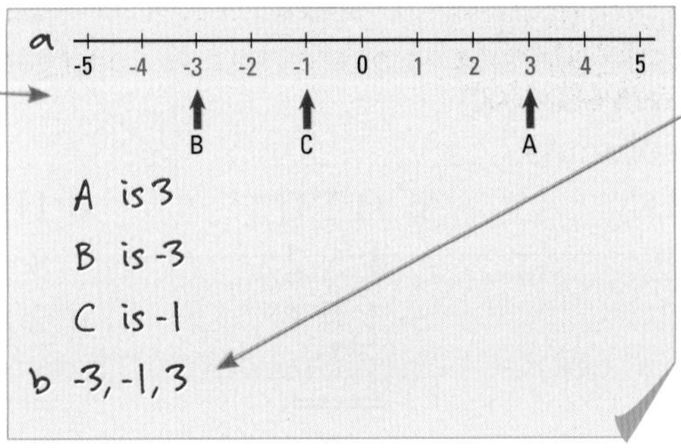

Amber remembers to start with the smallest number.

Level 3

2 The number 483 can be made using these cards.

4	8	3

a Write down the smallest number you can make using all three cards.
b Write down the largest number you can make using all three cards.
c Write down the nearest number to 400 that you can make using all three cards.

2 Algebra

Sequences and functions

In the UK, houses are numbered in a sequence. The even numbered houses are located on the left hand side of the street as you walk away from the centre of town. The odd numbered houses are on the right.

What's the point? If the houses weren't ordered in a predictable sequence, the postman would have a hard time finding your house!

Check in

Level 2

1 **a** Write all the even numbers between 19 and 29.
b Write all the odd numbers between 10 and 20.

2 Draw the next shape in each of these patterns

a

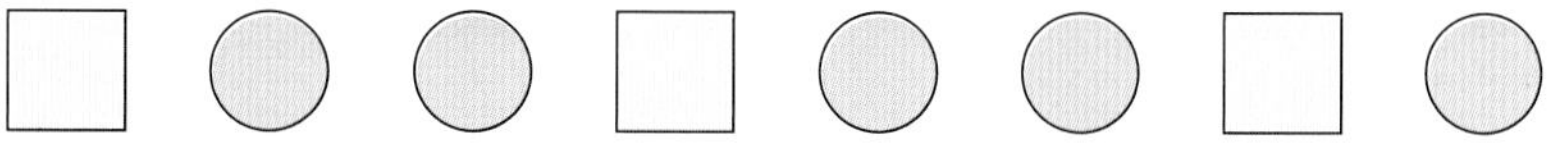

b

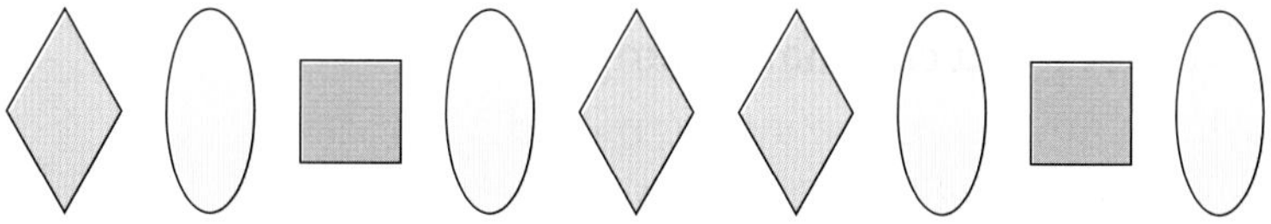

c W X Y Z W X Y Z W X

Level 3

3 Copy and complete these without using a calculator.

a $8 \div 2 = \square$ **b** $5 \times 3 = \square$ **c** $14 \div 2 = \square$ **d** $2 \times 6 = \square$

e $12 \div 4 = \square$ **f** $7 \times 3 = \square$ **g** $18 \div 3 = \square$ **h** $6 \times 4 = \square$

2a Sequences

- Write a number pattern as a sequence
- Find the next number in a sequence

Keywords
Pattern
Sequence
Rule
Terms

Jenny counts the number of leaves on this plant as it grows.

Number of leaves: 1 3 5 7 9

The plant is growing leaves in a **pattern**.

The pattern can be written as a **sequence** of numbers.

The **sequence** is 1, 3, 5, 7, 9

The sequence can be shown on a number line.

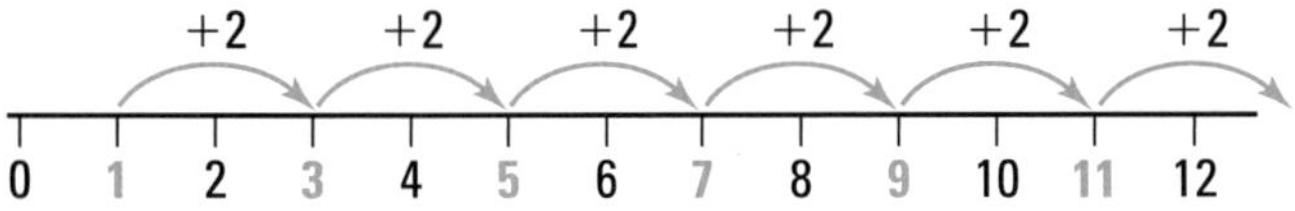

The plant is growing two new leaves each time.

example

Ted is knocking down this wall in a pattern.

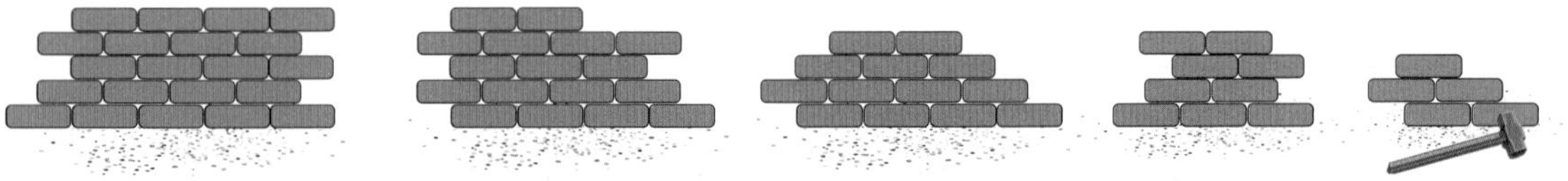

a Write this pattern as a sequence of numbers.
b Show this sequence on a number line.
c How many bricks does Ted knock down each time?
d How many bricks will be left after one more swing of Ted's hammer?

a The sequence is 21, 17, 13, 9, 5 — Count the bricks.

b

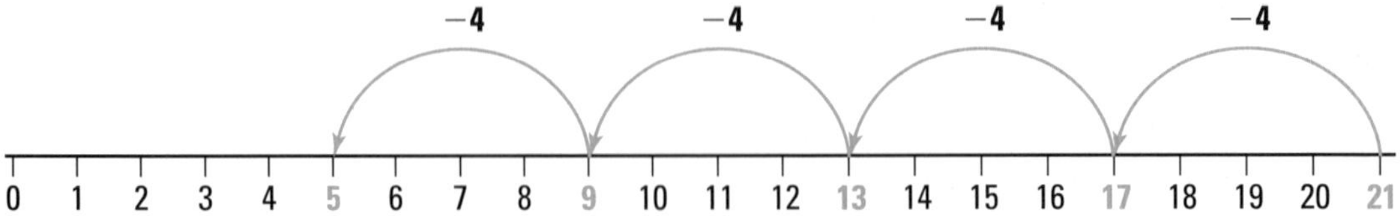

c There are four fewer bricks each time.
d The number of bricks left will decrease by 4, so $5 - 4 = 1$ brick left.

Exercise 2a

1 Write these patterns as number sequences.

a 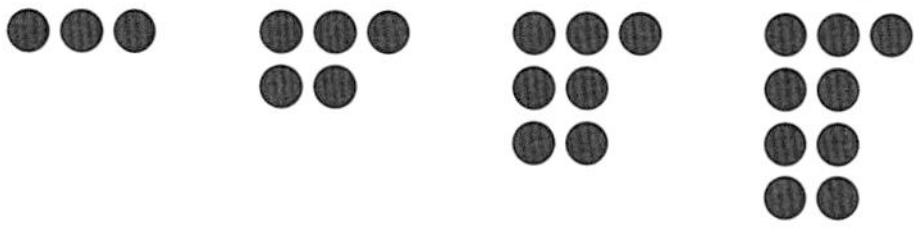

b 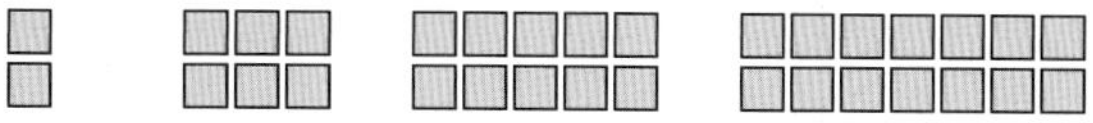

c 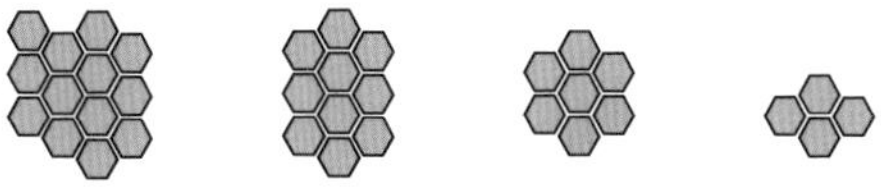

d 

2 Write the sequence shown on each number line.

a 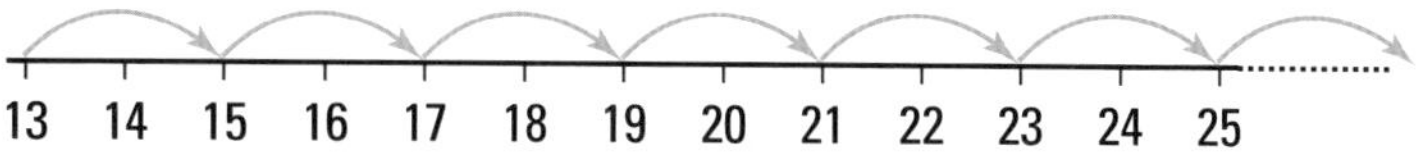

b 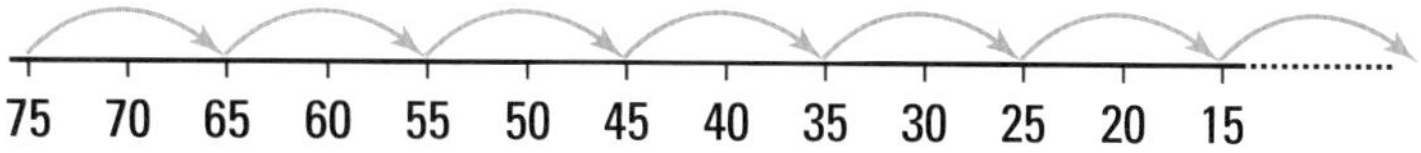

c 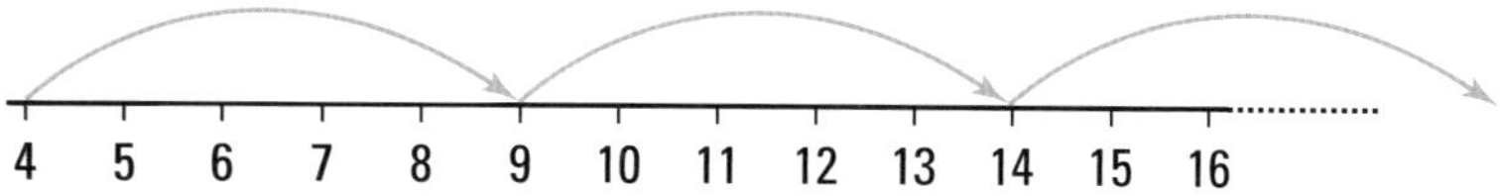

d What is the difference between the numbers in each sequence?

e Find the next number in each sequence.

3 Find the next two numbers in each sequence.

a 5, 8, 11, 14, ..., ...

b 7, 13, 19, 25, ..., ...

c 32, 28, 24, 20, ..., ...

d 2, 4, 8, 16, ..., ...

challenge

The numbers in the ring are some of the numbers in a sequence. Some numbers are missing.

Write the sequence in order and fill in the missing numbers.

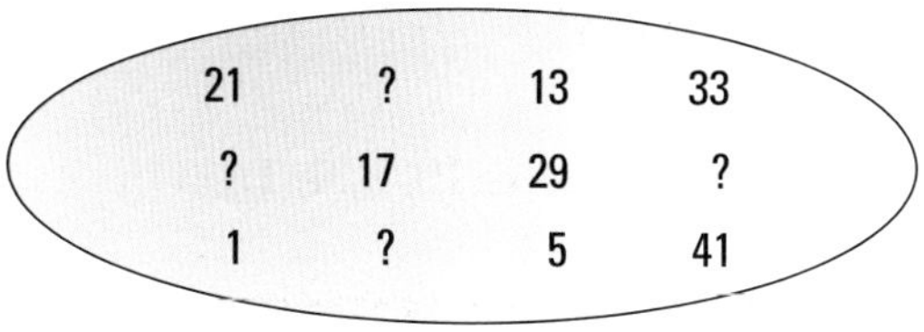

2b Describing sequences

- Find a rule to describe a sequence

Keywords
Describe Rule
Pattern

- The **rule** of a sequence tells you how to get to the next number.

- You **describe** a sequence with the first number and the rule.

  Start at 10 and −2 each time. 10, 8, 6, 4, 2
  −2 −2 −2 −2

The boss says, 'Start at 0 and add 2!'

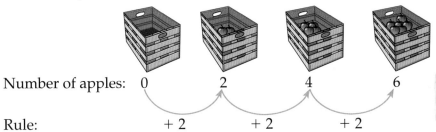

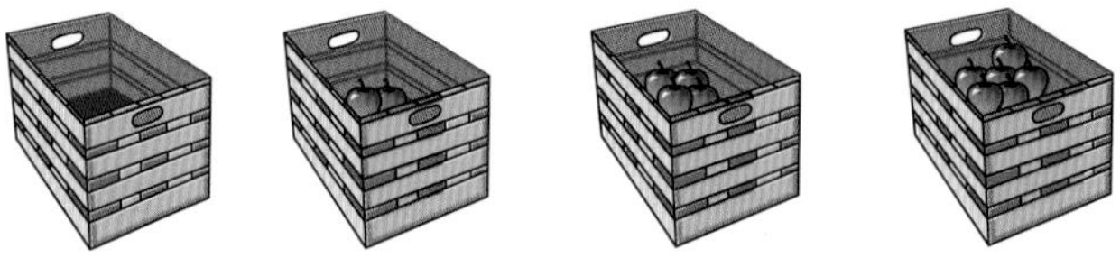

Number of apples: 0 2 4 6

Rule: + 2 + 2 + 2

The rule is +2 because 2 more apples were added each time.

'Work faster! Start at 4 and multiply by 2!'

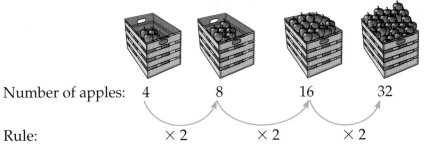

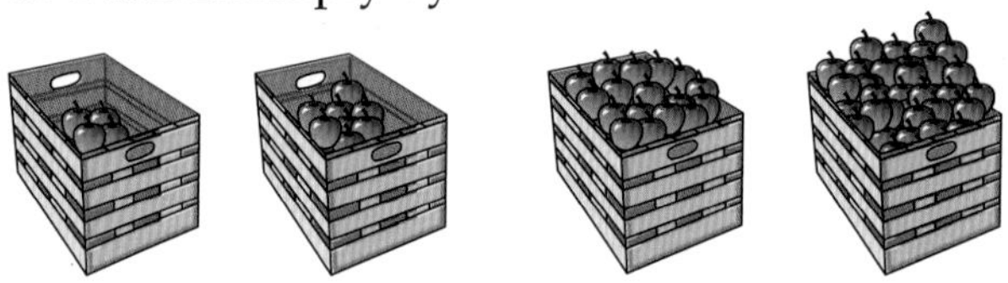

Number of apples: 4 8 16 32

Rule: × 2 × 2 × 2

The rule is ×2 because the number of apples is doubled each time.

example

Describe these sequences.

a

b

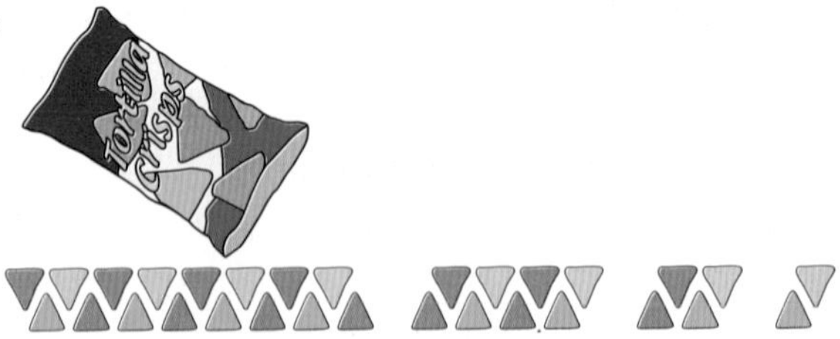

a The sequence is 10, 7, 4, 1.
The rule is −3.
'Start at 10 and −3.'

b The sequence is 16, 8, 4, 2.
The rule is ÷2.
'Start at 16 and ÷2.'

Exercise 2b

1 **a** Look at these tile patterns.

i

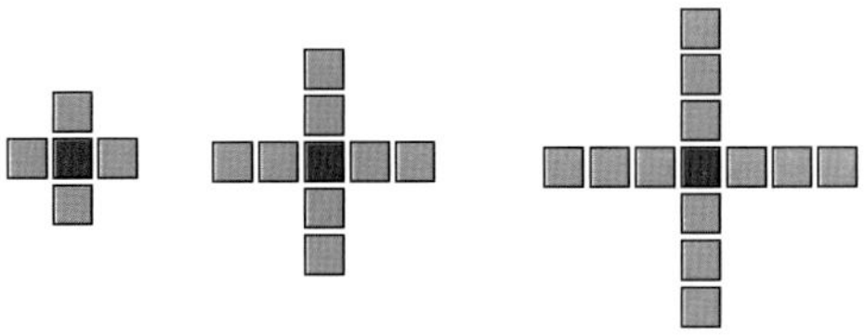

ii

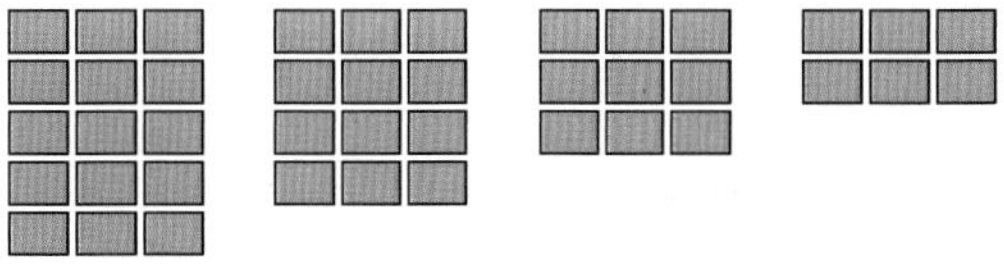

iii

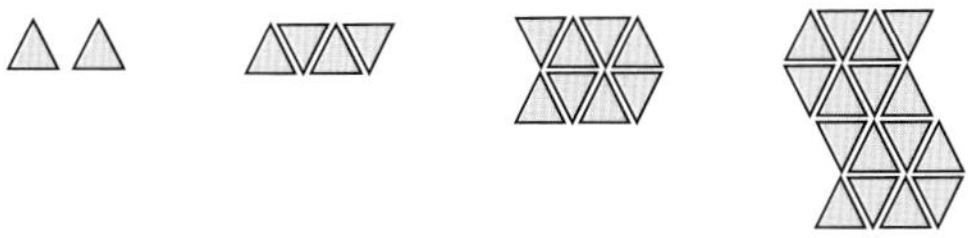

iv

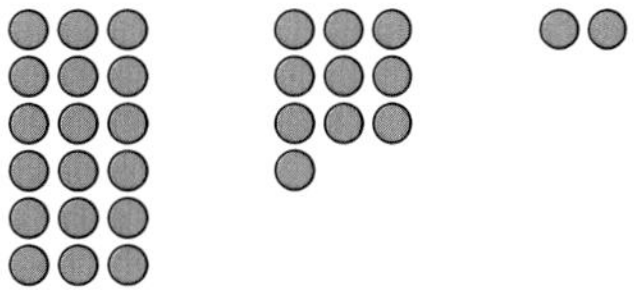

b Write each pattern as a number sequence.

c Give the rule for each.

d Describe each sequence using 'Start at ___ and ___.'

e Find the next two numbers in each sequence.

2 Match each description with a sequence.

'Start at 100 and ÷ 2'	100, 50, 0, −50, −100
'Start at 1 and + 7'	100, 50, 25, 12.5
'Start at 100 and × 2'	100, 200, 400, 800, 1600
'Start at 100 and − 50'	1, 3, 9, 27, 81
'Start at 1 and × 3'	1, 4, 7, 10, 13, 16
'Start at 1 and + 3'	1, 8, 15, 22, 29

3 Write a description for each sequence.

a 1, 2, 4, 8 ...

b 1, 3, 9, 27...

c 8, 11, 14, 17...

d 5, 25, 125, 625...

e 24, 12, 6, 3...

f −9, −6, −3, 0...

challenge

James saw this Roman tiling pattern on a trip to the local museum. Unfortunately, the rest of the pattern is lost. How many ways could you continue the pattern?

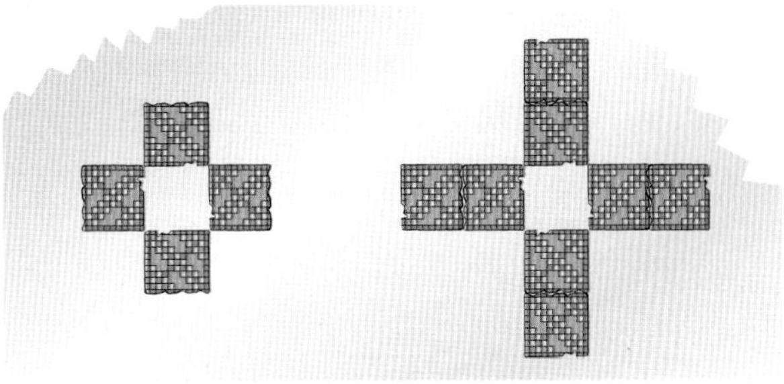

2c Using rules

- Use a rule to find more numbers in a sequence

Keywords
Number line
Rule
Term

Jenny knows that a plant grows two more leaves each week.
The **rule** is 'add 2 leaves'.

She uses this rule to draw the pattern of the plant's growth.

Jenny doesn't know where to start so she could draw lots of patterns using the rule 'add 2 leaves.'

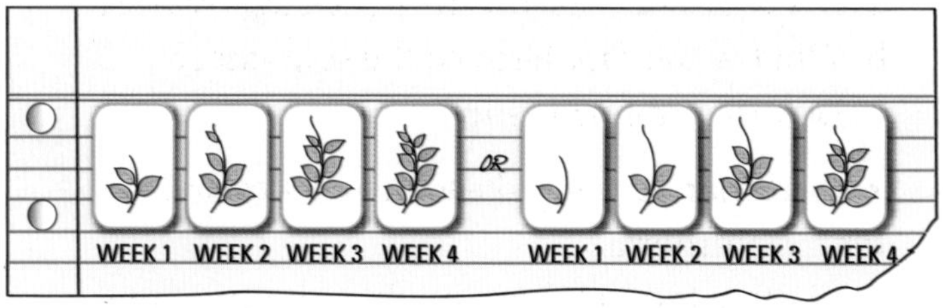

Jenny notices that the plant first sprouts two leaves.
She can now draw the sequence.

The number of leaves on the plant each week are called the **terms**.

2 4 6 8 10

- The numbers in a sequence are called the **terms.**

1st Term	2nd Term	3rd Term	4th Term	5th Term
2	4	6	8	10

The first term of a sequence is the starting number.

example

Draw two different tile patterns using the rule 'add 3'.
Draw five **terms**.

Pattern A

1st Term 2nd Term 3rd Term 4th Term 5th Term

Pattern B

example

Write the sequence described by 'Start at 29 and – 3'. Stop at the 4th term.

Use a number line. The sequence is 29, 26, 23, 20

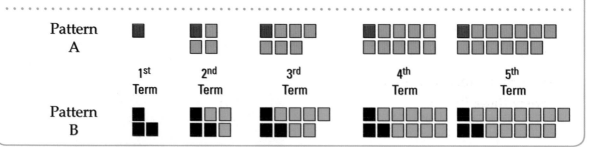

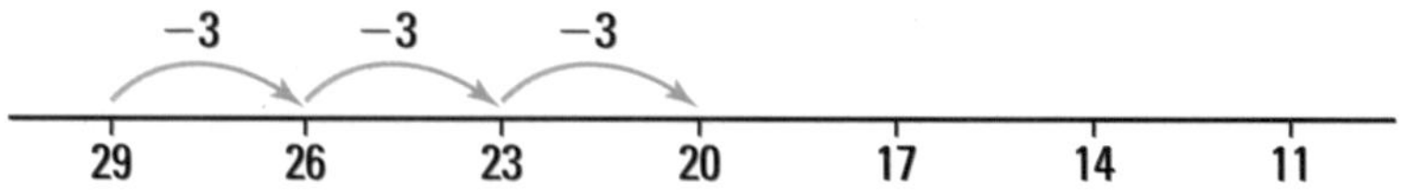

Exercise 2c

1 **a** Draw any pattern of tiles that has the rule 'add 4'. Draw four terms.

b Write your pattern as a sequence of numbers.

Use tiles like this: 

2 This plant loses three leaves each week.

a Draw the pattern for the next three weeks.

b What is the first term of the sequence?

c Describe this sequence.

3 A workman is using these instructions to tile a bathroom.
Draw five terms following these instructions.

Instructions
Start with 1 tile.
Multiply by 2 to get the next term.

4 Write a sequence for each description.

a 'Start at 6 and +4' ___, ___, ___, ___, ___

b 'Start at 80 and ÷2' ___, ___, ___, ___

c 'Start at 2 and ×3' ___, ___, ___

5 A lift starts on the 2nd floor of a building.
It stops every three floors.
There are 20 floors in the building.
Write the journey of the lift as a sequence.

You could start with a number line.

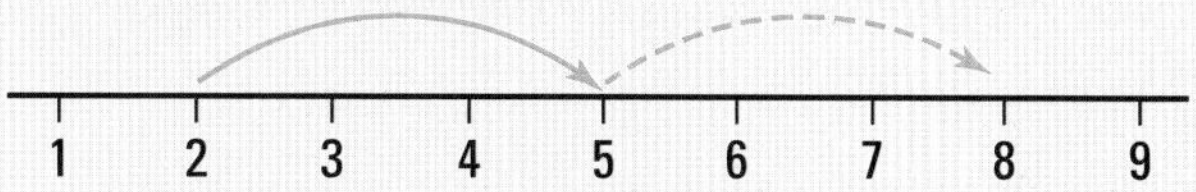

challenge

These two lifts work in the same building.

The building has 20 floors.

The North lift **starts at floor 1** and stops at **every three** floors.

The South lift **starts at floor 3** and stops at **every two** floors.

a Write each lift's journey as a sequence.

b On which floors do both lifts stop?

c Which floors have no stop?

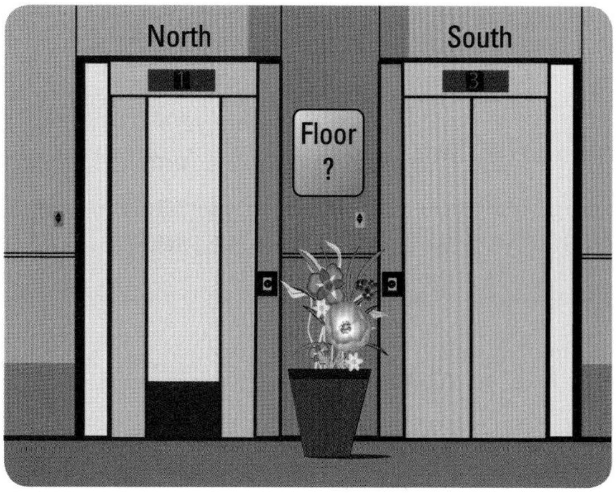

2d Sequences with negative numbers

- Use negative numbers in a sequence

Keywords
Debt
Negative

Debt is a **negative** number.
If you owe someone money, you are in debt to them.
You can pay them back using a sequence.

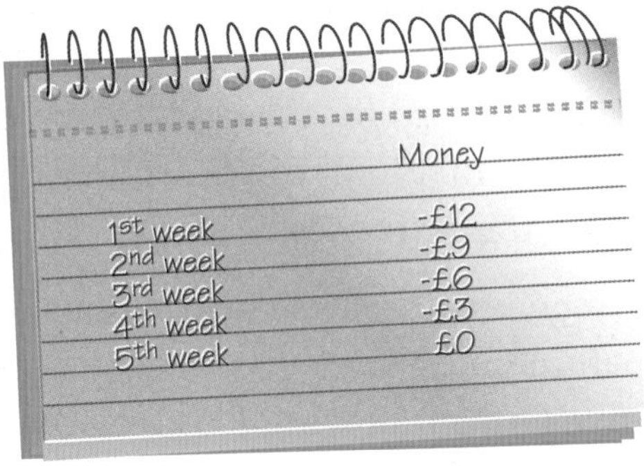
Money
1st week -£12
2nd week -£9
3rd week -£6
4th week -£3
5th week £0

Johnny owes his dad £12.
He has **negative** £12.
He pays his dad back £3 per week.
He describes the sequence as:
'Start at -12 and add 3.'

p. 6

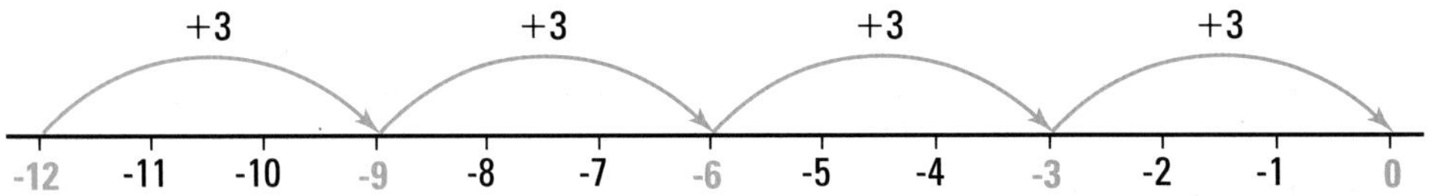
+3
+3
+3
+3
-12 -11 -10 -9 -8 -7 -6 -5 -4 -3 -2 -1 0

Out of debt means he doesn't owe money.

He will be out of debt after 4 weeks.

example

Maria is paying off her debt using this sequence.
-£16, -£12, -£8, -£4

a How much does she pay back each week?
b When will she have paid off her debt?

a The rule is add 4
She pays back £4 each week.
b The 5th term is 0 so she paid off her debt in Week 5.

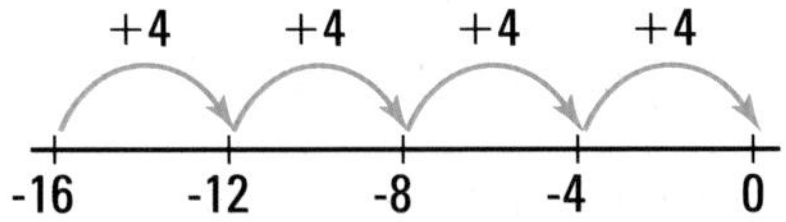

- **You can find the first term of a sequence by working backwards.**

p. 254

example

Write the first term of this sequence.
….., 2, 7, 12, 17

The rule is add 5.
Work backwards from the second term. This means −5.
The first term is 2 − 5 = -3

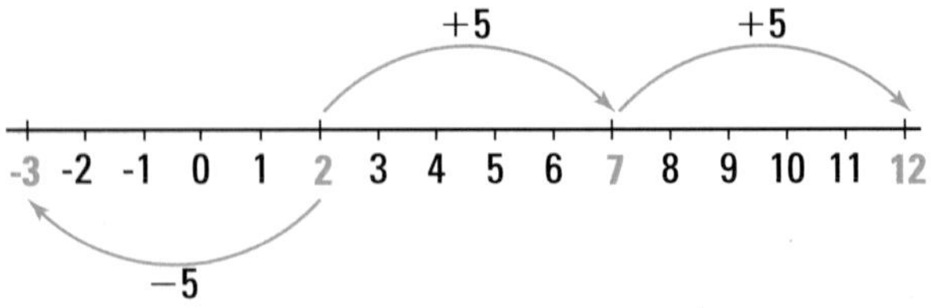

Exercise 2d

1 Use these number lines to help you find the missing terms of each sequence.

a -10, -7 ....., ..., ...

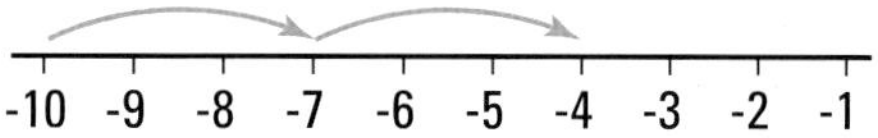

b -15, -12, -9, ..., ...

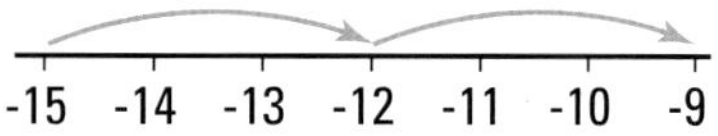

c ....., -3, -1, 1, ...

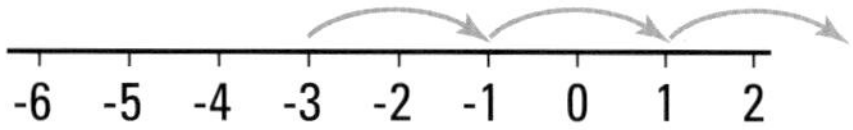

d ....., -7, -4, -1, ..., ...

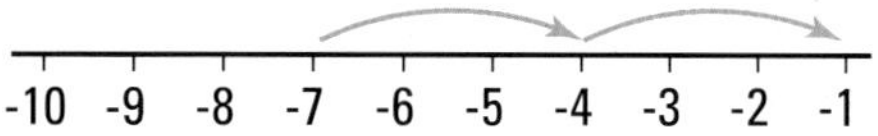

e ....., ..., -4, -2, 0

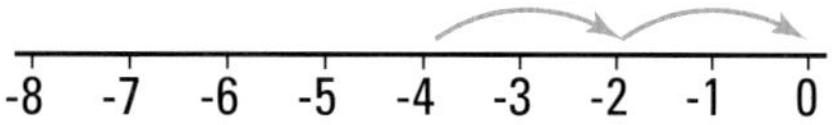

f ....., -50, -30, ..., ..., ...

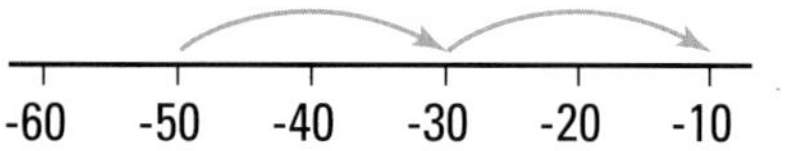

g Write the rule for each sequence.

2 Use the number lines to help you find the missing terms.

a 2, 0, -2, -4, ...

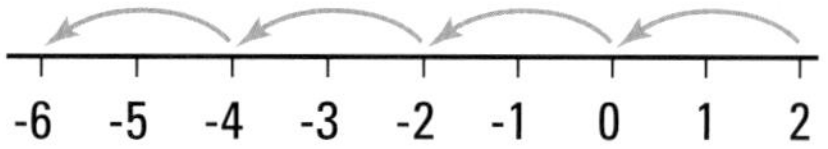

b ....., 1, -2, -5, ..., ..., ...

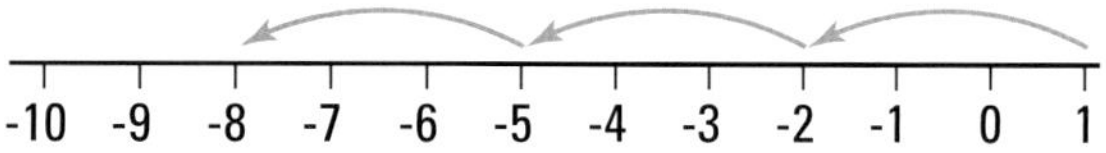

3 An ice cube is heated.
Its temperature is recorded every minute on this table.
Copy the table and fill in the missing temperatures.

Time (minutes)	0	1	2	3	4	5	6
Temperature (°C)			-2	2	6	10	

challenge

Sam records his spending.

If he promises not to spend any more until September, when will he pay off his debt?

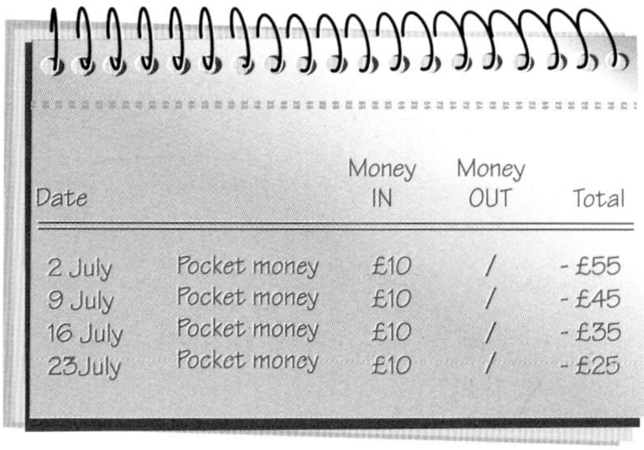

Date		Money IN	Money OUT	Total
2 July	Pocket money	£10	/	- £55
9 July	Pocket money	£10	/	- £45
16 July	Pocket money	£10	/	- £35
23July	Pocket money	£10	/	- £25

2e Functions

- Find an output when you know an input to a function

Keywords
Function *Output*
Input *Rule*

- A **function** uses a **rule**.

The **input** goes in. The function works on the input. The **output** comes out.

Input

1
2
3
4

Output

3 1 + 2
4 2 + 2
5 3 + 2
6 4 + 2

example

Send each input through the function +5.

Input

a 1
b 2
c 3
d 10

Output

a 6 1 + 5
b 7 2 + 5
c 8 3 + 5
d 15 10 + 5

example

Send each input through the function ×2.

Input

a 10
b 5
c 4

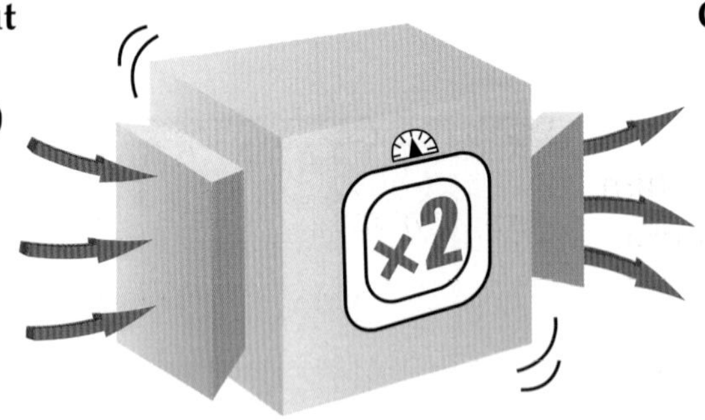

Output

a 20 10 × 2
b 10 5 × 2
c 8 4 × 2

Exercise 2e

1 Find the output for each function machine.

a 4 → ×2 → b 6 → +4 → c 12 → ÷2 →

d 8 → +3 → e 7 → ×10 → f 9 → −3 →

2 Send each input through the function ×5.

Input

a 3

b 5

c 7

d 10

Output

3 Send each input through the function +8.

Input

a 8

b 14

c 22

d 50

Output

4 A train ticket costs £5 per day.
How much would you pay if you travelled

a 1 day b 2 days

c 5 days d 10 days?

Set up a function machine to help you.

×5

challenge

A train ticket costs £30 per week.
Bradley has a rail card which gives him £10 back if he buys tickets for 4 weeks.
Draw a function machine to find out how much Bradley spends.

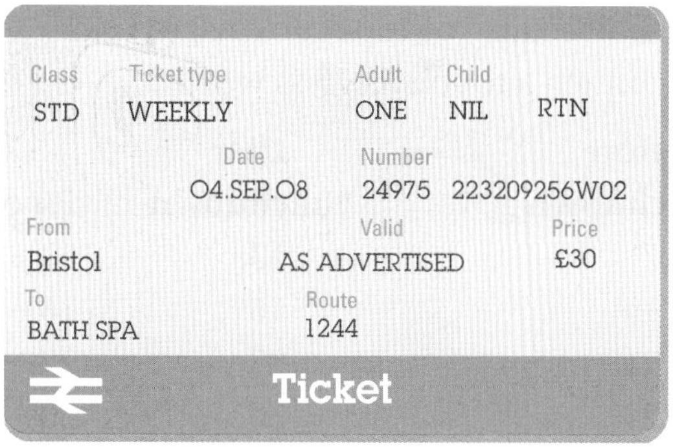

2f Mapping

- Complete a mapping when you know the rule

Keywords
Input
Mapping
Output

Each **input** has an **output**.

- A **mapping** shows you how an input matches to an output.

Input		Output	
1		3	
2	×3	6	This mapping shows ×3.
3		9	'Multiply by 3' is the rule.

example

In rugby, a try scores 5 points.
Complete this mapping for rugby scores.

before try		after try
0		5
5	+5	10
8		13
19		24

Add 5 to each 'before try' score.

example

Use this mapping of American Football scores, or touchdowns, to find how much a touchdown is worth?

before touchdown		after touchdown
7		13
10	?	16
21		27
24		30

Find each difference.
$13 - 7 = 6$
$16 - 10 = 6$
$27 - 21 = 6$ The mapping shows +6.
$30 - 24 = 6$ A touchdown is worth 6 points.

p. 250

Exercise 2f

1 Fill in the numbers missing from each mapping.

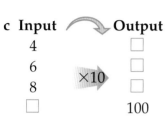

a

Input		Output
3		9
5	×3	□
□		30
8		□

b

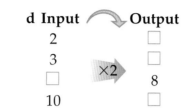

Input		Output
1		□
3	×5	15
5		□
9		□

c

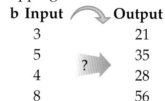

Input		Output
4		□
6	×10	□
8		□
□		100

d

Input		Output
2		□
3	×2	□
□		8
10		□

2 Work out the relationship for each mapping.

a

Input		Output
4		16
2	?	8
10		40
8		32

b

Input		Output
3		21
5	?	35
4		28
8		56

3 Copy and complete each mapping.

a Double your money!

before		after
£50		£100
£25	×2	□
£110		□
□		£80

b Half price sale!

before		after
£4		£2
£16	÷2	□
£100		□
£80		□

challenge

a Use this recipe to write a mapping.

sugar → **eggs**

b If you used 5 cups of sugar, how many eggs would you use?

Recipe

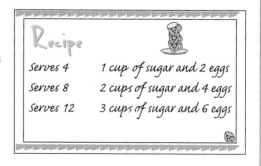

Serves 4	*1 cup of sugar and 2 eggs*
Serves 8	*2 cups of sugar and 4 eggs*
Serves 12	*3 cups of sugar and 6 eggs*

2 Consolidation

2a

1 Write the missing number in each sequence.

a 8, 10, __ , 14, 16

b 1, __ , 14, 21, 28

c 21, 18, 15, 12, __

d 2, 4, 6, __ , 10

e __ , 6, 18, 54, 162

2b

2 Match the sequences on the right with the statements on the left.

'Multiply by 3'	105, 80, 55, 30
'Add 35'	45, 80, 115, 150
'Divide by 4'	768, 192, 48, 12
'Multiply by 5'	25, 75, 225, 675
'Subtract 25'	12, 60, 300, 1500
'Divide by 6'	5400, 900, 150, 25

2c

3 Write the first six terms of each sequence described below.

a 'Start at 6 and $\times$5.'

b 'Start at 12 000 and $\div$2.'

c 'Start at 200 000 and $\div$5.'

2d

4 Use the number lines to help you find the missing terms.

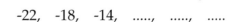

a

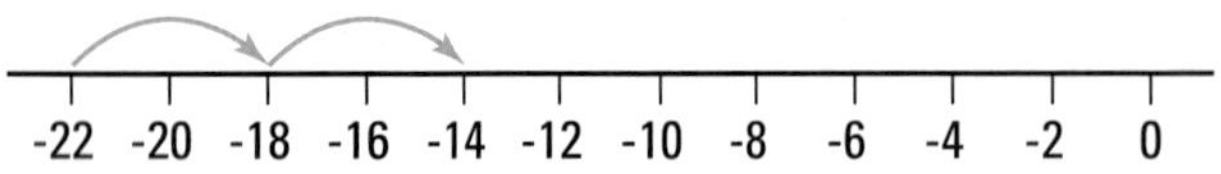

-22, -18, -14, ..., ..., ...

b

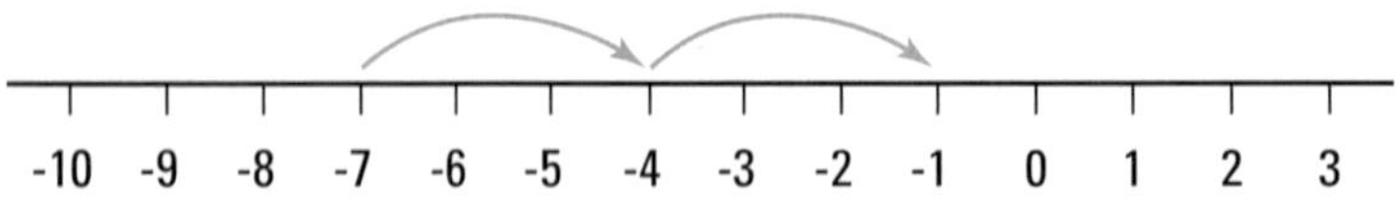

....., -7, -4, ..., ..., ...

c

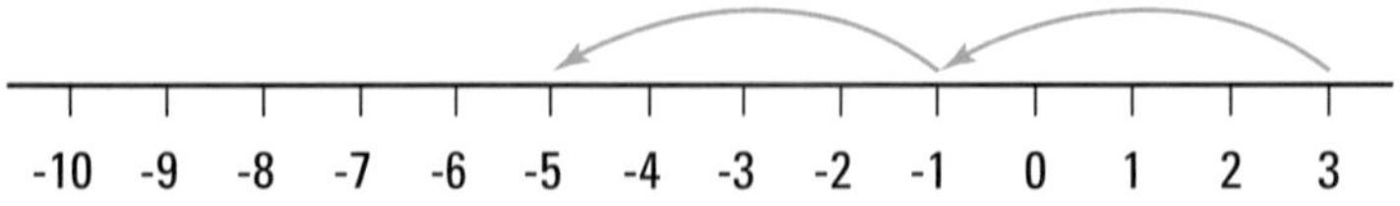

3, ..., -5 ....., ..., ...

2e

5 Put each input through the function machine and give each output.

a Input: 2, 3, 4, 5, 6 → ×4 → Output

b Input: 45, 35, 25, 15, 5 → ÷5 → Output

c Input: 30, 24, 18, 12, 6 → ÷3 → Output

d Input: 2, 4, 6, 8, 10 → ×10 → Output

2f

6 Copy and complete each of these mappings.

a −15

Input	Output
60	□
45	□
30	15
15	□

b ×5

Input	Output
2	□
4	□
6	□
8	40

c ÷4

Input	Output
32	□
24	□
16	4
8	□

7 Find the rule for each of these mappings.

a ?

Input	Output
4	11
8	15
16	23
19	26

b ?

Input	Output
50	25
32	16
28	14
16	8

c ?

Input	Output
8	2
24	18
30	24
35	29

2 Summary

Key indicators

- Use a function machine **Level 3**
- Predict numbers in a sequence **Level 3**

Level 4

1 One pound (£1) is about the same as two dollars ($2).

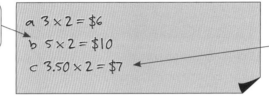

Use the function machine to change these amounts to dollars

a £3
b £5
c £3.50

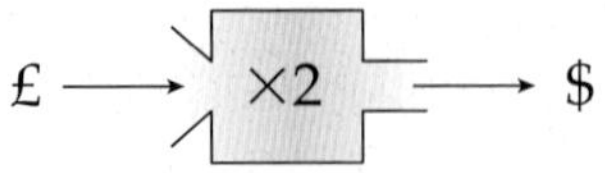

Naira's answer ✔

Naira multiplies each number by 2.

a $3 \times 2 = \$6$
b $5 \times 2 = \$10$
c $3.50 \times 2 = \$7$

Naira knows 3.50 is the same as $3\frac{1}{2}$ and $3\frac{1}{2} \times 2 = 7$.

Level 3

2 A sequence of numbers decreases by 3 each time.

Write the missing numbers in the sequence below.
You can use the number line on the right to help you.

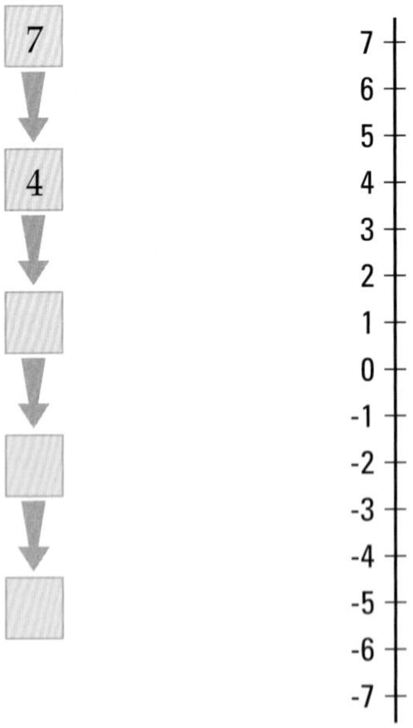

Key Stage 3 2007 3–5 Paper 1

3 Shape

Measures

A clock is a device for measuring time. People didn't start using clocks every day until the Industrial Revolution. They needed to keep track of when to start work at the factories and how many hours they had worked each day.

What's the point? You need to read a clock accurately or you'll be late (or early)!

Check in

Level 2

1 What time is it?

a

b

c

Level 3

2 Cog A turns. When it does, the other five cogs turn as well.

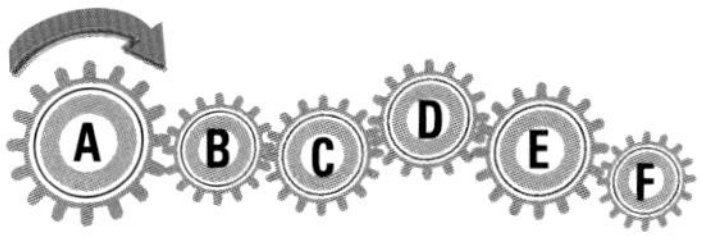

Cog A turns in a **clockwise** direction.

a Will cog B turn in a **clockwise** direction or an **anticlockwise** direction?

b Which direction will cog C turn in?

c Which direction will cog F turn in?

3a Measuring lines

- Choose between mm, cm, m, and km
- Measure lengths in centimetres and millimetres

Keywords
Centimetre *Metre*
Divisions *Metric*
Kilometre *Millimetre*
Length

The four common **metric** units of length are

Millimetres
very small lengths

Centimetres
small distances

Metres
bigger distances

Kilometres
very big distances

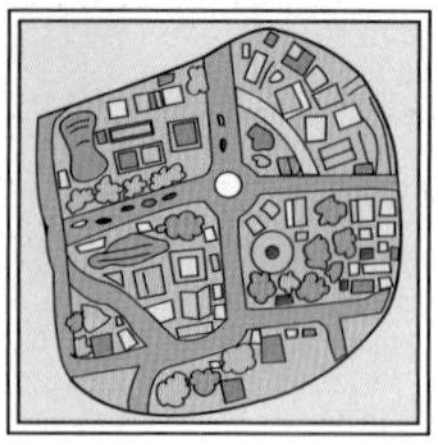

10 millimetres (mm) ⇒ 1 centimetre (cm)
100 centimetres ⇒ 1 metre (m)
1000 metres ⇒ 1 kilometre (km)

When measuring or drawing a line, you must start your measurement at the zero mark.

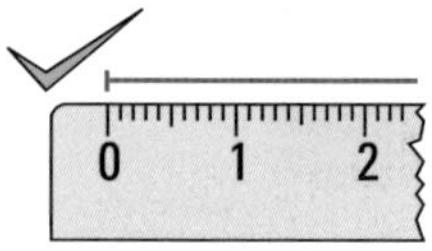

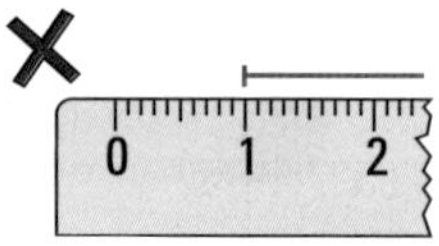

Each **centimetre** is divided into 10 smaller parts.

Each large numbered length is a **centimetre**.

Each smaller length is a **millimetre**.

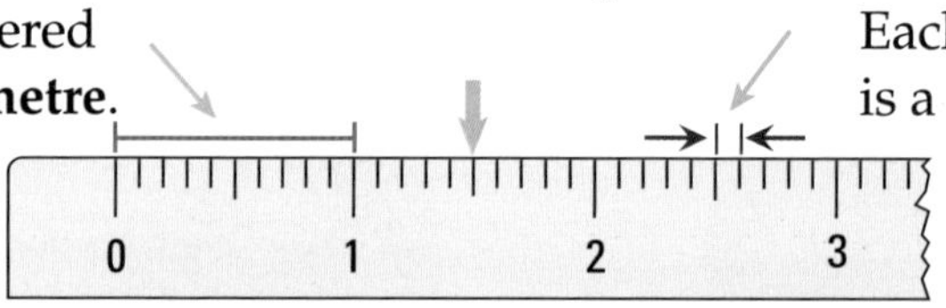

example

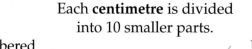

What is the length of this line?

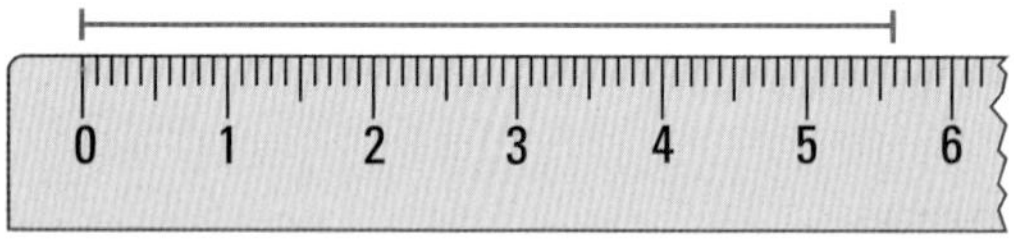

This line is 5 cm and 6 mm long.

Write this as 5.6 cm.

The decimal point shows this is 5 whole cm and $\frac{6}{10}$ cm

example

Which unit would you use to measure each of these?

a your hand
b a pen tip
c the distance from London to Leeds
d a door frame

a centimetres Your hand is about 15 cm
b millimetres A pen tip is about 3 mm
c kilometres The distance is about 315 km
d metres A door frame is about 2 m

Exercise 3a

1 Which of these units would you use to measure parts **a–h**?

millimetre	centimetre	metre	kilometre

a the length of your little finger
b the distance from your home to school
c the length of your classroom
d the width of your exercise book
e the thickness of a pencil
f the thickness of a 2p coin
g the length of a football pitch
h the distance from the earth to the moon

2 Give the length of each line by reading the ruler.

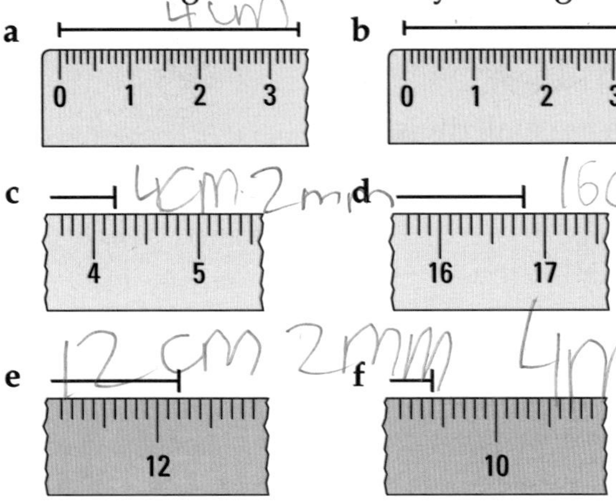

Did you know?

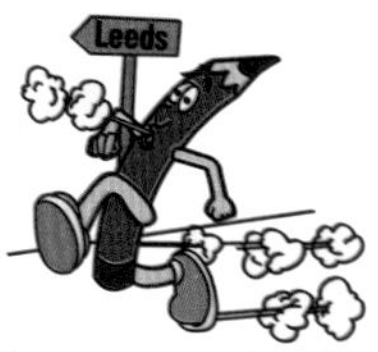

An average lead pencil will draw a line 48 km long.

3 Use a ruler to measure each line in centimetres and match it to a measurement from the box.

a ├──────────┤
b ├────────────┤
c ├─────────┤
d ├─────────────┤
e ├───────────┤
f ├──────────┤

A	6.9 cm	B	7.5 cm
C	7.2 cm	D	6.6 cm
E	5.9 cm	F	6.3 cm

4 Draw these lines accurately.
Write the measurement beside each line you draw.

a 3 cm **b** 7 cm **c** 45 mm
d 58 mm **e** 11.2 cm **f** 9.9 cm

puzzle

Which blue line is longer?

Check your estimate with a ruler.

3b Reading scales

- Read different scales accurately

Keywords
Scales
Measurements
Instruments

- **Scales** show measurements on a display.

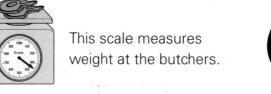

This scale measures weight at the butchers.

This scale measures petrol in a car.

The green scale shows intervals of 10.
The arrow is pointing to a number between 20 and 30.
The numbers in between 20 and 30 are shown as small divisions.

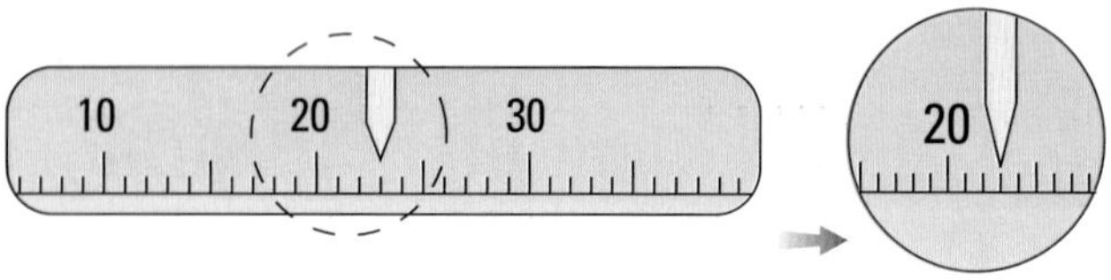

Count on from 20.
The arrow is pointing at 23.

The blue scale is numbered in ones.
There are 10 small divisions between each number.
Each small division is one tenth or 0.1.
The arrow is pointing to a number between 3 and 4.

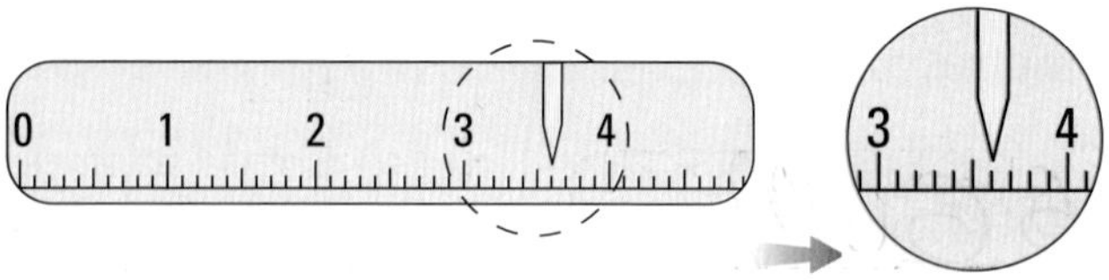

The arrow is pointing at 3 whole units and 6 tenths.
This is written 3.6.

example

What reading is shown on this scale?

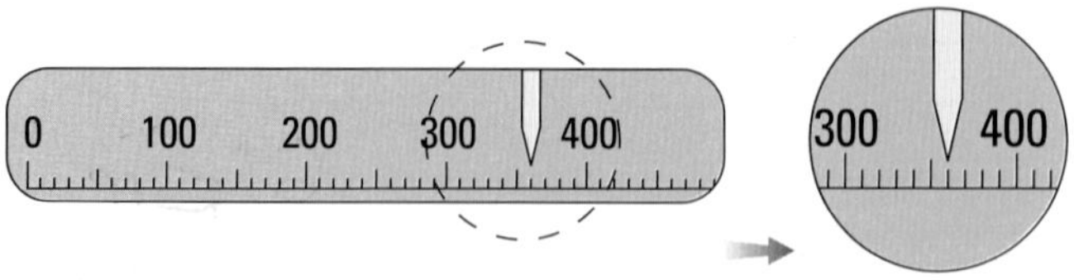

First, determine the intervals.	Intervals of 100 with 10 small divisions between each number.
Then find the value of each small division.	$100 \div 10 = 10$ Each small division = 10
The arrow is pointing between 300 and 400. Count on from 300.	You count 6 small divisions. Each small division is 10. $6 \times 10 = 60$
The reading on the scale is 360.	$300 + 60 = 360$

Exercise 3b

1 Look carefully at each dial. Decide which is the best guess.

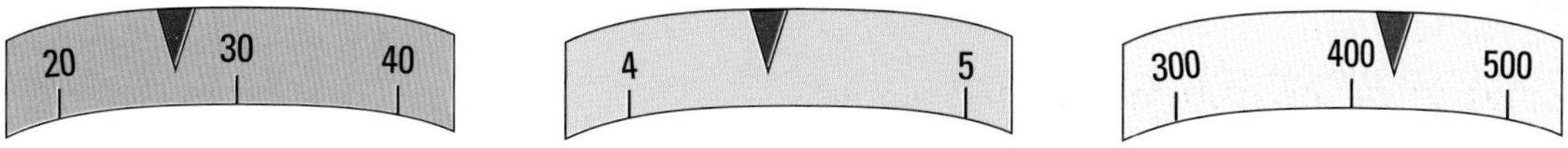

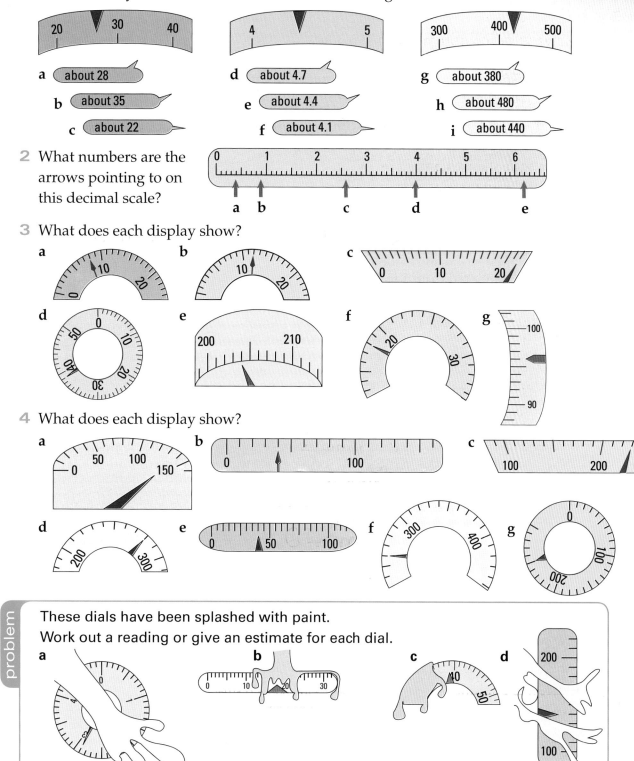

a about 28
b about 35
c about 22

d about 4.7
e about 4.4
f about 4.1

g about 380
h about 480
i about 440

2 What numbers are the arrows pointing to on this decimal scale?

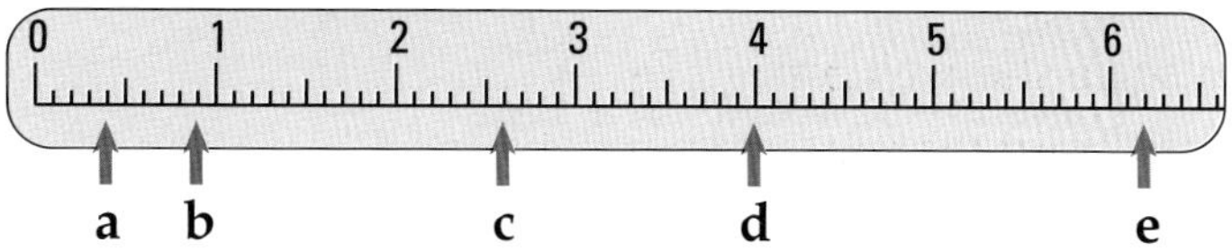

3 What does each display show?

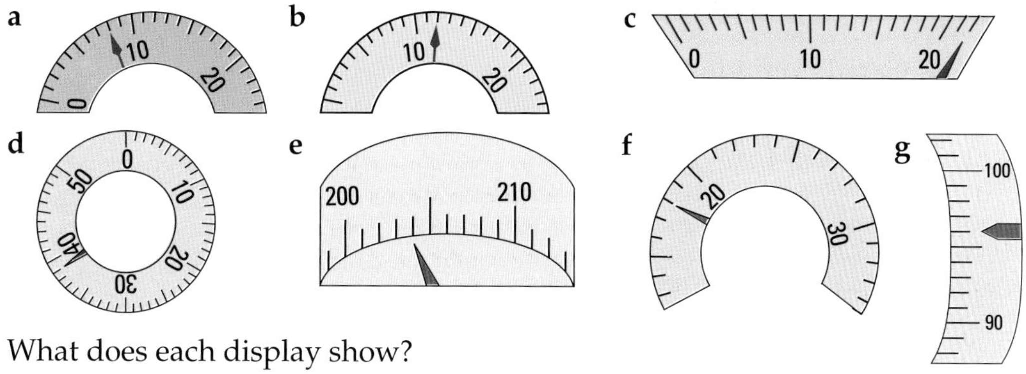

4 What does each display show?

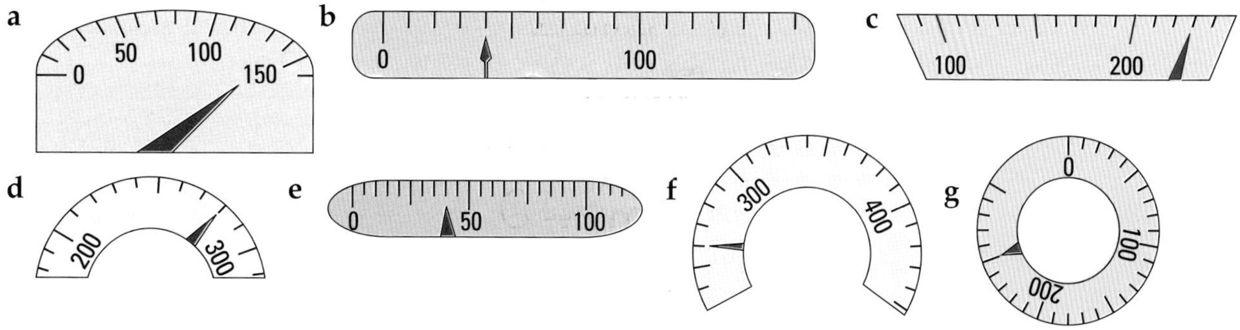

problem

These dials have been splashed with paint.
Work out a reading or give an estimate for each dial.

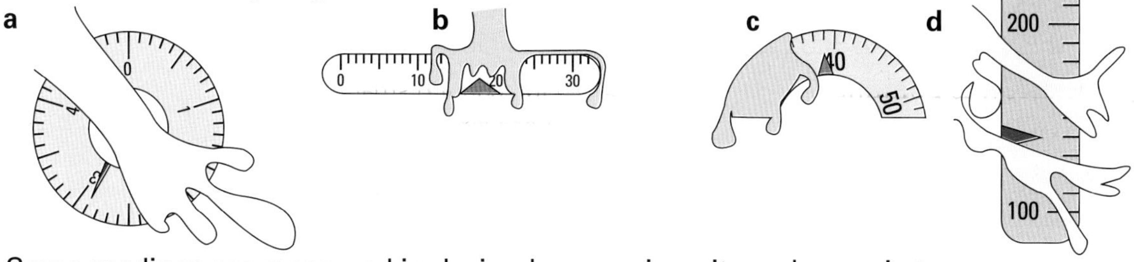

Some readings are measured in decimals, some in units and some in tens.

3c Time

- Tell the time in different ways

Keywords
a.m. *p.m.*
Clock *Time*
Digital

You measure time on scales.
You should know these units of times.

Second	There are 60 seconds in a minute.
Minute	There are 60 minutes in an hour.
Hour	There are 24 hours in a day.
Day	There are 7 days in a week.
Week	There are 52 weeks in a year.
Month	There are 12 months in a year.
Year	There are 365 days in a year (and 366 in a leap year).

Clocks and calendars are scales.

You read the time on a clock or a calendar.

A clockface is numbered from 1 to 12.

You use **a.m.** for times before midday. You use **p.m.** for times after midday.

The clock shows 8.30 a.m.

The clock shows 8.30 p.m.

- You can also use the 24-hour clock.

The hours before midday read the same.
The hours after midday count on from 12.

This clock shows 8.30 a.m.

This clock shows 8.30 p.m.

Exercise 3c

1 Which of these units of time would you use to measure parts **a–f**?

seconds	minutes	hours	days	weeks	months	years

a tying your shoe lace
b you are asked how old you are
c the amount you sleep each night
d the length of your summer holidays
e the time it takes to run 100 metres
f the time it takes to boil an egg

2 Here are the timings of Kim's day.

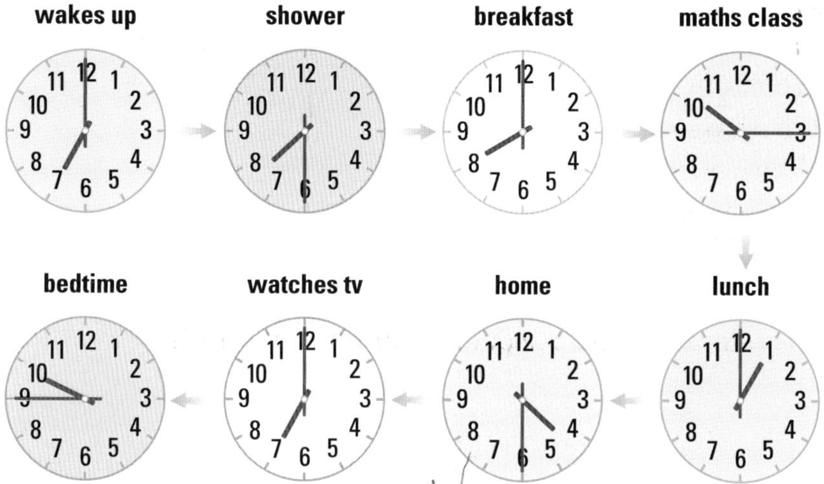

a What is Kim doing at 7 p.m.?
b Does Kim have lunch at 1 a.m. or 1 p.m.?
c What is she doing at eight o'clock?
d Where is Kim at a quarter past ten in the morning?
e What is Kim doing at 7.30 a.m.?
f What is Kim doing at half past four in the afternoon?
g What time does Kim go to bed?

Did you know?

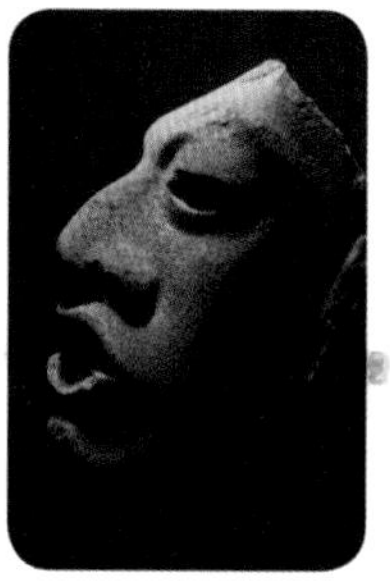

The Mayan civilisation in what is now Mexico used a system of 60 to record time.

3 Match the times on the clockface with the same time on a digital clock.

challenge

Work out your age in hours to the nearest hour.
Use a calculator to help you.

3d Shapes

- Know the names of simple shapes
- Know if a shape is regular or not

Keywords
Parallel
Regular
Sides

You need to know these shapes

Circle — **Square** — **Rectangle** — **Trapezium**

p. 144

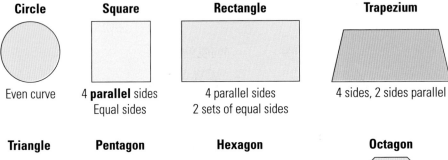

- Circle: Even curve
- Square: 4 **parallel** sides, Equal sides
- Rectangle: 4 parallel sides, 2 sets of equal sides
- Trapezium: 4 sides, 2 sides parallel

Triangle — **Pentagon** — **Hexagon** — **Octagon**

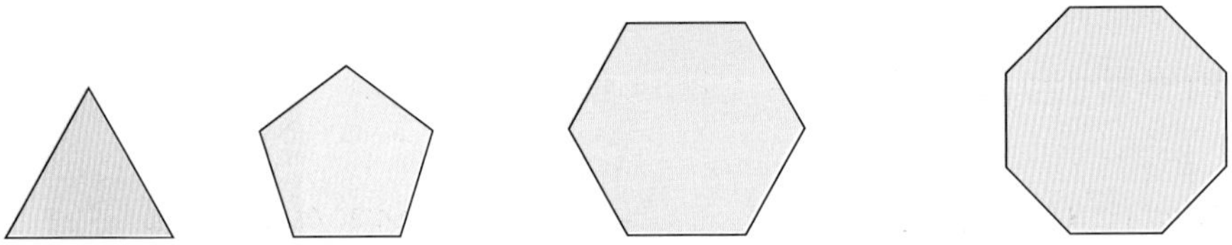

- Triangle: 3 sides
- Pentagon: 5 sides
- Hexagon: 6 sides
- Octagon: 8 sides

- If a shape is **regular**, all of its sides are the same length.

example

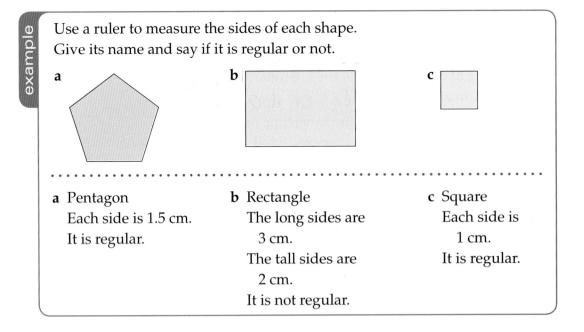

Use a ruler to measure the sides of each shape.
Give its name and say if it is regular or not.

a

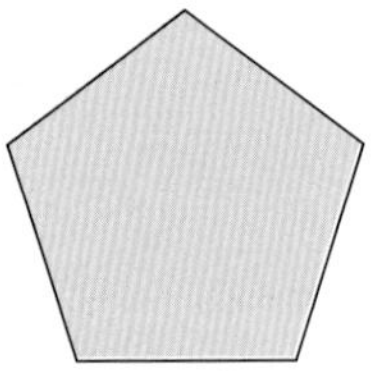

b

c

a Pentagon
Each side is 1.5 cm.
It is regular.

b Rectangle
The long sides are 3 cm.
The tall sides are 2 cm.
It is not regular.

c Square
Each side is 1 cm.
It is regular.

Exercise 3d

1 Give the name of each shape.

a 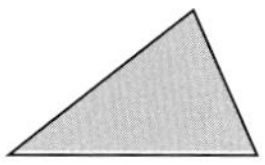

b 

c 

d 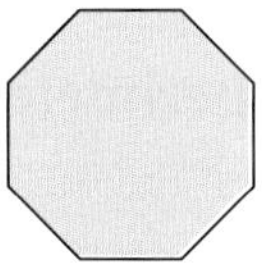

e 

f 

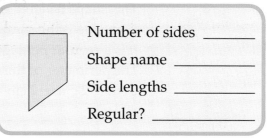

g 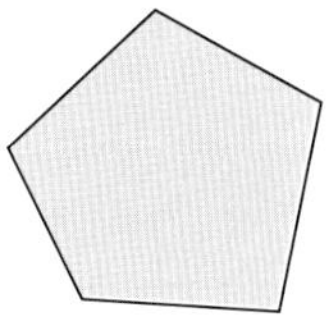

h 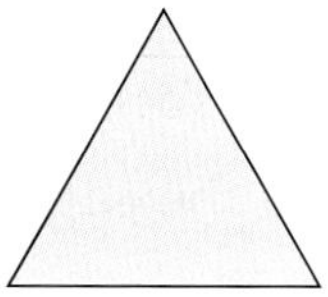

i 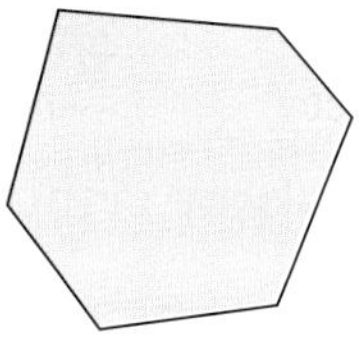

2 Measure the sides of each shape and fill in the missing information.

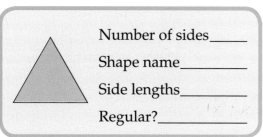

a 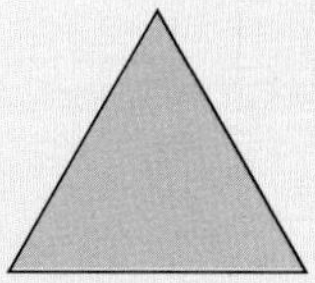

Number of sides_____

Shape name_________

Side lengths_________

Regular?___________

b 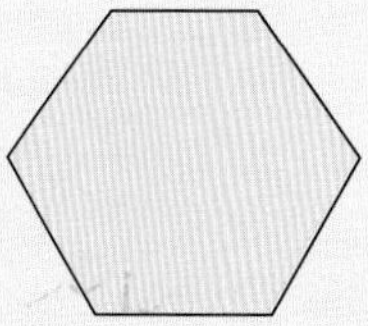

Number of sides _____

Shape name _________

Side lengths _________

Regular? ___________

c 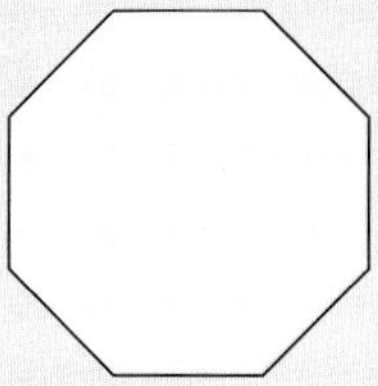

Number of sides _____

Shape name _________

Side lengths _________

Regular? ___________

d 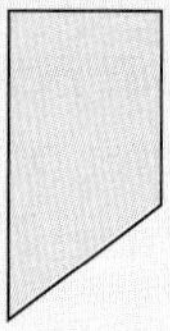

Number of sides _____

Shape name _________

Side lengths _________

Regular? ___________

challenge

Is this shape a square?
Why or why not?

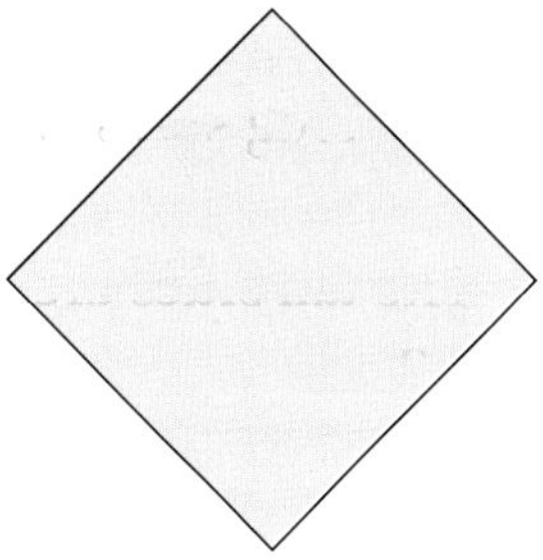

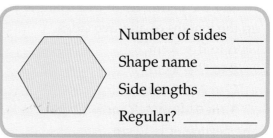

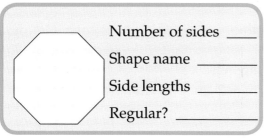

3e Perimeter

- Calculate the perimeters of simple shapes

Keywords
Edge
Perimeter
Regular

Rita is painting a white line around the edge of this table-tennis table.

When finished, the white line will go around the **perimeter** of the table.

- The **perimeter** of a shape is the distance around the **edge**.

example

What is the perimeter of this shape?

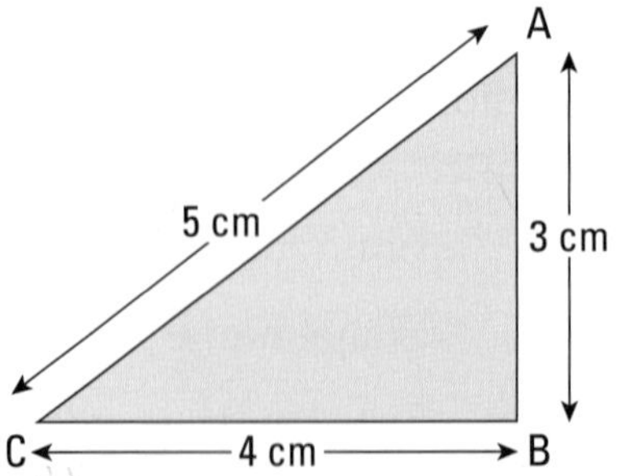

To find the perimeter of this triangle you add up the lengths of all three sides.

A to B = 3 cm
B to C = 4 cm
C to A = 5 cm
3 cm + 4 cm + 5 cm = 12 cm

The perimeter is 12 cm

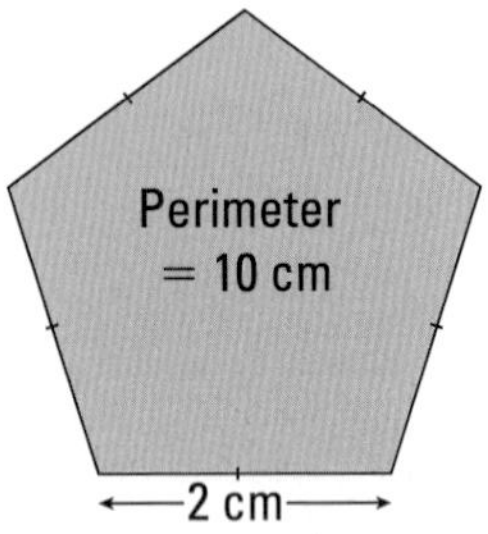

This shape has five sides.
Each side is the same length.
It is a **regular** pentagon.
The perimeter of this pentagon is:
2 cm + 2 cm + 2 cm + 2 cm + 2 cm = 10 cm

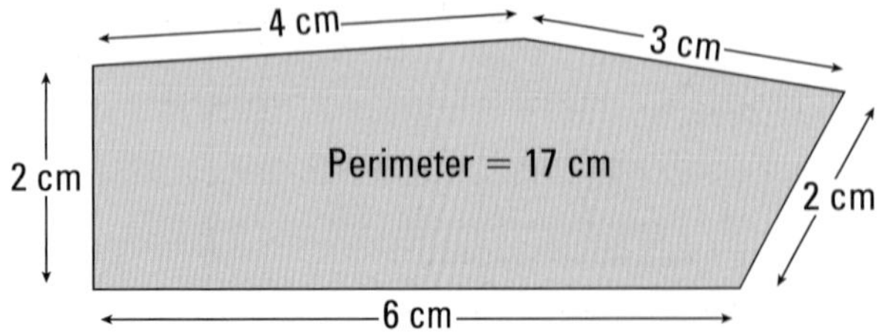

This shape has five sides.
The sides are not all the same length.
This pentagon is **not** regular.
The perimeter of this pentagon is:
4 cm + 3 cm + 2 cm + 6 cm + 2 cm = 17 cm

Exercise 3e

Don't use a ruler for the exercises on this page.

1 What is the perimeter of each shape?
Give your answers in centimetres (cm).

a
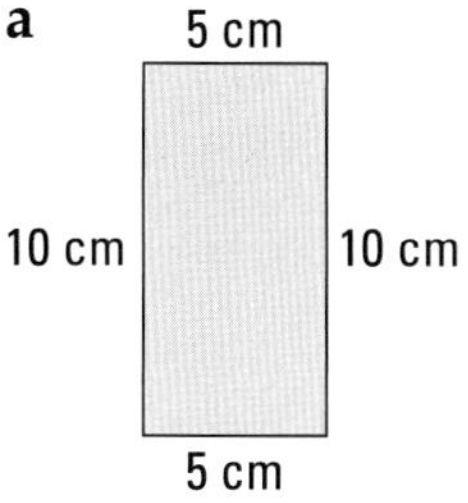

b
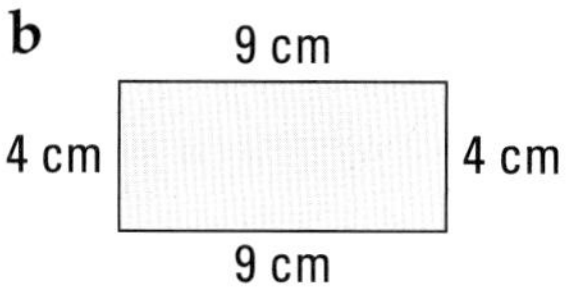

c
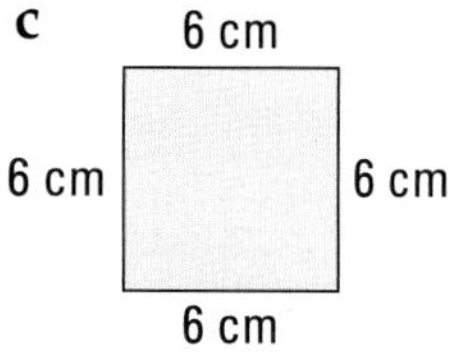

d
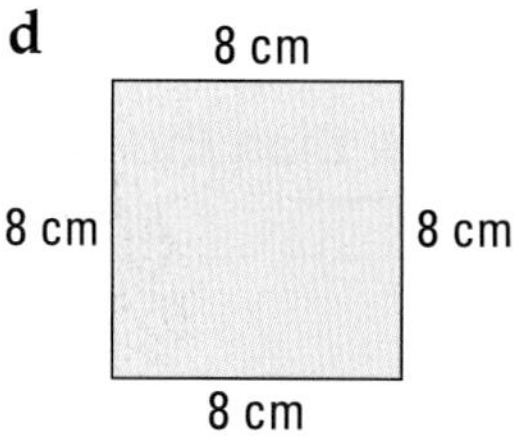

2 What is the perimeter of each **regular** polygon?
Remember, the sides are all the same length.

a
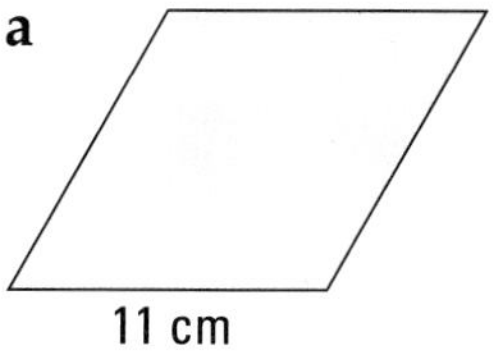

b
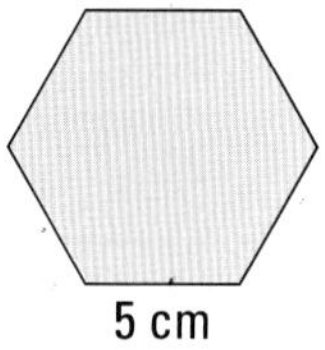

c
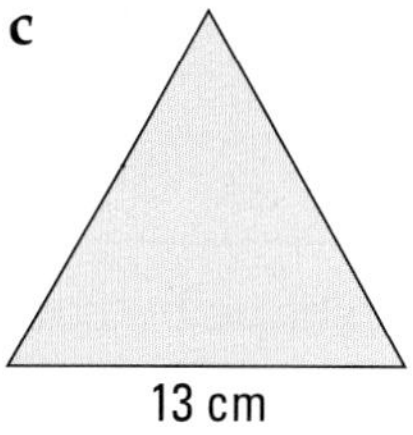

d
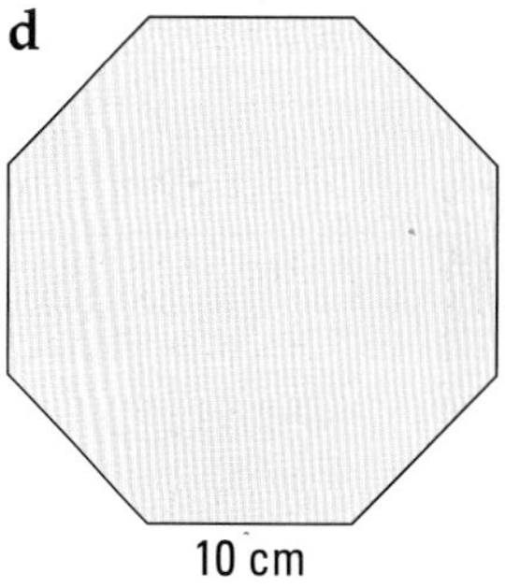

3 These polygons are **not regular**. What is the perimeter of each?

a
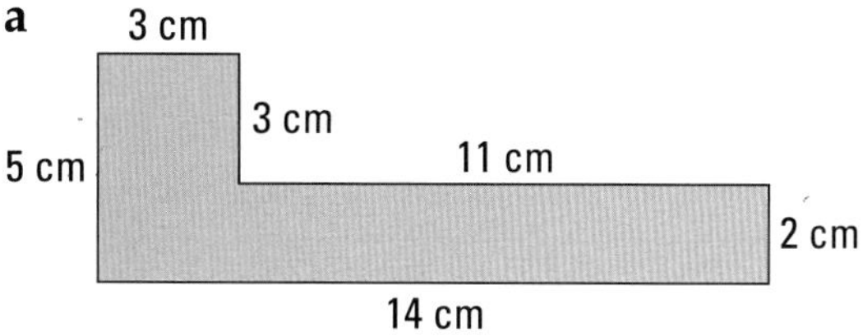

b
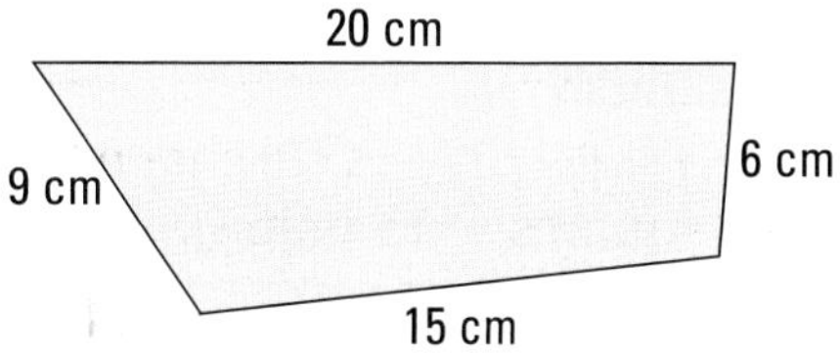

4 This netball court is made of rectangles.
Find the perimeter of
a the full court
b each third of the court.

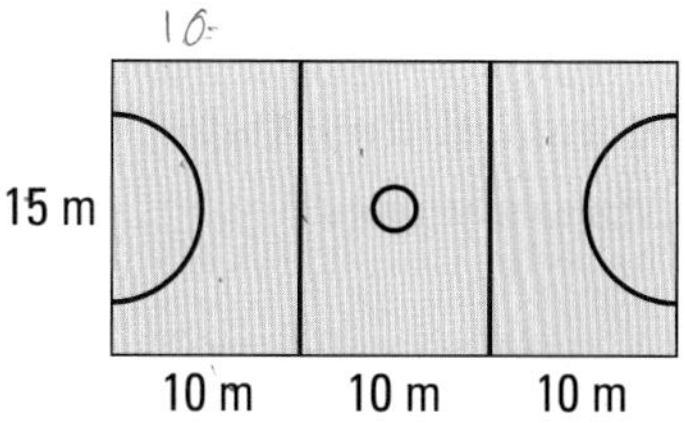

challenge

a The perimeter of this triangle is 35 cm.
What is the length of the missing side?

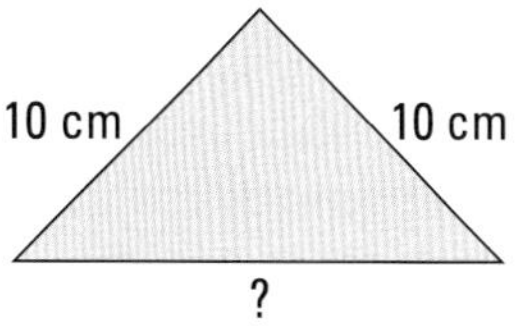

b This is a square. The perimeter is 20 cm.
What is the length of each side?

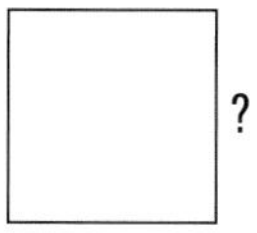

3f Area

- Find the areas of shapes by counting squares

Keywords
Area *Square units*
Length *Width*

- **Area** measures the space inside a 2-D shape.

The sheet of paper has a smaller area than the table-top.

The table-top has a smaller area than the kitchen floor.

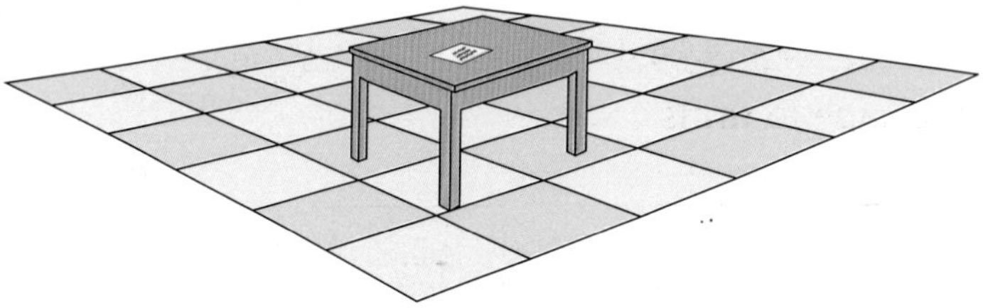

- Area is measured by finding how many **square units** (units²) would cover a shape.

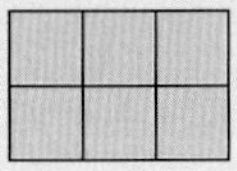

This shape is made of 6 squares. Its area is 6 $units^2$.

example

Give the area of each shape by counting squares.

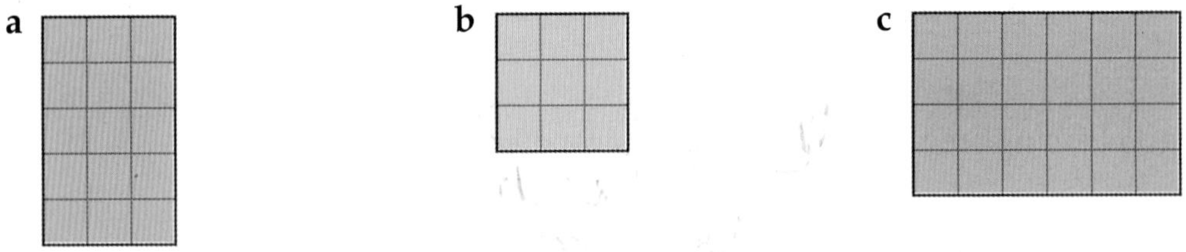

a 15 squares = 15 $units^2$ **b** 9 squares = 9 $units^2$ **c** 24 squares = 24 $units^2$

- You can guess about the area of a shape if it covers parts of squares.

example

Give the area of this shape by counting squares.

Count the whole squares. 24 squares
Count the half squares. About 6 half squares, so 3 whole squares
Add them together. 24 + 3 = 27 squares
The area is about 27 $units^2$.

Exercise 3f

1 How many squares are there in each shape?

a

b

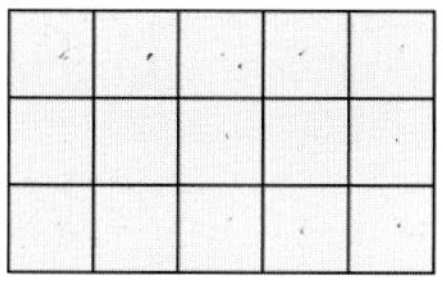

c

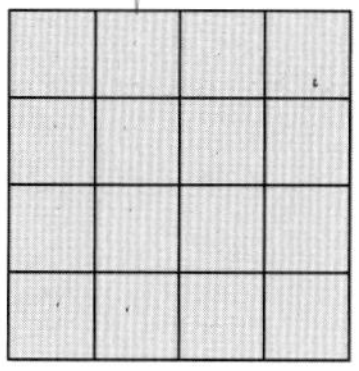

d

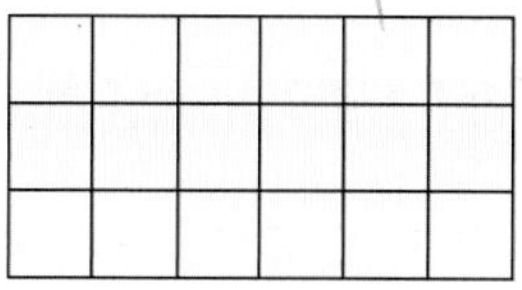

2 Mira has a bag of tiles. She arranges the tiles into rectangles.
Give the area of each shape in units^2.

a

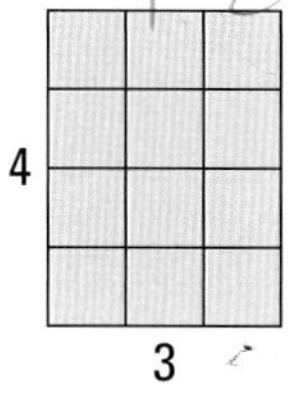

b

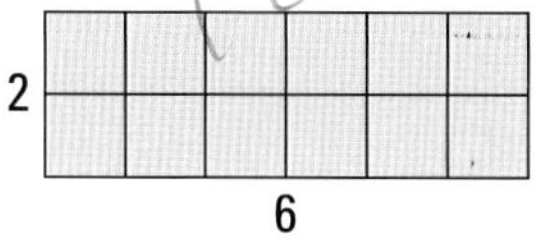

c

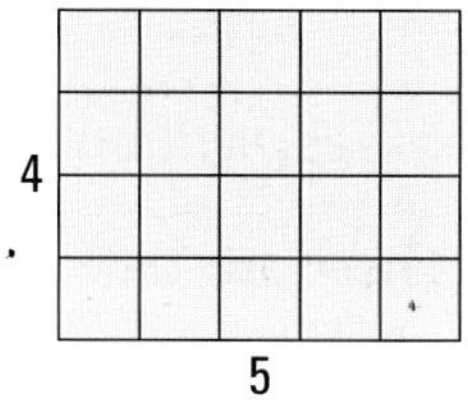

d

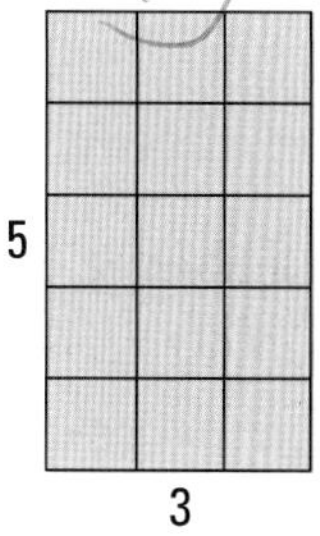

3 What is the area of each shape? Give your answer in units^2.

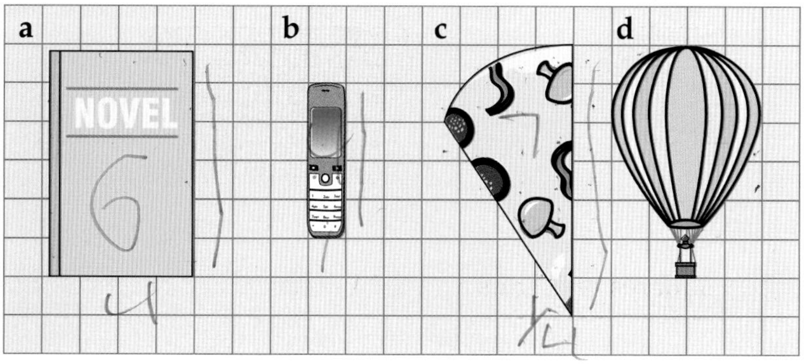

challenge

These areas have been paved with square slabs.
Not all of the paving can be seen.
Work out how many slabs are used in each area.

a

b

c

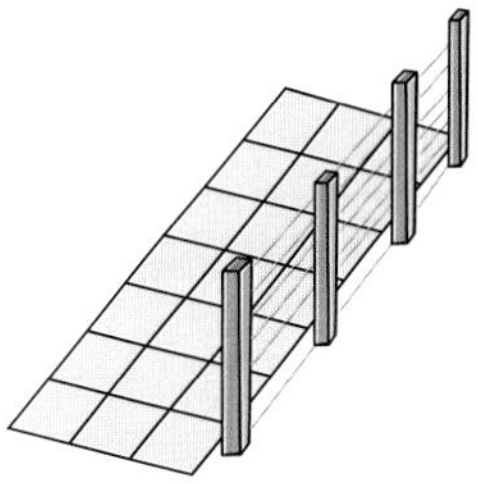

Angles

- Tell the difference between types of angles
- Estimate angles in degrees

Keywords

Acute, *Angle*, *Anticlockwise*, *Clockwise*, *Obtuse*, *Right angle*

You can turn in two directions:

Clockwise

From 12 to 3 is a $\frac{1}{4}$ turn.

Anticlockwise

From 12 to 6 is a $\frac{1}{2}$ turn.

The hands of a clock move in a clockwise direction.

- **You measure turns in degrees, written ° for short.**

There are 360° in a full turn.

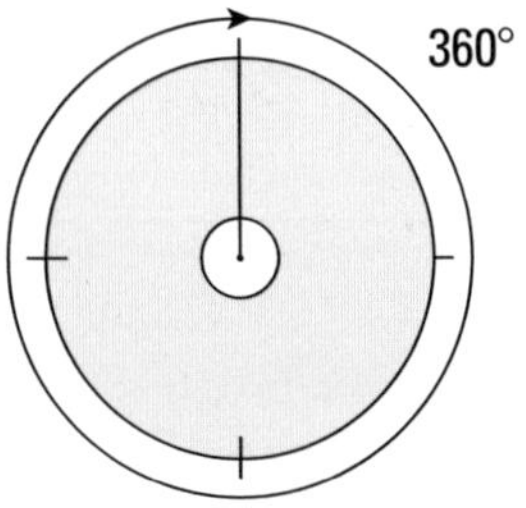

There are 180° in a half turn.

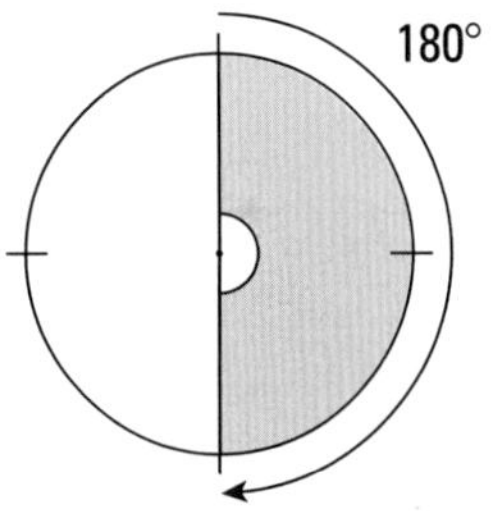

There are 90° in a quarter turn.

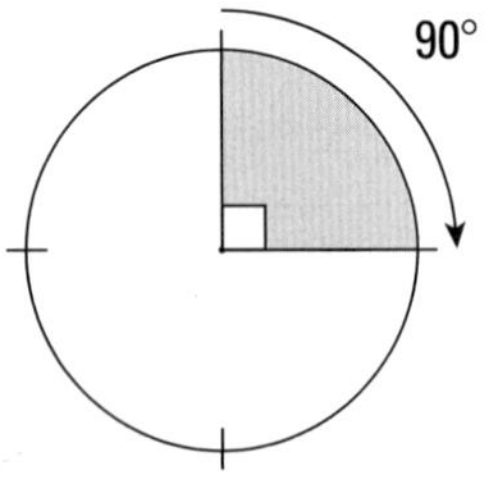

This is a right angle.

- **An angle is a measure of turn.**

p. 138

An **acute** angle is smaller than 90°.

A **right angle** is exactly 90°.

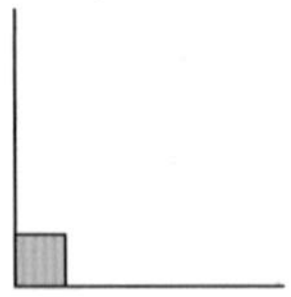

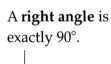

You mark a right angle with a square.

An **obtuse** angle is between 90° and 180°.

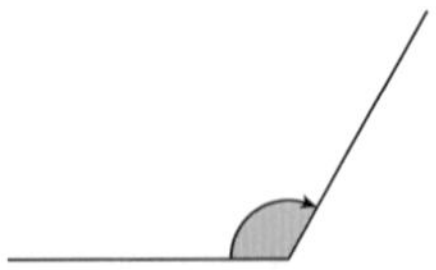

A straight line is exactly 180°.

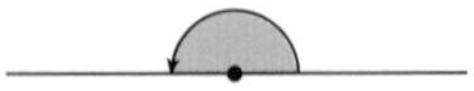

example

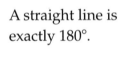

Which one of these angles measures 130°?

a

b

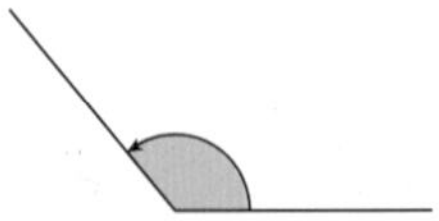

a This angle is an acute angle so it is less than 90°. It cannot be 130°.

b This angle is an obtuse angle so it must be 130°.

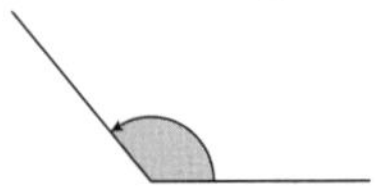

Exercise 3g

1 Name each of these angles. Choose your answer from this list.

acute   right   obtuse   straight line

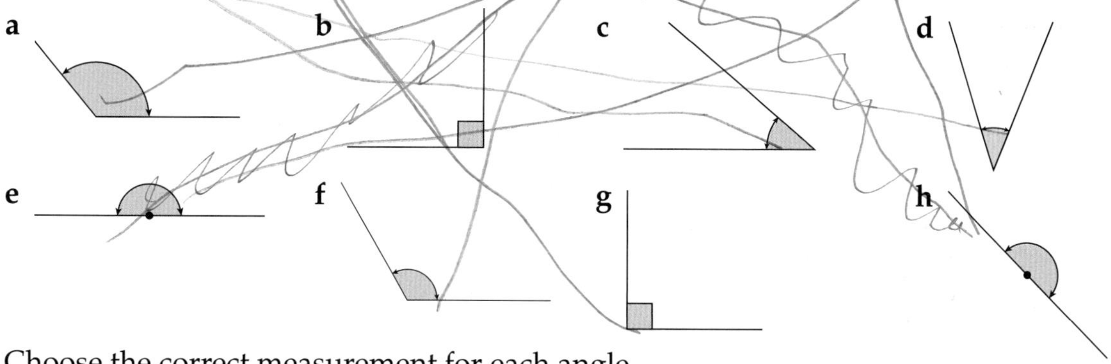

2 Choose the correct measurement for each angle.

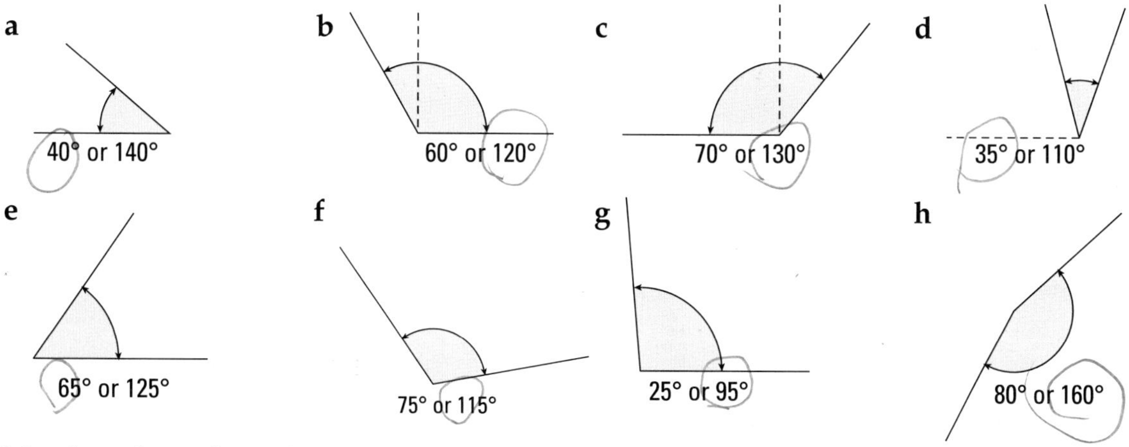

3 Match each angle with a measurement from this list.

180°   20°   90°   155°   75°   120°

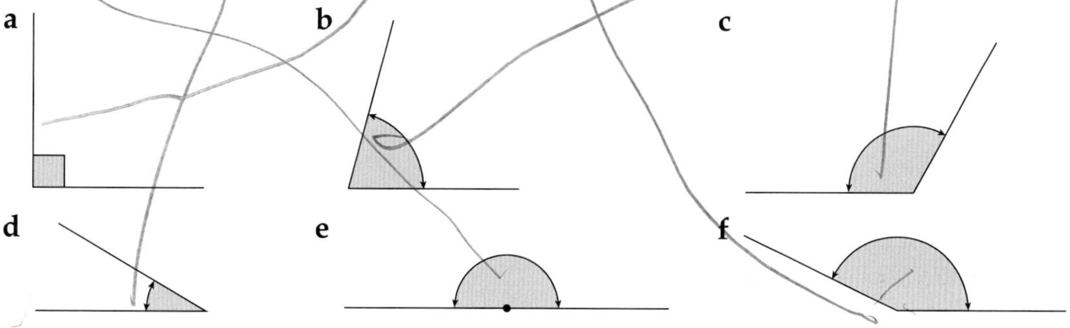

challenge

Alex has measured five angles. Which measurements are wrong?
Do not measure.

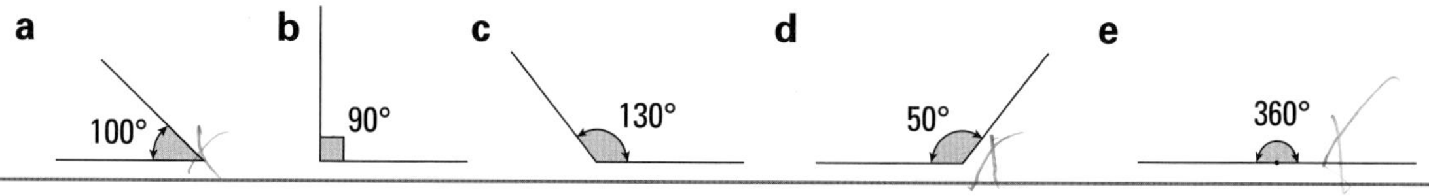

3 Consolidation

3a

1 Draw a line of each length.
Write the measurement beside each line that you draw.

a 10 cm **b** 9 cm **c** 13 cm
d 10.5 cm **e** 11.4 cm **f** 8.2 cm

2 Measure the length of each of these lines.

a ______________________________

b __________________________

c ____________________

3b

3 What number are the arrows pointing to on each scale

a

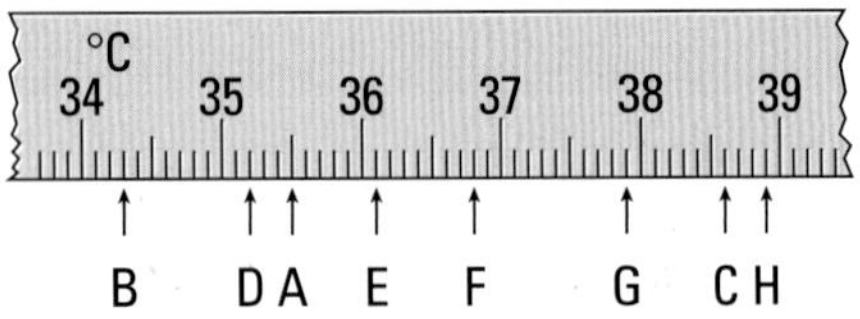

b

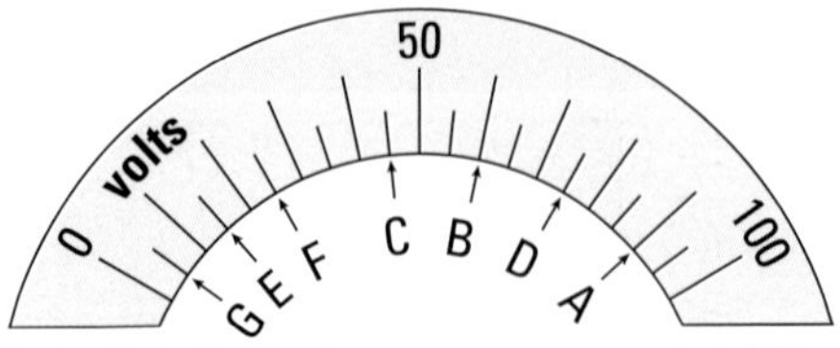

3c

4 Write each of these times using the 24-hour clock.

a

p.m.

b

p.m.

c

a.m.

d

p.m.

e

p.m.

f

a.m.

3d

5 Find the perimeter of each of these shapes.

a

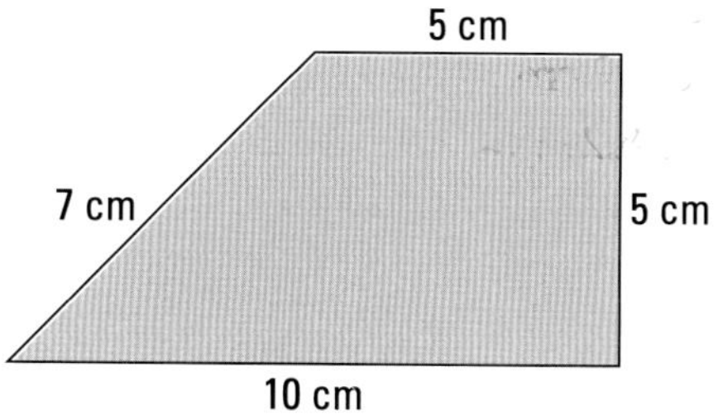

b

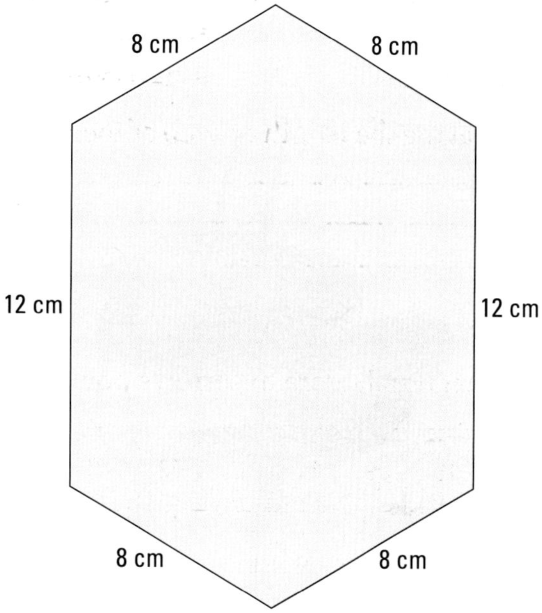

c

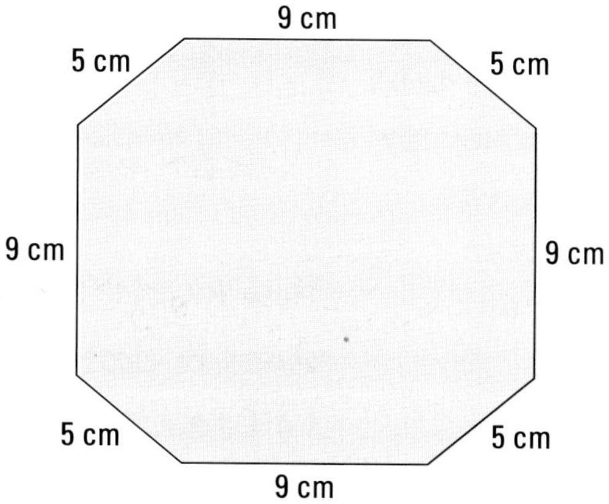

3e

6 Find the area of each rectangle by counting squares. Which one of the rectangles has an area different to the other two?

a

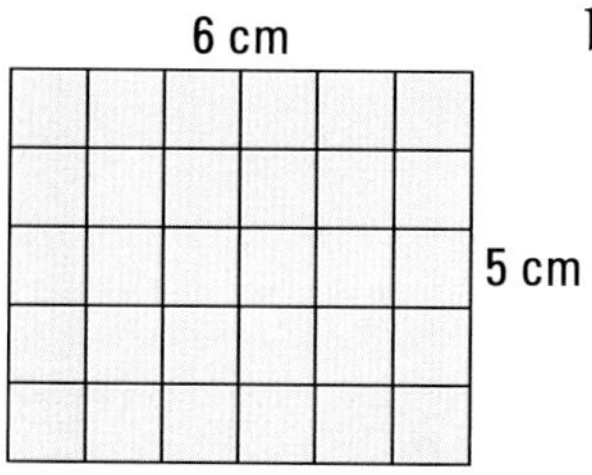

b

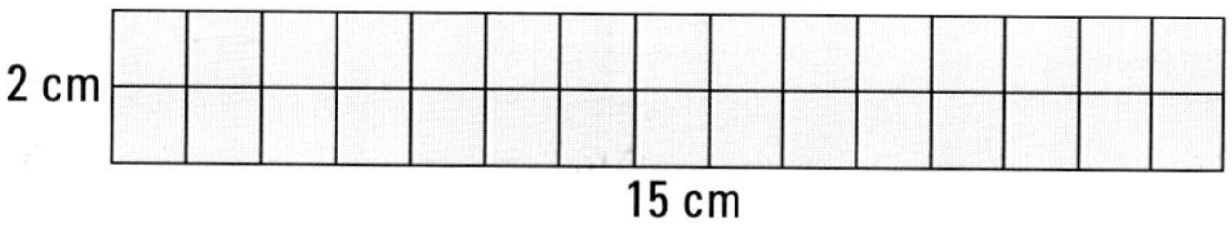

c

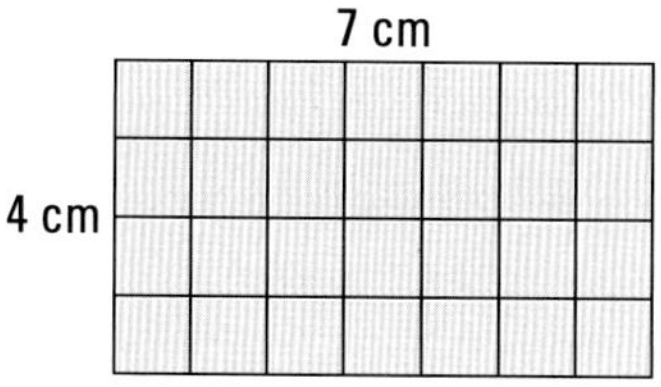

3f

7 What kind of angle is each of these?

a

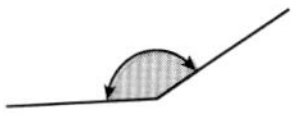

b

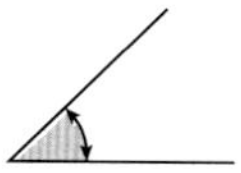

c

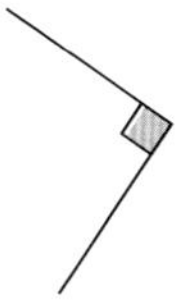

d

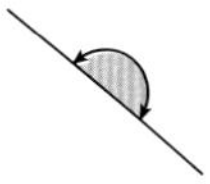

Maths Life

Meet your match!

Owning an animal involves much more than just love and affection. This is what each of these animals expects from its owners.

FISH

Food: 1 g per day, £5 for 100 g
Space: 20 litre tank
Time: 1 hour every two weeks to clean the tank

How much does it cost to feed a fish each day?

CAT

Food: 100 g tin per day, 25p per tin
Vet: £30 twice a year
Space: 100 m^2 in or out
Time: 30 minutes per day to play

DOG

Food: 200 g per day, £1.70 per kg
Vet: £100 per year
Space: 300 m^2 garden
Time: 2 x 30 minute walks per day

TORTOISE

Food: 60 g leaves per day
Vet: £20 per year
Space: 5 m^2 indoor tank, 10 m^2 garden
Time: 30 minutes per day

How much space does a tortoise need in total?

1 Which animal needs

a the most space
b the least time
c the most food per day?

2 Which animal would be a match if you had

a £150 to spend each year
b house with a 20m^2 garden
c no garden?

Which animal would you choose? Why?

3 Summary

Key indicators

- Measure area in square centimetres (cm^2) Level 4
- Calculate the perimeter and area of rectangles Level 4

Level 4

1 A square is shown.

a Measure one of the sides.

b Calculate the perimeter of the square.

Russell's answer ✓

Russell uses a ruler to measure one of the sides.

a 3.5 cm

b $3.5 \times 4 = 14$ cm

Russell knows the perimeter is the distance around the outside of the shape.

Level 4

2 Here is a shaded shape on a centimetre square grid.

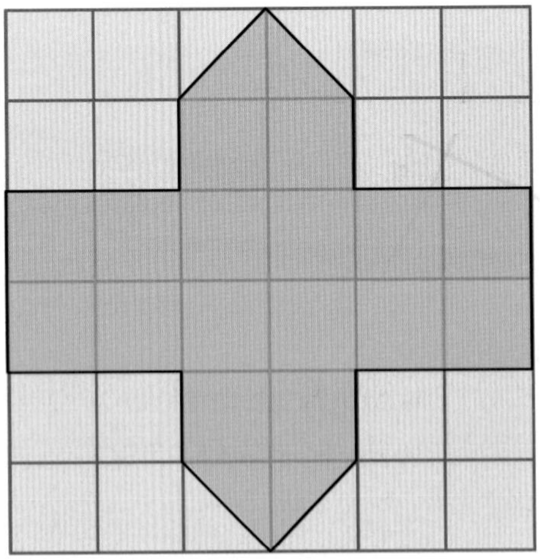

a What is the area of the shaded shape?

b Draw a rectangle on centimetre square grid paper that has the same area as the shaded shape.

Key Stage 3 2004 3–5 Paper 2

4 Number

Fractions and decimals

Before 1971, the UK system of money counted pounds, shillings and pence instead of just pounds and pence as we use now. There were 12 pence in a shilling and 20 shillings in a pound, so there were 240 pence in a pound!

What's the point? Our modern money is based on 100 pence in a pound. Ask an older friend or family member if they remember the old system of money. Do they find modern money easier to use than the old system?

Check in

Level 2

1 How many equal parts has each rectangle been divided into?

a

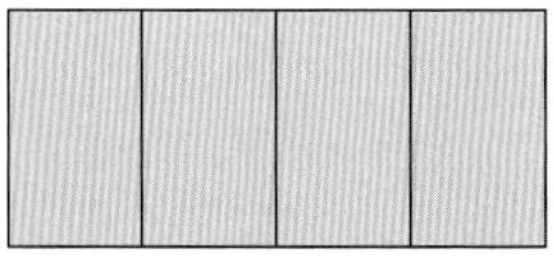

b

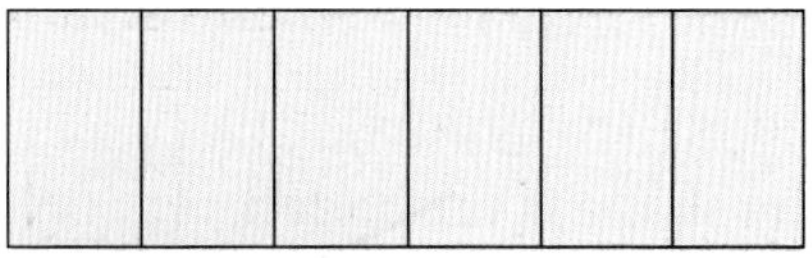

c

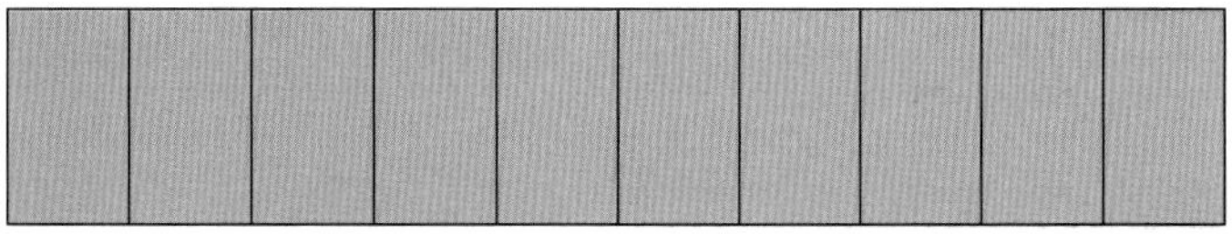

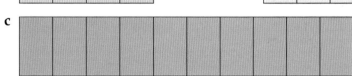

2 Vicky puts a £1 coin into a change machine.
The machine exchanges the £1 coin for other coins that have a value of £1. Write the number of coins if all the exchanged coins are

a 10p **b** 50p **c** 1p **d** 20p

Level 3

3 Use multiplication facts to copy and complete these.

a $7 \times 2 = \square$ **b** $4 \times 5 = \square$ **c** $\square \times 3 = 15$ **d** $6 \times \square = 60$

e $\square \times 4 = 8$ **f** $10 \times \square = 70$ **g** $3 \times 9 = \square$ **h** $\square \times 5 = 25$

4a Fraction notation

- Find a fraction of a shape which is divided into equal parts

Keywords
Denominator Fraction
Equal Numerator

- A **fraction** is a part of a whole.

This cake has been divided into three **equal** parts.
Each person will get $\frac{1}{3}$ (one third) of the cake.

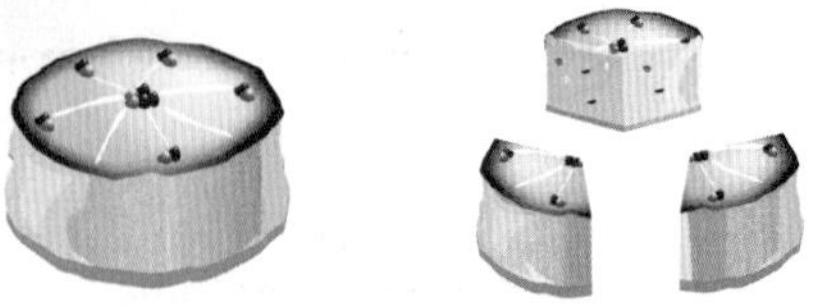

- The **numerator** is on top. It tells us how many parts of the fraction we are working with.

- The **denominator** is on bottom. It tells us how many equal parts something has been divided into.

example

What fraction of this shape is shaded?

There are **six** equal parts.
One part is shaded.
The shaded fraction is $\frac{1}{6}$ (one sixth).

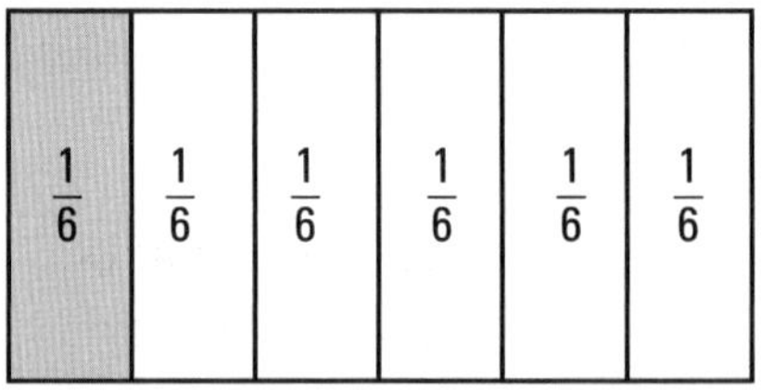

This shape is divided into five equal parts.
Each part is $\frac{1}{5}$ (one fifth).
Two parts are shaded.
p. 168
The fraction shaded is $\frac{2}{5}$ (two fifths).
$\frac{3}{5}$ (three fifths) of the shape is unshaded.

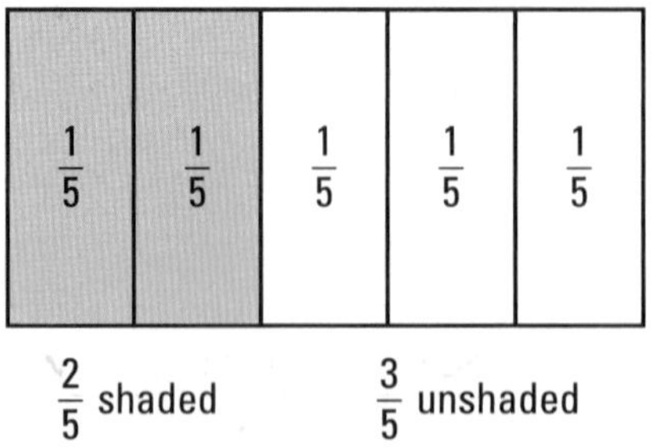

example

a What fraction of this pizza has mushrooms?
b What fraction of this pizza is plain?

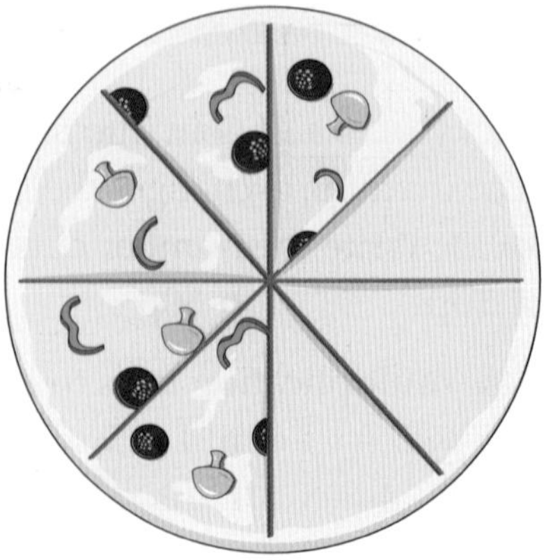

a There are eight parts.
Five parts out of eight have mushrooms.
The fraction of this shape with mushrooms is $\frac{5}{8}$ (five eighths).

b Three parts out of eight are plain.
The fraction of the pizza that is plain is $\frac{3}{8}$ (three eighths).

Exercise 4a

1 At the Cookery Club students are making pizzas.
Charlie and his three friends are going to eat his pizza.
There are four people to share equally.
What fraction will each person have?

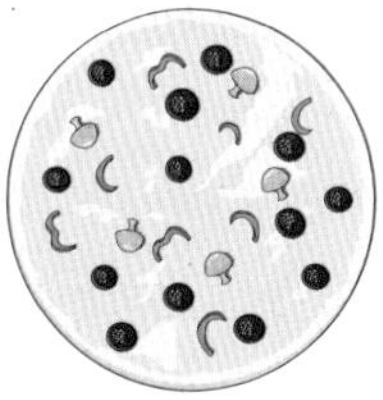

2 What fraction of each shape is shaded?

a 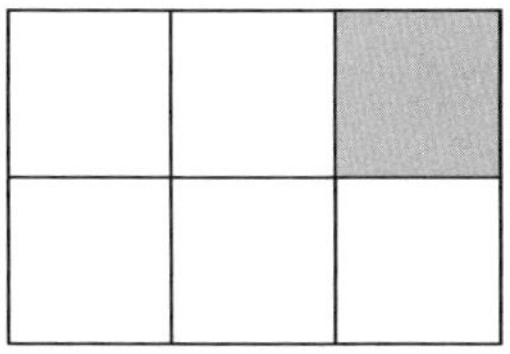 **b** 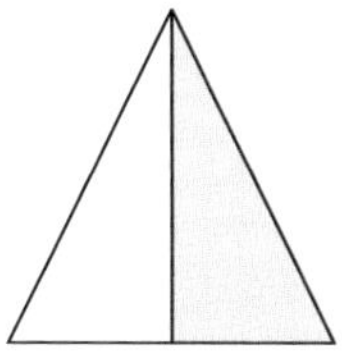 **c** 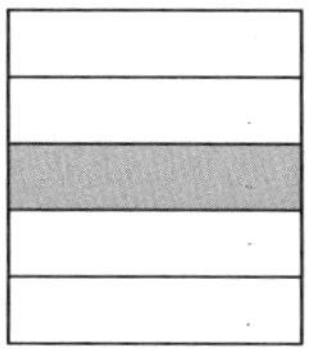 **d** 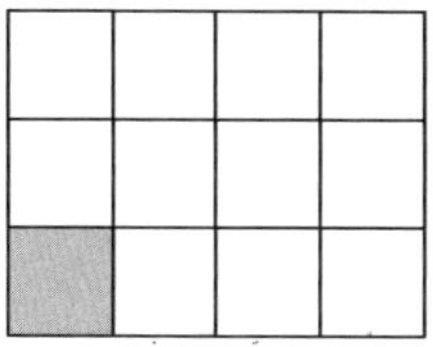

3 Nisha baked a cake. She has cut it into eight equal pieces.
She eats some of the cake.

a What fraction has she eaten?

b What fraction of the cake is left?

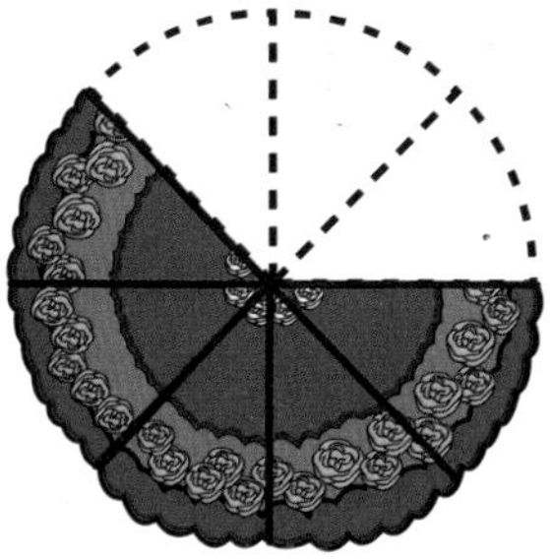

4 What fraction of each shape is shaded?
What fraction of each shape is unshaded?

a 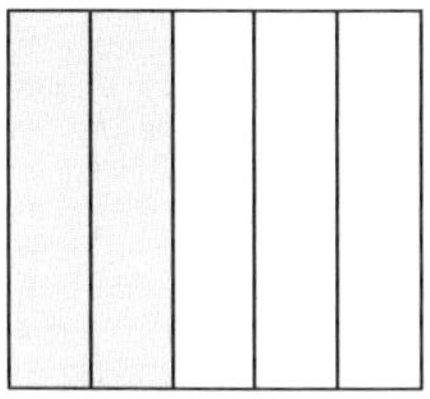 **b** 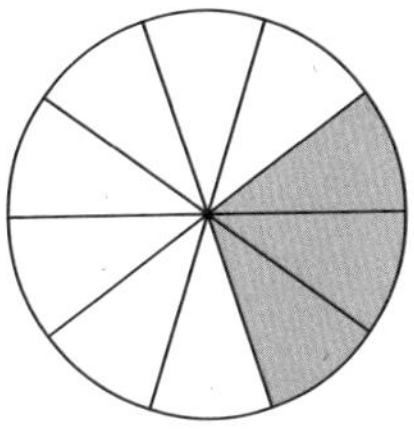 **c** 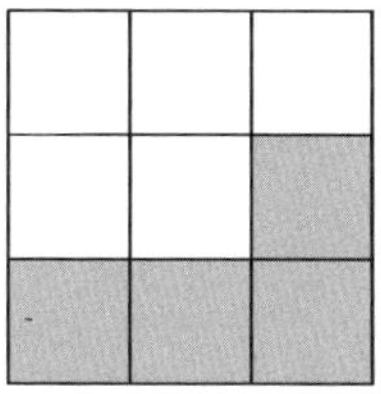 **d** 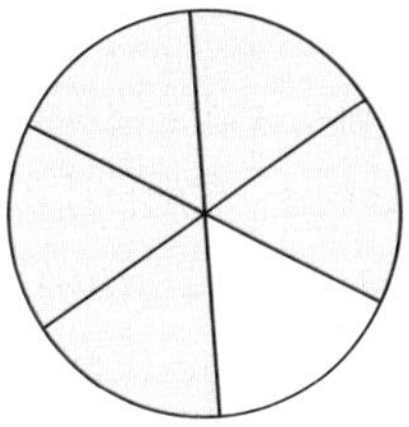

task

Match each shaded shape with its fraction.

$\frac{1}{4}$ $\frac{2}{3}$ $\frac{3}{4}$ $\frac{1}{5}$ $\frac{1}{8}$ $\frac{1}{10}$ $\frac{3}{5}$ $\frac{4}{7}$ $\frac{1}{6}$ $\frac{3}{8}$

a 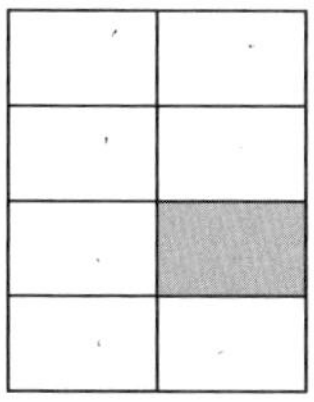 **b** 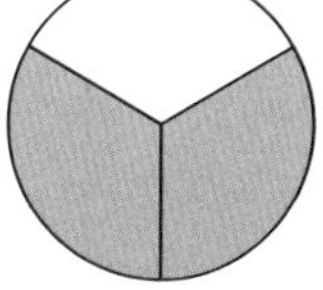 **c** 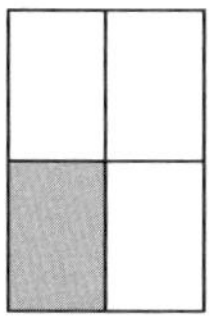 **d** 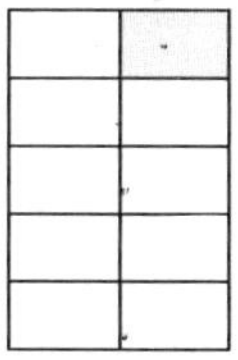 **e** 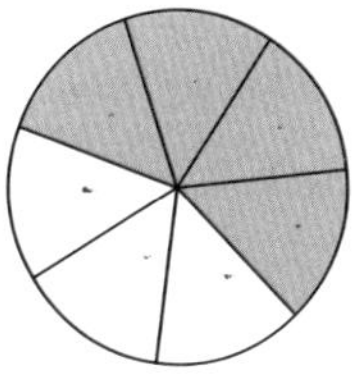

f 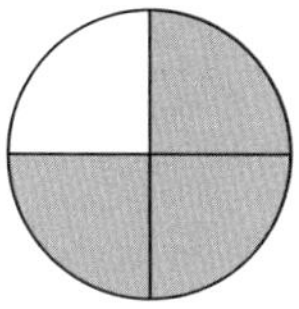 **g** 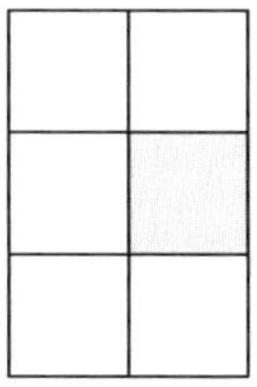 **h** 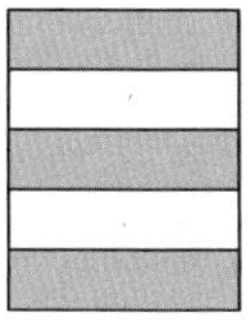 **i** 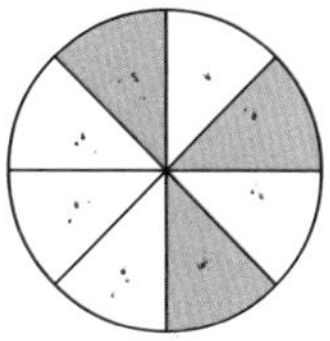 **j** 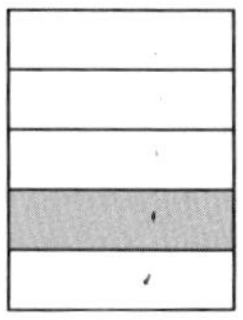

4b Equivalent fractions

- Find fractions which are equivalent to each other

Keywords
Denominator
Equivalent
Numerator

Sarah cuts a pizza into four equal parts.

Each slice is $\frac{1}{4}$ of the pizza.

Sarah notices that $\frac{2}{4}$ are the same as $\frac{1}{2}$.

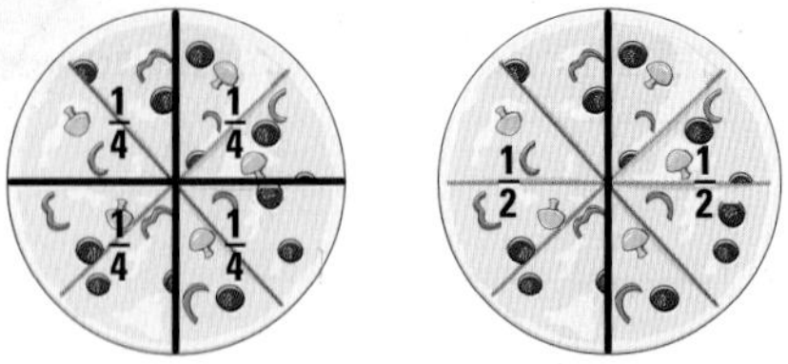

- Fractions which are the same but have different names are **equivalent fractions.**
  $\frac{2}{4}$ is equivalent to $\frac{1}{2}$.

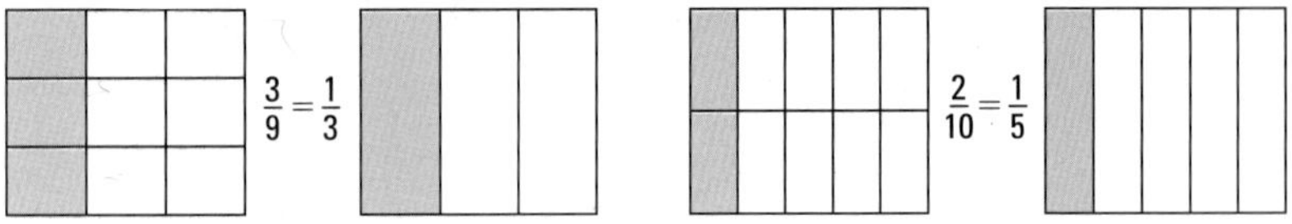

$\frac{3}{9}$ is equivalent to $\frac{1}{3}$. $\frac{2}{10}$ is equivalent to $\frac{1}{5}$.

example

Match each shaded shape with its equivalent fraction.

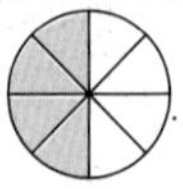
→ $\frac{1}{2}$ is equivalent to $\frac{4}{8}$ shaded.

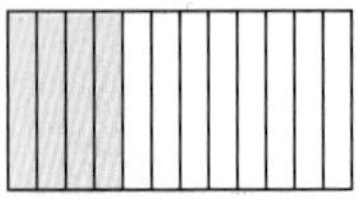
→ $\frac{1}{3}$ is equivalent to $\frac{4}{12}$ shaded.

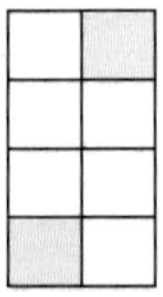
→ $\frac{1}{4}$ is equivalent to $\frac{2}{8}$ shaded.

- You multiply or divide the **denominator** and the **numerator** by the same number to make equivalent fractions.

$\frac{3}{9} = \frac{1}{3}$ (numerator ÷3, denominator ÷3) $\frac{1}{5} = \frac{2}{10}$ (numerator ×2, denominator ×2)

example

Which drawing has $\frac{1}{4}$ shaded?

a
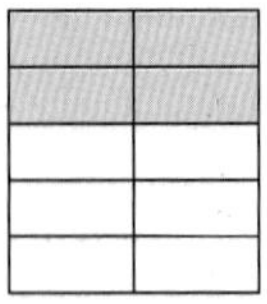
b
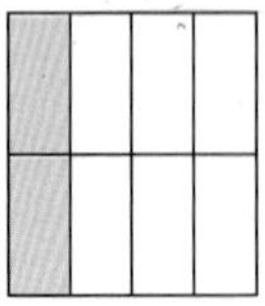
c
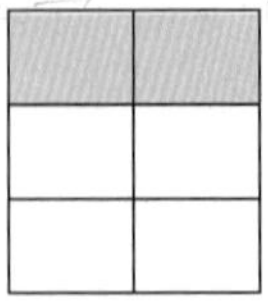

Drawing **b** shows $\frac{1}{4}$ shaded.

$\frac{2}{8} = \frac{1}{4}$ (numerator ÷2, denominator ÷2)

Exercise 4b

1 Match each shaded shape with its equivalent fraction $\frac{1}{2}$, $\frac{1}{3}$ or $\frac{1}{4}$

a

b

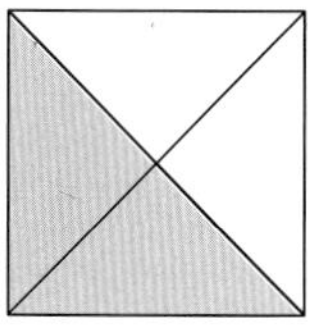

c

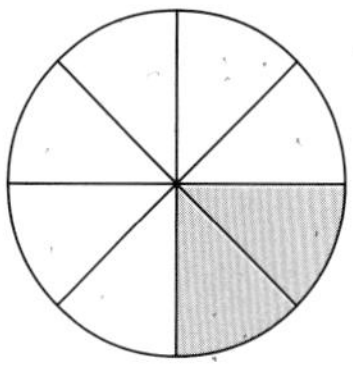

d

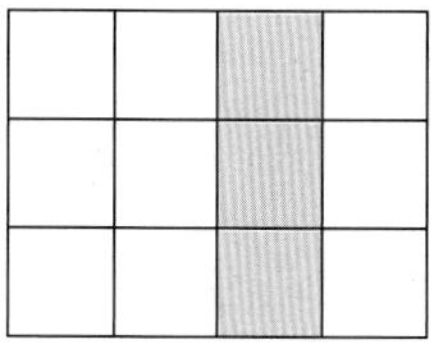

e

f

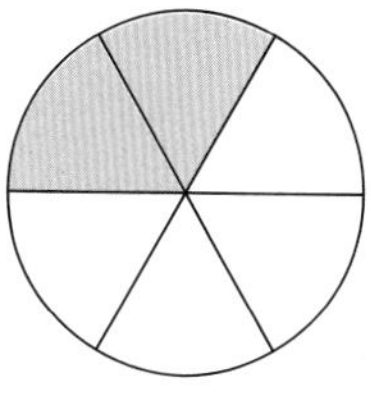

g

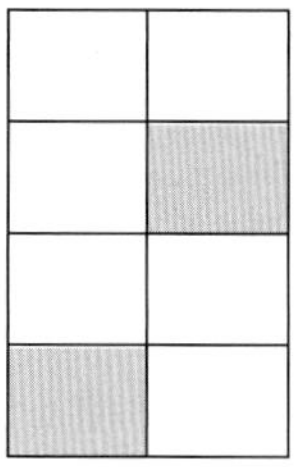

h

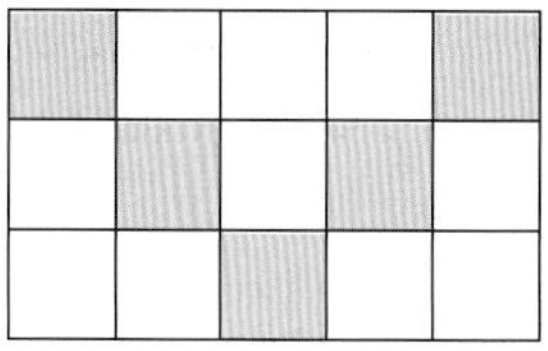

2 Write an equivalent fraction for each.

a

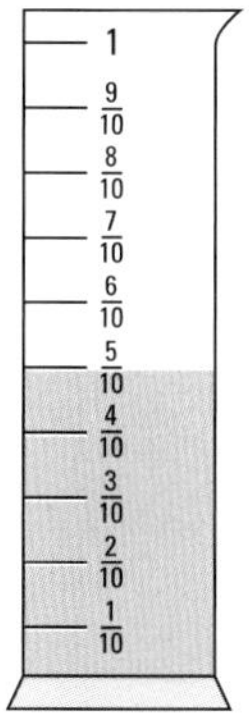

b

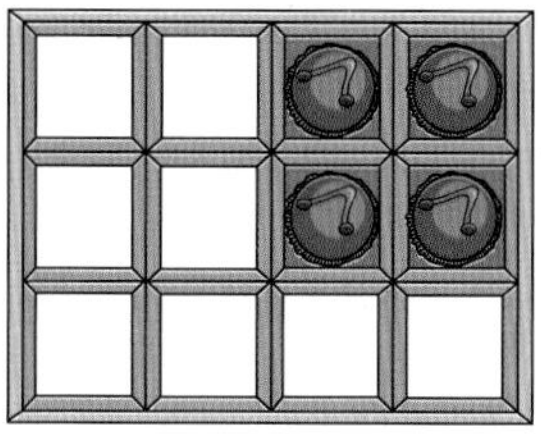

c

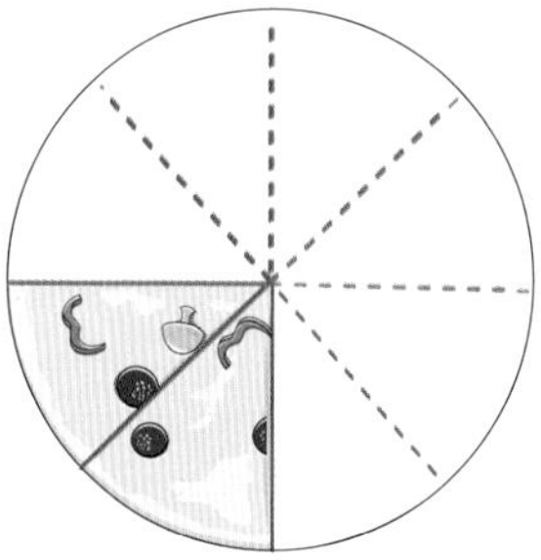

Did you know?

At least $\frac{7}{10}$ of the human body is water.

3 Use multiplication or division to copy and complete these pairs of equivalent fractions.

a $\frac{2}{6} = \frac{1}{\square}$ **b** $\frac{2}{4} = \frac{\square}{2}$ **c** $\frac{1}{\square} = \frac{3}{6}$

d $\frac{1}{3} = \frac{3}{\square}$ **e** $\frac{4}{12} = \frac{1}{\square}$ **f** $\frac{10}{20} = \frac{\square}{2}$

task

Karen baked a cherry pie and an apple pie. She cut the cherry pie into 7 equal pieces and the apple pie into 5 equal pieces.

If she ate $\frac{3}{7}$ of the cherry pie and $\frac{2}{5}$ of the apple pie, which pie has the most leftover?
Draw the pies to help you.

4c Improper fractions

- Change improper fractions to mixed numbers
- Change mixed numbers to improper fractions

Keywords
Denominator
Improper fraction
Mixed number
Numerator

Howda bakes two pies at the Cookery Club.
She cuts each pie in half $\left(\frac{1}{2}\right)$.

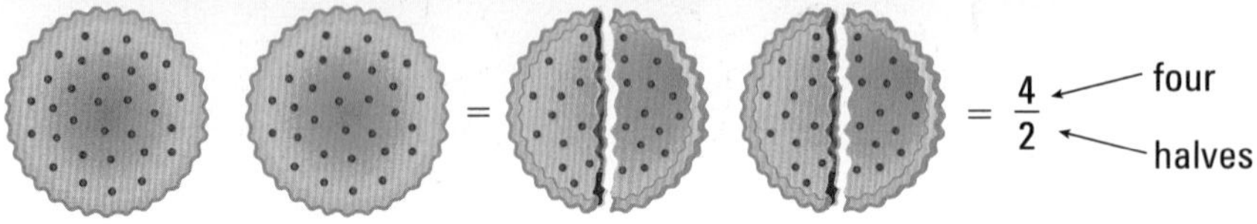

The two pies are shared into four halves $= \frac{4}{2}$.
This is an **improper fraction**.

- An improper fraction has a **numerator** greater than the **denominator**. Its value will be greater than 1.
  $\frac{5}{3}$ is an improper fraction.

Howda cooked more pies and cut each pie into four quarters $\left(\frac{1}{4}\right)$.
Each student takes a piece of pie.
This is left over:

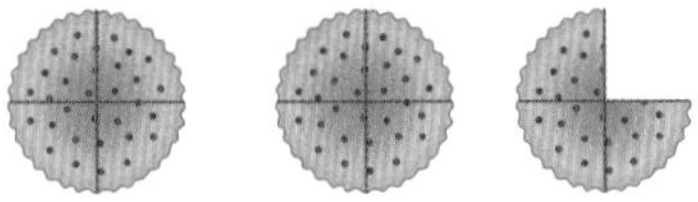

There are eleven quarters left over.
As an improper fraction this is $\frac{11}{4}$.
As a **mixed number** this is $2\frac{3}{4}$.
There are two whole pies and $\frac{3}{4}$ of a pie left.

- A mixed number contains a whole number and a fraction.
  $2\frac{3}{4}$ is a mixed number.

example

Change the improper fraction $\frac{7}{3}$ into a mixed number.

$\frac{7}{3}$ makes 2 whole pies with $\frac{1}{3}$ left over.
$\frac{7}{3}$ as a mixed number is $2\frac{1}{3}$.

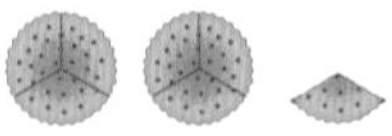

3 goes into 7 two times with $\frac{1}{3}$ left over.

example

Change the mixed number $2\frac{1}{3}$ into an improper fraction.

$2\frac{1}{3}$ means 2 wholes with $\frac{1}{3}$ left over.
Each whole makes 3 thirds. 2 wholes are $2 \times 3 = 6$ thirds.
There is one third left over so $6 + 1 = 7$ thirds or $\frac{7}{3}$.
$2\frac{1}{3}$ as an improper fraction is $\frac{7}{3}$.

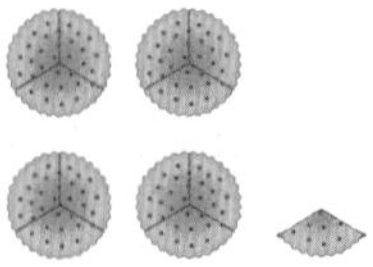

Exercise 4c

1 Show each amount as an improper fraction.

a 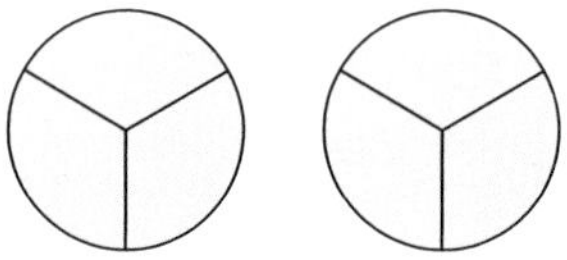 $= \frac{\square}{3}$

b 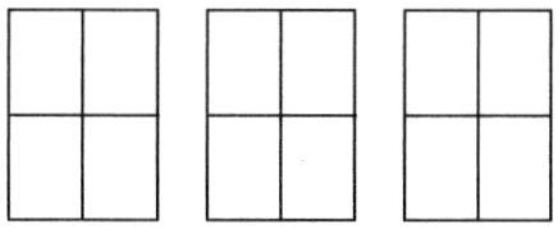 $= \frac{\square}{4}$

c 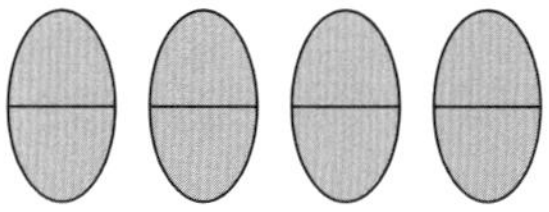 $= \frac{\square}{\square}$

d 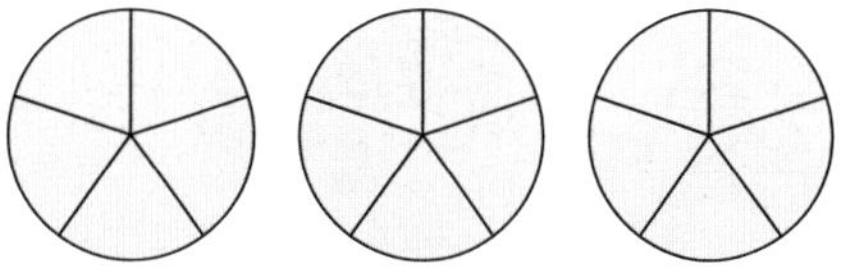 $= \frac{\square}{\square}$

2 Show each amount as a mixed number.

a 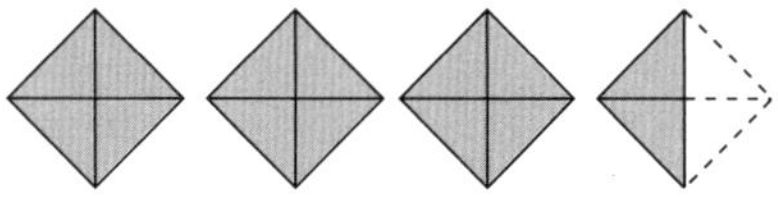 $= 3\frac{\square}{\square}$

b 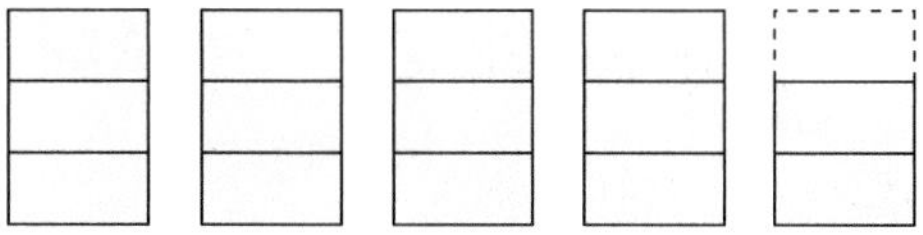 $= \square$

c 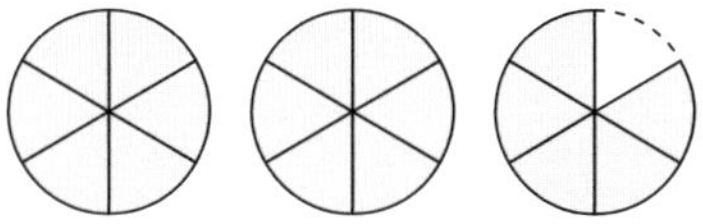 $= \square$

d 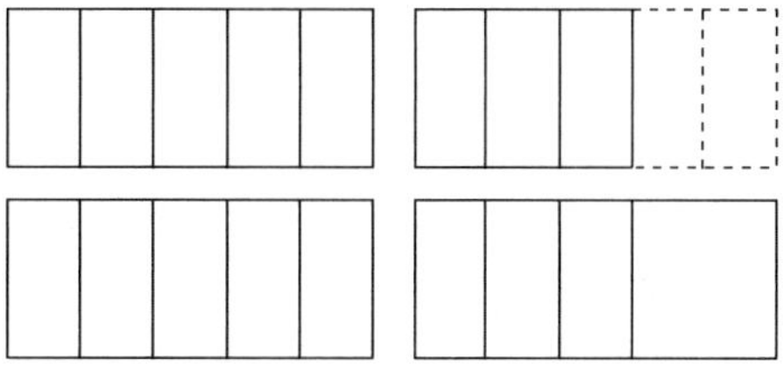 $= \square$

3 Show each amount as **a** an improper fraction **b** a mixed number.

i 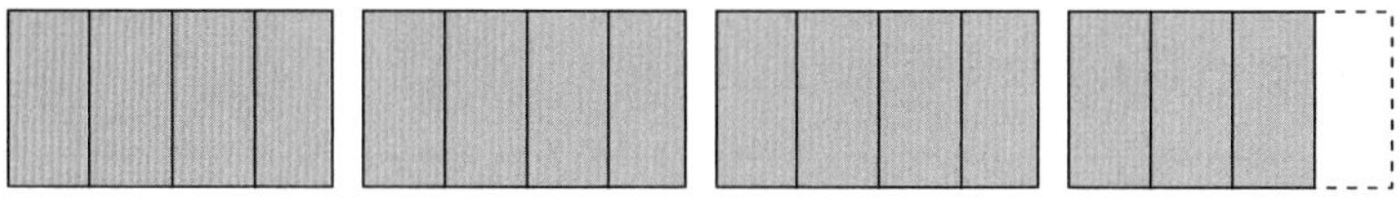

ii 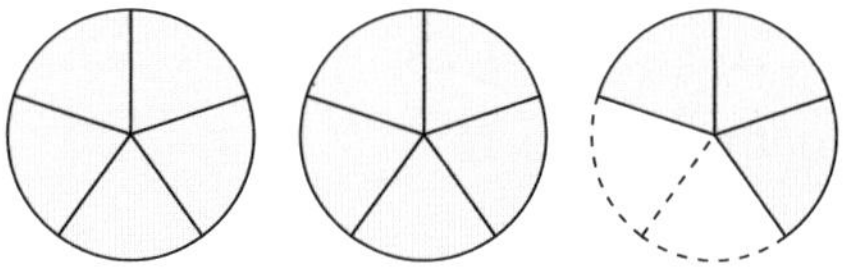

iii 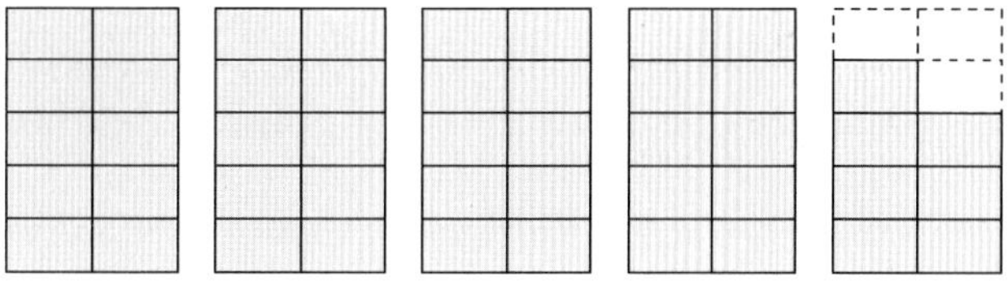

4 Convert these improper fractions to mixed numbers.

a $\frac{5}{2}$ **b** $\frac{10}{3}$ **c** $\frac{9}{2}$ **d** $\frac{9}{4}$ **e** $\frac{13}{5}$

5 Convert these mixed numbers to improper fractions

a $1\frac{1}{2}$ **b** $1\frac{1}{4}$ **c** $2\frac{1}{2}$ **d** $2\frac{2}{3}$ **e** $3\frac{4}{5}$

puzzle

Howda bakes some cakes.
She cuts each cake into five equal pieces.
She has 25 pieces when she has finished.
How many cakes did Howda bake?

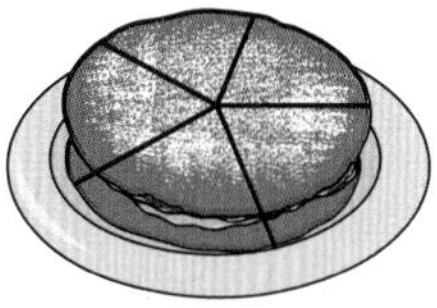

4d Decimals

- Use decimals to write money

Keywords
Decimal
Tenth
Whole

p. 4²

- A **decimal** is a part of a **whole**.

Gaz shares £1 equally between two charities.

£0.50 = 50p

£0.50 + £0.50 = £1.00

If Gaz shares another £1 between 10 charities, how much would each charity get?

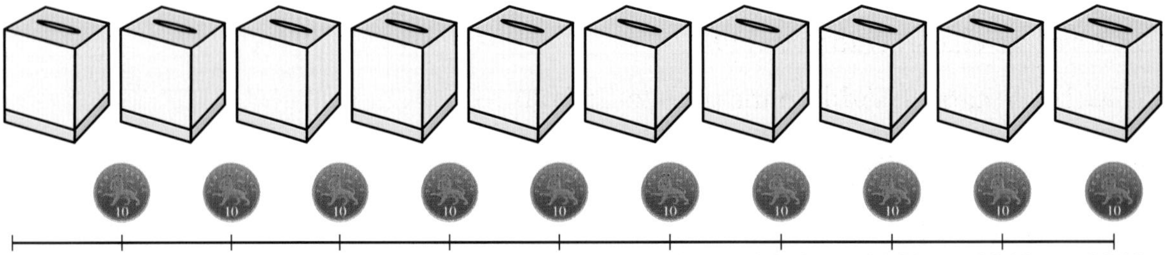

£1.00 divided by 10 is £0.10.
Each charity gets a **tenth** of the pound.

£0.10 = 10p
£0.10 is one tenth of a pound.

- You can add decimals, but make sure you keep the decimal points lined up.

example

Write each amount as a decimal number.

a 

b 

a Add

0.10	10p = £0.10
0.10	
+0.10	Line up the decimal
£0.30	points!

b Add

0.50	50p = £0.50 = five tenths
0.20	20p = £0.20 = two tenths
0.20	
+0.10	
£1.00	The decimals add to a whole number.

Exercise 4d

1 Write each amount as a decimal number.

a 

b 

c 

d 

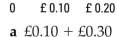

2 Write each of these as a decimal.

a ten pence
b twenty pence
c fifty pence
d eighty pence

3 Use the number line to help you add these amounts.

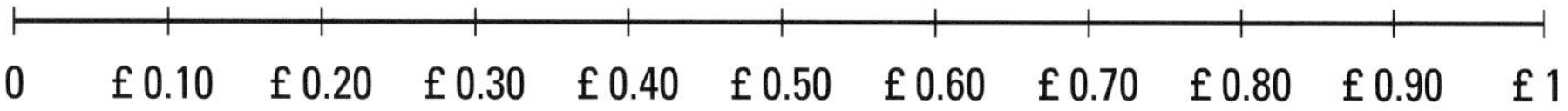

a £0.10 + £0.30 **b** £0.40 + £0.50 **c** £0.20 + £0.70
d £0.50 + £0.50 **e** £0.20 + £0.80 **f** £0.40 + £0.40

4 Gaz put his change into piles of £1.

Is each pile correct? Add up the piles to find out.

a 

3 × 20p 4 × 10p

b 

2 × 10p

c 

2 × 20p

d 

7 × 10p

5 Use these coins,  to make up each amount.

The first is done for you.

a £0.30 ⟶ 

10p + 10p + 10p OR 20p + 10p

b £0.70 **c** £0.40 **d** £0.80 **e** £0.60

challenge

The Reading Bus Company does not give change to customers. How can Stuart make exact change for his £0.80 fare with these coins?

4e Adding decimals

- Add up money using different coins
- Use decimals to write money

Keywords
Decimal
Hundredths
Tenths

Joydip puts his change in a bank every night.
He counts his coins into stacks of 100 pence.

100p = £1.00
1p = £0.01 = 1 **hundredth** of a pound

100 × 1p coins | 50 × 2p coins | 20 × 5p coins | 10 × 10p coins

Joydip has four stacks of 100p. He has £4.00.

Joydip finds more change in the sofa cushions.

8 × 1p | 2 × 2p | 3 × 5p

£0.08
£0.04
+ £0.15
£0.27

He now has £4.00
+ £0.27
£4.27

Line up the decimal point.

2 tenths and 7 hundredths

example

Write each amount as a decimal.

a 

b 

a Add
0.01   1p = £0.01
0.01
0.05   5p = £0.05
+ 0.05
£0.12

b Add
0.50   50p = £0.50 = five tenths
0.50
0.20   20p = £0.20 = two tenths
0.05
+0.04   0.01 + 0.01 + 0.01 + 0.01
£1.29   The decimals add to more than a whole.

example

Add these decimal amounts.

a £0.15 + £0.30 + £0.50   **b** £0.55 + £0.40 + £0.32

a 0.15
0.30
+ 0.50
£0.95   Nine tenths and five hundredths

b 0.55
0.40
+ 0.32
£1.27   One whole, two tenths and seven hundredths

Exercise 4e

1 Use the number line to help you add these decimals.

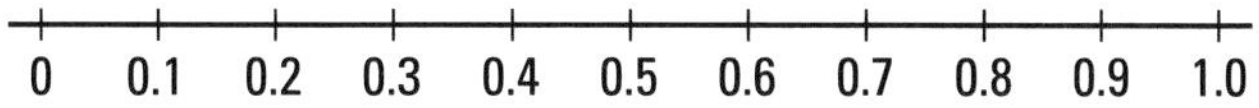

a 0.1 + 0.4 **b** 0.3 + 0.5 **c** 0.2 + 0.6
d 0.8 + 0.1 **e** 0.7 + 0.3 **f** 0.9 + 0.1

2 Write each amount as a decimal.

a 

b 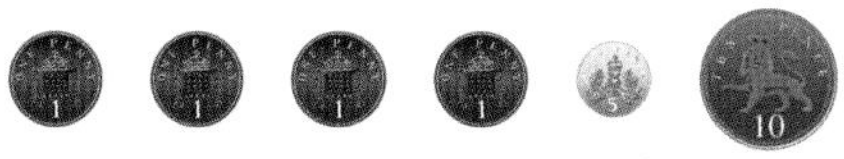

c 

d 

3 Write each of these as a decimal.
a ten pence and two pence
b fifty pence and one pence
c forty pence and eight pence
d eight pence

4 Use the number line to help you add these decimals.

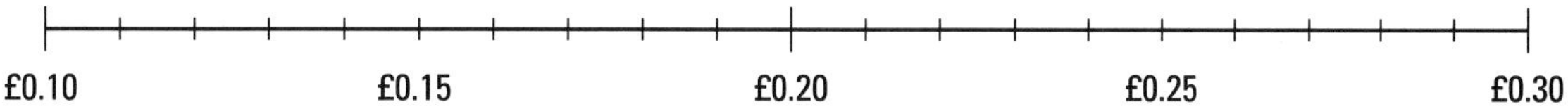

a £0.10 + £0.02 **b** £0.20 + £0.05 **c** £0.10 + £0.08
d £0.15 + £0.05 **e** £0.18 + £0.02 **f** £0.22 + £0.08

Remember to line up the decimal point.

5 Write each amount as a decimal number.

a 

b 

challenge

Martin found these lost coins on the pavement.
a Write this amount as a decimal.
b If Martin already had £1.91 in his pocket, how much does he have now?
c A pack of crisps costs 60p. How many packs of crisps can Martin buy?

4f Fractions and decimals

- Write decimals using tenths and hundredths
- Change fractions to decimals and decimals to fractions

Keywords
Decimal, Divide, Equal, Equivalent, Fraction, Tenth

Fractions show less than a whole. $\frac{1}{10}$ is a fraction.
Decimals also show less than a whole. 0.1 is a decimal.

- Fractions are **equivalent** to decimals.
  $\frac{1}{10}$ is equivalent to 0.1. They both read 'one **tenth**'.

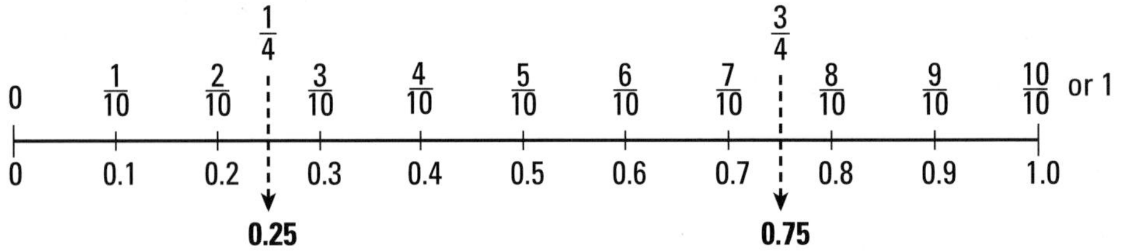

$\frac{1}{4}$ is equivalent to 0.25. $\frac{3}{4}$ is equivalent to 0.75.

example

For each shape, write the shaded part
i as a fraction
ii as a decimal.

a 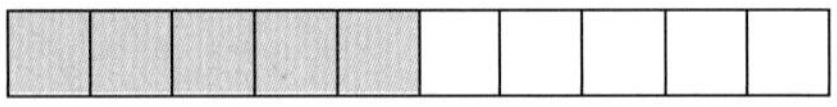

b 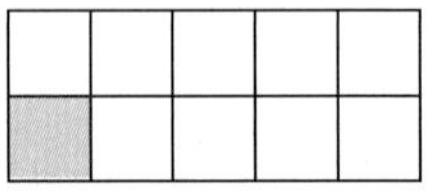

c 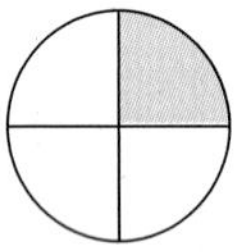

a i $\frac{5}{10}$ **ii** 0.5

b i $\frac{1}{10}$ **ii** 0.1

c i $\frac{1}{4}$ **ii** 0.25

This hundred square is **divided** into 100 **equal** parts.

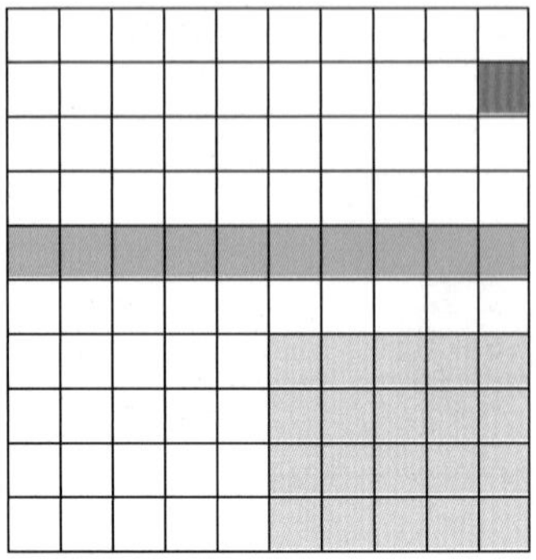

Each square is $\frac{1}{100}$ as a fraction.
This pink square is 0.01 as a decimal.
Each row of 10 squares is $\frac{1}{10}$ as a fraction.
This green row of 10 squares is 0.1 as a decimal.
$\frac{20}{100}$ of the squares are shaded blue.
0.20 is shaded blue.

Exercise 4f

1 Answer the four questions about each shape. The first one is done for you.

i What fraction is shaded? **ii** What fraction is not shaded?

iii What decimal is shaded? **iv** What decimal is not-shaded?

a 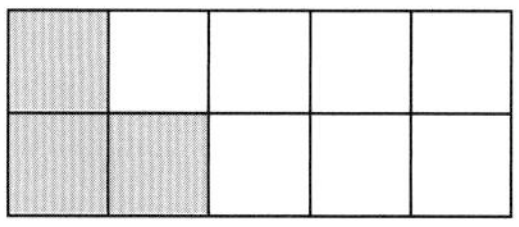

i $\frac{3}{10}$ is shaded **ii** $\frac{7}{10}$ is not shaded

iii 0.3 is shaded **iv** 0.7 is not shaded

b 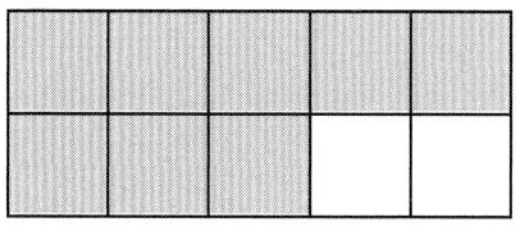

c 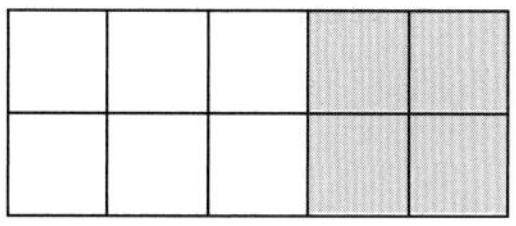

d 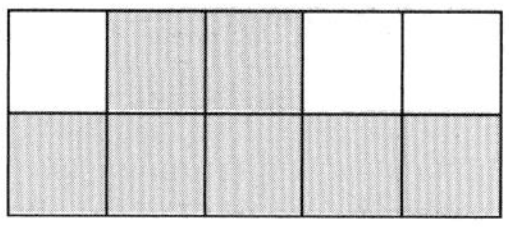

2 Give the decimal equivalent to each of these.

a $\frac{3}{10} = 0.\square$ **b** $\frac{9}{10} = 0.\square$ **c** $\frac{5}{10} = 0.\square$ **d** $\frac{6}{10} = 0.\square$

3 Give the fraction equivalent to each of these.

a $0.1 = \frac{\square}{\square}$ **b** $0.8 = \frac{\square}{\square}$ **c** $0.4 = \frac{\square}{\square}$ **d** $0.7 = \frac{\square}{\square}$

4 This hundred square is divided into 100 equal parts.

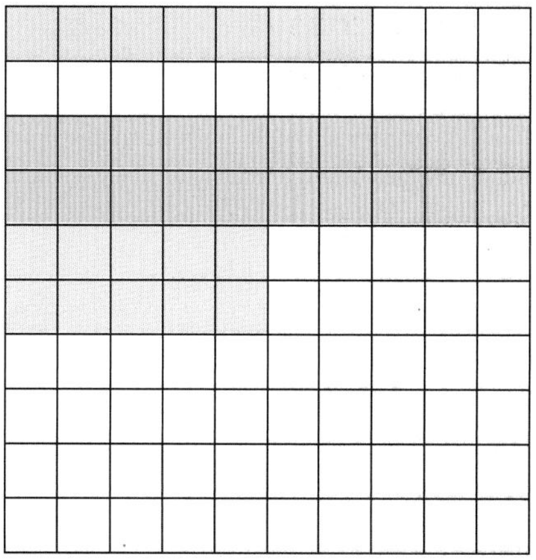

a Describe the area shaded blue as
i a fraction **ii** a decimal.

b Describe the area shaded pink as
i a fraction **ii** a decimal.

c Describe the area shaded green as
i a fraction **ii** a decimal.

d Describe the area shaded yellow as
i a fraction **ii** a decimal.

puzzle

Four cakes have been cut into eight different sized pieces. Which pieces go together to make the four cakes?

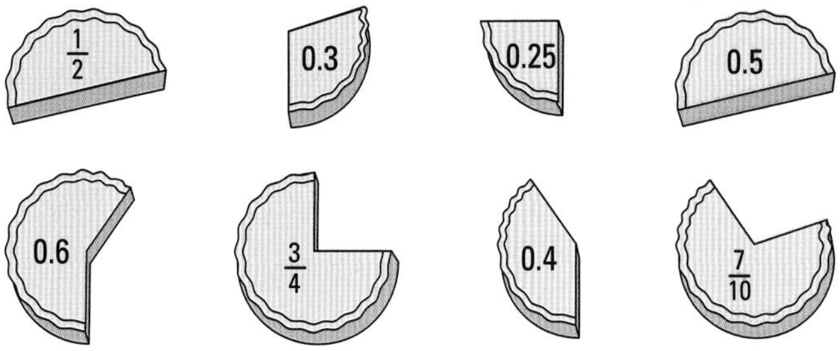

4 Consolidation

4a

1 What fraction of each shape is shaded?

a

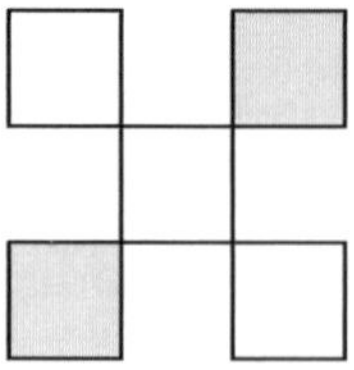

b

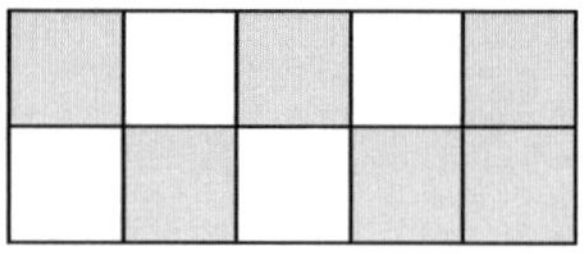

c

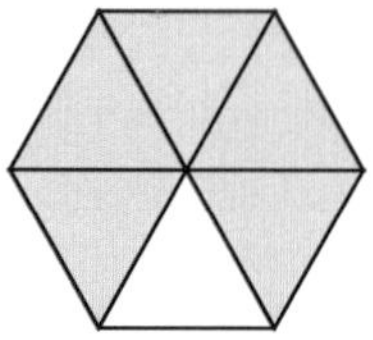

d

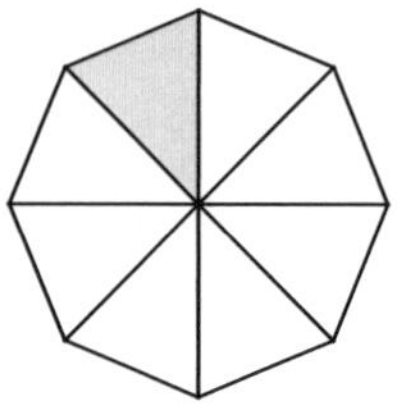

e

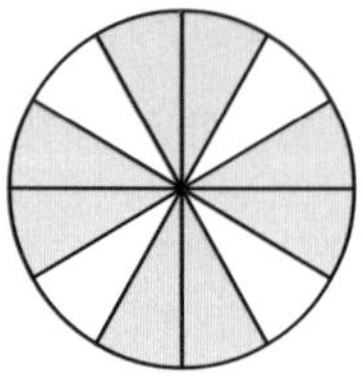

4b

2 Put these equivalent fractions into pairs as shown in the example.

÷2

$\frac{4}{10} = \frac{2}{5}$

÷2

$\frac{3}{9}$ $\frac{10}{20}$ $\frac{3}{12}$ $\frac{2}{10}$ $\frac{10}{100}$ $\frac{2}{16}$

$\frac{1}{4}$ $\frac{1}{2}$ $\frac{1}{10}$ $\frac{1}{8}$ $\frac{1}{5}$ $\frac{1}{3}$

4c

3 Write these whole numbers as improper fractions.

a $4 = \frac{\square}{2}$ **b** $3 = \frac{\square}{3}$ **c** $6 = \frac{\square}{2}$ **d** $2 = \frac{8}{\square}$ **e** $5 = \frac{15}{\square}$

4 Write these improper fractions as whole numbers.

a $\frac{6}{2}$ **b** $\frac{8}{4}$ **c** $\frac{10}{2}$ **d** $\frac{15}{3}$ **e** $\frac{12}{3}$

5 Write these improper fractions as mixed numbers.

a $\frac{7}{2}$ **b** $\frac{8}{3}$ **c** $\frac{9}{2}$ **d** $\frac{9}{4}$ **e** $\frac{11}{3}$

6 Convert these mixed numbers into improper fractions.

a $2\frac{1}{2} = \frac{\square}{\square}$ **b** $3\frac{1}{2} = \frac{\square}{\square}$ **c** $2\frac{1}{4} = \frac{\square}{\square}$ **d** $3\frac{1}{3} = \frac{\square}{\square}$ **e** $2\frac{2}{5} = \frac{\square}{\square}$

4d

7 Write each of these as decimals.

a three tenths
b seven tenths
c nine tenths
d six tenths

8 Use the number line to help you add these decimals.

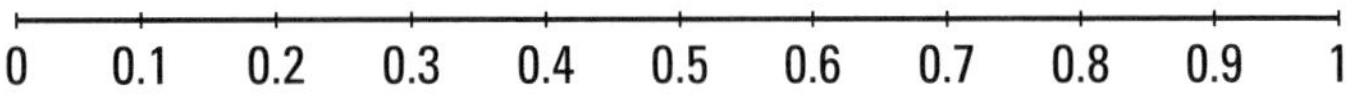

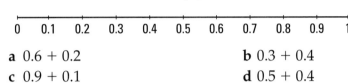

a 0.6 + 0.2 **b** 0.3 + 0.4
c 0.9 + 0.1 **d** 0.5 + 0.4

4e

9 Write each of these as decimals.

a seven tenths and two hundredths
b three tenths and one hundredth
c two tenths and nine hundredths
d one hundredth

10 Use the number line to help you add these decimals.

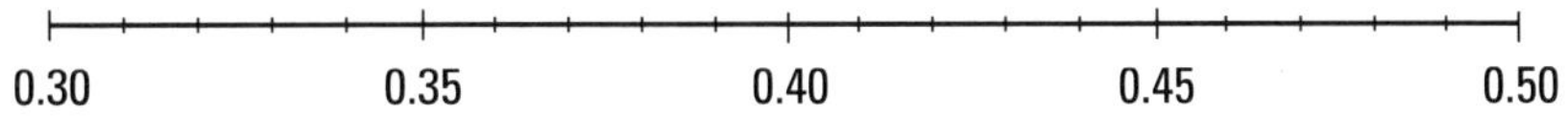

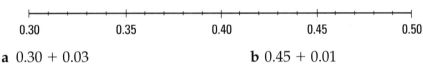

a 0.30 + 0.03 **b** 0.45 + 0.01
c 0.35 + 0.06 **d** 0.30 + 0.09

4f

11 These rectangles are divided into equal squares.
Describe each area, A to F, as

a a fraction
b a decimal.

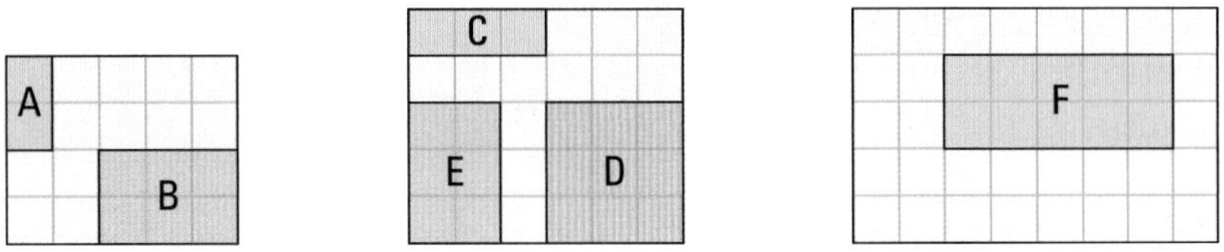

4 Summary

Key indicators

- Use decimal notation for money **Level 3**
- Identify equivalent fractions Level 4
- Compare and order decimals Level 4

Level 4

1 This shape is made from identical triangles.

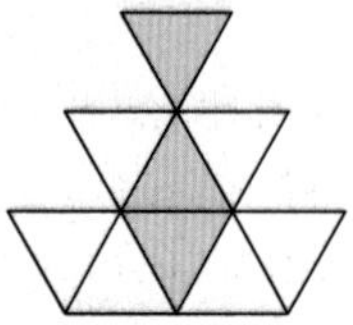

Circle the fraction of the shape that is shaded.

$\frac{1}{2}$ $\frac{1}{3}$ $\frac{1}{4}$ $\frac{1}{5}$ $\frac{1}{6}$

Nia's answer ✔

Nia decides there are 9 triangles altogether and 3 of these triangles are shaded.

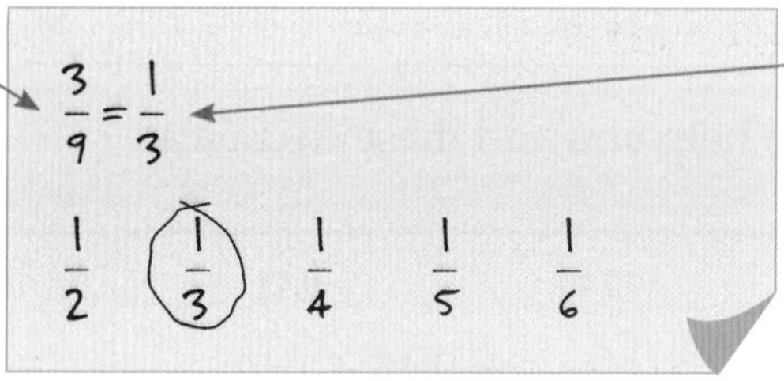

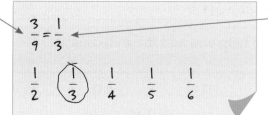

Nia divides 3 by 3 and 9 by 3.

Level 3

2 **a** Jack buys four apples.
He pays with a £2 coin.
He gets £1.20 change.

How much does one apple cost?

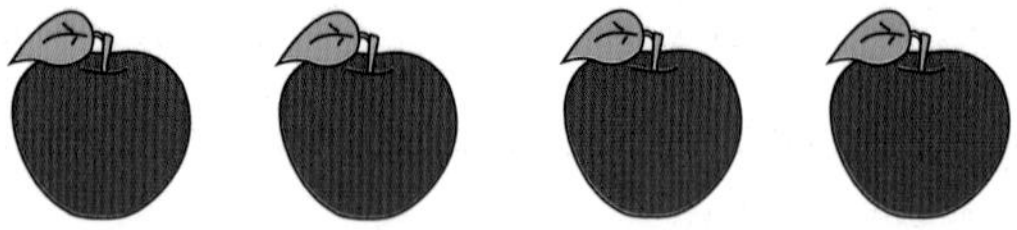

b Oranges cost 15p each.
Raj has a £1 coin.

What is the greatest number of oranges Raj can buy with £1?

Year 7 2007 3–4 Paper 1

5 Data

Representing data

Florence Nightingale was a famous nurse during the Victorian era. However, she was also a famous statistician. She is considered the first person to use clearly presented charts and graphs to argue a point. As a result, she improved hygienic conditions in the London hospitals.

What's the point? Clearly presented data backs up your ideas and helps you to get what you want!

Check in

Level 2

1

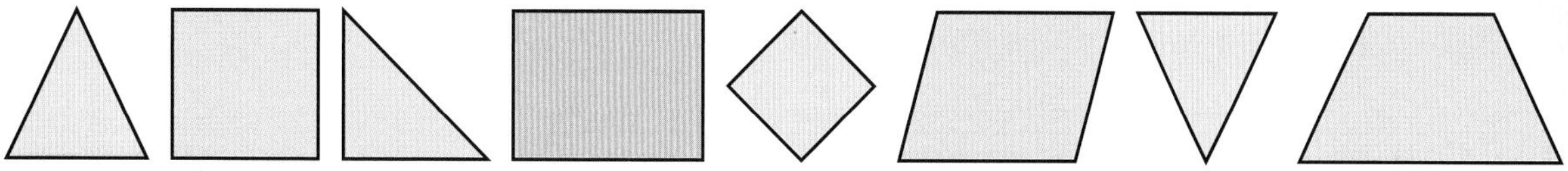

a Copy and complete this table by drawing each of these coloured shapes in the correct box below.

Shapes with 3 sides	Shapes with 4 sides

b Draw a similar table to sort the shapes by colour. You will need three boxes.

Level 3

2 Work out these sums mentally.

a $3 + 2 + 7 + 8$

b $4 + 9 + 8 + 6 + 2$

c $10 + 7 + 12 + 13 + 5$

d $8 + 11 + 3 + 15 + 9 + 20$

5a Data in lists and tables

- Use data in lists and tables

Keywords
Data
Lists
Tables

You often need to make sense of **data** in **lists** and **tables**.

- A list shows data in a clear way. You can answer questions about the data in a list.

example

At the end of a meal in a restaurant four friends received the bill.

a How many drinks were served?

b If the four friends share the bill equally, how much should each person pay?

CARLA'S RESTAURANT
YOUR RECEIPT

STARTER	3.75
STARTER	3.75
MAIN COURSE	8.90
MAIN COURSE	7.95
MAIN COURSE	8.20
MAIN COURSE	8.75
DESSERT	4.20
DESSERT	4.20
DESSERT	4.75
DRINK	2.60
DRINK	2.60
DRINK	2.60
DRINK	1.75
*********************	******
TOTAL	64.00
*********************	******

THANK YOU - CALL AGAIN SOON

a There were four drinks altogether

We can simply count the number of drinks shown on the bill.

b Divide the total by four.
Each person pays £16.

To divide by four, just halve the total, and then halve again.

p. 212

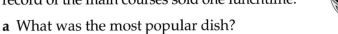

- Tables are used to organise lists of data.

example

The manager at Carla's Restaurant keeps a record of the main courses sold one lunchtime.

a What was the most popular dish?

b How many main courses were served altogether?

Dish	Total
Dover Sole	7
Lasagne	4
Chef's Salad	8
Stuffed Courgette	2
Crab Cakes	4

a The chef's salad was the most popular dish. Look at the totals in the table. There were more chef's salads sold than any other dish.

b Add together the totals for each dish. There were 25 main courses sold.

Exercise 5a

1 Look at the restaurant bill shown in the first example on the page opposite.

a How many starters were served?

b How much did the most expensive dessert cost?

c How can you tell that the four friends all had different main courses?

d The friends paid £70 for the meal, including a tip. How much was the tip?

2 Look at the table in the second example on the page opposite.

a How many people ordered lasagne?

b What was the least popular dish?

c What was the second most popular dish?

3 This list shows the prices for a range of furniture. How much would each of the following people spend?

a Hari buys a 2-seater settee and a reclining armchair.

b Antonio buys a 3-seater settee, a corner unit and a 2-seater settee.

c Jane buys two armchairs and a 3-seater settee.

4 The table shows the number of minutes Jenna spent doing her homework.

Sunday	Monday	Tuesday	Wednesday	Thursday	Friday	Saturday
75	30	45	25	60	0	0

a What was the total amount of time that Jenna spent doing homework?

b On which day did she do the most homework?

c On which days did she do no homework?

challenge

Sam noted the time he spent doing homework. He spent 30 minutes doing homework on Monday, and the same on Tuesday. He did one hour of homework on Wednesday, and 75 minutes on Thursday. On Friday he spent just 15 minutes on homework, but on Saturday he did 90 minutes. He did no homework on Sunday.

a Make a table to show the number of minutes of homework Sam did each day.

b Find the total time Sam spent on his homework.

5b Reading and drawing pictograms

- Understand pictograms and draw them

Keywords
Data
Group
Pictogram

Diagrams make it easy to see patterns in **data**.

- A **pictogram** shows data as a series of pictures.

example

A teacher recorded the number of computers in three classrooms.

What was the total number of computers in the three classrooms?

p. 123

Key: = 1 Computer

There were 5 computers in Room 17, 3 in Room 18 and 4 in Room 19.
The total number of computers was 5 + 3 + 4 = 12 computers.

- With larger numbers, one symbol can stand for a **group** of things.

example

Andy's teacher asked him to record the number of books in each classroom. Andy wrote the data down in a list, but his teacher wanted a pictogram. Use Andy's data to create a pictogram showing the number of books in each classroom.

First, choose a symbol to represent your data.

Then choose a suitable key. **Key:** = 10 Books

10 books per symbol works well

Next, determine how many symbols you will need to represent the data for each room.

30 ÷ 10 = 3 symbols
40 ÷ 10 = 4 symbols
15 ÷ 10 = 1.5 symbols

The symbol stands for 5 books.

Finally, draw your pictogram.

Don't forget to give a key.

Key: = 10 Books

Exercise 5b

1 This pictogram shows the number of people living in three houses in a street.

a Create a table to show the number of people living in each house.

b Work out the total number of people living in the three houses.

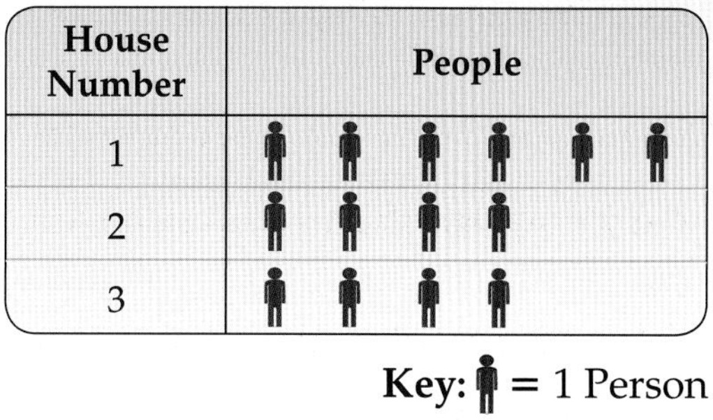
House Number
People
1
2
3
Key: = 1 Person

2 Celine bought some cans of food for her cat. She bought 2 cans of beef flavour, 2 cans of tuna flavour and 5 cans of chicken flavour. Draw a pictogram to show this information.

3 The pictogram shows the number of houses in three villages.

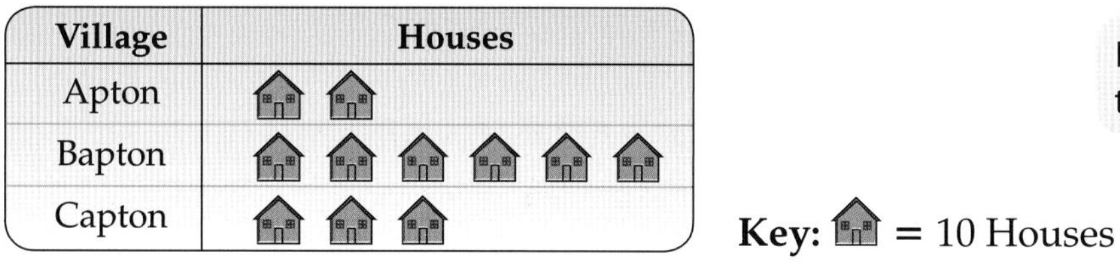
Village
Houses
Apton
Bapton
Capton
Key: = 10 Houses

Look carefully at the key for the pictogram.

a Work out the number of houses in each village.

b Find the total number of houses in the three villages.

4 A pictogram uses this symbol  to represent 20 cars.
How would you show

a 40 cars **b** 100 cars **c** 30 cars

5 The pictogram shows the number of meals served in Max's restaurant.

a How many meals were served on Tuesday?

b How many meals were served on Thursday?

c How many meals were served altogether?

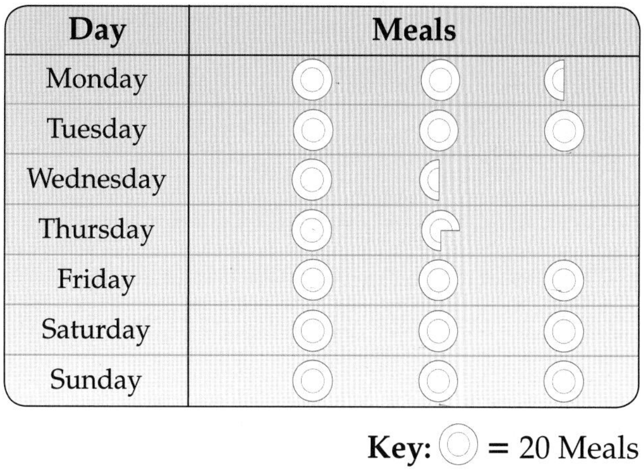
Day
Meals
Monday
Tuesday
Wednesday
Thursday
Friday
Saturday
Sunday
Key: = 20 Meals

research

Pictograms are commonly used in newspapers and magazines to represent data visually.
Be on the look out for examples and bring them in to share with the class.

5c Reading and drawing bar charts

- Understand bar charts and draw them

Keywords
Axis
Bar chart

- A **bar chart** is another way to represent a set of data.
  A scale shows what each bar represents.

- When you draw a bar chart:
  - Leave gaps between the bars.
  - Write a label on each **axis**.
  - Make sure that the vertical axis has a clear scale.

The lines that form the sides of the chart are axes.

The horizontal axis goes across. The vertical axis goes up.

- You can use data from a pictogram or table to draw a bar chart.

7A's favourite drinks

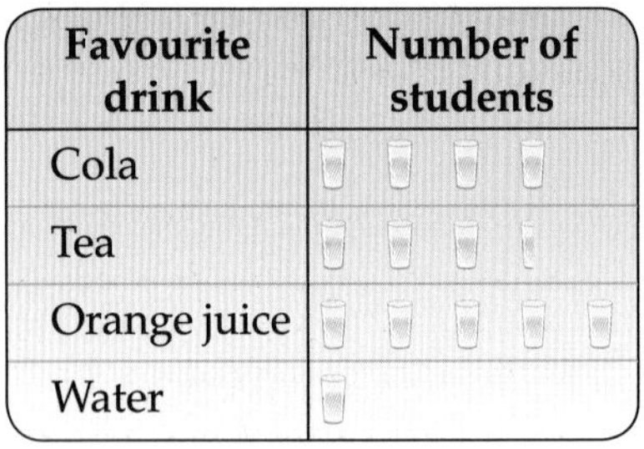
Favourite drink
Number of students
Cola
Tea
Orange juice
Water

Key: [glass] means 2 students

7A's favourite drinks

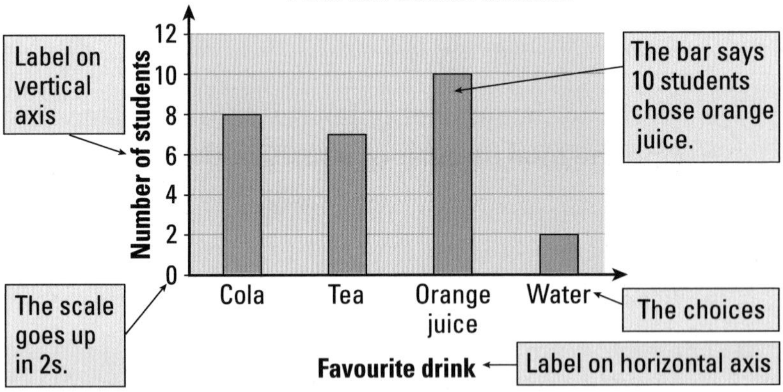

example

The bar chart shows the number of computers in four classrooms.

a Which room has the most computers?

b How many computers are there altogether?

p. 122

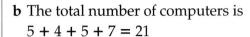

a Room 24 has the most computers

p. 214

b The total number of computers is
$5 + 4 + 5 + 7 = 21$

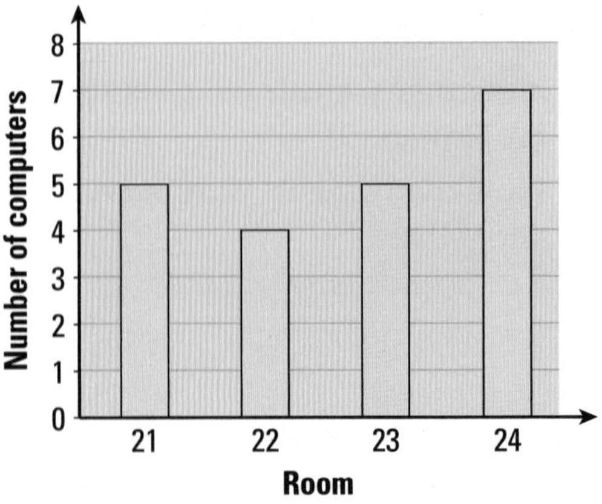

Exercise 5c

1 This bar chart shows the number of students in each class who play football.

   a How many students in class 7A play football?

   b Which class has the most football players?

   c Which class has the least football players?

   d How many students play football in total?

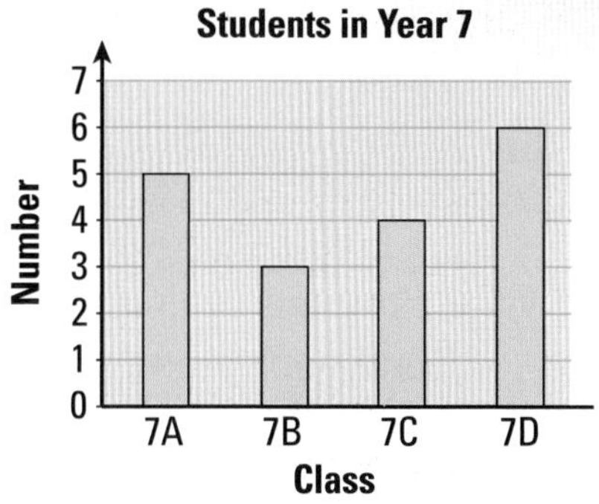

Students in Year 7

2 This bar chart shows the number of minutes that Jane spent on homework each day.

   a When did Jane do the most homework?

   b When did she do no homework?

   c How much time did she spend on homework in total?

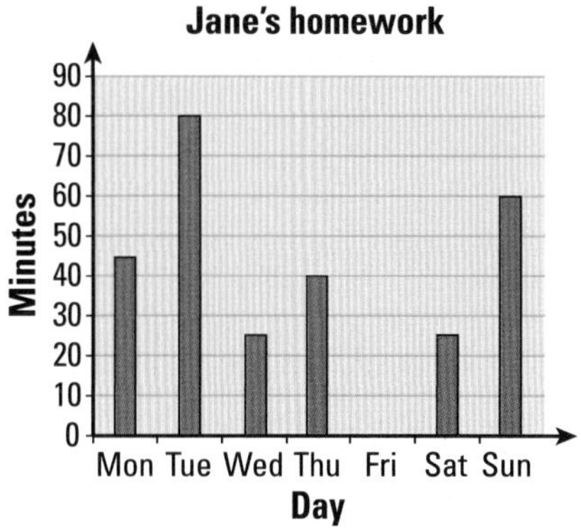

Jane's homework

3 This table shows the number of people who were absent from class 7C at Clearview High School. Draw a bar chart for this set of data.

Day	Monday	Tuesday	Wednesday	Thursday	Friday
Absence	3	2	0	1	2

4 This pictogram shows the number of people who ate at a restaurant. Draw a bar chart for this data.

Day	People
Monday	○ ○ ○ ◖
Tuesday	○ ○ ◗
Wednesday	○ ○ ○
Thursday	○ ○ ◠
Friday	○ ○ ○ ○ ○
Saturday	○ ○ ○ ○ ○
Sunday	○ ○ ○ ◗

Key: ○ = 4 people

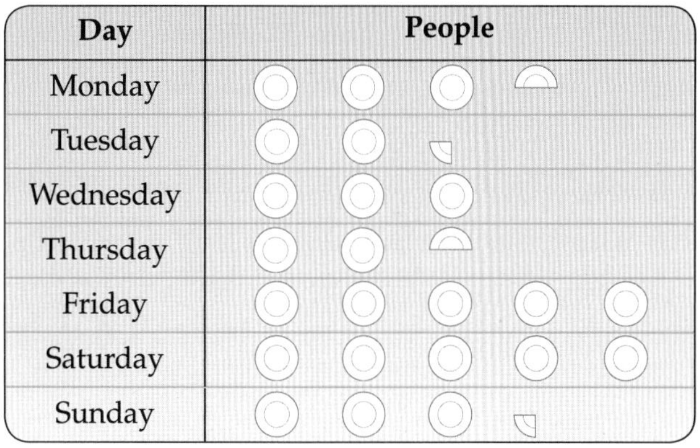

discussion

Bar charts are also used in newspapers and on TV to show data.
Think about where you see them in print and on which programmes they are used on TV.

Discuss your examples.

5d Line graphs

- Take data from line graphs

Keywords
Axis
Line graph
Time

A **line graph** is useful for showing how things change over time.

- When you read a line graph:
  - **Time** goes along the horizontal **axis.**
  - The vertical axis shows what you are measuring.
  - The points show the data that you are given.
  - The points are joined with a line.

p. 124
p. 214[2]

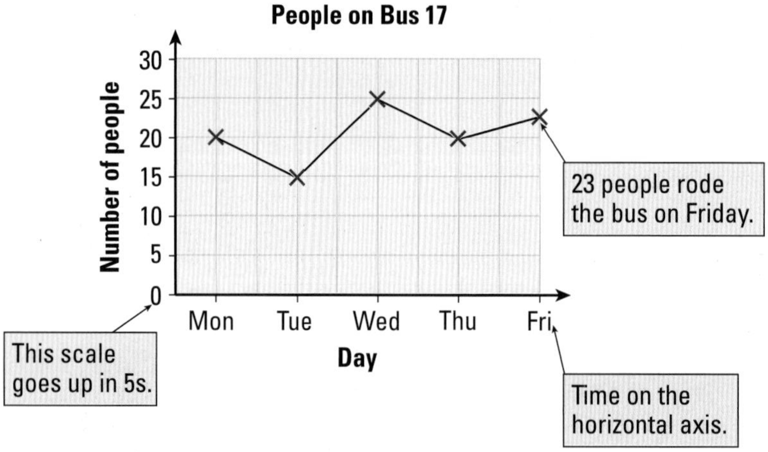

example

James drew a line graph to show the temperature of his oven.

a What time was the oven turned on?

b What was the highest temperature in the oven?

c What time was the oven switched off?

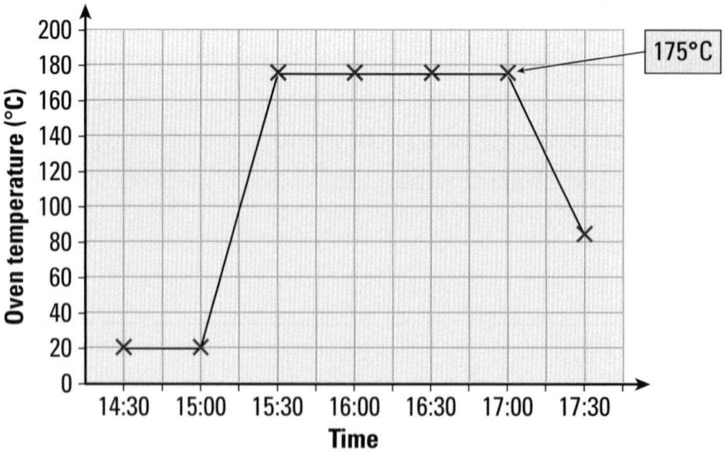

a The oven was turned on at 15:00 (3 p.m.). The line rises at 15:00.

b The highest temperature was 175 °C. Look at the highest points on the graph.

c The oven was turned off at 17:00 (5 p.m.). The line begins to fall at 17:00.

Exercise 5d

1 This line graph shows the height of a hot air balloon.

a What time did the balloon take off?

b What was the greatest height that the balloon reached?

c How long did the whole flight last?

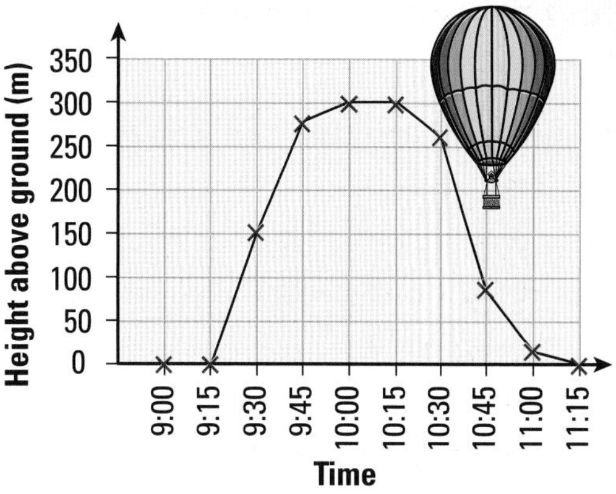

2 This line graph shows how the outside temperature changed one summer day.

a What was the temperature at 10 a.m.?

b What was the highest temperature recorded?

c At what times was the temperature 15 °C?

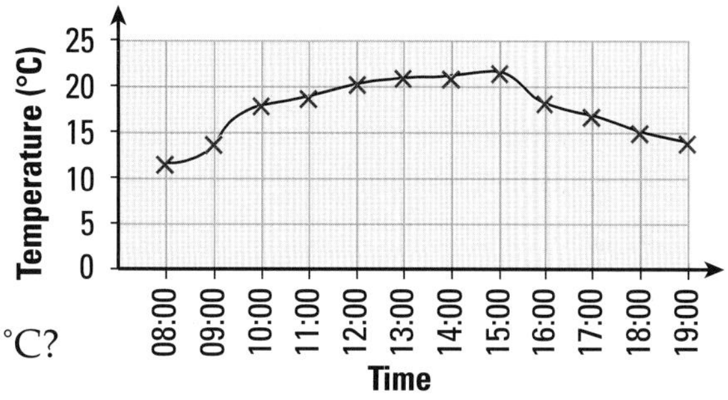

3 Grandad planted a tree when he was young and measured it every 10 years.

a How tall was the tree in 1970?

b Use your line graph to find when the tree was exactly 10 m tall.

c What was the height of the tree in 1995?

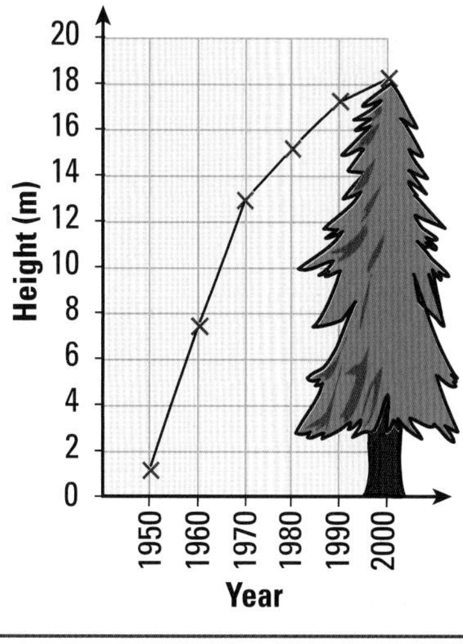

challenge

This line graph shows the average daily maximum temperature for a part of Libya. The highest temperature ever recorded was in Al' Aziziyah, Libya at 57.7 °C.

Where would that temperature be on this chart? What would that do to the line?

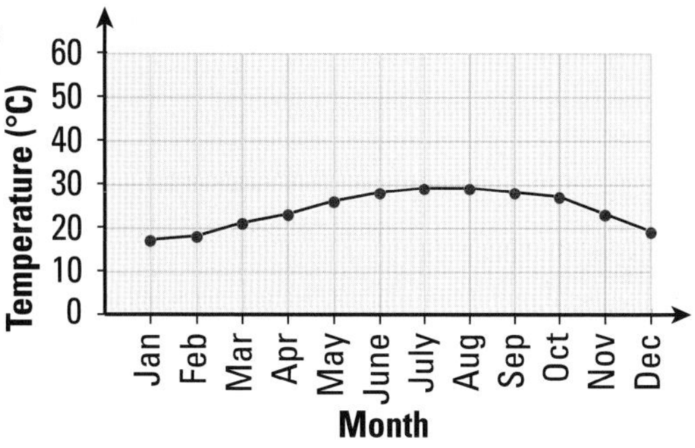

5e Pie charts

- Take data from pie charts

Keywords
Pie chart

- A **pie chart** shows you how a total is divided up into its parts.
- A whole circle represents the total.
- The slices of the pie show you how big the parts are.

Favourite pie

10 people chose chocolate pie.

5 people chose apple pie.

3 people chose cherry pie.

example

This pie chart shows the types of films that a cinema showed one month.

a How many types of film are there?

b Which type of film was shown the most?

Types of film

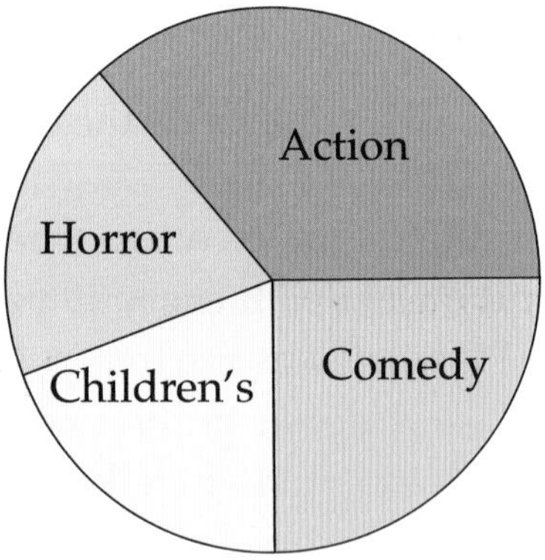

a 4 types of film

There are 4 pie slices.

p. 125

b Action films were shown most.

Action has the biggest pie slice.

- You can make good guesses from a pie chart and can write one part as a fraction or percentage of the whole pie.

example

This pie chart shows the flavours of ice cream served one day in a shop.

What part of the total did each flavour represent?

Ice cream flavours

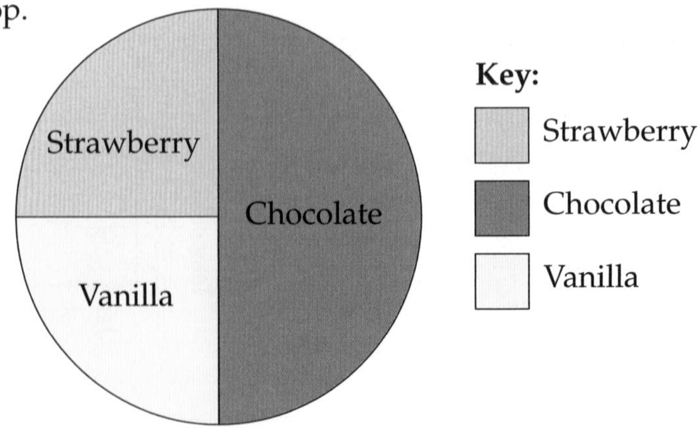

It looks like

Chocolate $\frac{1}{2}$, Vanilla $\frac{1}{4}$, Strawberry $\frac{1}{4}$

The key helps to label the pie slices.

Exercise 5e

1 This pie chart shows class 7A's eye colours.

a How many types of eye colour are shown?

b Which eye colour did the least number of students have?

c Which eye colour did the most number of students have?

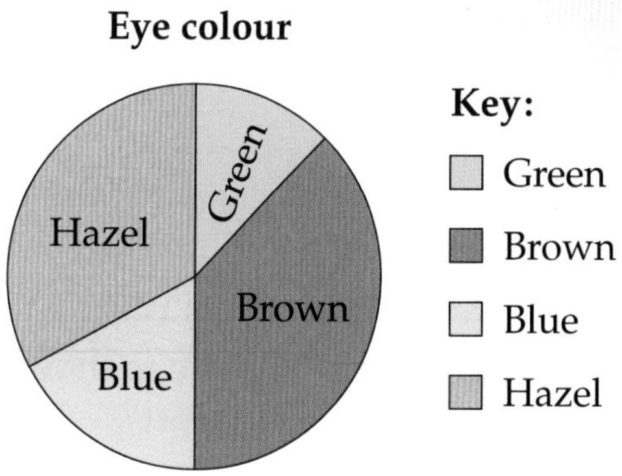

2 Camilla carried out a survey to find out what kind of pet her classmates have. The pie chart shows her results.

Guess the fraction of the class who own

a only a dog

b only a cat

c neither a dog nor a cat.

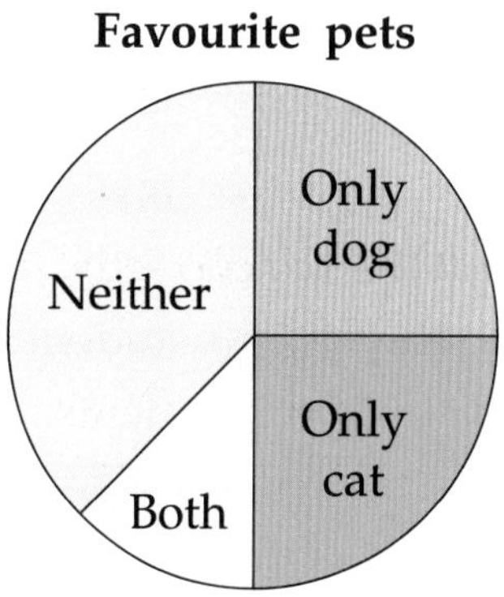

3 This pie chart shows how the Barnes family spent their money one month.

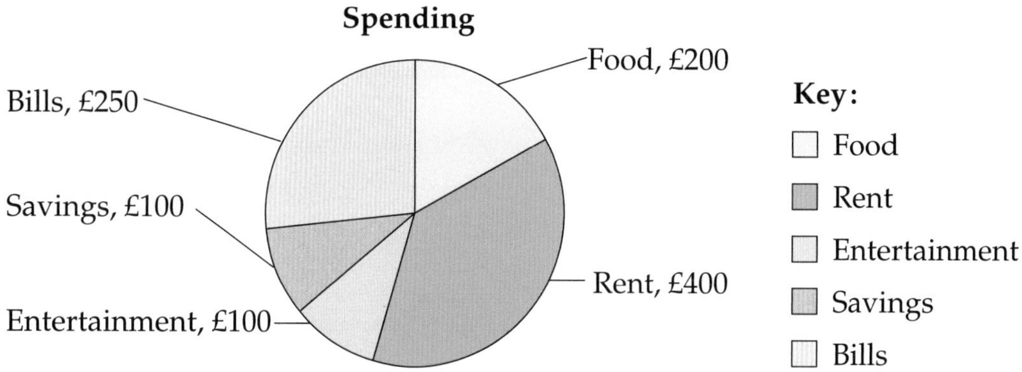

a How much did they spend on food?

b Which category shows about $\frac{1}{4}$ of the money spent?

c Which category is the largest?

discussion

Why are these charts called 'pie charts' and not 'pizza charts' or 'cake charts'? Use the Internet to find out.

5f Reading diagrams

- Read different kinds of charts and graphs

Keywords
Axis *Key*
Diagram *Scale*

- When reading a diagram with a **key**, you need to read the key correctly.

Pie charts and pictograms use keys.

example

Sara drew this pictogram to show her classmates' favourite sports.

Andrew said, 'This diagram is wrong. You can't have half a student!'

Is Andrew correct?

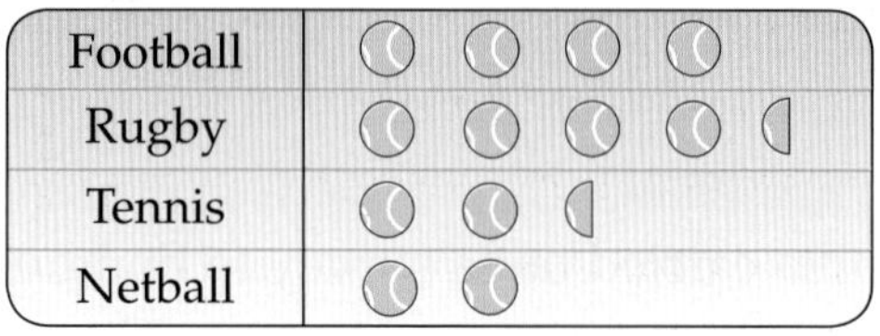

Key: = 2 students

He hasn't read the key correctly.
Andrew read **Key:** = 1 student instead of the correct key **Key:** = 2 students.

p. 122

- When reading a **diagram** with a **scale**, you need to:
  - Use the correct **axis**
  - Read the scale correctly.

Bar charts and line graphs use scales.

example

This line graph shows the attendance at Meadway School.

a Which week had the lowest attendance?

b What was the highest attendance?

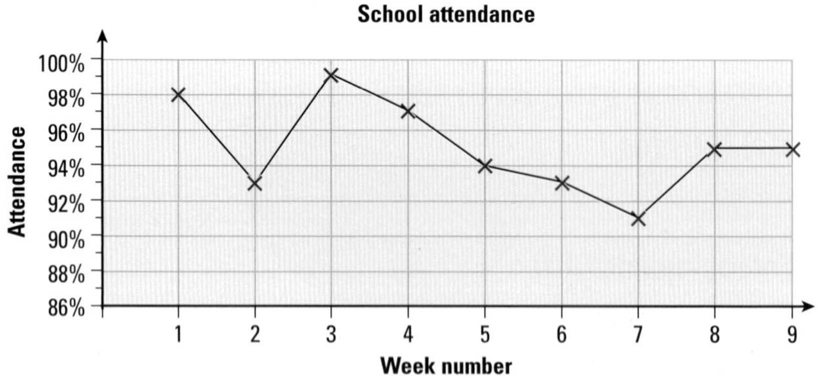

a The lowest attendance was in week 7.

The question asks **when** the lowest attendance was.

b The highest attendance was 99%.

The question asks **what** the highest attendance was.

Exercise 5f

1 This bar chart shows the number of boys and girls in four classes.

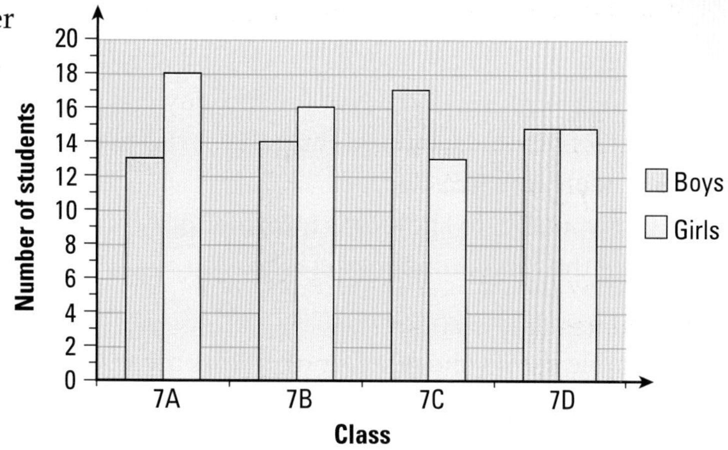

The blue bars represent boys and the green bars represent girls.

a How many boys are there in class 7B?

b Which class has equal numbers of boys and girls?

c Which class has more boys than girls?

2 Steve drew this line graph to show the number of songs he downloaded each month.

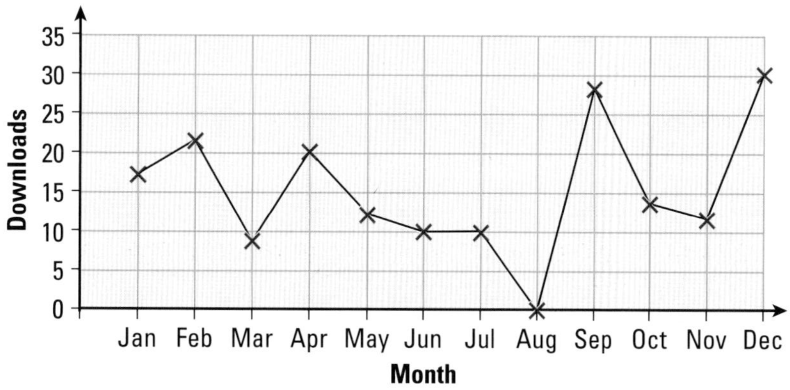

a How many songs did Steve download in April?

b In which month did Steve download no songs?

c What was the greatest number of songs he downloaded in a month? When did this happen?

3 This pie chart shows the flavours of ice creams sold in a shop one day.

a How many different flavours of ice cream were sold?

b Which flavour made up about half of the ice creams sold?

c Which was the least popular flavour?

Ice cream flavours

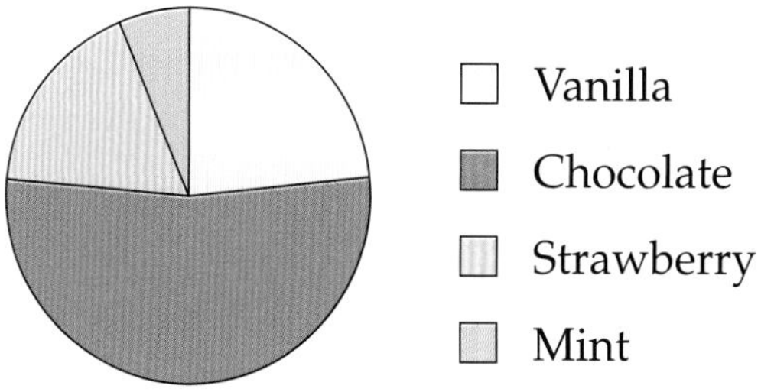

discussion

You have now seen data displayed with lists, tables, pictograms, bar charts, line graphs and pie charts.
Which way do you think is the most clear?
Which way do you think is the most confusing?

5 Consolidation

5a

1 Ben recorded the number of times his computer crashed. It crashed three times on Monday, and twice on Tuesday. On Wednesday his computer crashed five times, but on Thursday it did not crash at all. On Friday there were four crashes.

a Draw a table to show this information.

b Find the total number of crashes.

5b

2 The table shows the number of credits awarded to students in Year 7 at Hollybank High School.

Class	**7W1**	**7W2**	**7W3**	**7W4**
Credits	8	7	4	6

Draw a pictogram to show this information.
Make sure you choose a good symbol!

5c

3 This table shows the number of pieces of homework that Kelly was set each day.

Day	**Monday**	**Tueday**	**Wednesday**	**Thurday**	**Friday**
Pieces of homework	2	3	2	4	5

Draw a bar chart to represent this set of data.

5d

4 This line graph shows how the temperature in a room changed.

a At what time was the temperature 18°C?

b What was the temperature at 10:00?

c How many hours did it take for the temperature to drop from 21°C to 15°C?

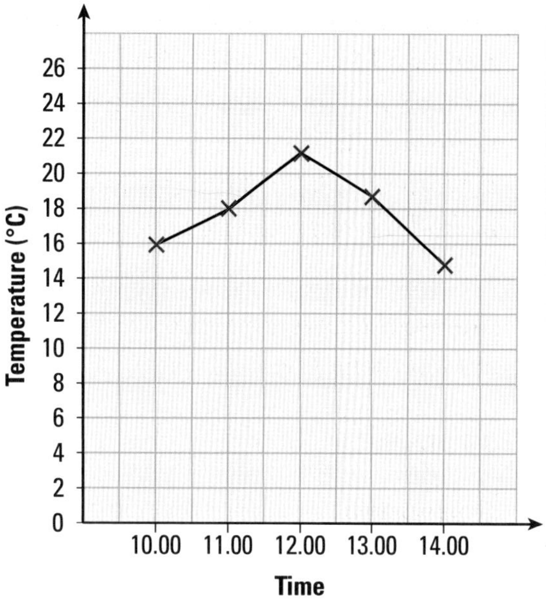

5e

5 This pie chart shows the methods used to generate electricity in the USA.

a What method is $\frac{1}{4}$ of the total?

b What method is $\frac{1}{2}$ of the total?

c What two methods together make up $\frac{1}{4}$ of the total?

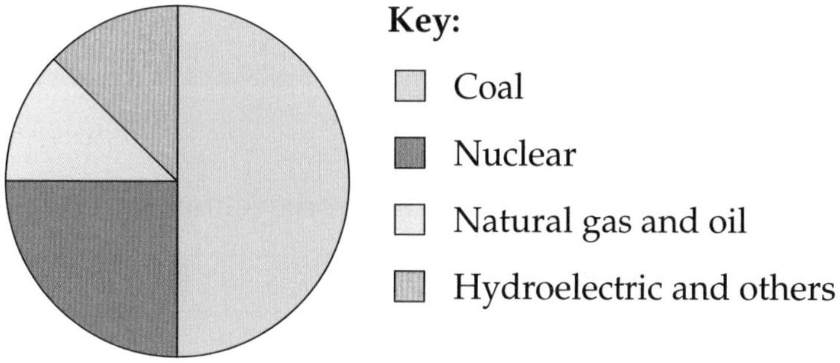

5f

6 This bar chart shows the number of points awarded to five competitors by the judges in a talent show.

a Which competitor was awarded most marks?

b The two competitors with the least marks have to face a public vote.
Which competitors are these?

c What was the total number of marks awarded by the judges?

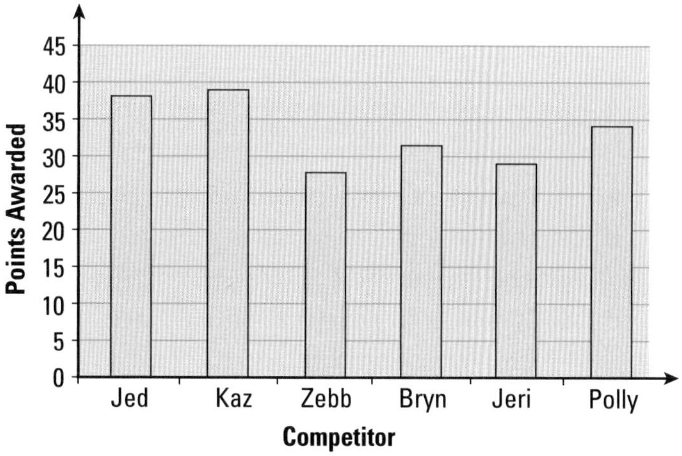

5 Summary

Key indicators

- Construct and interpret graphs and charts **Level 3**
- Interpret information in tables and charts **Level 4**

Level 3

1 Sami does a survey of the colour of 10 cars.
She draws a pictogram, but forgets to write the key.

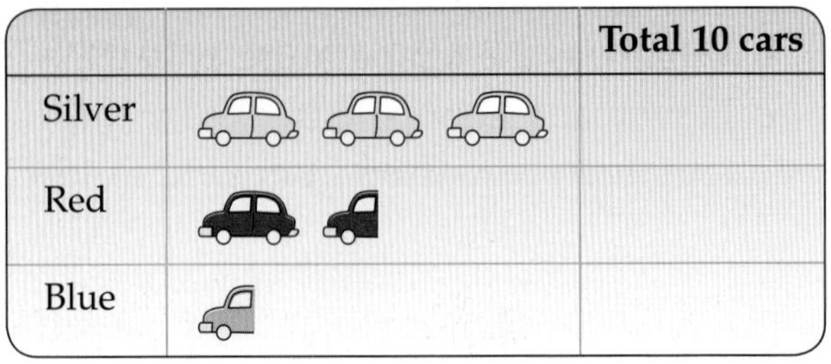

a How many cars does  represent?

b How many silver cars did Sami see?

Ella's answer ✔

Ella checks that 6 + 3 + 1 = 10.

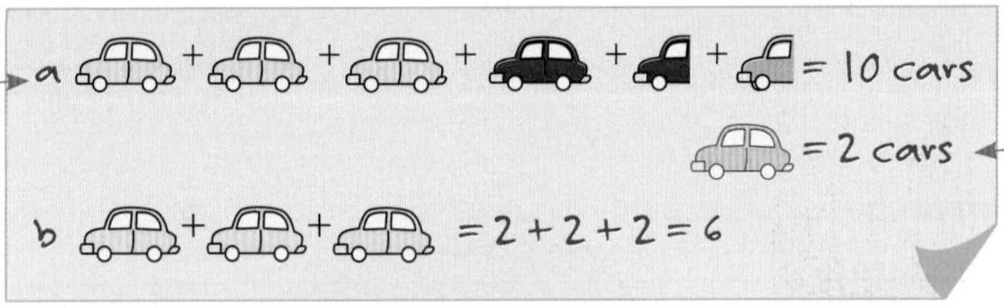

Ella knows the two half cars together make a whole car.

Level 3

2 Look at the information about recycling places in one town.

Recycling place	Glass	Cans	Plastic	Paper	Clothes	Shoes
Supermarket A	✔	✔		✔	✔	✔
Supermarket B	✔					
Supermarket C	✔	✔	✔			✔
Car park D	✔			✔	✔	
Car park E	✔	✔				
Road F	✔	✔		✔		

a How many of these places recycle paper?

b One of these places recycles plastic.
Which place is this?

c Molly wants to go to one of the places to recycles cans and clothes.
Which place should she go to?

Year 7 3–4 2007 Paper 1

6 Algebra

Operations and symbols

Symbols are drawings that represent ideas or words. You don't need to know how to read to know what the symbol stands for.

What do these symbols stand for?

What's the point? You can use symbols to represent numbers in maths. You don't need to know what the number is to use it in your calculations.

Check in

Level 2

1 Three friends each have 20 marbles. Write the number of marbles that each friend now has if

a Lynda gives away 3 marbles.
b John buys 4 more marbles.
c Pat shares her marbles between 5 friends.

You do not need to work out the answers to this question.

Level 3

2 Work out the value of each of these symbols.

a 6 + ♥ = 8 **b** ? + 3 = 10 **c** 10 − ☺ = 5 **d** 3 × ∗ = 12

e ♣ × 2 = 6 **f** 15 − ⊗ = 9 **g** ♦ ÷ 2 = 4 **h** 4 ÷ ▲ = 4

3 Work out these calculations mentally.

a 12 + 13 + 14
b 2 × 3 × 4
c 20 − 10 − 5
d 18 ÷ 3 ÷ 2

- Use more than one operation in a calculation

Keywords
Addition *Operation* *Division* *Subtraction* *Multiplication*

- An **operation** tells you what to do in a calculation.
  $\div$, $\times$, $+$, $-$ are operations

$\div$	**Division** shows how many times one number goes into another.	3 girls and 5 boys split into 2 teams. $\frac{3+5}{2} = \frac{8}{2} = 8 \div 2 = 4$ per team
$\times$	**Multiplication** saves time instead of addition.	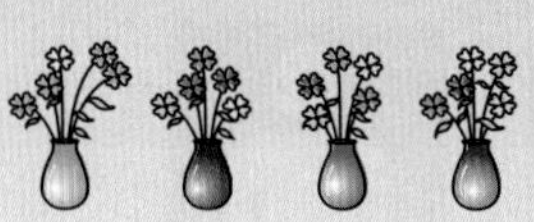 Four vases with five flowers each $4 \times 5 = 20$ flowers
$+$	**Addition** combines numbers to get a total.	£500 + £500 = £1000 
$-$	**Subtraction** takes one number out of another to get a difference.	NATIONAL BANK Bank Statement Money In £ 950 – Money Out £ 850 New Balance £100

example

Work out these calculations.

a $\frac{20+4}{2}$ **b** $75 + 15 - 5$ **c** $8 \times 4 \times 2$

a $\frac{20+4}{2} = \frac{24}{2}$
$= 24 \div 2$
$= 12$

b $75 + 15 - 5 = 90 - 5$
$= 85$

c $8 \times 4 \times 2 = 32 \times 2$
$= 64$

Exercise 6a

1 Work out these calculations.

a $15 + 30$ **b** 12×5 **c** $29 - 13$

d $45 \div 9$ **e** 11×7 **f** $52 - 21$

2 Work out these calculations.

a $4 + 20 - 5$ **b** $4 \times 5 \times 2$ **c** $25 - 12 - 8$

d $6 + 21 + 19$ **e** $81 \div 9$ **f** $12 - 6 + 15$

g $5 \times 5 \times 4$ **h** $36 \div 4 \div 3$ **i** $45 \div 3 \div 5$

3 In each of these divisions do the operation on the top line first.

a $\frac{12 + 2}{2}$ **b** $\frac{34 + 1}{5}$ **c** $\frac{55 - 10}{8}$

d $\frac{15 \times 4}{2}$ **e** $\frac{27 + 13}{5}$ **f** $\frac{27 - 13}{8}$

g $\frac{80 + 40}{12}$ **h** $\frac{45 + 45}{15}$ **i** $\frac{25 + 45}{5}$

j $\frac{12 \times 5}{20}$ **k** $\frac{16 \times 5}{2}$ **l** $\frac{90 \times 2}{20}$

Did you know?

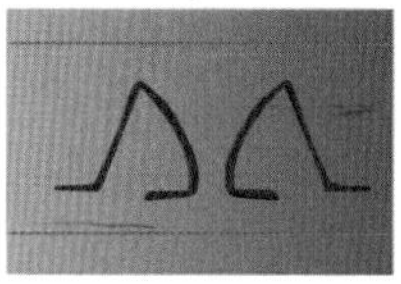

Ancient Egyptians used symbols of legs walking forward for addition and legs walking backwards for subtraction.

4 Work out the answers to these calculations.
Each calculation has two operations.

a Add 50 to 25 and then divide by 3

b Take 5 from 21 and then divide by 4

c Divide 60 by 5 and then add 8

d Multiply 9 by 5 and then divide by 15

e Divide 35 by 7 and then subtract 5

5 a Daniel has £5 and Lucy has £13.
They decide to share out the money equally.
How much do they each get?

b Samira has £150 in her bank account and spends £35 on a new pair of trainers. How much money does she have left?

c 12 friends each give £1.50 to buy ice creams.
Each ice cream costs 75p.
How many can they buy altogether?

challenge

Work out

$12 + 3 - 4 + 5 + 67 + 8 + 9$

Do you see anything interesting?

6b Order of operations

- Do calculations where the order of doing them matters

Keywords
Order of operations

Ali sees that there are two ways to do this calculation:
$6 \times 4 + 18$

You can multiply 6 by 4 and then add 18.
$6 \times 4 = 24$ now,
$24 + 18 = 42$

OR you could add 4 to 18 first and then multiply your answer by 6.
$4 + 18 = 22$ and
$22 \times 6 = 132$

Which one is correct?

- You always follow this **order of operations** in calculations.

  'Divide or Multiply before you Add or Subtract'

$6 \times 4 + 18$	Multiply first.
$24 + 18 = 42$	Then add.

Warning! Your calculator may not follow this order so be careful.

example

Work out these calculations.

a $5 \times 9 - 22$ **b** $10 + 20 \div 5$ **c** $6 \times 4 + 18 \div 2$

a $5 \times 9 - 22 = 45 - 22$
$= 23$
Multiply first: $5 \times 9 = 45$

b $10 + 20 \div 5 = 10 + 4$
$= 14$
Divide first: $20 \div 5 = 4$

c $6 \times 4 + 18 \div 2 = 24 + 9$
$= 24 + 9$
$= 33$
Multiply and divide first: $6 \times 4 = 24$ and $18 \div 2 = 9$
Then add.

Exercise 6b

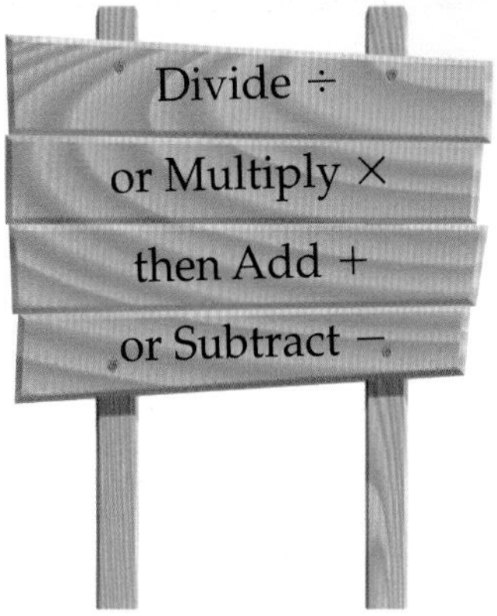

1 Work out these calculations. Show your work.

a $4 \times 5 - 16$ **b** $12 + 32 \div 4$ **c** $50 + 12 \div 3$
d $6 \times 9 + 4$ **e** $21 \div 7 + 18$ **f** $45 - 9 \times 3$
g $40 \div 1 + 7$ **h** $64 + 40 \div 4$ **i** $31 + 2 \times 4$
j $45 - 36 \div 6$ **k** $18 \div 3 + 4$ **l** $50 + 15 \times 3$
m $100 - 9 \times 5$ **n** $12 + 32 \times 4$ **o** $80 \times 7 + 3$
p $50 - 7 \times 7$ **q** $27 - 21 \div 3$ **r** $65 + 6 \times 7$
s $14 \times 2 + 3$ **t** $16 \times 12 - 9$ **u** $54 \div 2 \times 2$

2 Work out these calculations with three operations.

a $16 \times 2 + 4 \times 2$ **b** $4 \times 4 + 12 \times 2$
c $36 \div 2 - 5 \times 2$ **d** $12 \times 5 - 2 \times 5$
e $35 \div 7 - 45 \div 9$ **f** $30 + 4 \times 3 + 15$
g $24 \div 3 + 4 \times 2$ **h** $15 - 2 \times 3 + 6$
i $20 - 4 + 3 \times 2$ **j** $33 \div 3 + 3 \times 3$
k $100 \div 5 - 16 + 4$ **l** $100 \div 10 - 1000 \div 100$
m $40 \times 2 - 6 \times 7$ **n** $48 \div 4 - 4 \times 2$
o $16 \div 4 \times 2 - 3$ **p** $27 \div 3 + 7 \div 7$
q $32 \div 2 + 5 \times 4$ **r** $55 \div 5 + 22 \div 22$
s $24 \div 3 + 2 \times 1$ **t** $70 \div 5 + 36 \div 36$

Show your work.
Or, you may want to use a calculator.

3 **a** Donna puts her age into code.
She says, 'To find my age divide 40 by 4, then add 10 divided by 5.'
How old is Donna?

b Ayesha and Charlotte wash car windows.
This morning Ayesha earned £20.
By teatime she had doubled this amount.
Charlotte earned £15 in the morning and three times this by teatime.
How much did the two girls earn altogether?

challenge

As I was going to St Ives, I met these things.

How many things did I meet?

Seven men

with one wife each

with two cats each

6c Using letters

- Know that letters can stand for numbers
- Use letters where the numbers are not known

Keywords
Amount
Symbol
Represent

Joel doesn't know how many marbles are in this bag.
He uses a letter to **represent** the number of marbles.

He uses the letter ***m*** to represent the number of marbles in the bag.

Joel gave away six of his marbles.

I had ***m*** marbles. I gave six marbles away so now I have $\boldsymbol{m - 6}$ marbles.

Jenny started with ***n*** marbles.
She won 10 more marbles in a game.

I have $\boldsymbol{n + 10}$ marbles.

Peta started with ***d*** marbles.
She shared them by dividing the marbles into two groups.

Now I have $\boldsymbol{d \div 2}$ marbles.

Michael had ***k*** marbles.
He doubled this **amount** in a game.

I have $\boldsymbol{k \times 2}$ marbles.

example

James has ***t*** sweets. He eats 10 of the sweets.
How many sweets has he now?

James has $\boldsymbol{t - 10}$ sweets.

p. 180

Exercise 6c

1 There are *s* fish in this school.
If 20 fish are caught by a fisherman,
how many fish will be left in the school?

2 Jeff has *m* pounds in his wallet.
He gives away half of his money to a charity.
How much money has Jeff now?

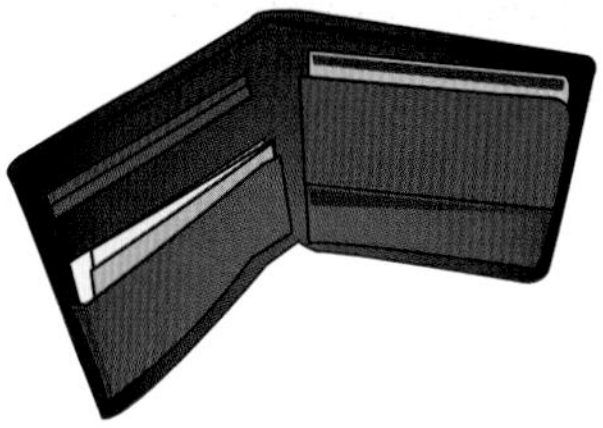

3 Each girl has *n* counters.

a If Dinesh adds 12 more, how many does she have?

b If Alice grabs 19 more counters, how many does she have?

c If Nicky trebles her number of counters, how many would she have then?

d If Tina divides her counters into six equal groups, how many counters would she have in each group?

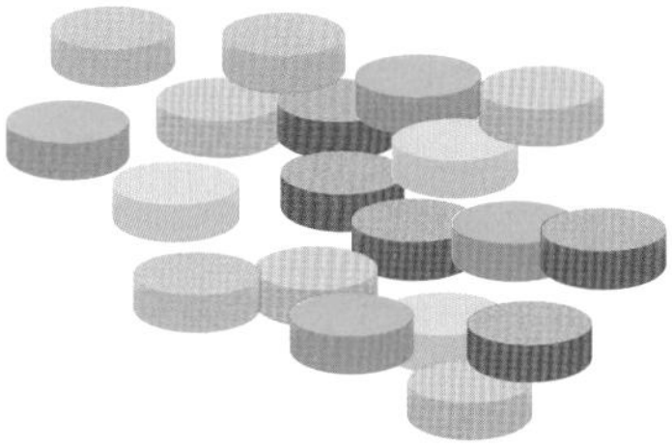

4 There are *j* biscuits in this packet.
There are some more on the plate.
How many biscuits are there altogether?

5 There are *g* trees in a forest.

a If 100 trees are cut down for Christmas, how many trees are left?

b How many trees will there be in five forests of the same size?

challenge

In her maths exams, Tracy answered ***P*** questions.
She got 25 of the questions right.

How many questions did Tracy get wrong?

6d Substitution

- Replace a letter by its numerical value to work out a problem

Keywords
Expression
Substitute
Value

Biscuits are sold in packets.
One gold packet holds 12 biscuits.

You can use a letter to represent the number of biscuits in the packet.

One gold packet holds n biscuits. $n = 12$

p. 186

The number of biscuits in two packets $= 2 \times n$
$= 2 \times 12$
$= 24$ biscuits

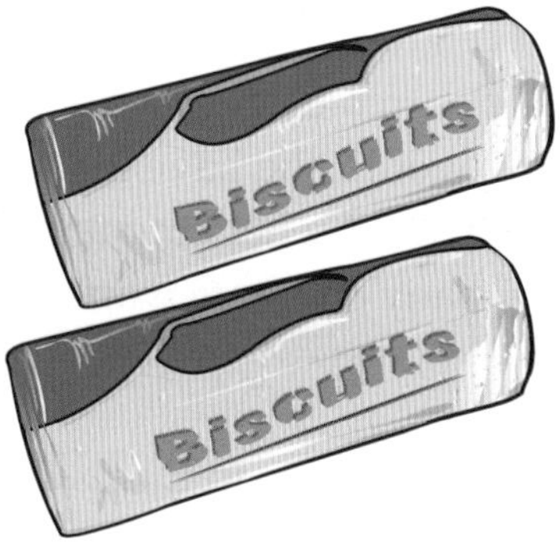

One green packet holds 20 biscuits.
You can say, 'One green packet holds m biscuits if $m = 20$.'

The number of biscuits in one green and one gold packet $= n + m$
$= 12 + 20$
$= 32$ biscuits

example

There are c chocolates in a box.

a How many chocolates are shown in this picture?

b If $c = 16$, how many chocolates are there altogether?

a $c + 5$ chocolates — One box and 5 chocolates

b There are $16 + 5$ chocolates. — $16 + 5 = 21$ chocolates

Exercise 6d

1 One green packet holds m biscuits. $m = 20$
One gold packet holds n biscuits. $n = 12$
How many biscuits are in

a two green packets
b two gold and one green packet
c three gold packets plus five extra biscuits
d $n + 1$ biscuits
e $n - 2$ biscuits
f $m + n + 5$ biscuits?

2 The number of sweets in a jar $= p$
a How many sweets are there in three full jars?
b If $p = 25$ how many sweets are there in three full jars?

3 The number of chocolates in each box $= h$
How many chocolates are shown in each picture?

a

b

c

d

e

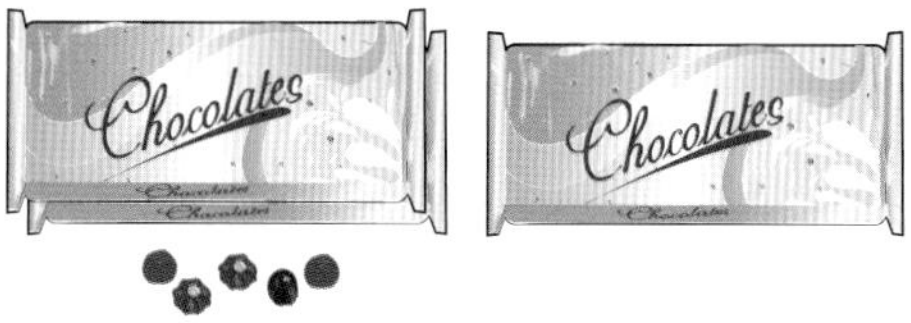

f If h is 30, how many chocolates are in each picture?

4 Work out these calculations when $n = 10$.

a $n + 5$	**b** $n + 16$	**c** $n - 3$	**d** $n - 10$
e $2 \times n$	**f** $5 \times n$	**g** $n \div 2$	**h** $n \times n$

challenge

There are k biscuits in the large green pack and j biscuits in the smaller red packet.
a How many biscuits would you have if you bought one large green pack and one small red pack?
b If $k = 20$ and $j = 15$, how many biscuits are there in one large green and one small red packet?
c You need 60 biscuits. How many of each pack of biscuits would you buy?

6a

1 Work out each calculation and say which of each group has a different answer.

a i $360 \div 5 \div 3$ **ii** $840 \div 6 \div 5$ **iii** $\frac{200}{25} \times 3$

b i $150 - 12 \times 9$ **ii** $111 - 9 \times 7$ **iii** $\frac{170}{5} + 14$

c i $155 + 27 - 106$ **ii** $133 - 95 + 34$ **iii** $250 - 115 - 63$

6b

2 Work out each calculation and say which of each group has a different answer.

a i $\frac{84}{7} + 12 \times 5$ **ii** $\frac{48}{3} + 8 \times 7$

iii $\frac{128}{8} + \frac{300}{5}$ **iv** $\frac{192}{4} + \frac{72}{3}$

b i $\frac{450}{6} - 13 \times 3$ **ii** $\frac{300}{5} - 8 \times 3$

iii $\frac{360}{4} - \frac{162}{3}$ **iv** $\frac{480}{8} - \frac{84}{3}$

3 Work out each calculation and say which of each group has a different answer.

c i $\frac{300}{27 + 23}$ **ii** $\frac{360}{31 + 14}$

iii $\frac{150}{60 - 35}$ **iv** $\frac{210}{99 - 64}$

d i $\frac{95 + 73}{12}$ **ii** $\frac{111 + 69}{15}$

iii $\frac{244 + 56}{25}$ **iv** $\frac{235 + 125}{30}$

6c

4 In a match box there are 50 matches.

How many matches are there in

a 2 boxes **b** 3 boxes **c** y boxes?

5 A bottle contains 100 tablets. How many tablets are there in

a 3 bottles **b** 4 bottles **c** t bottles

6d

6 Find the value of each expression if

★ = 4, ☺ = 3, □ = 2

a ★ + □ **b** ★ − ☺

c ☺ − □ **d** ★ + ☺ − □

e 2 × ★ **f** 2 × □

g 4 × ☺ **h** 4 × □

i 6 × ☺ **j** 10 × ☺

6 Summary

Key indicators

- Recognise number patterns **Level 3**
- Use inverse operations **Level 3**

Level 4

1 Work out the missing numbers.
Use the first line to help you.

a $14 \times 16 = 224$

$14 \times \square = 448$

b $832 \div 26 = 32$

$832 \div \square = 64$

Hayley's answer ✔

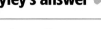

Hayley realises $224 \times 2 = 448$ and so she needs $16 \times 2 = 32$

a 32

b 13

Hayley realises $32 \times 2 = 64$ and so she needs $26 \div 2 = 13$

Level 3

2 Here is part of the 36 times table.

$1 \times 36 = 36$
$2 \times 36 = 72$
$3 \times 36 = 108$
$4 \times 36 = 144$
$5 \times 36 = 180$
$6 \times 36 = 216$
$7 \times 36 = 252$
$8 \times 36 = 288$
$9 \times 36 = 324$
$10 \times 36 = 360$

Use the 36 times table to help you work out the missing numbers.

$288 \div 8 =$

$180 \div 36 =$

$11 \times 36 =$

Key Stage 3 2007 3–5 Paper 1

7 Number

Calculation and measure

November
2008
Mon Tue Wed Thu Fri Sat Sun
1 2
3 4 5 6 7 8 9
10 11 12 13 14 15 16
17 18 19 20 21 22 23
24 25 26 27 28 29 30

One month, instead of asking for pocket money, what if you asked for 1p the first day and then double each day from then on? So, one penny today. Tomorrow you will get 2p. The next day 4p, the next day 8p, then 16p, then 32p. Each day you will double the amount over the 30 days.

What's the point? That's £10 737 418.24!!! See, you **can** use your knowledge of maths to your advantage!

Check in

Level 3

1 Which operation sign is missing from each of these problems (+, −, × or ÷)?

a 10 □ 3 = 30 **b** 12 □ 4 = 8 **c** 8 □ 4 = 2

d 11 □ 9 = 20 **e** 13 □ 2 = 26 **f** 19 □ 11 = 8

g 20 □ 10 = 2 **h** 6 □ 6 = 36 **i** 12 □ 4 = 3

2 Double each of these numbers.

a 6 **b** 10 **c** 13 **d** 25 **e** 50

3 Halve each of these numbers.

a 8 **b** 12 **c** 20 **d** 28 **e** 80

4 Copy out these headings. Put each word under the correct heading.

Measure of length	Measure of weight	Measure of time

second metre day
gram millimetre
year tonne hour
kilometre century
week centimetre kilogram

7a Rounding and estimating

- Round a number to the nearest 10 or 100

Keywords
Estimate
Nearest
Round

- **Rounding** makes numbers easier to work with.

Round down Round up

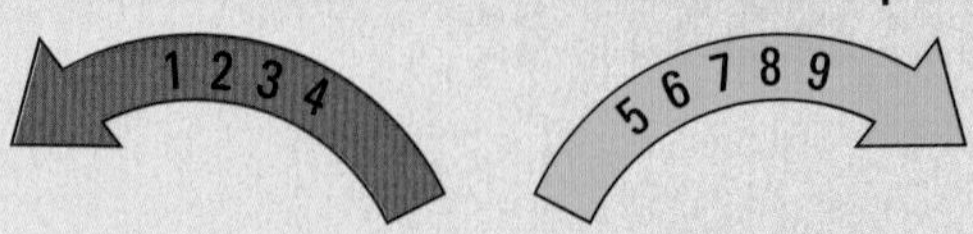

Five is actually in the middle but you round up.

- You can round to the **nearest** 10.

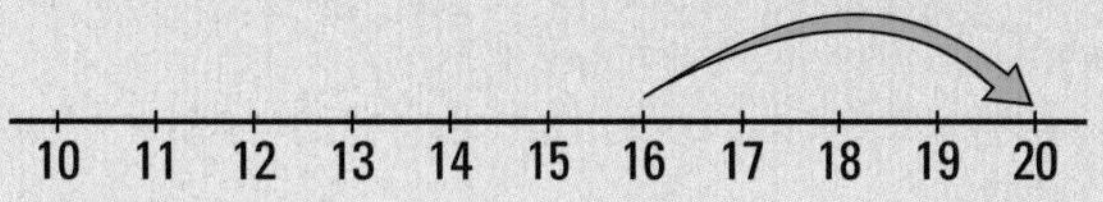

16 rounds up.
The nearest 10 is 20.

example

Round to the nearest 10.

a 8
b 25
c 184

a 8 rounds up — The nearest '10' is 10.
b 25 rounds up — The nearest '10' is 30.
c 184 rounds down — The nearest '10' is 180.

- You can round to the nearest 100 or 1000.

example

Round 832

a to the nearest 100
b to the nearest 1000

a 832 rounds down — The nearest '100' is 800.
b 832 rounds up — The nearest '1000' is 1000.

p. 14

- You can **estimate** first to find what the answer might be before you find the actual answer. This will help you to see if you've made a mistake.

example

Solve 251 + 97. Make an estimate first.

Estimate first
251 is close to 250.
97 is close to 100.

$$\begin{array}{r} 250 \\ +100 \\ \hline 350 \end{array}$$

Estimate answer is 350

Actual answer

$$\begin{array}{r} {}^{1}251 \\ +\ 97 \\ \hline 348 \end{array}$$

This is close to the estimate answer. ✔

Exercise 7a

1 Round the pink number to the nearest 10.

a
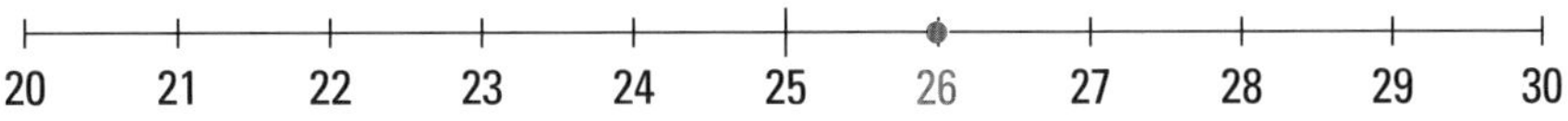

b
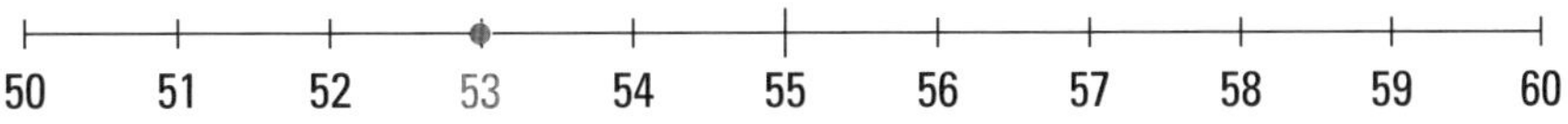

c
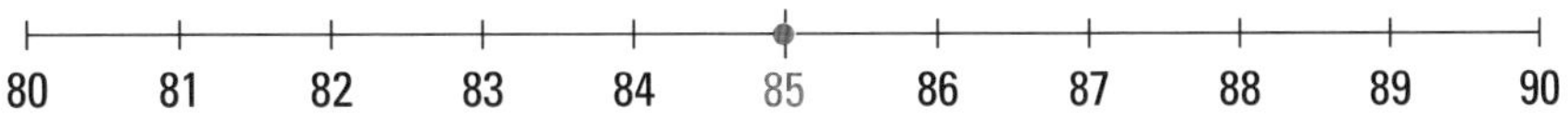

2 Round each number to the nearest 10.

a 13 **b** 27 **c** 35 **d** 66
e 51 **f** 112 **g** 239 **h** 215

3 Round each number to the nearest 100.

a 231 **b** 388 **c** 810 **d** 555
e 495 **f** 786 **g** 123 **h** 450

4 Chlöe is 130 cm tall and Amir is 160 cm tall.

a Give an estimate for Ben's height.
b Give an estimate for Laura's height.

5 Bags of charcoal are sold in three sizes:
2 kg bags, 5 kg bags and 10 kg bags.

a Give an estimate for the cost of a 5 kg bag.

Did you know?

Justin Gatlin lost the Men's 100 m World Record due to a rounding error.

problem

The height of each person has been rounded to the nearest 10 cm.

The actual heights of the six people are:

144 cm | 154 cm | 161 cm | 165 cm | 184 cm | 185 cm

Match each person with their actual height.

7b Mental methods of multiplication

- Multiply a whole number by 10 and 100
- Use mental methods to multiple two whole numbers

Keywords
Digit *Jotting*
Double *Multiply*
Half *Partition*

p. 16 There are many mental methods you can use when multiplying.

Quick multiplying by 10 and 100

To **multiply** 46 by 10, move the **digits** one place left.

H	T	U
	4	6
4	6	0

Answer: $46 \times 10 = 460$

To multiply 46 by 100, move the digits two places to the left.

Th	H	T	U
		4	6
4	6	0	0

Answer: $46 \times 100 = 4600$

Use zeros to fill gaps in the T and U columns

Partitioning

When you **partition** you split numbers into simpler numbers.

16×5

Split 16 into 1 ten and 6 units.

16×5 → $10 \times 5 = 50$
16×5 → $6 \times 5 = 30$

Answer: $50 + 30 = 80$

Doubling and halving

13×8

Double the first number and **halve** the second one. Repeat this.
Make **jottings** to help.

Answer: $13 \times 8 = 104$

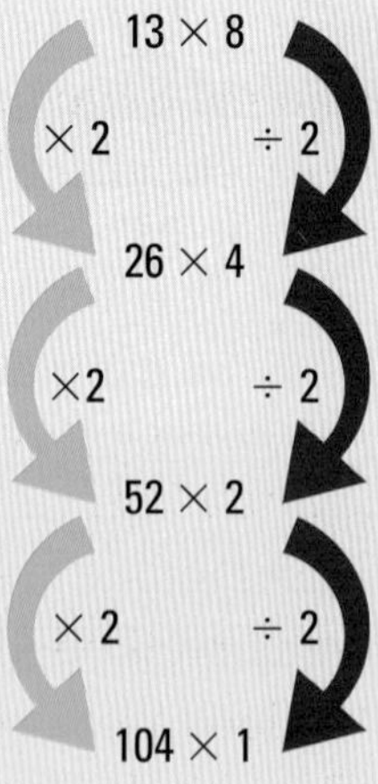

Repeated **addition**

5.6×3

Add three lots of 5.6.

$5.6 + 5.6 + 5.6 =$ **16.8**

$5.6 \times 3 = 16.8$

Exercise 7b

1 Fill in the missing numbers.

a 2 × □ = 8 **b** 5 × □ = 20 **c** 3 × 6 = □ **d** □ × 10 = 40

e 7 × 3 = □ **f** □ × 2 = 16 **g** 5 × □ = 35 **h** □ × 4 = 32

2 Put each number through the function machine to multiply it by 10.

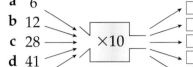

Input → ×10 → **Output**

a 6 → □
b 12 → □
c 28 → □
d 41 → □
e 80 → □

Input → ×10 → **Output**

f 65 → □
g 82 → □
h 123 → □
i 108 → □
j 222 → □

3 Multiply each number by 100.

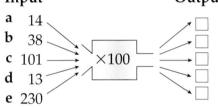

Input → ×100 → **Output**

a 14 → □
b 38 → □
c 101 → □
d 13 → □
e 230 → □

4 Complete these multiplication problems.
Make jottings to show your working out.

a 20 × 5 **b** 30 × 6 **c** 40 × 5 **d** 20 × 12 **e** 40 × 10

f 15 × 4 **g** 13 × 3 **h** 18 × 4 **i** 22 × 5 **j** 30 × 6

5 Freya is out at the shops and needs to do some quick multiplying.
She doesn't have a calculator and so must use her head.
Which method should she use for each calculation?
Use the method to find the answer.

a 'Onions are 10p each. I need 13 onions. How much does that cost?'

b 'Bread is £1.20 a loaf. I need 3 loaves. How much does that cost?'

c 'Carrots come in bunches of 6. I need 14 bunches for my rabbits. How many carrots is that?'

investigation

There are patterns in the 9 times table.
The digits in the answer always add up to 9.
The 10s column increases by 10 each time;
the 1s column decreases by 1 each time.

Continue the 9 times table and see what happens.

Part of the 9 times table
1 × 9 = **9** (9 = 9)
2 × 9 = **18** (1 + 8 = 9)
3 × 9 = **27** (2 + 7 = 9)
4 × 9 = **36** (3 + 6 = 9)
5 × 9 = **45** (4 + 5 = 9)

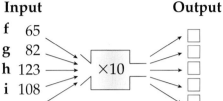

7c Written methods of multiplication

- Make an estimate of the answer before finding the exact answer
- Multiply two whole numbers together using the partitioning and grid methods

Keywords
Column
Diagonal
Digit
Multiple
Partition
Remainder
Row

- Make an estimate before you start a problem
  235 × 4 235 is close to 250
  So, 250 × 4 = 1000

The Partitioning Method

The problem is 235 × 4

235 is 'broken up' into hundreds, ten and units.

Multiply each part of the number by 4.

Add the parts together.

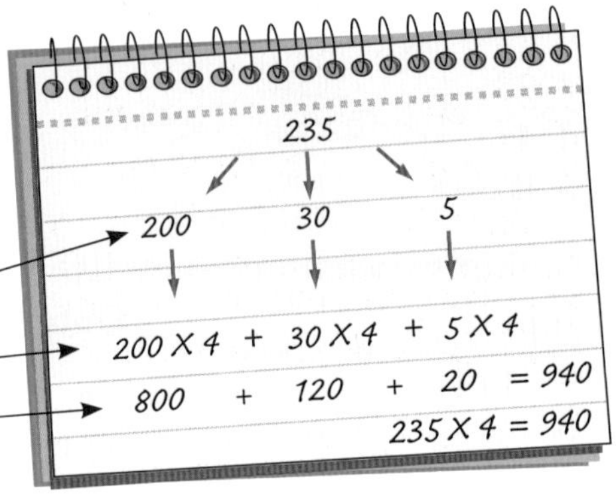

p. 236

The Grid Method

The problem is 426 × 6

The number to be multiplied is 'broken up' into hundreds, tens and units and arranged around the grid.

Multiply the hundreds, the tens and then the units.

Add the parts together to give the answer.

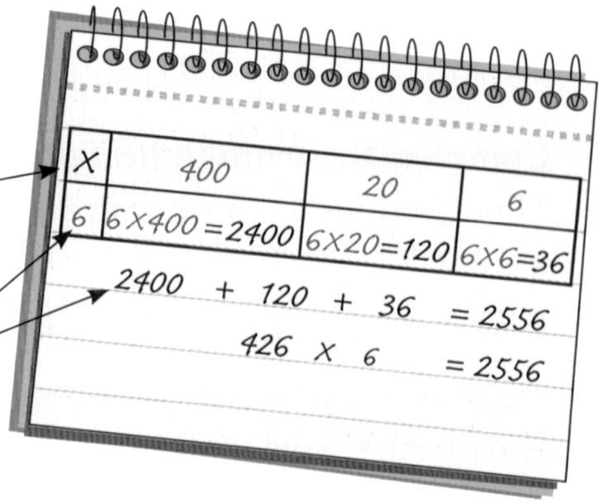

example

Work out an estimate for each problem.

a Use partitioning to solve 432 × 3. **b** Use the grid method to solve 181 × 6.

a An estimate is 400 × 3 = 1200

432 = 400 + 30 + 2

400 × 3 + 30 × 3 + 2 × 3

1200 + 90 + 6 = 1296

1296 is close to the estimate.

b An estimate is 200 × 5 = 1000

181 = 100 + 80 + 1

×	100	80	1
6	6 × 100 = 600	6 × 80 = 480	6 × 1 = 6

600 + 480 + 6 = 1086

1086 is close to the estimate.

Exercise 7c

1 Use the number line to help you answer these questions.

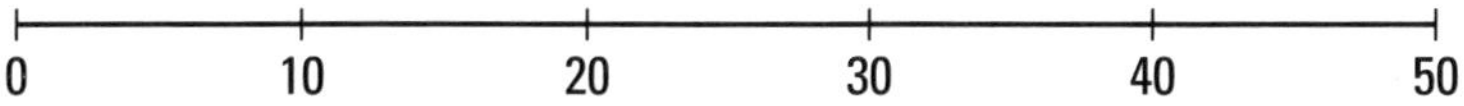

a Is 18 nearer to 10 or 20? **b** Is 22 nearer to 20 or 30?
c Is 3 nearer to 0 or 10? **d** Is 46 nearer to 40 or 50?
e Is 34 nearer to 30 or 40? **f** Is 29 nearer to 10 or 40?

2 Work out an **estimate** for each problem.
Use partitioning to answer each question and compare it with your estimate.

a 23×4 **b** 43×4 **c** 52×3 **d** 74×5
e 126×3 **f** 236×3 **g** 319×5 **h** 285×6

3 Use the grid method to complete these multiplications.
The first two problems have been started for you.

a 324×5

×	300	20	4
5	$5 \times 300 = 1500$	$5 \times 20 = 100$	$5 \times 4 = 20$

$1500 + 100 + 20 = \square$
$324 \times 5 = \square$

b 267×3

×	200	60	7
3	?	?	?

c 215×3 **d** 423×4 **e** 527×5
f 187×6 **g** 134×4 **h** 326×3

investigation

Doubling and **halving** is known as Russian multiplication.
The problem is 13×12.

Work down the page in two columns.

Halve the number in this column, ignoring remainders, until you get to '1'.

Cross-out any row that begins with an even number.

Add the remaining numbers in the right-hand row to get the answer.

Double the numbers in this column.

÷2	×2
13	12
~~6~~	~~24~~
3	48
1	96
	156

$13 \times 12 = 156$

Try these:

a 20×10
b 12×15

Mental and written methods of division

- Use multiplication tables to help with division
- Jump backwards on a number line to help with division

Keywords
Division
Multiplication

- You can use a number line to help you to divide.

$28 \div 4$

p. 238

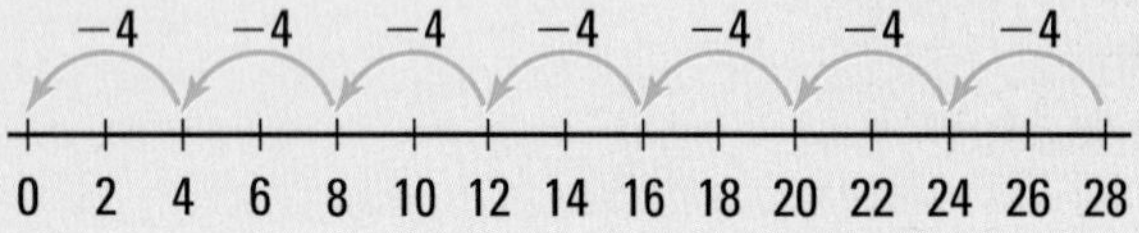

There are seven jumps, so $28 \div 4 = 7$.

example

Divide $48 \div 12$

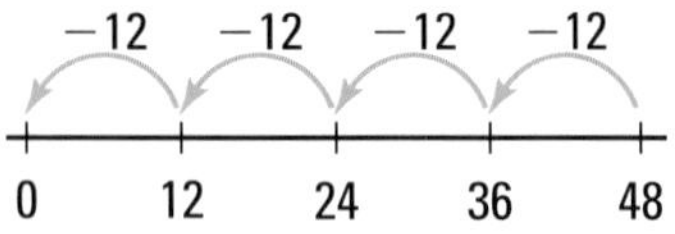

There are four jumps of 12 in 48 $\quad 48 \div 12 = 4$

Shah has seen a link between **multiplication** and **division**. He is looking at a part of the 4 times table.

He uses it to see how many times 4 divides into 28.

$4 \times 7 = 28 \quad$ so $28 \div 4 = 7$

Four divides into 28 seven times.

×	4
1	4
2	8
3	12
4	16
5	20
6	24
7	28

- When you divide by 10, you move the digits one place to the right.

p. 4

$20 \div 10$

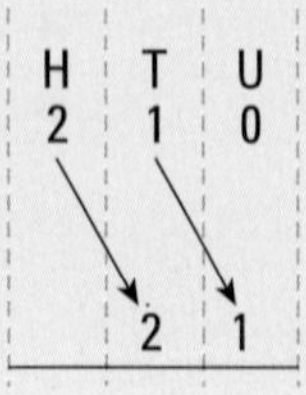

Notice that the digits move to the right.

Exercise 7d

1 Use the multiplication grid to help with these division problems.

a 28 ÷ 7
b 24 ÷ 8
c 45 ÷ 5
d 32 ÷ 8
e 72 ÷ 9
f 54 ÷ 6
g 42 ÷ 6
h 63 ÷ 7
i 81 ÷ 9

×	1	2	3	4	5	6	7	8	9	10
1	1	2	3	4	5	6	7	8	9	10
2	2	4	6	8	10	12	14	16	18	20
3	3	6	9	12	15	18	21	24	27	30
4	4	8	12	16	20	24	28	32	36	40
5	5	10	15	20	25	30	35	40	45	50
6	6	12	18	24	30	36	42	48	54	60
7	7	14	21	28	35	42	49	56	63	70
8	8	16	24	32	40	48	56	64	72	80
9	9	18	27	36	45	54	63	72	81	90
10	10	20	30	40	50	60	70	80	90	100

2 Complete these division problems.

a 80 ÷ 10 **b** 100 ÷ 10 **c** 120 ÷ 10 **d** 390 ÷ 10
e 25 ÷ 10 **f** 48 ÷ 10 **g** 165 ÷ 10 **h** 103 ÷ 10

3 Use number lines to sketch out these divisions.

a 12 ÷ 4 **b** 16 ÷ 8 **c** 28 ÷ 7 **d** 35 ÷ 5
e 27 ÷ 9 **f** 66 ÷ 11 **g** 39 ÷ 13 **h** 45 ÷ 15

4 Starting with 3, follow the numbers that 3 will divide into exactly. Which letter do you reach? Repeat this for 7, 6 and 5.

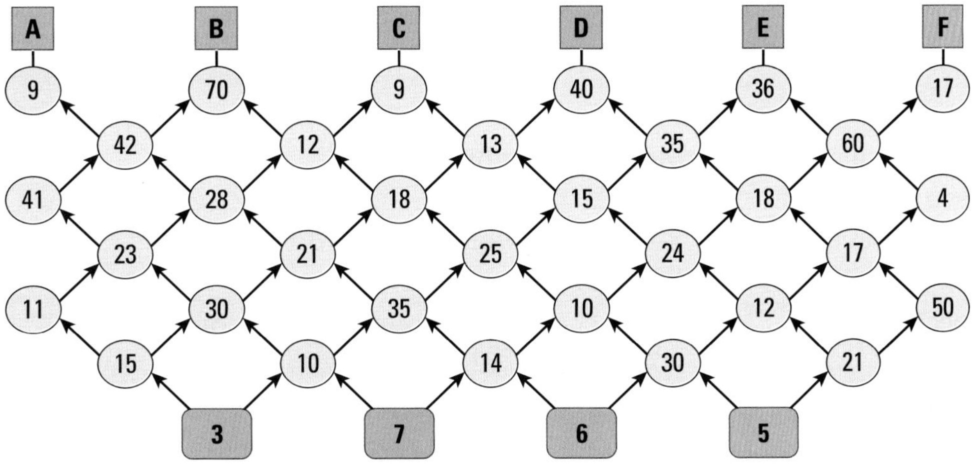

problem

Tanya has five boxes containing cups.
Each box contains a different number of cups.
She wants the same number of cups in each box.
How many should she have in each box?

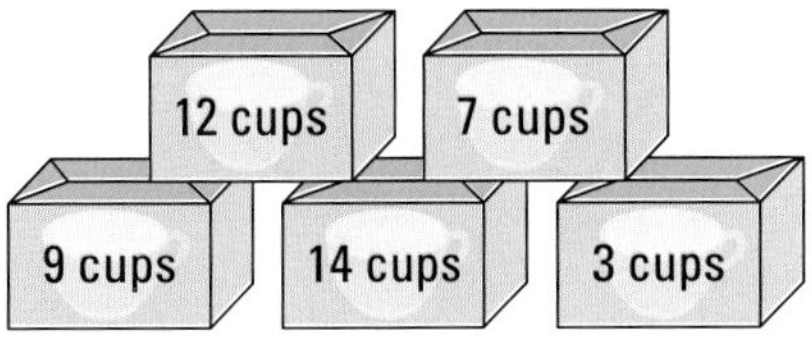

7e Division problems

- Divide by a whole number
- Sometimes have an answer with a remainder

Keywords
Divide *Remainder*
Equal *Share*

- You use division when you **share** something.
  Jack shares 12 tickets **equally** between his four friends.
  $12 \div 4 = 3$ They have three tickets each.

- You can also think of division as grouping.
  12 students get into groups of 4.
  $12 \div 4 = 3$ There are three groups altogether.

p. 234

- Whole numbers do not always **divide** exactly.

Betty shares 14 cakes onto three plates. She has two cakes left over.

As a division sum this would be: $14 \div 3 = 4 \text{ r } 2$

'r' stands for **remainder**.

- You can break larger division problems into smaller steps.

example

A necklace needs three beads.
Maggie has 72 beads.
How many necklaces can she make?

You need to work out $72 \div 3$
You know that $10 \times 3 = 30$
Subtract as many groups of 30 as you can:

$$72 \div 3 \qquad \begin{array}{r} 72 \\ \underline{-\ 30} = 10 \times 3 \\ 42 \\ \underline{-\ 30} = 10 \times 3 \\ 12 = \ \ 4 \times 3 \end{array}$$

So there are: $10 + 10 + 4 = 24$ groups of 3 in 72.
Maggie can make 24 necklaces from 72 beads.

Exercise 7e

1 Answer these division problems. Share equally.

17 apples

5 bags

a How many apples are placed in each bag?
b How many are left over?

32 sweets

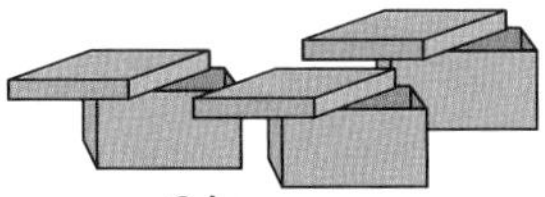

3 boxes

c How many sweets are placed in each box?
d How many are left over?

23 pound coins

4 friends

e How many coins does each person get?
f How many are left over?

2 Answer these division problems. Give a remainder.

a 8 ÷ 3 **b** 11 ÷ 5 **c** 10 ÷ 4 **d** 19 ÷ 4 **e** 28 ÷ 5
f 23 ÷ 3 **g** 36 ÷ 10 **h** 21 ÷ 6 **i** 32 ÷ 7 **j** 50 ÷ 9

3 Pete is making necklaces. He uses five beads on each necklace. How many necklaces can he make if he has

a 35 beads? **b** 85 beads? **c** 125 beads?

4 A carpenter needs to cut each rod into three equal lengths. When she has finished how long will the marked lengths be?

a
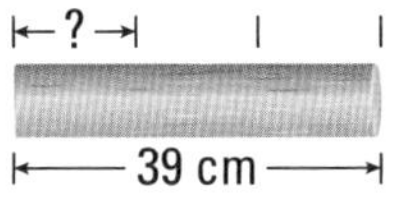

b
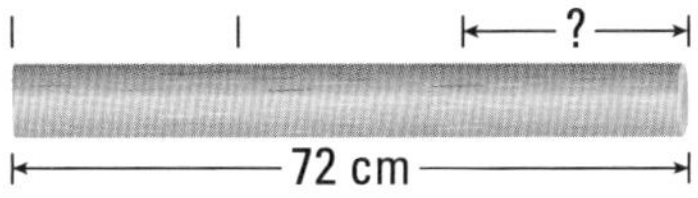

c
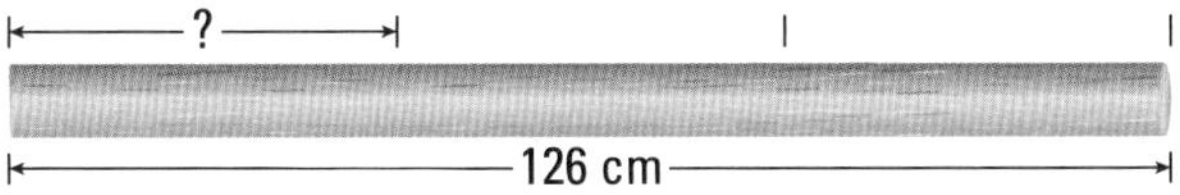

5 Eggs are packed in boxes of six.
How many boxes do you need to pack 138 eggs?

6 Divide these numbers. Jot down your working.

a 132 ÷ 3 **b** 124 ÷ 4 **c** 176 ÷ 4 **d** 130 ÷ 5
e 186 ÷ 6 **f** 132 ÷ 4 **g** 255 ÷ 5 **h** 288 ÷ 9

problem

The Sky Walker big dipper holds eight passengers.
Sixty-eight people are waiting to travel on the Sky Walker.
How many trips will the Sky Walker make so that everyone has a ride?

7f Calculator skills

- Read money as a decimal on a calculator
- Round decimal numbers to 1 and 2 decimal places

Keywords
Decimal place (dp)
Rounding

p. 14

Some calculator answers are not practical.
Shirts cost £8.70 in the sale.
Jamal wants to know how much 16 shirts will cost.
He uses his calculator.

16 ÷ 8.7 → [1] [6] [÷] [8] [.] [7] [=] → 1.83908046

There are too many digits here for an amount of money.
This answer needs to be **rounded** to 2 decimal places (dp).

Look at the third decimal place. 1.83(9)
9 rounds up 1.84
The answer rounded to 2 dp is 1.84 or £1.84

example

Use your calculator to find each answer. Give your answer to 2 dp.

a £7.30 ÷ 8 **b** £50.85 ÷ 12

a Type [7] [.] [3] [÷] [8] [=]
7.3 ÷ 8 = 0.91(2)5
To 2 dp = 0.91
£7.30 ÷ 8 = £0.91

You don't need to type the zero for pence.
Look at the third decimal place.
2 rounds down so the 1 doesn't change.

b Type [5] [0] [.] [8] [5] [÷] [1] [2]
50.85 ÷ 12 = 4.23(7)5
To 2 dp = 4.24
£50.85 ÷ 12 = £4.24

Look at the third decimal place.
7 rounds up and changes the 3 to 4.

- When writing your answer remember to put a zero into the single pence place, and the pound sign → £6·80

example

Add £4.20 and £1.20 on a calculator.

The calculator display will show: 5.4

There are no single pence in the answer.

You would write your answer as £5.40

Exercise 7f

1 Use the number line to round these numbers to the nearest 10.

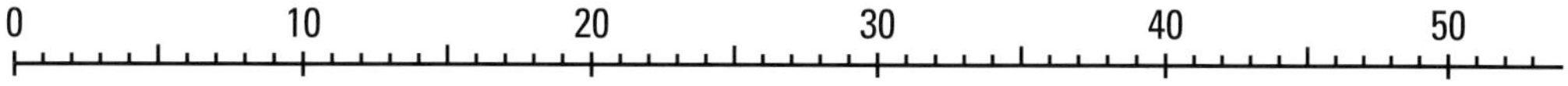

a 21 **b** 3 **c** 45
d 18 **e** 52 **f** 15

2 Use the number line to round these numbers to the nearest whole one.

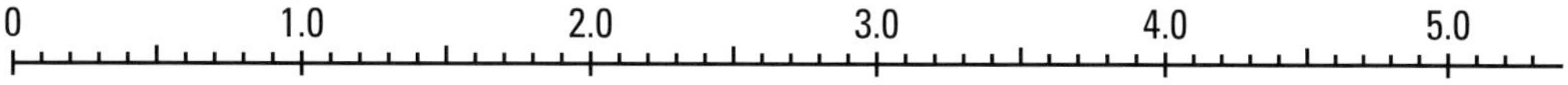

a 2.8 **b** 0.6 **c** 4.5
d 3.4 **e** 5.3 **f** 0.3

3 Round these calculator answers to 2 decimal places (2 dp).

a 0.143 **b** 0.639 **c** 6.129
d 2.032 **e** 1.375 **f** 4.2384

4 Use your calculator to answer these division problems.
Round your answer to 2 dp.
The first has been worked through for you.

a £3.27 ÷ 4 → 3 . 2 7 ÷ 4 = 0.8175
→ Rounded to 2 dp = £0.82

b £7.53 ÷ 9 **c** £3.79 ÷ 3 **d** £16.54 ÷ 8 **e** £0.79 ÷ 4

5 Use your calculator to answer these money problems.

a £2.26 + £3.54 **b** £8.47 − £2.07
c £2.20 × 4 **d** £6.80 ÷ 4
e £0.79 + £15.11 **f** £9.47 − £8.07
g £4.60 × 6.50 **h** £16 ÷ 2.5

Did you know?

Until 2006, one million Turkish Lira was worth about 40p, so almost everybody in Turkey was a millionaire!

problem

Use a calculator to answer these problems.

a Josh and his two friends earn £40, cleaning windows.
Can the money be shared out **exactly** between the three of them?

b Tara opens her money box and finds:
eleven 1p coins, six 2p coins, three 5p coins,
seven 10p coins, four 20p coins, nine 50p coins
and three £1 coins.
How much has she in total?

7g Metric units

- Choose a metric unit for length, mass and capacity

Keywords
Capacity *Mass*
Length

Units of **length** and distance

millimetres (mm) **centimetres** (cm) **metres** (m) **kilometres** (km)

1 mm × 10 = 1 cm 1 cm × 100 = 1 m 1 m × 1000 = 1 km

a grain of sugar

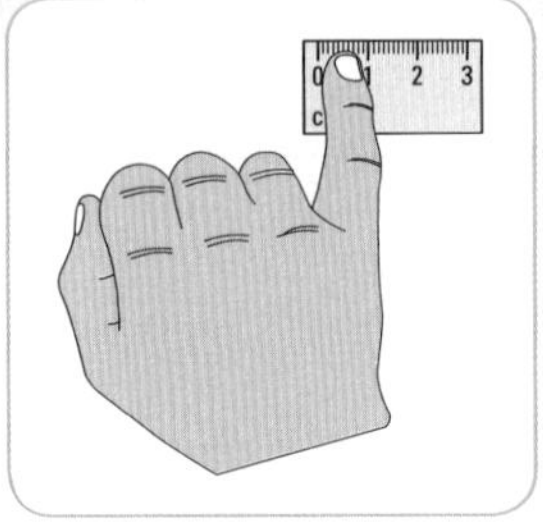

your little finger

height of a table

a 15 minute walk

Units of **mass**

gram (g) **kilogram** (kg) **tonne** (t)

1 g × 1000 = 1 kg 1 kg × 1000 = 1 t

a postage stamp

a bag of sugar

a shire horse

Units of **capacity**

millilitre (ml) **litre** (ℓ)

1 ml × 1000 = 1 litre

Capacity is the amount of liquid a container will hold.

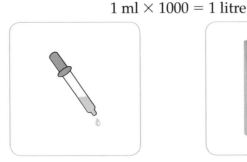

an eyedropper

a carton of fruit juice

example

A bag of flour weighs 1 kg.
200 g of flour is removed from the bag.
How many grams are left?

1 kg is equivalent to 1000 g
1000 g − 200 g = 800 g
There are 800 g of flour left in the bag.

Exercise 7g

1 Match each measurement with its short form.

kilogram	millimetre	gram
millilitre	metre	centimetre
litre	tonne	kilometre

ℓ	km	t	kg	cm	g	mm	ml	m

Did you know?

The A380-800 Air bus weighs 275 tonnes, holds 310 000 litres of fuel and has 530 km of electric cables.

2 Complete each sentence by choosing the correct unit from the list above.

a A bag of crisps weighs 50 __.

b The world's tallest man was over 2.7 __ tall.

c A mug holds 250 __ of tea.

d The moon is 384 403 __ from Earth.

e Mount Everest is 8848 __ high.

f Dad filled his car with 40 __ of petrol.

g James weighs 62 __.

h The distance around my head is 56 __.

3 Paul has a one litre bottle of Cola.
How many 100 ml glasses can he fill from the bottle?

4 The Speedee Delivery van is making deliveries.
The map shows the journey of the van.

a How far does the van travel on its journey?

b The van uses one litre of fuel each 11 km.
How many litres does the van use on this journey?

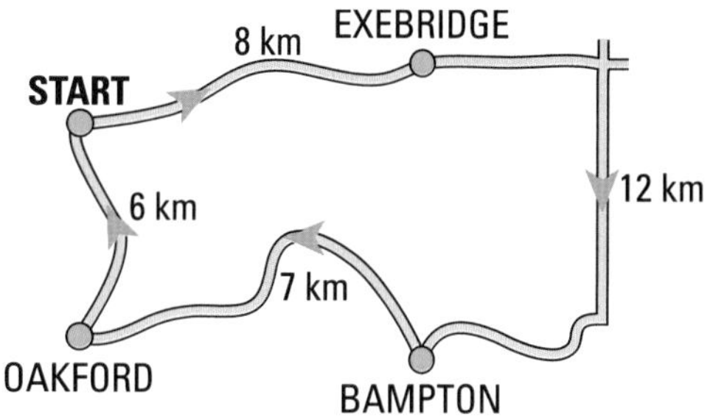

challenge

How much will each item on this shopping list cost?

7h Measuring and accuracy

- Make an estimate by comparing two objects
- Make an estimate of a measurement

Keywords
Accurate
Estimate
Instrument

- Most situations require an **accurate** answer.

In the Olympic 100 m sprint final you would expect very accurate times.

Yuliya Nesterenko from Belarus won the 2004 Olympic gold medal for the Women's 100 m in 10.93 seconds.

- You use **instruments** for accurate measurement.

Clocks, measuring tapes, scales, thermometers and electronic recording devices are instruments which measure.

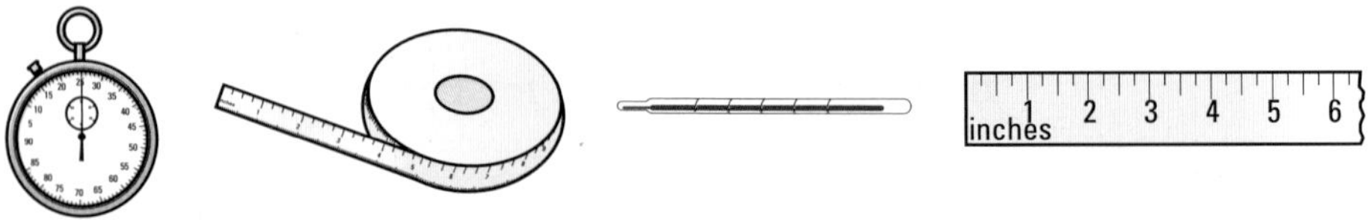

- Sometimes you **estimate** when the true answer is not known.

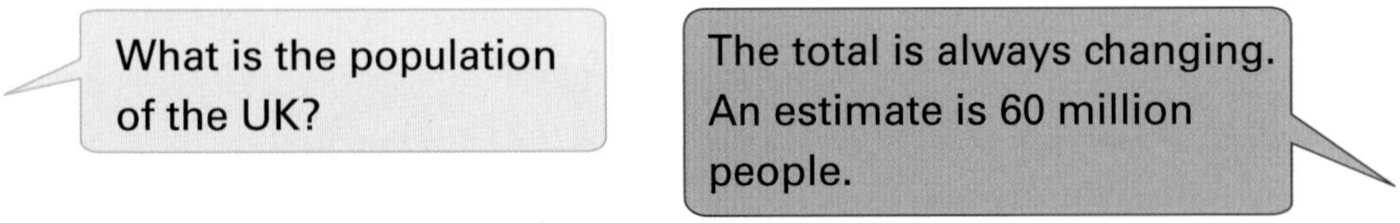
What is the population of the UK?
The total is always changing. An estimate is 60 million people.

example

Estimate

a the height of your teacher
b the weight of your pencil case
c the distance from home to school.

---

a An estimate could be 1.75 m
b An estimate could be 1 kg
c An estimate could be 2 km

These estimates will differ for every student.

Exercise 7h

1 Use the picture below to help you estimate.

a Who is the tallest?
b Who is the oldest?
c Who weighs the least?
d Who is the shortest?
e Who is the youngest?
f Who do you think broke the window, and how?

2 Which of these involve estimates? Which need to be accurate?

a

How many peas in the jar? 20p a guess.

b

What percentage did I get in my Maths test, Sir?

c

d

It must be 3m tall.

e

f

How many people are here today, Dad?

g

h

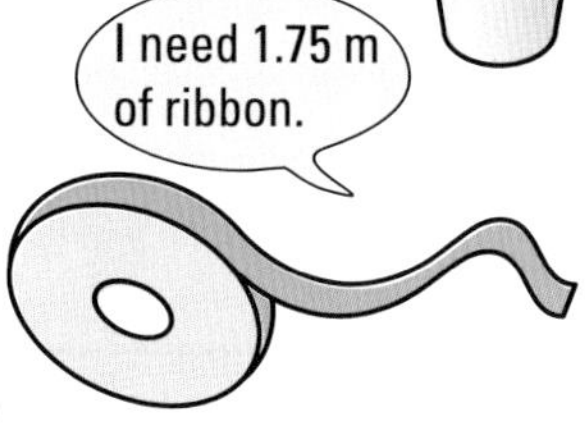
I need 1.75 m of ribbon.

challenge

A car's petrol tank holds 30 litres.
The car travels 1800 km on each tank of petrol.
How many kilometres can the car travel with one litre of petrol?

7 Consolidation

7a

1 Round each number to the nearest ten.

a 54 b 149 c 65 d 612 e 98 f 185 g 102

2 Round each number to the nearest whole number.

a 4.7 b 8.1 c 5.4 d 11.8 e 19.5 f 25.4

7b

3 Multiply each number by 100.

a 31 b 346 c 84

4 Use partitioning to solve these multiplications.
The first is done for you.

a $32 \times 6 = (30 \times 6) + (2 \times 6)$

$180 + 12 = 192$

$32 \times 6 = 192$

b 24×5 c 43×4 d 26×6

5 Use the method of doubling and halving to multiply each of these by 4.

a 33 b 75 c 24

6 Complete these multiplications using repeated addition.

a 2.5×4 b 7.2×3 c 14.2×4

7c

7 Use the grid method to solve these. The first is done for you.

a $215 \times 5 =$

×	200	10	5
5	5 × 200 = **1000**	5 × 10 = **50**	5 × 5 = **25**

$= 1000 + 50 + 25 = 1075$

$215 \times 5 = 1075$

b 136×3 c 243×5 d 167×3

7d

8 Divide each of these numbers by 10.

a 50 b 307 c 370 d 54 e 120 f 1005

9 Do these division problems in your head.

a $6 \div 3$ b $27 \div 9$ c $48 \div 8$ d $18 \div 2$ e $16 \div 4$

7e

10 For each of these give the answer and the remainder if there is one.

a 99 ÷ 3 **b** 68 ÷ 5 **c** 170 ÷ 5 **d** 161 ÷ 3 **e** 101 ÷ 10

f 204 ÷ 6 **g** 111 ÷ 9 **h** 31 ÷ 2 **i** 92 ÷ 4 **j** 161 ÷ 7

11 A small ferry boat can only carry 9 passengers. If 52 people are waiting how many "full" journeys will the boat have to make and how many passengers will be carried on the last journey?

7f

12 Use a calculator to answer these. Write the full calculator display.

a 5.24 + 0.22 **b** 6.09 + 3.41 **c** 1.04 × 3

d 25.24 ÷ 4 **e** 1.60 × 5 **f** 25.57 ÷ 5

13 Use a calculator to answer these money problems.
Remember to use the £ sign and give your answers to 2 decimal places.

a £4.46 + £6.14 **b** £1.50 + £6.60

c £3.51 + £2.09 **d** £4.18 + £5.82

7g

14 Sarah has 5 kg of fruit salad.
How many 500 g portions can she serve?

15 Farmer Jones has 4000 kg of seeds.
How many tonnes of seeds does he have?

7h

16 Complete these statements about yourself. Estimate your answer.
I live about __________ from my school. By the time I leave school I will have made this journey __________ times! It takes me about __________ to get here each morning. There are around __________ students in the whole school, and __________ in my Year Group.

7 Summary

Key indicators

- Start to read scales on measuring equipment **Level 3**
- Make estimates based on metric units **Level 3**
- Multiply and divide whole numbers by 10 or 100 **Level 4**

Level 3

1 **a** Choose the best estimate for the width of a car.

A 2 centimetres **B** 2 metres

C 2 millimetres **D** 2 kilometres

b Choose the best estimate for the weight of a calculator.

A 100 milligrams **B** 100 grams

C 100 kilograms **D** 100 tonnes

Erin's answer ✔

Erin decides that 2 metres is about the same as 2 paces.

a 2 metres
b 100 grams

100 mg isn't even 1 gram.
100 kg is 100 bags of sugar.
100 t is 100 small cars.

Level 3

2 **a** Look at this scale.

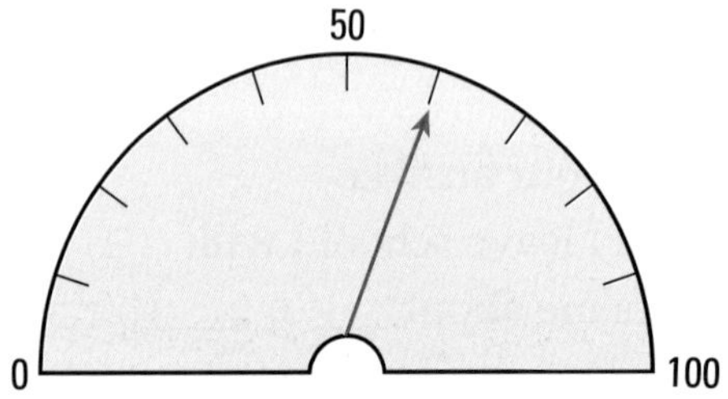

What value does the arrow point to on the scale?

b Here is a different scale.

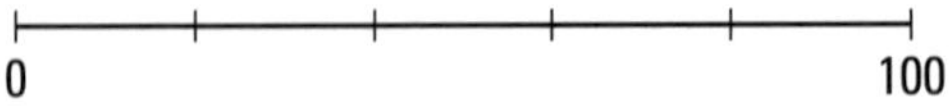

Draw an arrow (↓) so that it shows the same value as the arrow in part **a**.

Key Stage 3 2003 3–5 Paper 1

8 Data

Data and probability

An insurance policy protects you from losing everything in a disaster. If you are insured and do have a disaster, the insurance company will pay for repairs. Insurance companies use probability to work out how much of a risk there is for fire, flood and theft.

What's the point? If you live next to a river which floods every year, there is a high probability that it will flood again. You will have to pay more for your insurance policy.

Check in

Level 3

1 A pictogram uses the symbol  to represent 10 cars.

a Which of these represents 20 cars?

i  **ii**  **iii** 

b Which of these represents 5 cars?

i  **ii**  **iii** 

Level 4

2 This pie chart shows the amount of time Clare spent on her homework on Thursday.

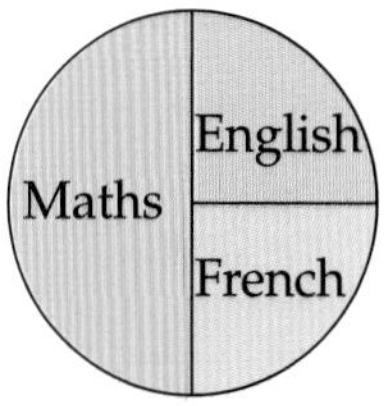

a What fraction of her time did Clare spend on English?

b Clare spent 40 minutes on all of her homework on Thursday. How long did she spend on mathematics?

3 Write the decimal number that each arrow is pointing to.

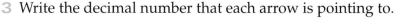

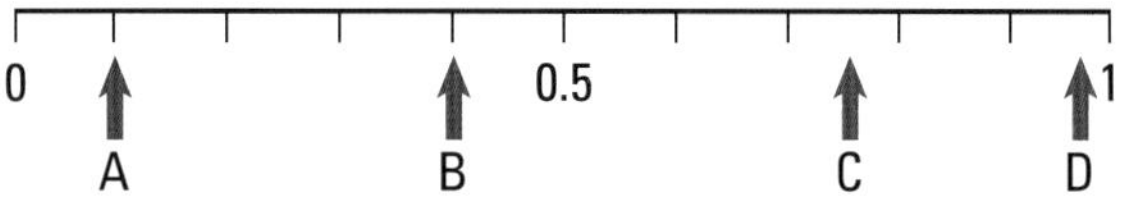

8a Interpreting diagrams

- Read various charts and graphs to extract information

Keywords
Bar chart *Pictograms*
Line graph *Pie chart*

p. 84

- You need to recognise, read and make sense of a range of statistical diagrams.
  - **Bar charts** and **pictograms** compare totals.
  - **Line graphs** show how things change over time.
  - **Pie charts** show how big the parts of a total are.

- When you are reading any statistical diagram:
  - Understand what the diagram shows and how it works.
  - Read the axes and scales carefully.
  - Interpret the data correctly.

example

The head of Year 7 at Dunmore High School produced these charts.

a In which week were the most credits awarded?

b Which class has the most students?

p. 78

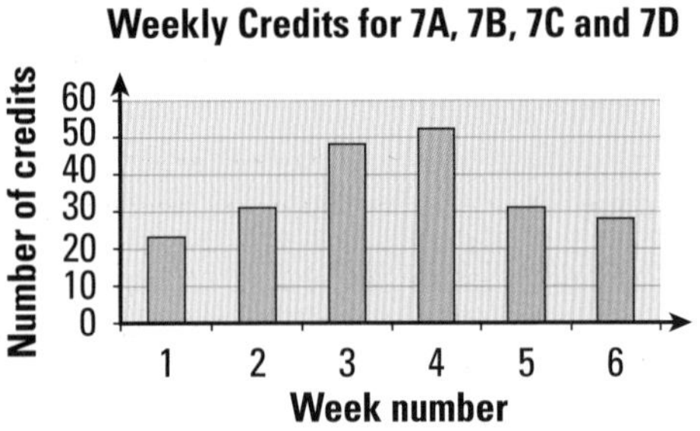

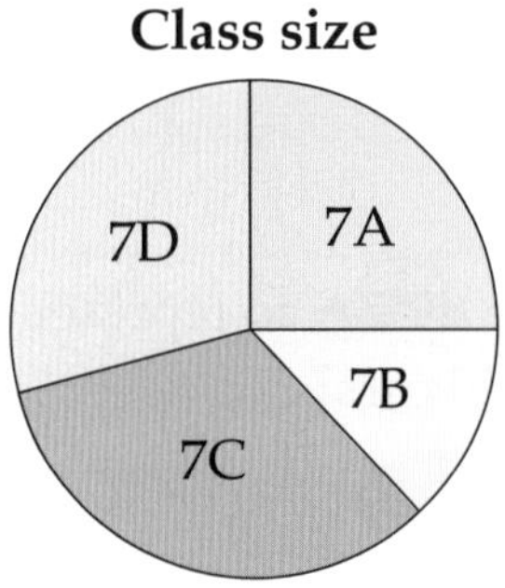

a The bar chart shows the weekly totals.
The highest total was 52, in week 4.

b The slice of pie for Class 7C is the biggest, so Class 7C has the most students.

Exercise 8a

1 From the list, choose what kind of diagram could show you this information.
You can choose more than one answer.

Pictogram | Bar chart | Line graph | Pie chart

a a car's speed during a journey
b the most popular ice cream flavour
c the number of pets each student has, using symbols
d a quarter of students like fish and chips

p. 76

2 This pictogram shows the number of people attending an after-school club.
a Which day was the busiest?
b How many people attended the club in total?
c The club has to close one day a week because of staff shortages. Which day should it close? Explain your answer.

Key: (symbol) = 10 People

3 The bar chart shows students' pets.

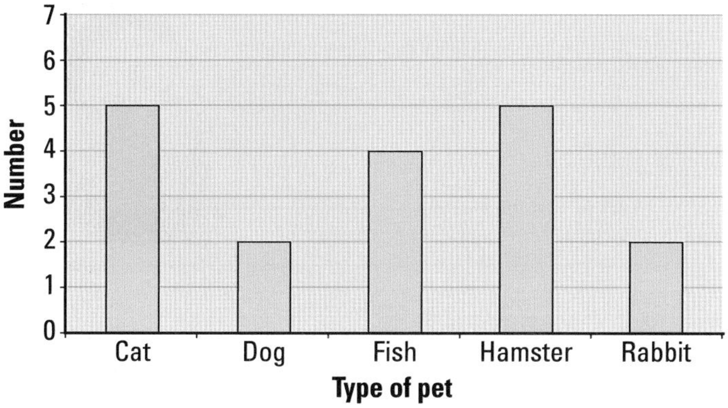

a How many dogs did the students own?
b Which was the most popular kind of pet?
c How many pets did the students own in total?
d Explain why you **cannot** use this chart to find out the total number of students in the class.

discussion

The deputy headteacher at Passmore School wants to draw a diagram to show the number of absences at the school each term for the last year.
What sort of diagram should she use? Explain your answer.

Interpreting data

- Make sense of the information taken from graphs and charts

Keywords
Certain
Interpreting

- **Interpreting** a diagram means making sense of the data shown in the diagram and explaining what it tells you.

example

This line graph shows the temperature of the water in a kettle.

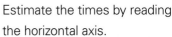

a How many times was the kettle switched on?

b When was the kettle switched on?

c How many times did the water boil?

p. 80

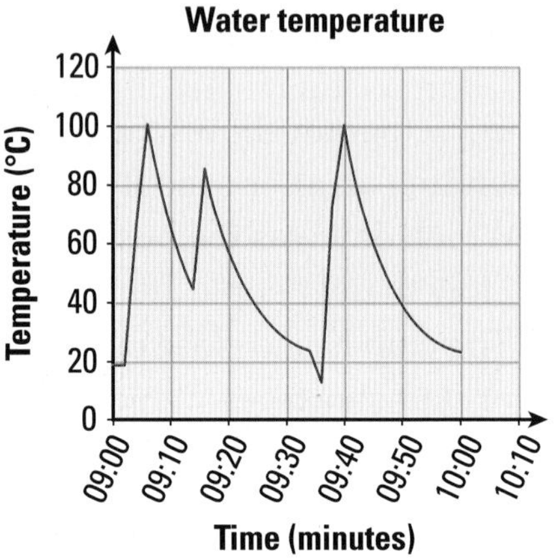

a The kettle was switched on three times.

The temperature rises three times.

b The kettle was switched on at about 09:02, 09:14 and 09:36.

Estimate the times by reading the horizontal axis.

c The water boiled twice; the second time it was switched on, it was switched off again before it boiled.

Water boils at 100 °C.

- Sometimes you cannot be **certain** how to interpret a diagram. You might want to suggest a possible explanation.

example

In the diagram above, the temperature dips before the kettle is switched on the third time.
Suggest a possible reason for this.

One possible reason is that the kettle was filled with cold water from the tap before it was switched on.

We cannot be sure about this, but it is a reasonable suggestion.

Exercise 8b

1 This bar chart shows the number of students who picked the different options available for a school activities day.

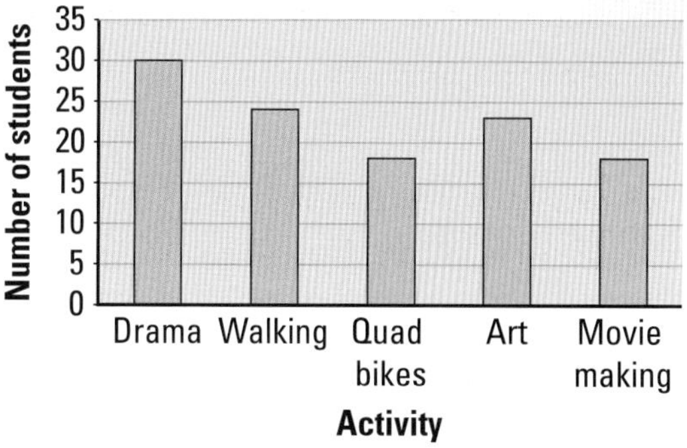

a Which was the most popular option?

b How many students will need to travel away from the school for quad biking and walking?

c There are only 25 places available for Drama. How many of the people who chose drama will need to pick another activity?

2 This line graph shows a kite's height above ground level.

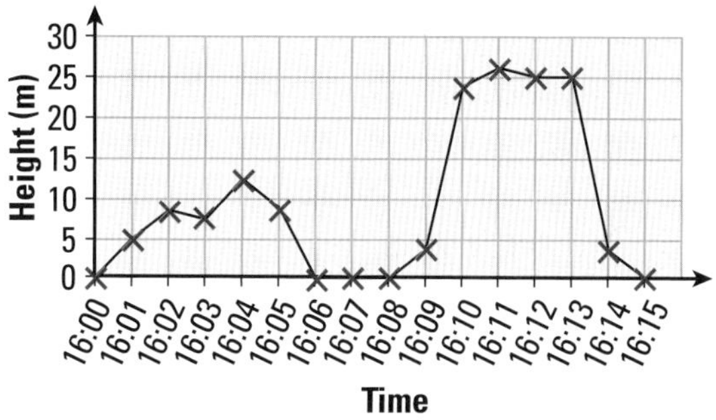

a At what time did the kite first take off?

b What was the kite's greatest height?

c How many times was the kite flown during the time shown?

d Which flight was the best? Explain your answer.

p. 82

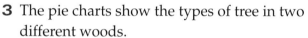

3 The pie charts show the types of tree in two different woods.

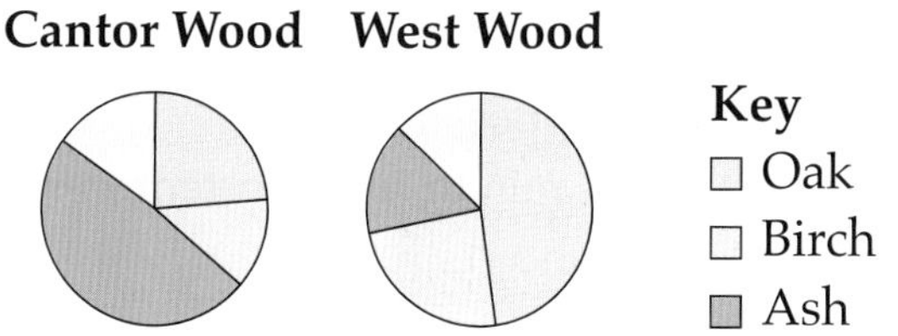

a What was the most common type of tree in each wood?

b Richard says, 'The charts show that there are more oak trees in Cantor Wood than there are in West Wood'. Explain why Richard is wrong.

c George says, 'The charts show that Cantor Wood has more oak trees than birch trees'. Explain why George is right.

discussion

Computer spreadsheets make it easy to produce very fancy '3-D' charts. What are the advantages and disadvantages of this kind of chart?

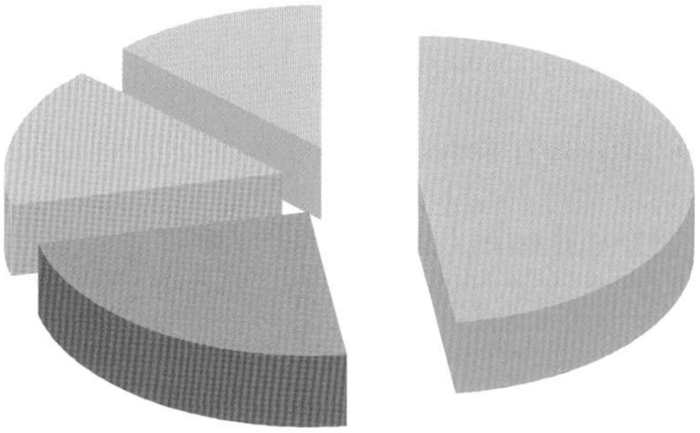

Introducing probability

- Decide if events are certain, impossible or uncertain

Keywords
Certain *Probability*
Impossible *Uncertain*
Likely

Some events are...

certain

This will definitely happen.

impossible

This will definitely not happen.

uncertain

This may or may not happen.

example

Give an example of an event that is
a certain **b** impossible **c** uncertain.

a The day after Tuesday will be Wednesday.
This is certain.
b You cannot teach a hamster to play chess.
This is impossible.
c It might rain in Manchester tomorrow.
This is uncertain.

You will be able to think of other examples.

- **Probability** is about how **likely** events in the future are.

example

Match each event with the probability that it will happen.

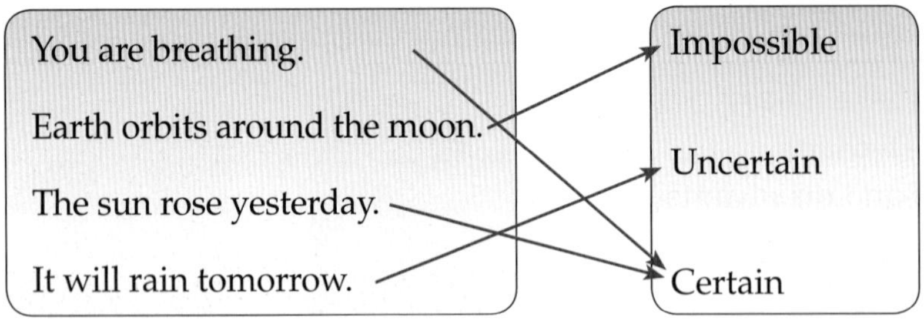

Exercise 8c

1 Are these events **certain, impossible** or **uncertain**?
Can you give a reason why?

a It will snow in London next Christmas Day.
b The sun will rise tomorrow.
c You can teach a worm to play the violin.
d If you flap your arms, you will fly.
e You will sleep tonight.
f A flipped coin will land on Heads.
g You will roll a 7 with a dice.

2 Karen places tokens labelled 1 to 100 in a bag and picks one out without looking.
Give an example of an event which is

a certain
b impossible
c uncertain.

3 Think about the events which happen to you.
Give an example of something which is

a certain
b uncertain
c impossible.
b Are some events more certain than others?

investigation

Insurance companies work with probability. The greater the chance of disaster means the greater the amount you pay for insurance.
Describe the probability of disaster in these situations using words.

a

b

c

8d More probability

- Use words to describe how likely an event might be

Keywords
Probability

- You can describe the **probability** of an event using words.

  It is certain the Sun will set tonight.

  It is very unlikely you will win the lottery.

example

Describe the probability of each event.

a It will snow in July.
b You fill flip a coin and get Heads.
c You are in maths class.

a This is almost impossible, but might happen!
b There is an evens chance this would happen.
c This is almost certainly the case!

- You can show a scale of probabilities like this:

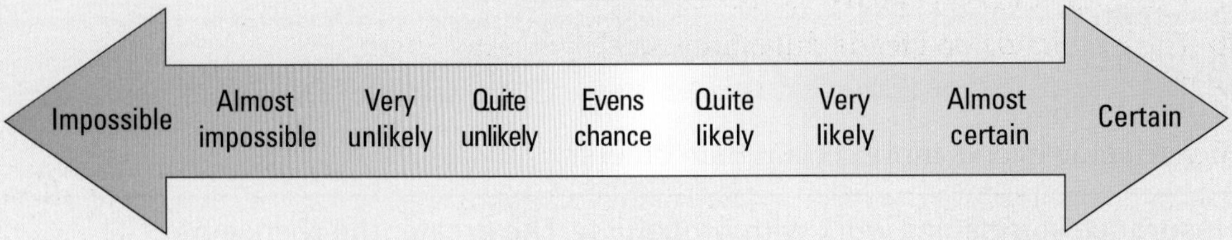

example

How likely are these events?

a If you spin a coin it will land on Heads.
b If you roll an ordinary dice, you will get a score of 7.
c It will rain in London within the next month.

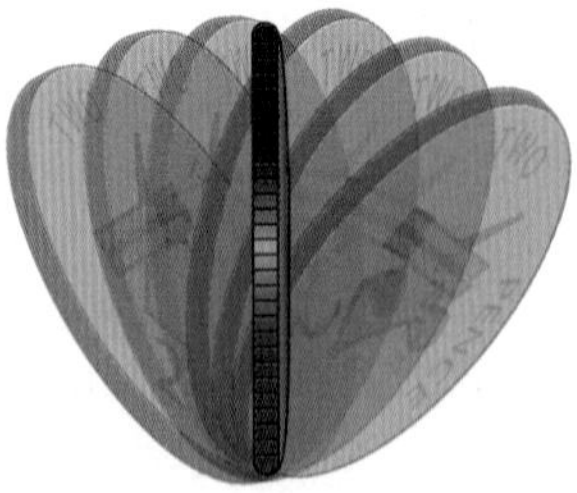

a There is an evens chance that a fair coin will land on heads.
b There is no 7 on an ordinary dice, so this event is impossible.
c London hardly ever has a rainless month, so this is very likely or almost certain.

Exercise 8d

1 Match each event with the probability that it will happen.

a You will watch TV tonight.	Impossible
b It will be dark tonight.	Very unlikely
c It will rain tomorrow.	Evens chance
d You will be a millionaire.	Very likely
e A sheep will win the Derby.	Certain

2 Sam rolls an ordinary six-sided dice.
Explain how likely he is to get a score that is

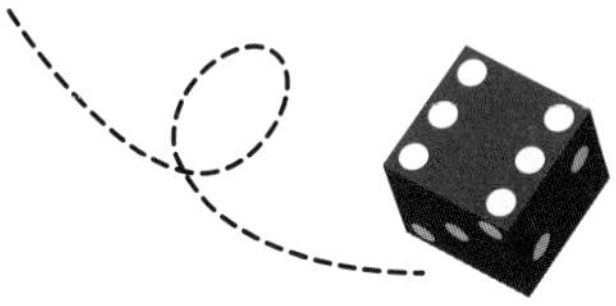

a less than 4
b an odd number
c a multiple of 3
d exactly 5

3 Dave spins an ordinary coin six times.
Explain in words how likely these results are.
a The coin lands on Heads six times.
b The coin lands on Heads three times and Tails three times.
c The coin lands on Tails eight times.

4 Carla places raffle tickets numbered 1 to 100 in a bag, and picks one out without looking. Give an example of an outcome that is

a certain
b impossible
c very likely (but not certain)
d very unlikely (but not impossible)

investigation

Put this list of events in order of probability, with the **most likely** events at the top of the list and the **least likely** ones at the bottom. Justify your answers.
a You will go swimming during the next week.
b You will use a computer in the next 24 hours.
c You will use a telephone within the next week.
d You will fly in a plane within the next week.
e You will have an English lesson tomorrow.

8e The probability scale

- Use a number scale from 0 to 1 to describe probabilities

Keywords
Certain
Evens chance
Impossibility
Probability
Probability scale

Because descriptions in words can be unclear, it is better to describe probabilities using numbers.

- The **probability scale** is used to give **probabilities** numerical values.

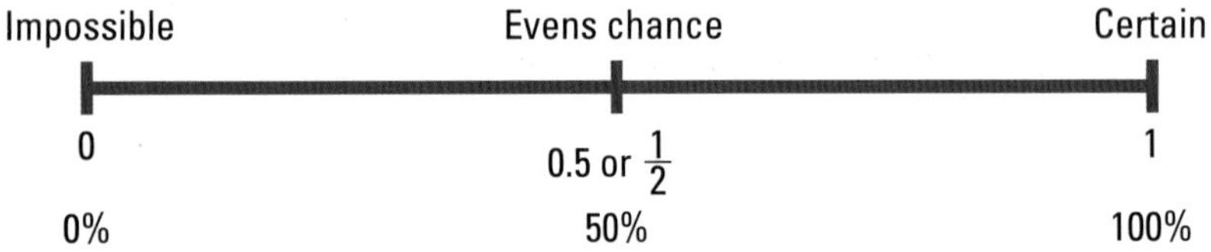

Probabilities can be given as fractions, decimals or percentages.

- Probabilities have a value between 0 and 1.
  An event that is
  – **certain** has a probability of 1 (100%)
  – **impossible** has a probability of 0 (0%)
  – **evens chance** has a probability of $\frac{1}{2}$ (0.5 or 50%).

example

What is the probability of each event?

a You can balance a pencil upright on its point.

b You get an odd score when you roll an ordinary dice.

c The sun will rise tomorrow.

a This is impossible. The probability is 0 (0%).

b This event has an evens chance.
The probability is $\frac{1}{2}$ (0.5 or 50%).

c This event is certain. The probability is 1 (100%).

'Almost certain' means a probability very close to 1, maybe $\frac{9}{10}$ (0.95 or 95%) or more.

'Quite unlikely' means a probability less than 0.5, maybe $\frac{3}{10}$ (0.3 or 30%) or $\frac{2}{10}$ (0.2 or 20%).

It's easier to use decimals or percentages for these probabilities.

Exercise 8e

1 Match up the purple probability cards with the correct yellow description cards.

0.1	0	0.5	0.99
Impossible	Almost certain	Unlikely	An evens chance

2 Match up the purple probability cards with the correct yellow description cards.

99% | 65% | 1% | 100%

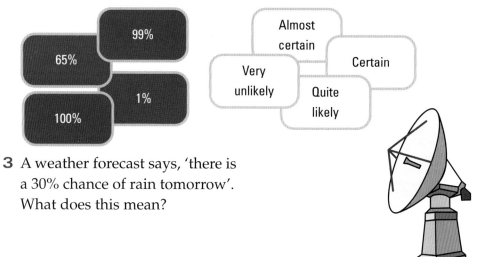

Almost certain | Certain | Very unlikely | Quite likely

3 A weather forecast says, 'there is a 30% chance of rain tomorrow'. What does this mean?

4 A game at a school fair has a poster saying, 'Every entry wins a prize'. What is the probability of winning the game? Explain your answer.

5 Suggest a probability (as a decimal) for each of these descriptions.

a An evens chance **b** Very likely

c Almost certain **d** Very nearly (but not quite) certain

e Certain

discussion

a Explain why it is easier to compare probabilities (using numbers) than probabilities (using words).

b Explain why it is easier to compare probabilities using percentages rather than fractions.

8a

1 The bar chart shows the number of boys and girls in five year groups.

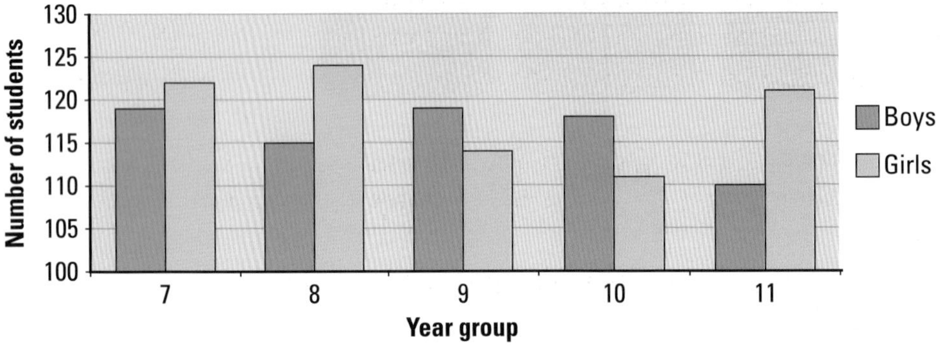

a List the year groups that had more boys than girls.

b Estimate the total number of girls in the five year groups.

c Estimate the total number of students in all five year groups.

d Explain which year group had the largest total number of students.

8b

2 This line graph shows the number of people sitting in a theatre.

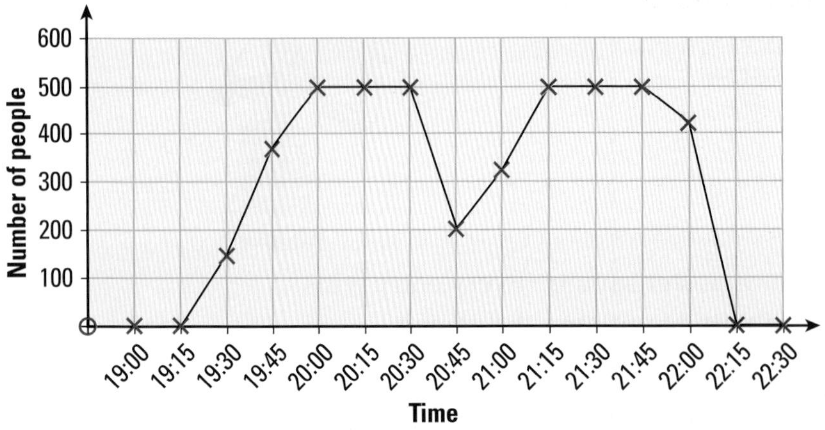

Estimate

a the time that the theatre opened

b the time the show started

c the length of the interval

d the number of people who left their seats during the interval.

8c

3 Use one of the words in the box to classify each of these events.

Certain
Impossible
Uncertain

a If you keep running for long enough you will tire out.
b If we go out any night after dark we will see a full moon.
c If I go out on a very cold morning I will see ice in a puddle.
d If I arrive at a level crossing and the barriers are down because a train has just passed through, and the barriers do not go up, then another train must be coming.
e If we look at the sun at 12 midday in the winter or 1 p.m. in the summer, we are looking due south.
f The year 2012 will be a leap year.
g Josiah says that where he lives in the west of Cornwall it gets dark at a later time than it does in London.

8d

4 Look at the events in question **3**.
Could you give a better probability if you used one of these words?
Give the events new probabilities from this list.

Almost impossible
Quite unlikely
Even chance
Very likely
Almost certain

8e

5 The dominoes shown here are shuffled and placed upside down on a table.

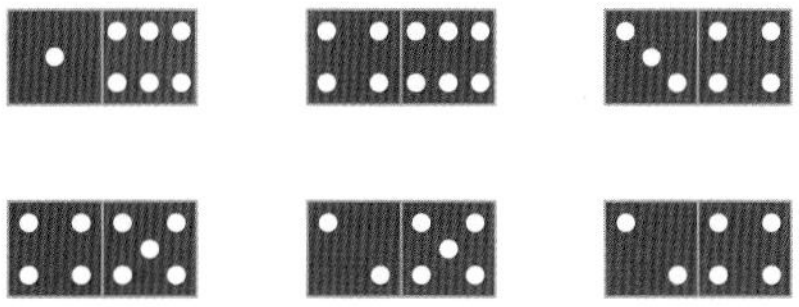

If one is then picked up, find the probability that it will have
a 7 dots
b an odd number of dots
c an even number of dots.

Choosing the right route

Valley Mountain Rescue held two fundraisers, a Cake Stall and a sponsored hike. Compare the events to see which raised the most money for the charity.

Cakes £1

Tea 50p

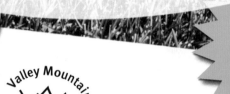

Valley Mountain Rescue

Cake Stall!

Saturday

15 April

1.30pm - 4.30pm

The Valley Community Centre

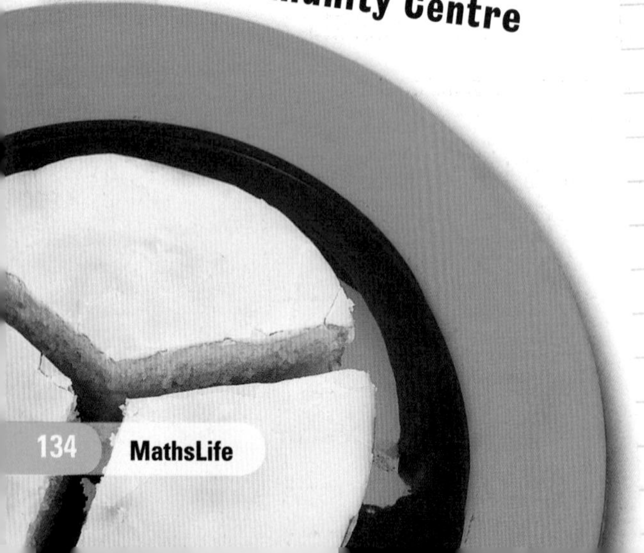

Cake Stall

Costs

Cake ingredients	£25
Tea bags	£5
Milk for tea	£5
Cups for tea	£5
Carrier bags	£4.50
Room rent	£25
Posters	£20
Total spent	£

Sales

133 Cakes sold	£
80 Teas sold	£
Extra donations	£22.50
Total earned	£
Total to charity	£

Use

Total earned
- Total spent

Total to charity

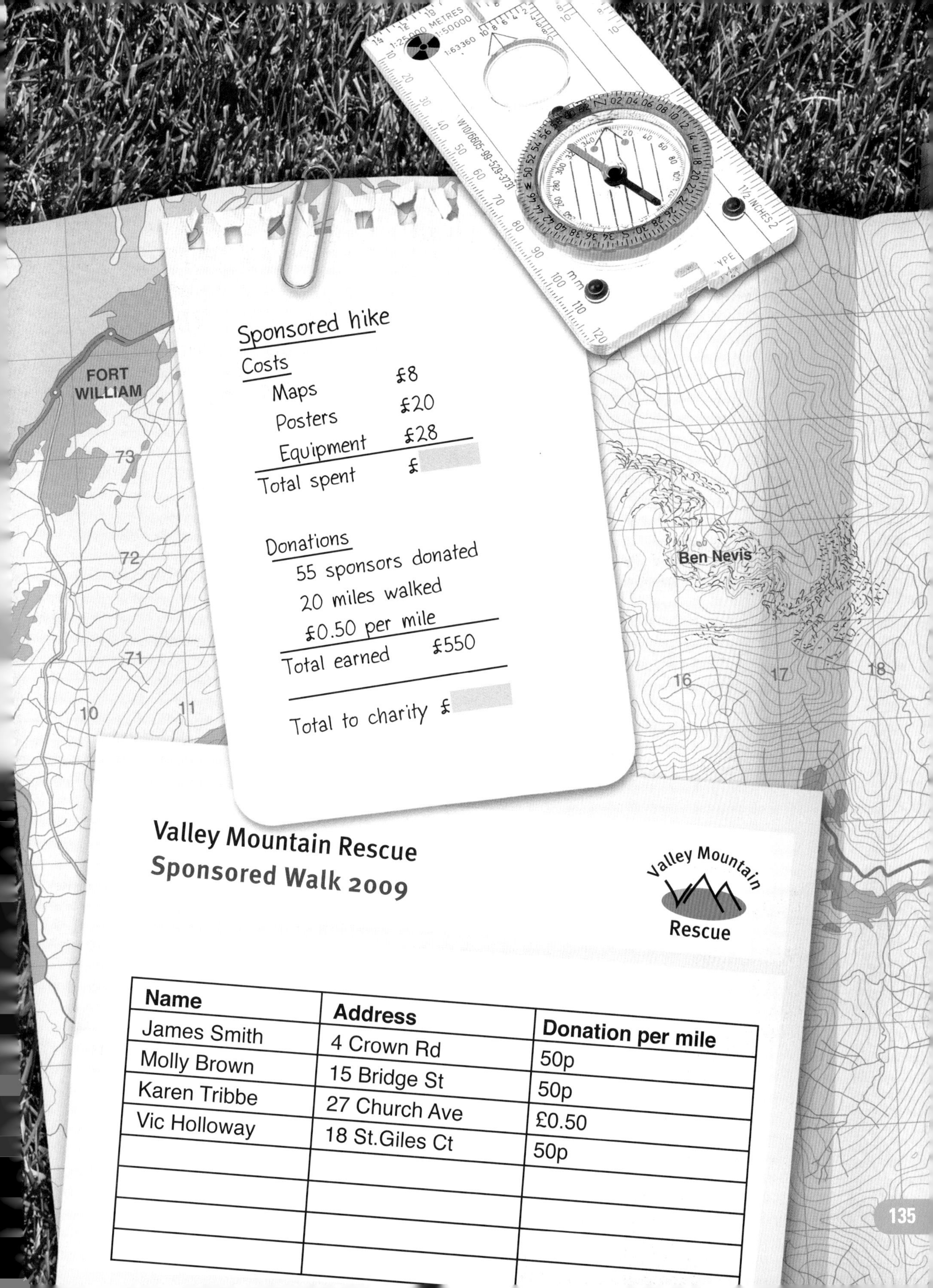

Sponsored hike

Costs

Maps	£8
Posters	£20
Equipment	£28
Total spent	£

Donations

55 sponsors donated
20 miles walked
£0.50 per mile

Total earned £550

Total to charity £

Valley Mountain Rescue
Sponsored Walk 2009

Valley Mountain Rescue

Name	Address	Donation per mile
James Smith	4 Crown Rd	50p
Molly Brown	15 Bridge St	50p
Karen Tribbe	27 Church Ave	£0.50
Vic Holloway	18 St.Giles Ct	50p

8 Summary

Key indicators

- Read diagrams like bar charts and line graphs **Level 3**
- Understand words associated with probability **Level 4**

Level 3

1 The number of students in John's class who had a packed lunch one week are shown in the bar chart.

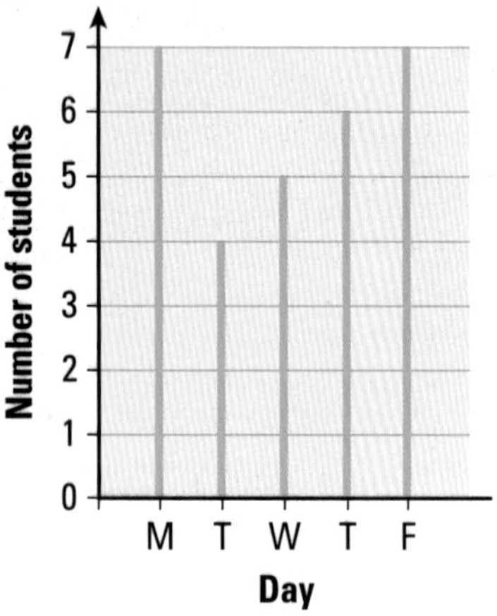

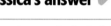

a How many students had a packed lunch on Wednesday?
b How many packed lunches were eaten during the whole week?

Jessica's answer ✔

Jessica reads the height of the bar for Wednesday.

a 5 students
b 7 + 4 + 5 + 6 + 7 = 29 packed lunches

Jessica adds the packed lunches for each day.

Level 4

2 The diagram shows a fair spinner divided into 8 equal sections. I am going to spin the pointer.

Write numbers on the blank sections so that there is a 50% chance that I will spin an odd number.

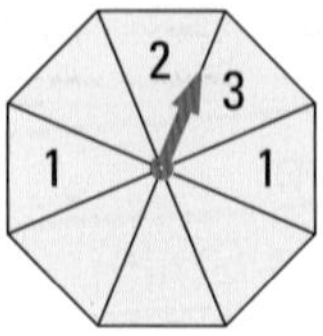

Year 7 3–4 2007 Paper 2

9 Shape

Angles

Ships use lighthouses to navigate around rocks or into harbours. The captain will measure the angle between the lighthouse and the ship and use maps, compasses and protractors to plot a clear route.

What's the point? Without tools to measure angles, the ship's captain would have to estimate and might just hit the rocks!

Check in

Level 3

1 Work out these without using a calculator.

a 180 − 60 = ☐ **b** 180 − 150 = ☐ **c** 180 − 35 = ☐ **d** 180 − 90 = ☐

e 360 − 200 = ☐ **f** 360 − 130 = ☐ **g** 360 − 185 = ☐ **h** 360 − 180 = ☐

2 Match each object with its shape below.

a Baked Bean tin **b** Dice **c** Box of washing powder **d** Football

A

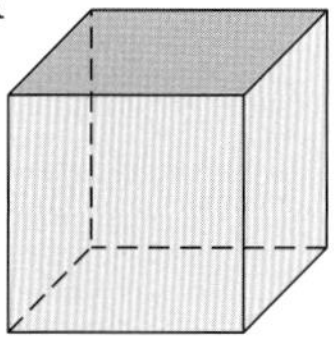

B

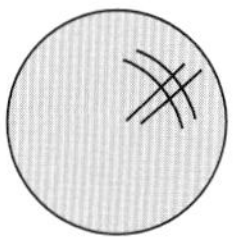

C

D

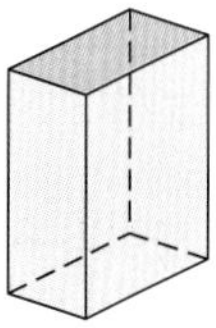

Level 4

3 Choose the best estimate for each angle.

a 25° or 80° **b** 80° or 120° **c** 70° or 90° **d** 100° or 160°

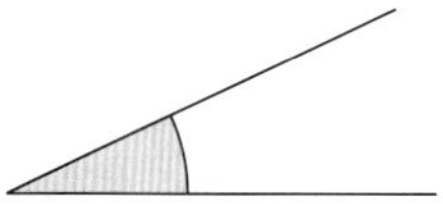

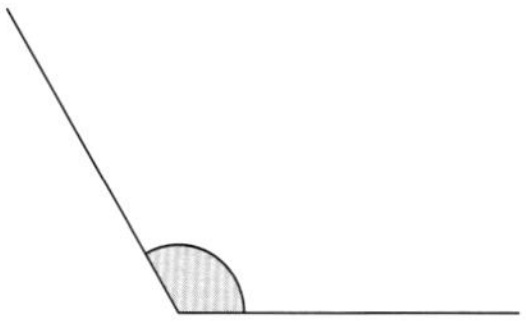

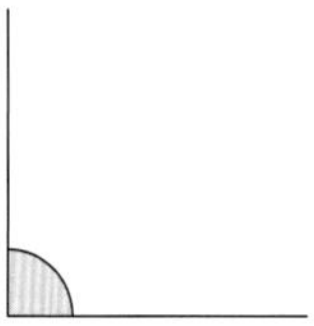

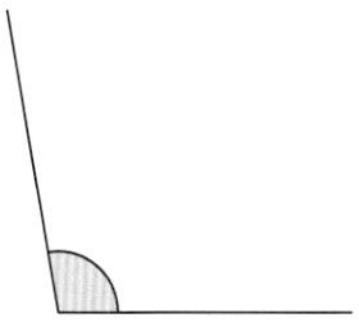

9a More angles

- Calculate angles on a straight line

Keywords
Acute *Obtuse*
Half *Straight*

Rory is on a swing.
As he swings higher, the angle of turn becomes greater.

p. 50

An **acute** angle. Less than 90°.

An **obtuse** angle. Greater than 90°, but less than 180°.

A **straight** line Exactly 180°, or **half** a turn.

. . . oops!

Rory notices that he swings 90° down and 90° back up to make a total swing of 180°.
He combines two angles to make a straight line.

p. 266

- You can combine angles by adding them.

example

Combine these angles by adding them. What is each new angle called?

a

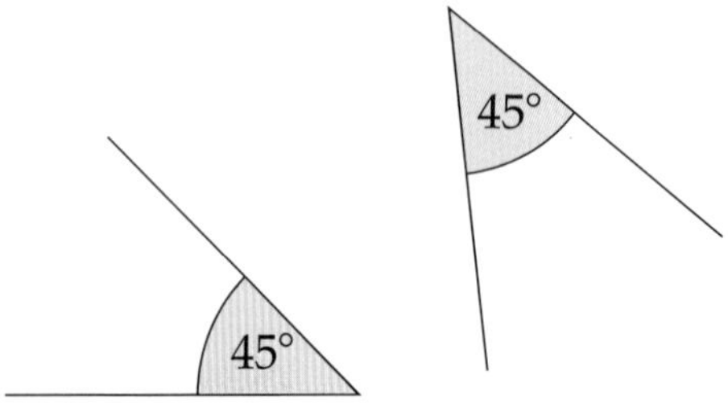

b

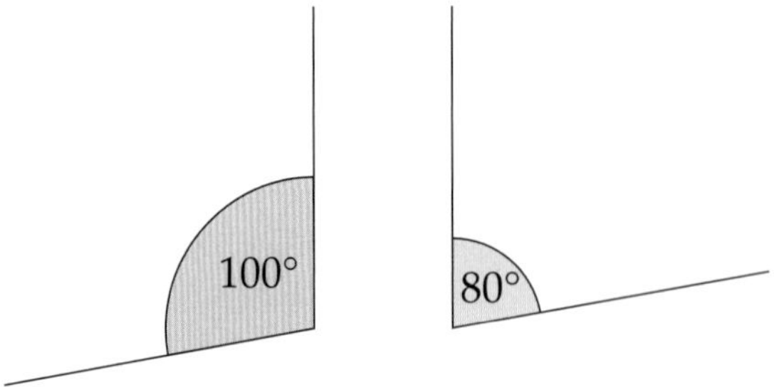

a 45° + 45° = 90°

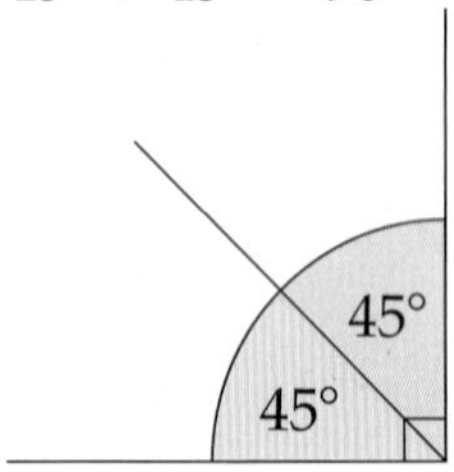

A 90° angle is a right angle.

b 100° + 80° = 180°

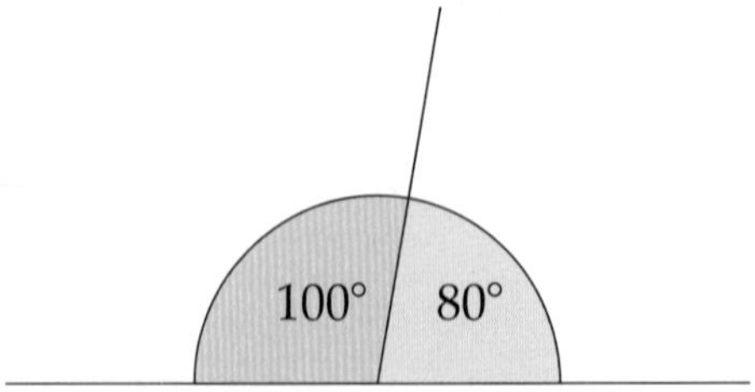

An 180° angle is a straight line.

Exercise 9a

1 Write if each angle is acute or obtuse.

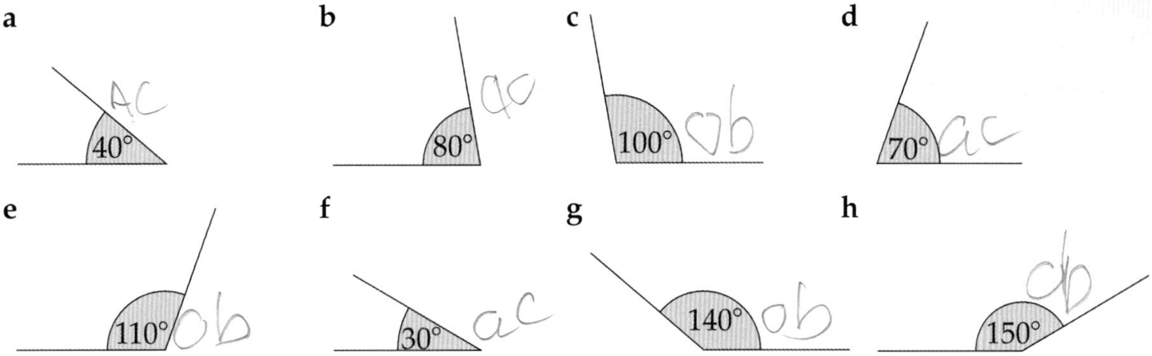

2 Find pairs of angles from question **1** that fit together to make a straight line.

There are 4 pairs.

3 How many more degrees does the pink line have to turn through to reach 90°? The first one is done for you.

a

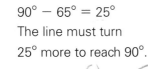

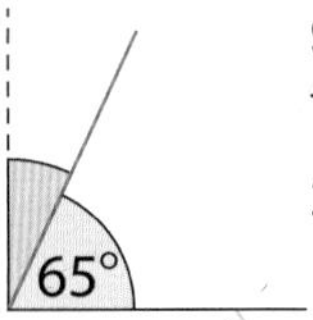

$90° - 65° = 25°$
The line must turn
25° more to reach 90°.

b

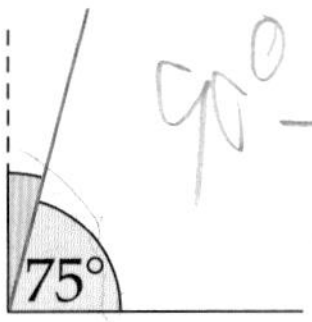

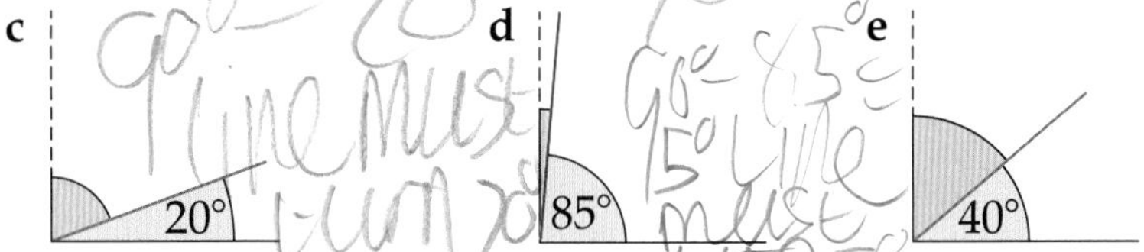

4 How many **degrees** does the pink line have to turn through to reach 180°?

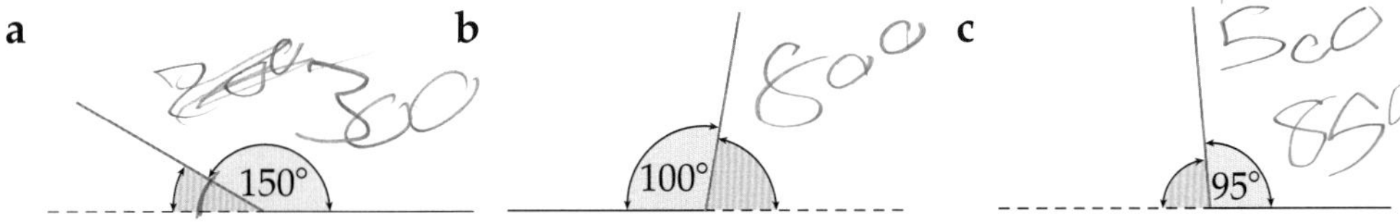

problem

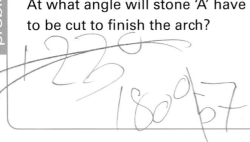

Ryan is building a stone arch.
At what angle will stone 'A' have to be cut to finish the arch?

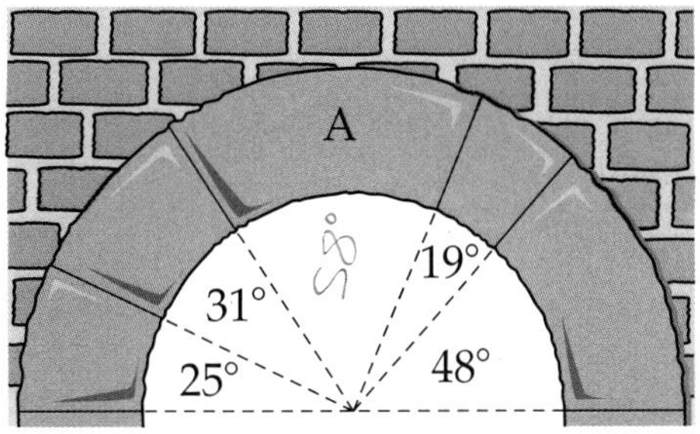

Angle measure

- Use a protractor to measure angles up to 180°

Keywords
Anticlockwise *Protractor*
Clockwise *Vertex*
Degree

- A **protractor** is a tool used to measure **angles**.
  It is numbered in 10s, and each small division is 1 **degree**.

- You read one scale **anticlockwise** and the other scale **clockwise**.

Line up the **vertex** of the angle with the cross line on the protractor.
This angle is 125°.

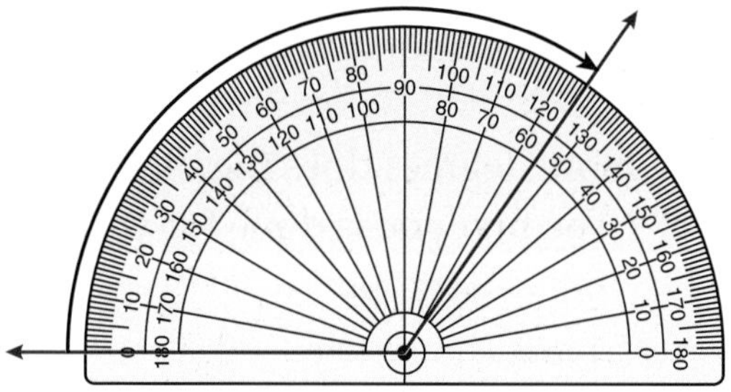

Read round the scale clockwise from zero.
The angle is 60°.

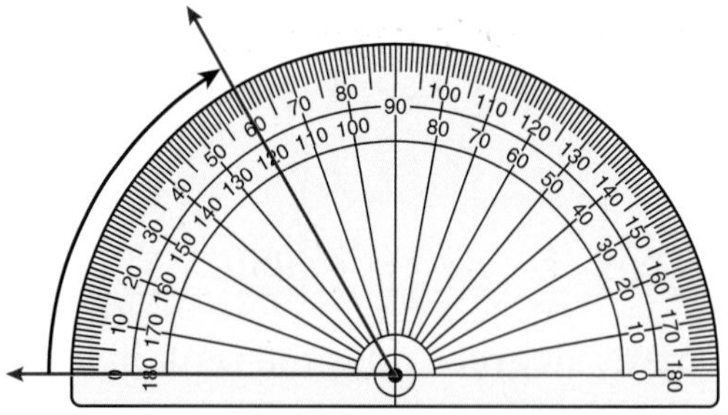

example

What angle is shown here?

Read round the scale anticlockwise from zero.
The angle is between 50° and 60°.
Count on from 50° to 55°.
The angle is 55°.

p. 270

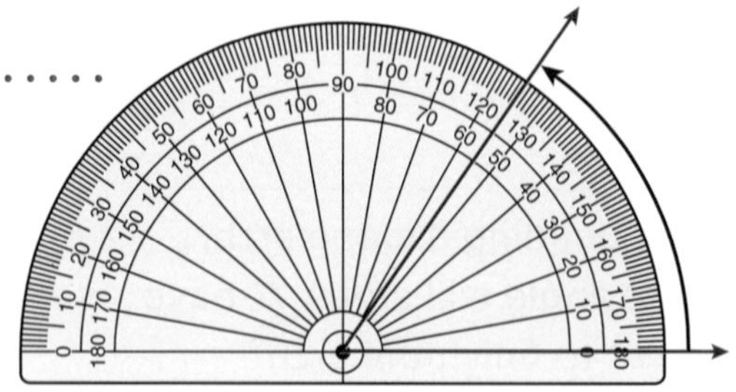

Exercise 9b

1 What is the size of each angle?
Give your answer in degrees (°).

a

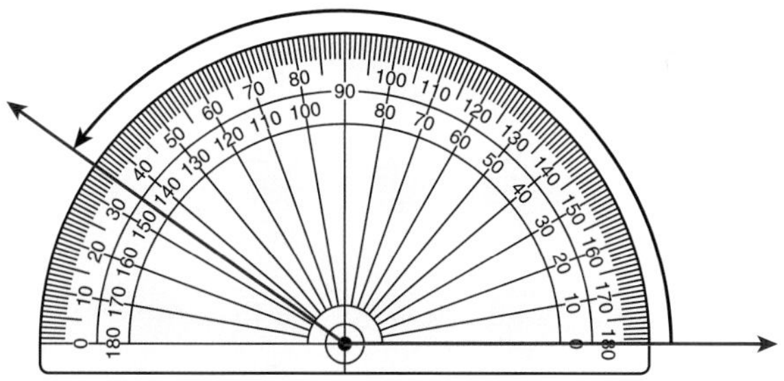

b

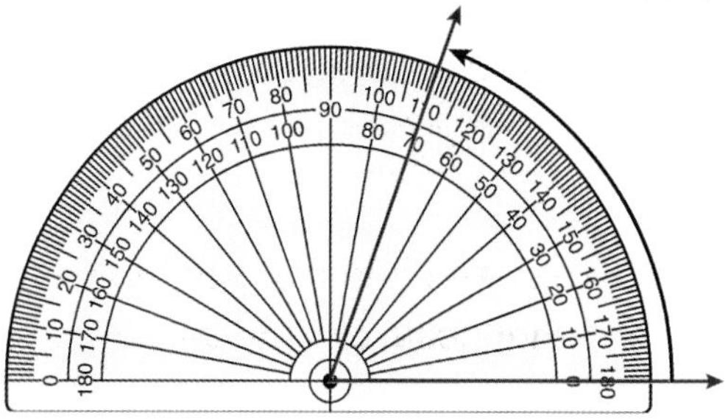

c

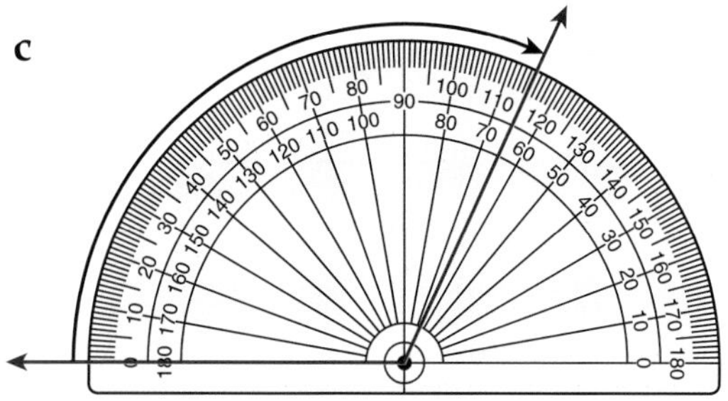

d

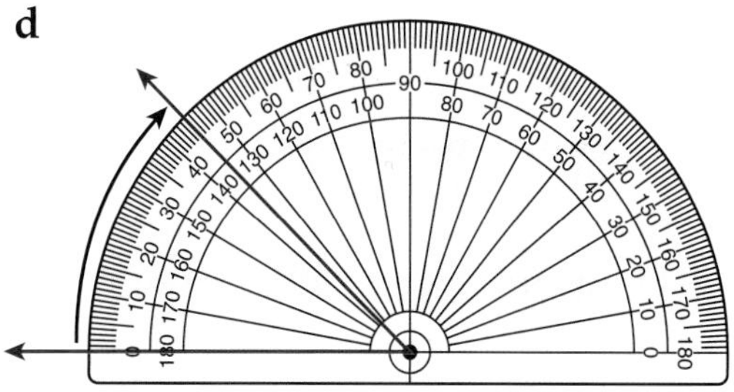

2 Measure these angles with a protractor.
Give your answer in degrees (°).

a

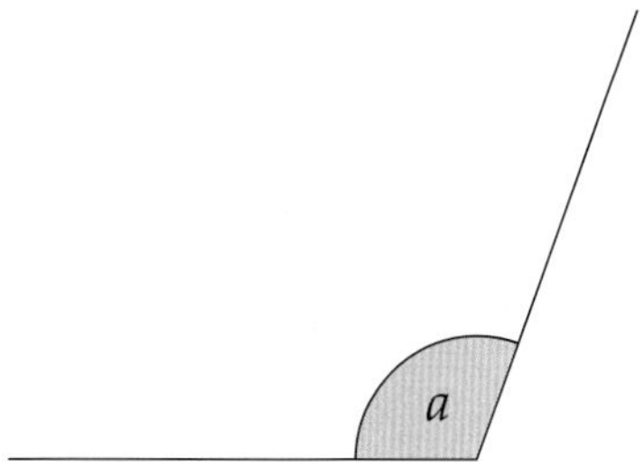

b

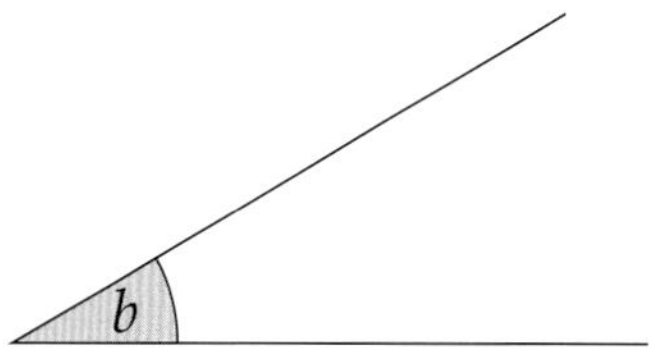

c

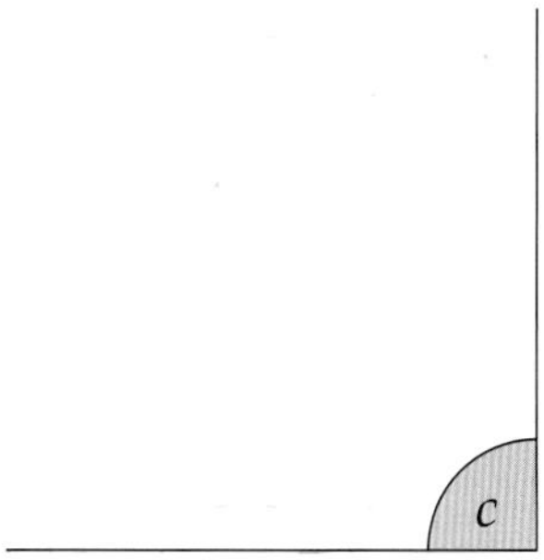

d

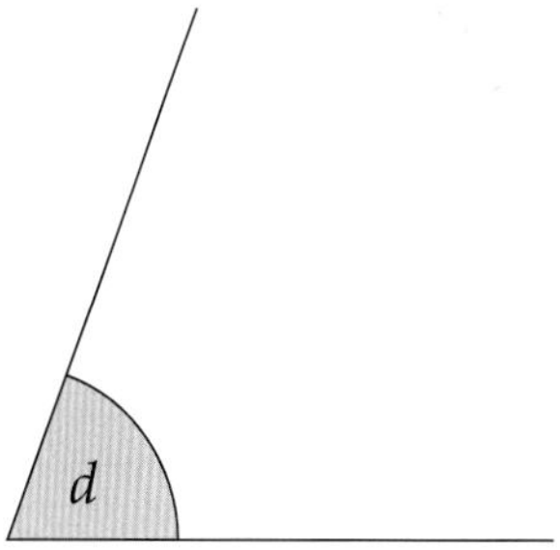

discussion

What could you do so you could measure this tiny angle with your regular sized protractor?
What is the size of the angle?

9b² Measuring and drawing angles

- Use a protractor to measure and draw angles up to 180°

Keywords
Angle
Degree
Protractor

You can measure an angle or draw an angle with a **protractor**.

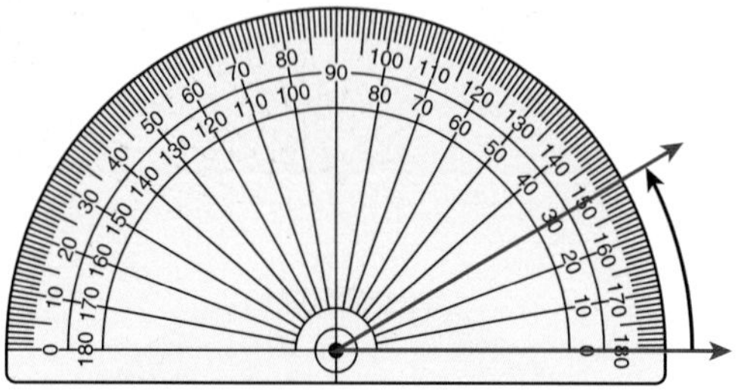

This angle is 30°.

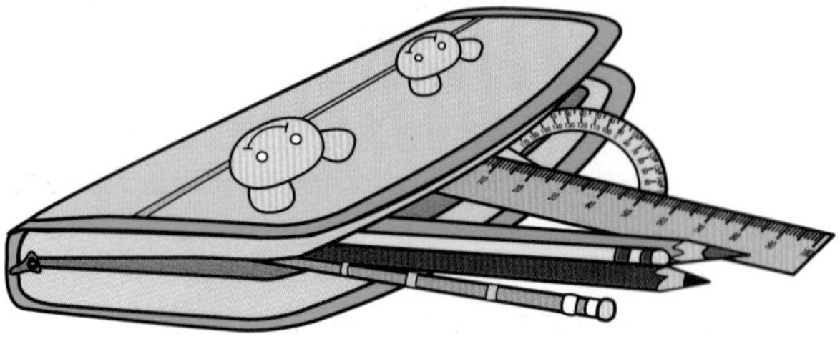

You will use a ruler, pencil and protractor.

example

Draw an angle of 60°.

1 Draw a line about 7 cm long.

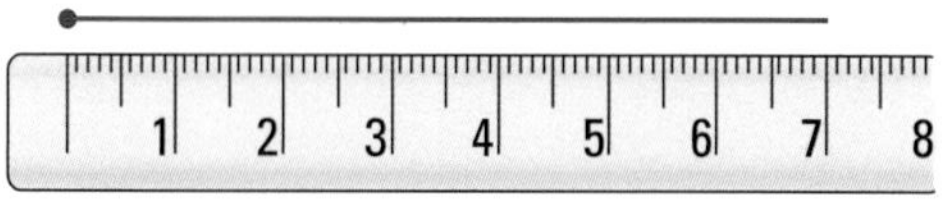

Put a dot at one end.

2 Place the protractor on the line.

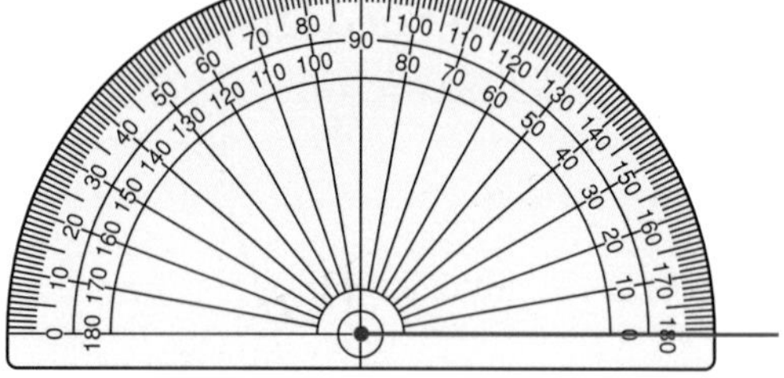

Make sure the cross-line is on top of the dot.

3 Read round the scale from 0.

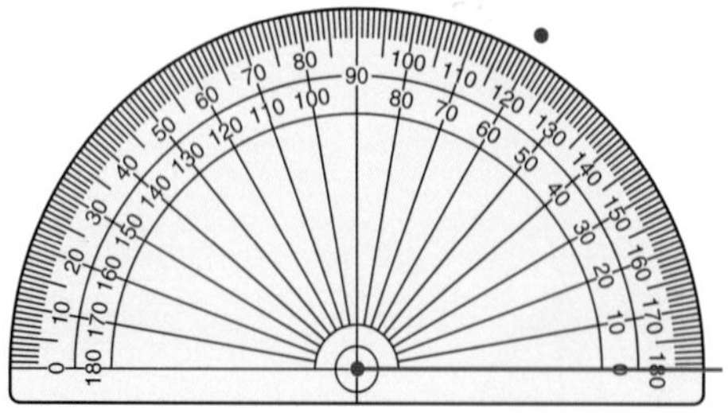

Mark 60° with a dot.

4 Join the dots to complete the angle.

This is an angle of 60°.

p. 270²

Exercise 9b²

1 What is the size of each angle?
Give your answer in degrees (°).

a

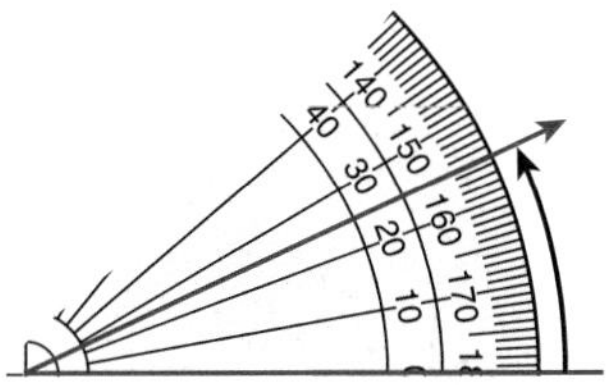

b

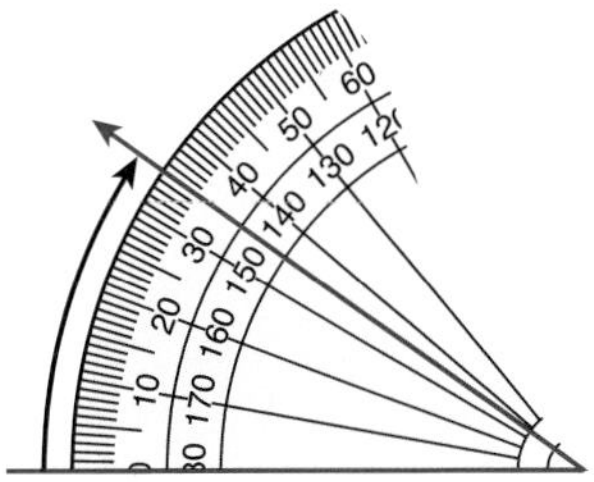

c

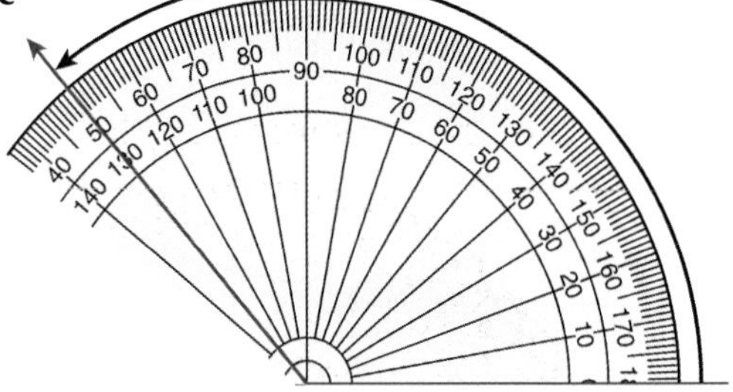

2 Measure each angle.
Give your answers in degrees (°).

a

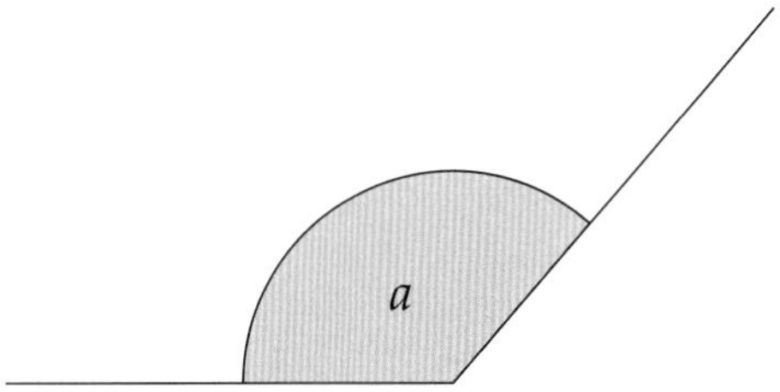

b

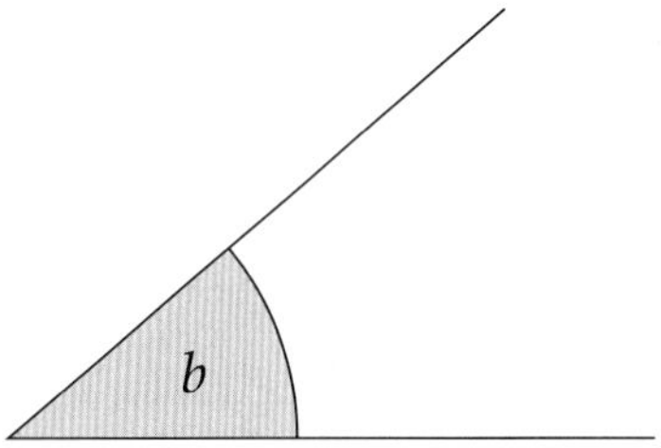

c

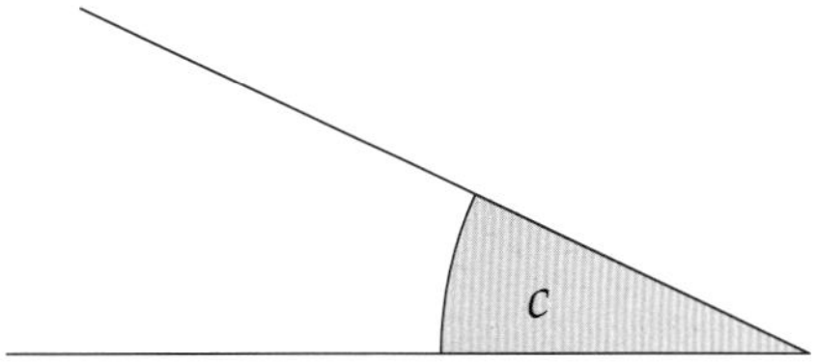

d

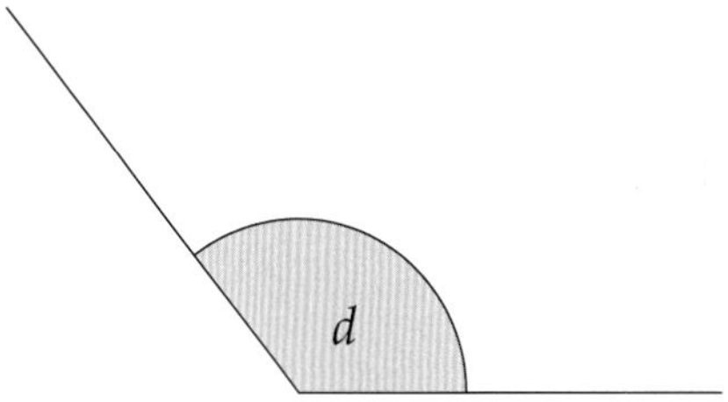

3 Draw these angles.

a 35°	**b** 60°	**c** 100°	**d** 135°	**e** 165°
f 20°	**g** 145°	**h** 55°	**i** 115°	**j** 85°

challenge

Michael is aiming a ball of paper at three waste paper bins.

Attempt **'a'**, at angle 30° missed.

Attempt **'b'**, at angle 60° missed.

Estimate the three angles he should launch the ball of paper at to land in bins 1, 2 and 3.

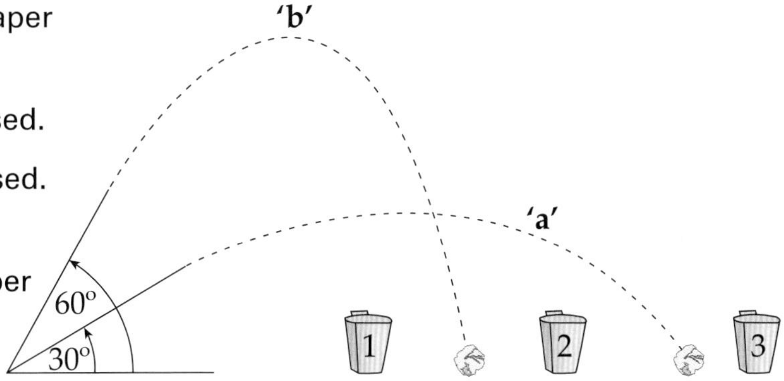

9c Calculating angles at a point

- Calculate angles that make a full turn of 360°

Keywords
Angle Quarter
Degrees (°) Rotate

Rory is on a roundabout.
Each time the roundabout goes one full turn,
Rory turns through an **angle** of 360°.

As the roundabout turns the angle increases.

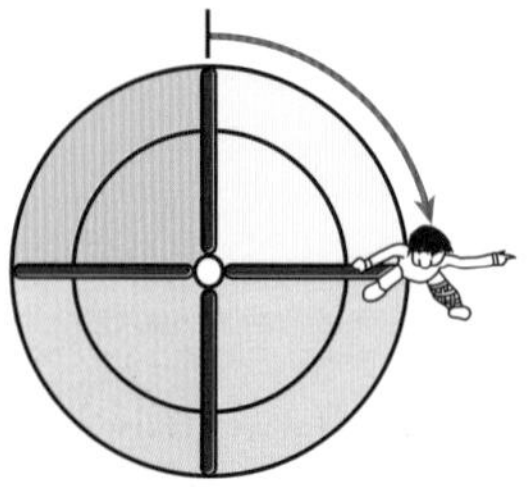

90° a **quarter** turn

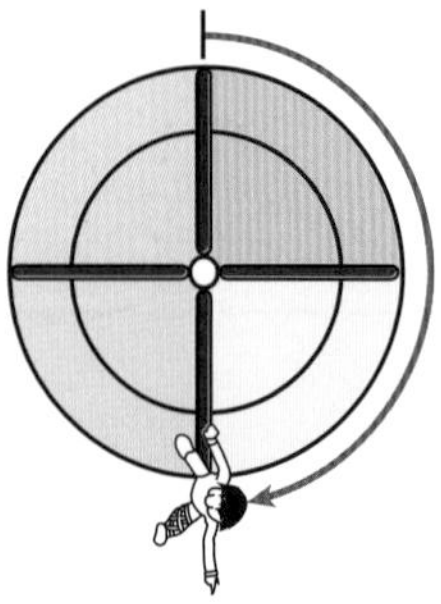

180° a half turn

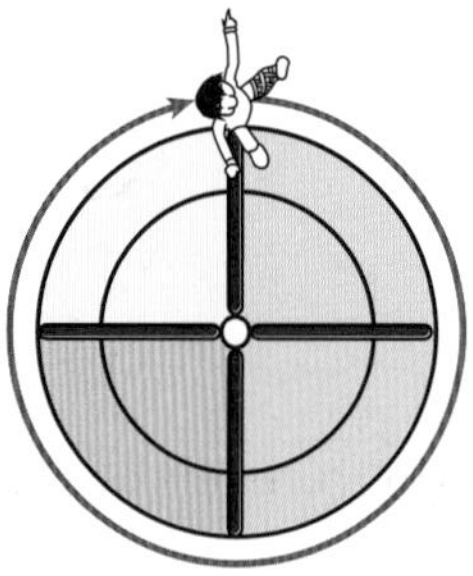

360° a complete turn

p. 266

- One complete turn is 360°.

At this point, Rory has turned 270°.
To finish one complete turn Rory must go
360° − 270° = 90°
Rory has to **rotate** another quarter turn.

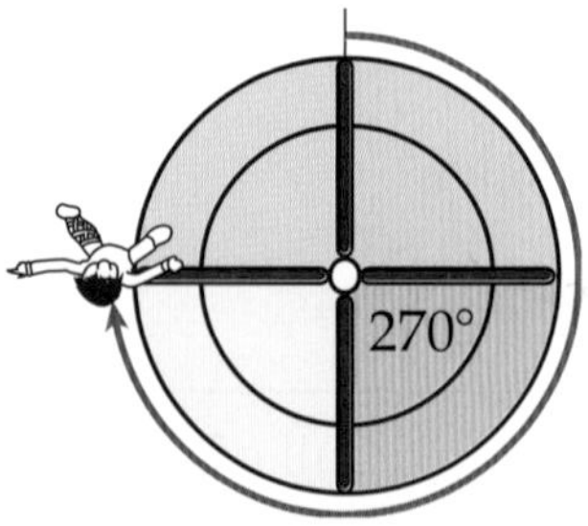

example

How many degrees does Rory need to turn through to reach 360°?

360° − 180° = 180°

Rory must turn 180° more to reach 360°.

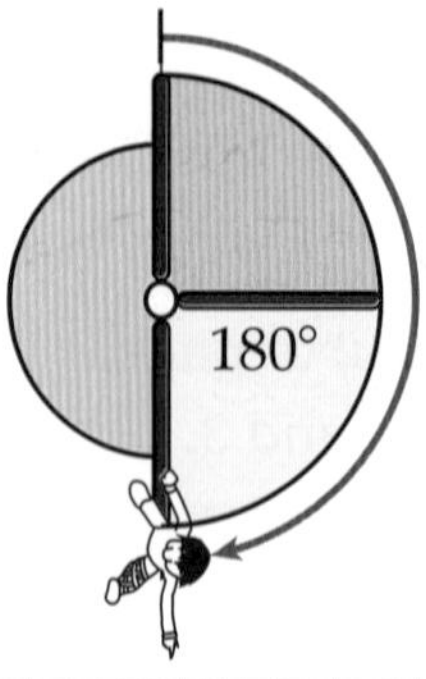

Exercise 9c

1 Answer these

a $360 - 200 = \square$ b $360 - 120 = \square$ c $360 - 230 = \square$ d $360 - 250 = \square$

e $100 + \square = 360$ f $260 + \square = 360$ g $\square + 60 = 360$ h $\square + 245 = 360$

2 How many degrees must Rory turn through to finish a complete turn?
Give an answer for each drawing.

a
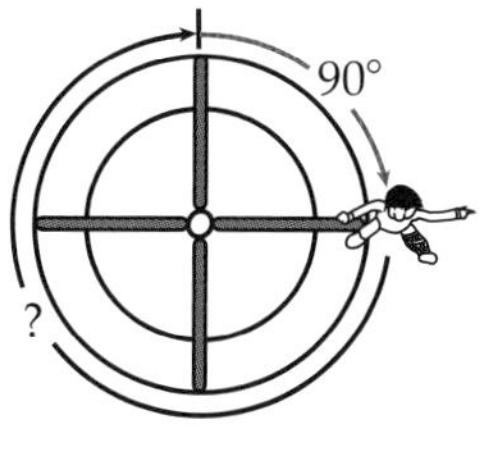

b
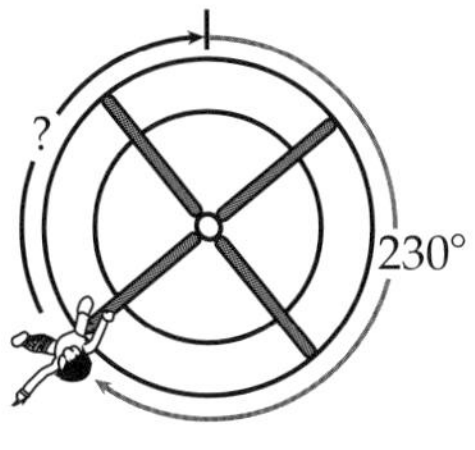

c
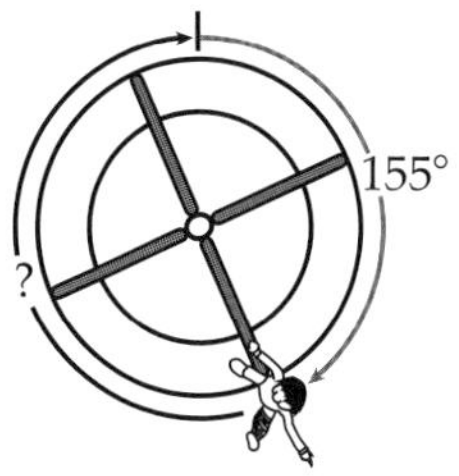

d
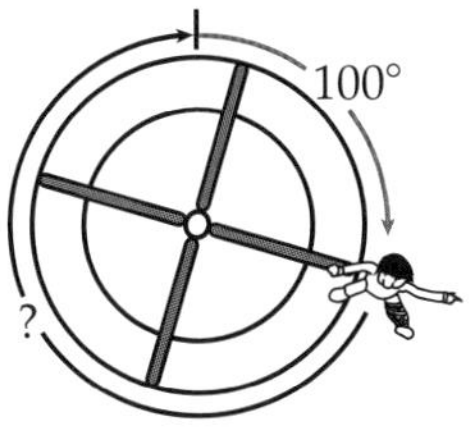

e
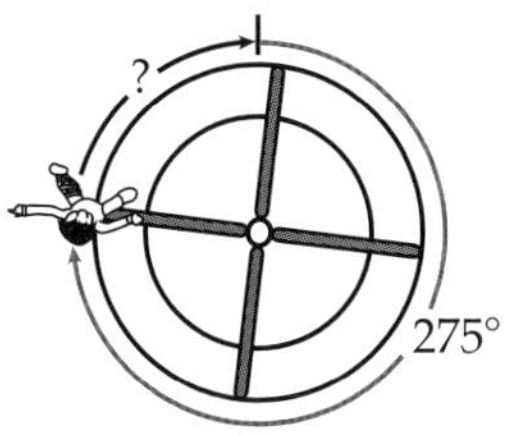

f
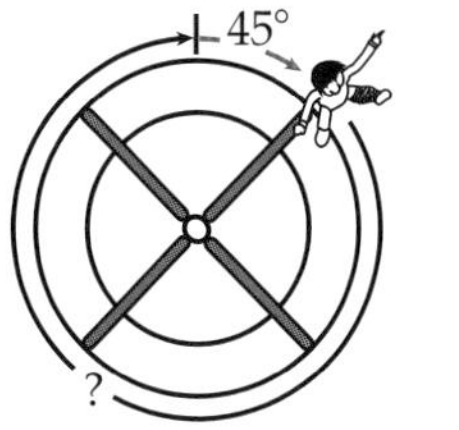

3 Find the missing angle for each of these.

a
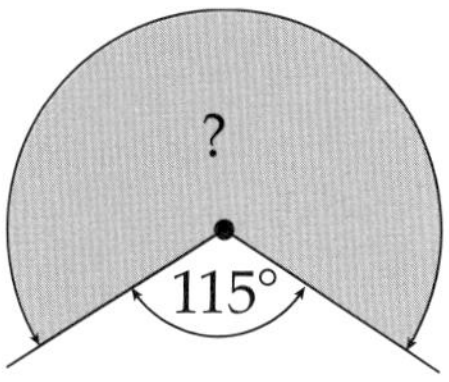

b
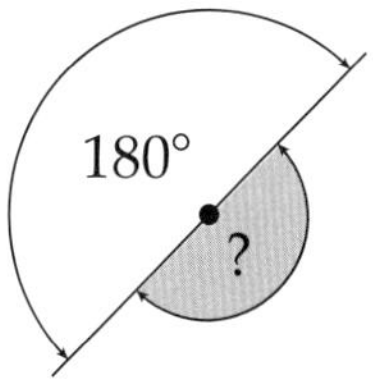

c
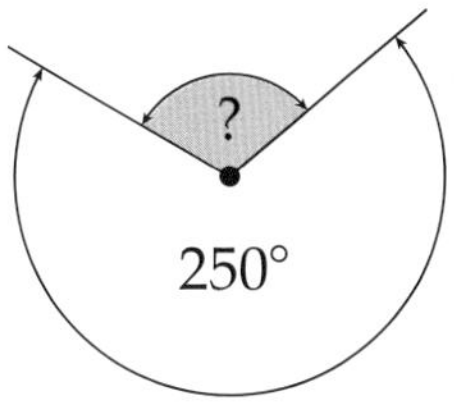

d
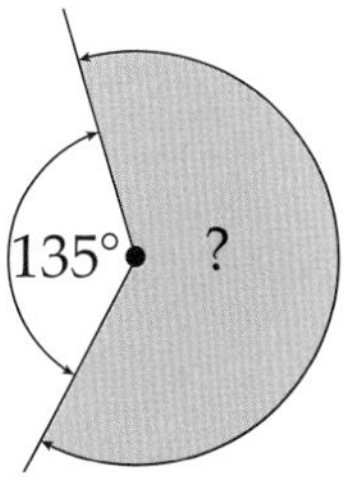

Did you know?

The world's biggest soccer ball was made for the 2006 World Cup Finals in Germany. The ball was 15 m high.

challenge

Choose three slices of cake that will make one whole cake when put together.

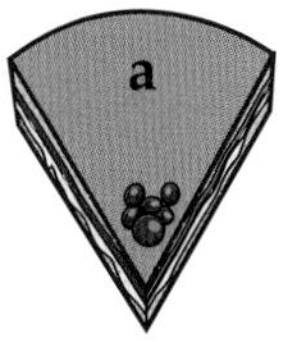

60°

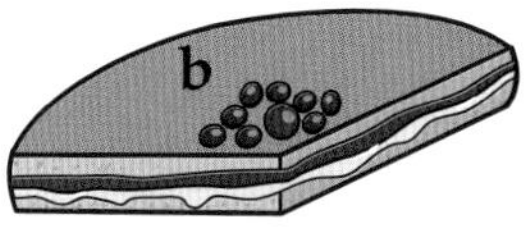

150°

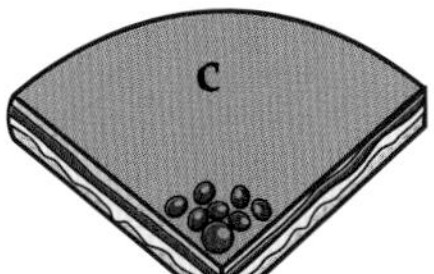

100°

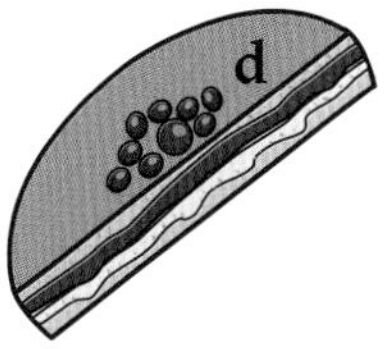

180°

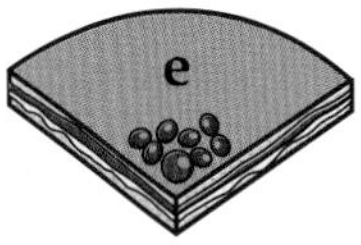

110°

9d Properties of triangles

- Know the names and recognise different types of triangle

Keywords
Angle *Right-angled*
Equilateral *Scalene*
Isosceles *Triangle*

p. 44

- A **triangle** is a three-sided shape that contains three **angles**.

p. 268

Isosceles

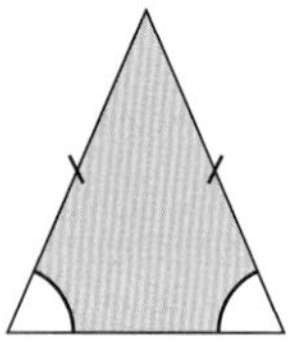

Two sides are equal.
Two angles are equal.

Right-angled

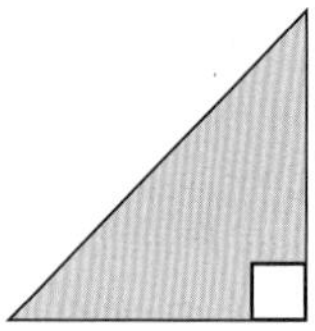

One angle is 90°.

Equilateral

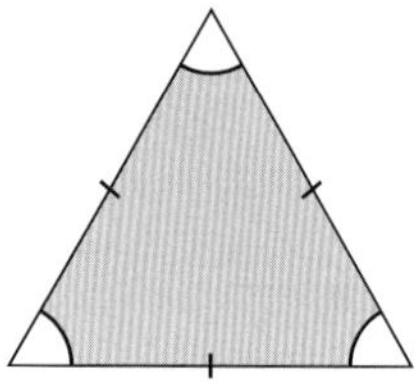

All sides are equal.
All angles are equal.

Scalene

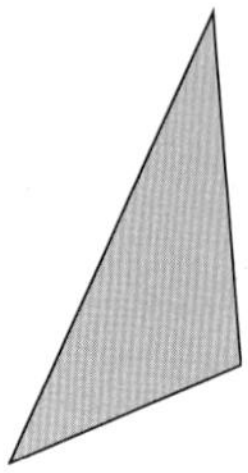

All sides different.
All angles different.

- You need to know these symbols:

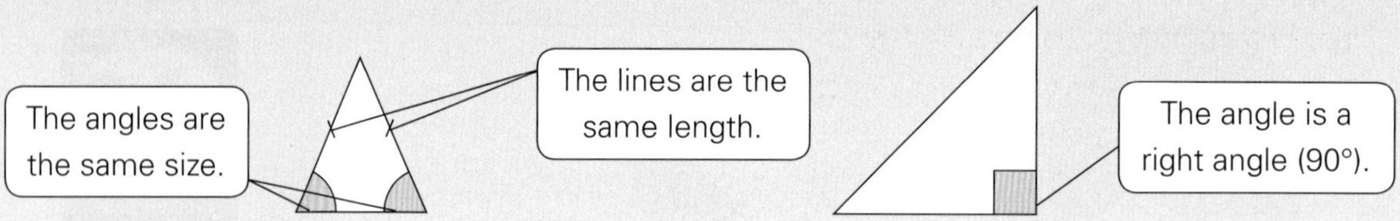
The angles are the same size.
The lines are the same length.
The angle is a right angle (90°).

example

What kind of triangle is each of these?

a

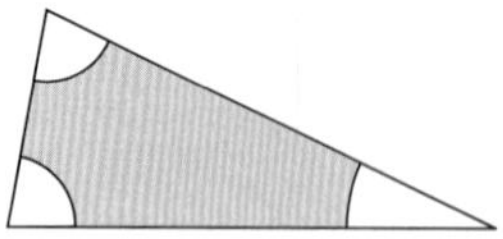

b

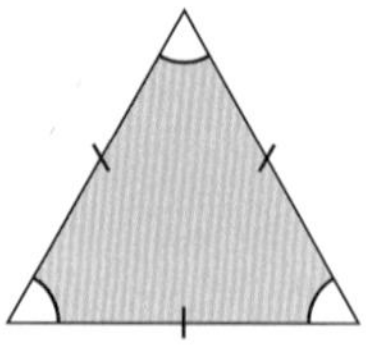

c

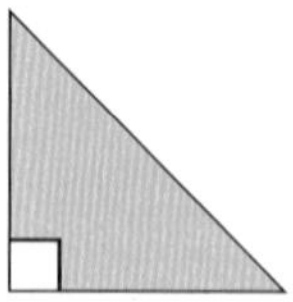

a Scalene.
All sides and angles are different.

b Equilateral.
All sides and angles are the equal.

c Right-angled triangle.
One angle is 90°.

Exercise 9d

1 Which of these shapes are triangles?

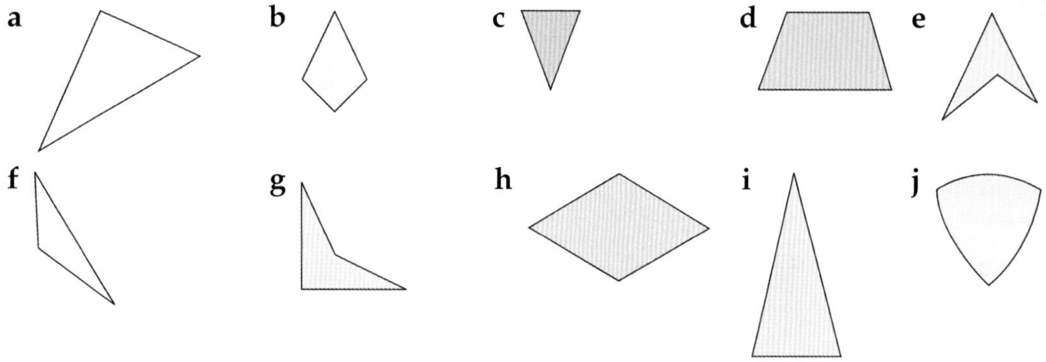

2 Name each triangle.

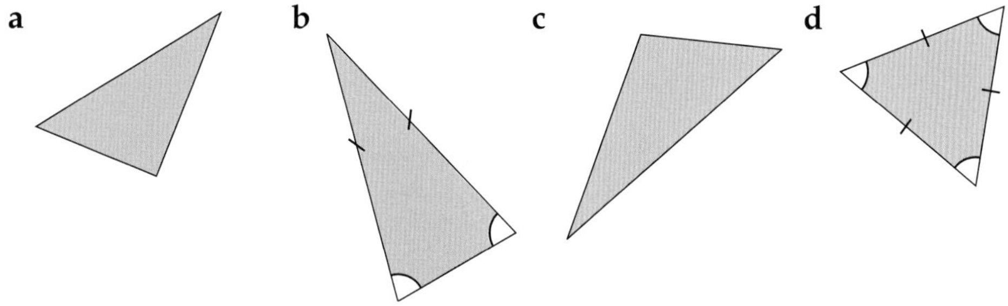

3 For each of these triangles:

a use a ruler to measure each side
b use a protractor to measure each angle
c name the type of triangle.

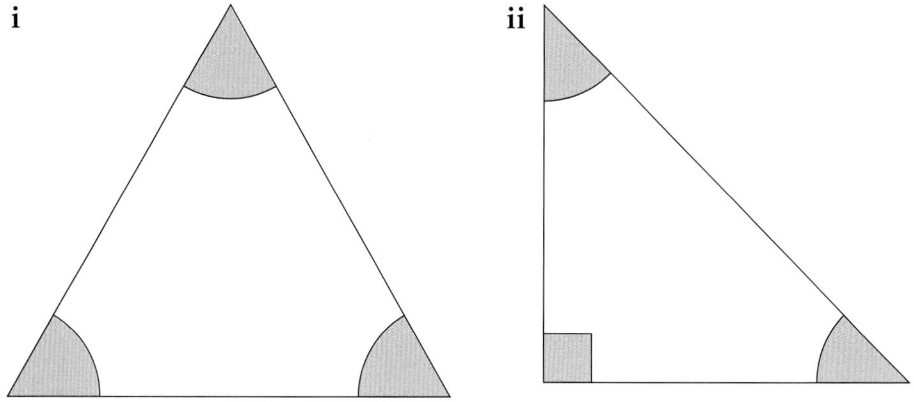

puzzle

Which three lines could you use to make:

a an isosceles triangle?
b an equilateral triangle?
c a scalene triangle

Line 1 ____________________
Line 2 __________
Line 3 ____________________
Line 4 ____________________
Line 5 ________________________

3-D shapes

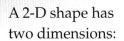

- Know the names and recognise different 3-D shapes

Keywords

3-D	*Faces*
Cone	*Prism*
Cube	*Pyramid*
Cylinder	*Sphere*
Edges	*Vertices*

A 2-D shape has two dimensions:

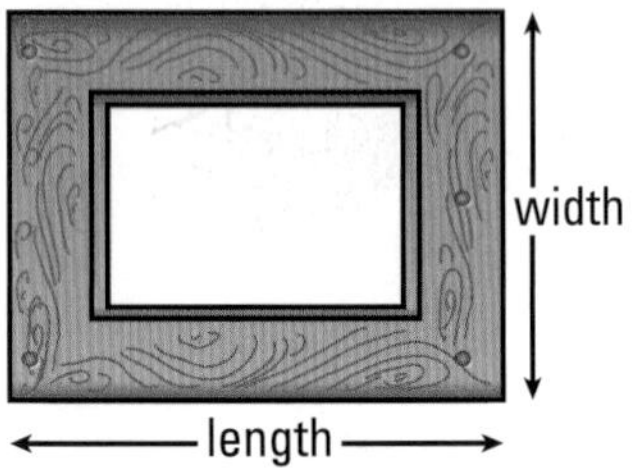

A flat shape

A **3-D** shape has three dimensions:

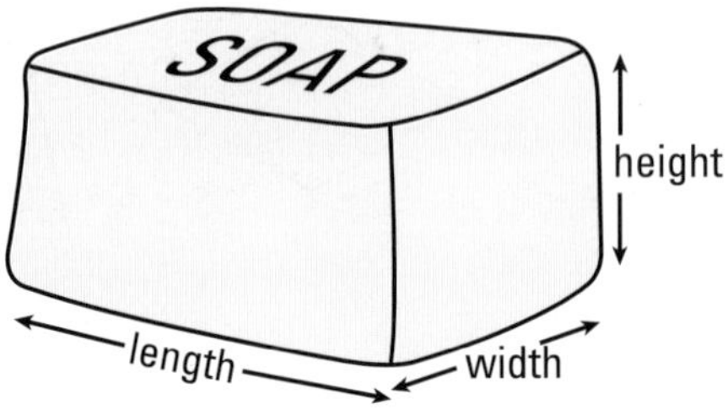

A solid shape

Here are some 3-D shapes.

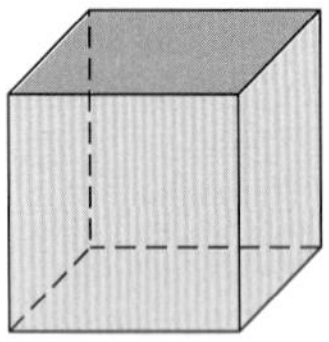

cube

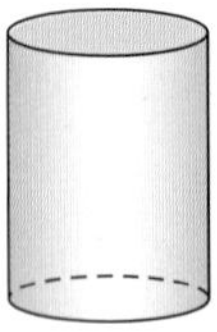

cylinder

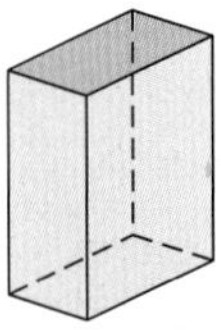

cuboid

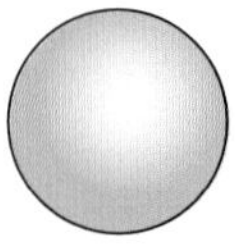

sphere

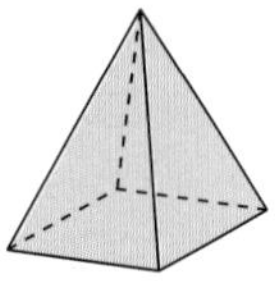

pyramid

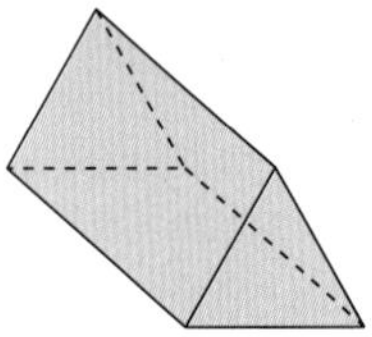

prism

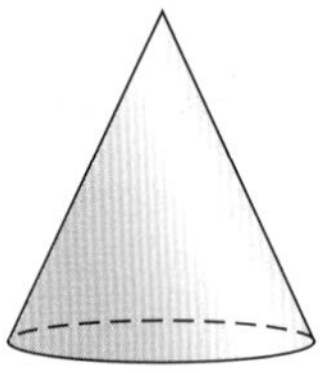

cone

- A 3-D shape has **faces, edges** and **corners.**

Corners are **vertices.**
Vertices is plural for vertex.

This cube has
6 faces – all squares
12 edges – all the same length
8 vertices or corners

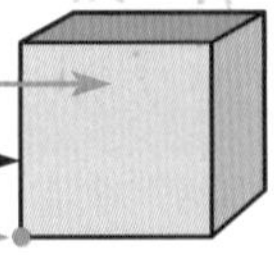

example

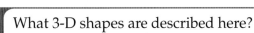

What 3-D shapes are described here?

a One curved face
No edges or corners

b Six rectangular faces
Edges not the same length

c Circular base and top
No straight edges

a

sphere

b

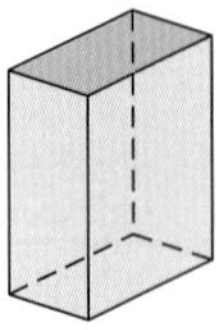

cuboid

c

cylinder

p. 274

Exercise 9e

1 Class 7W are making 3-D models of buildings near their school.
List the 3-D shapes used to make each model. The first is done for you.

a

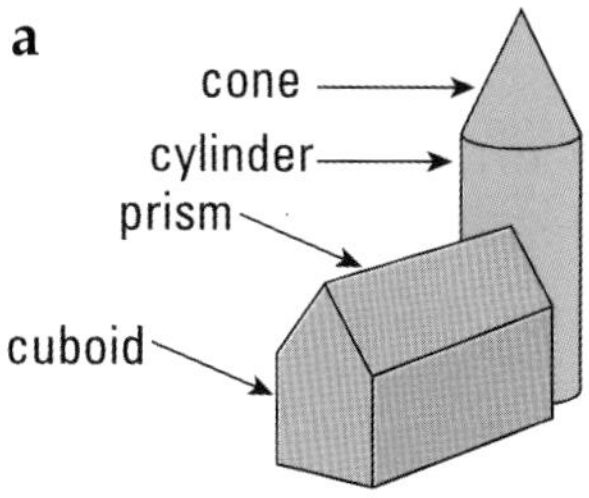

b

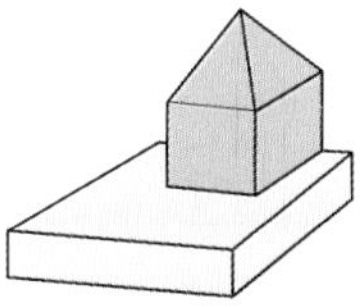

c

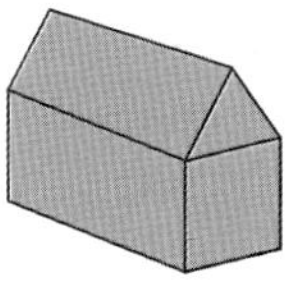

d

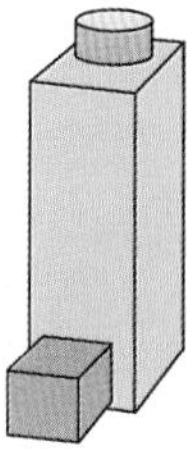

e

f

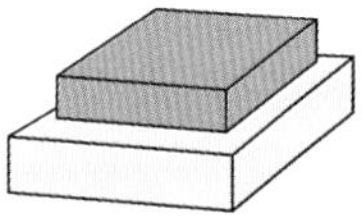

g

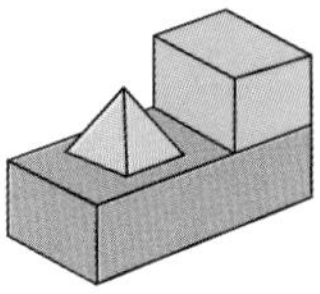

h

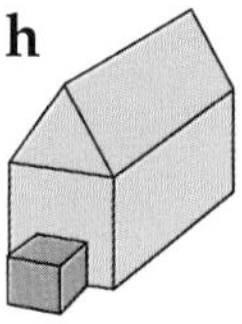

i

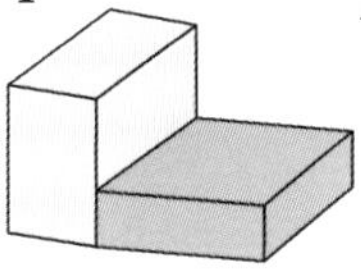

j

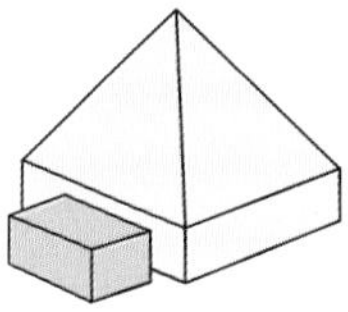

2 Here is an overhead view of the buildings near the school.
Match each 3-D model above with the 2-D view below.

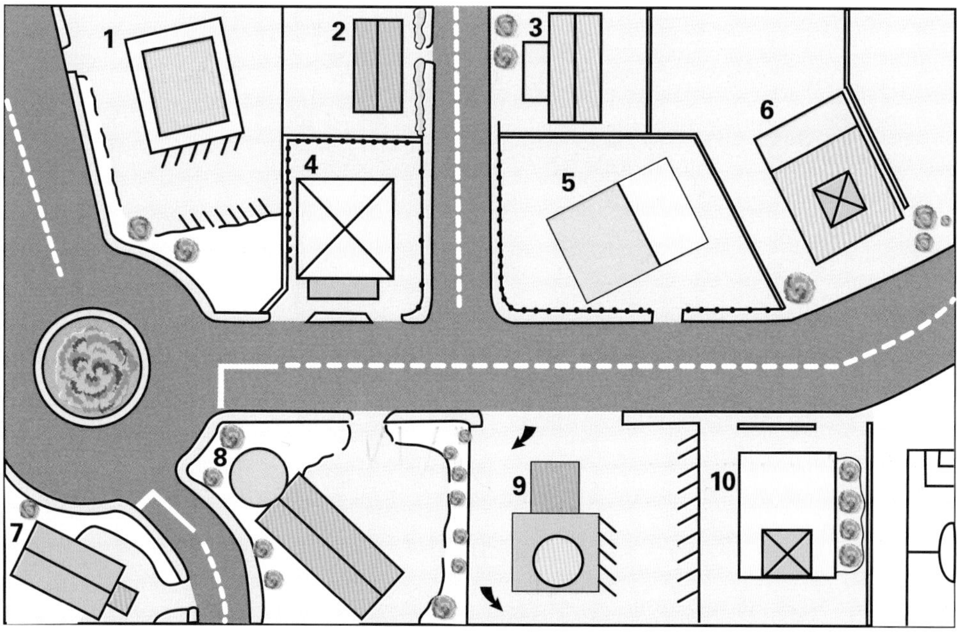

challenge

a Copy the cube and cuboid onto isometric paper.
Make sure the isometric paper is the right way up.

b Draw a 3-D shape made from three cubes.

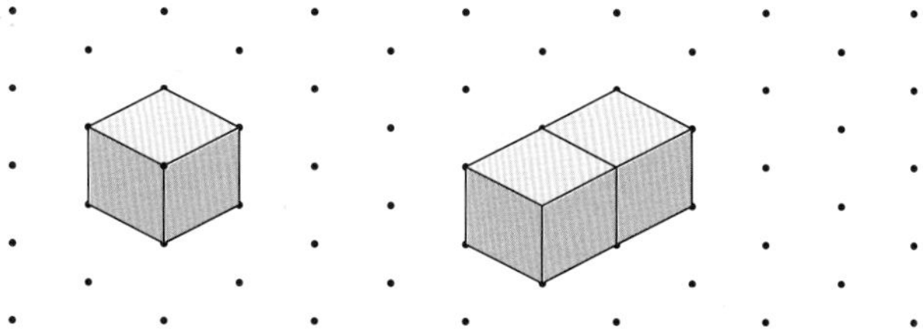

9a

1 Find the other angle on the straight line for each of diagram.

a

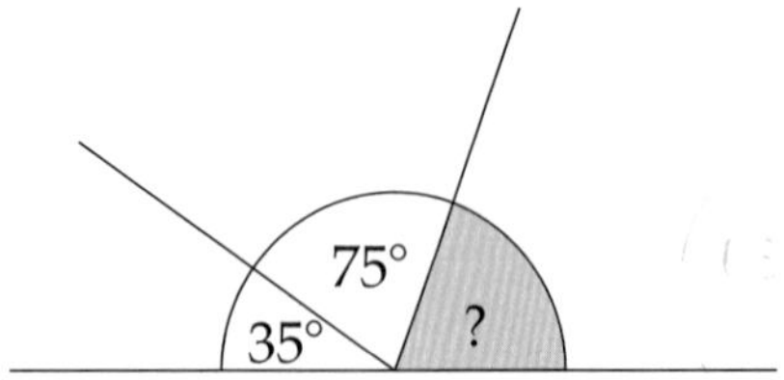

b

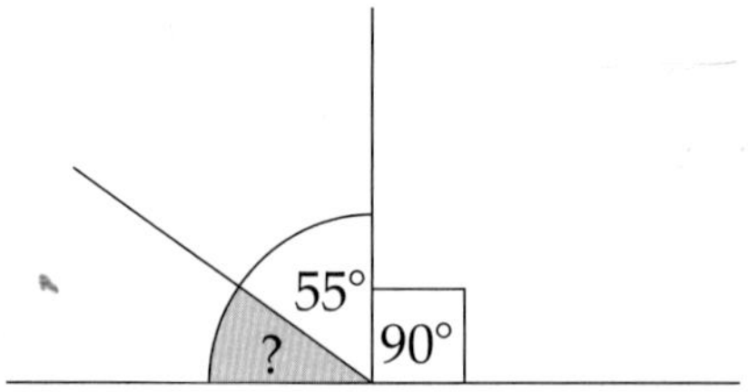

c

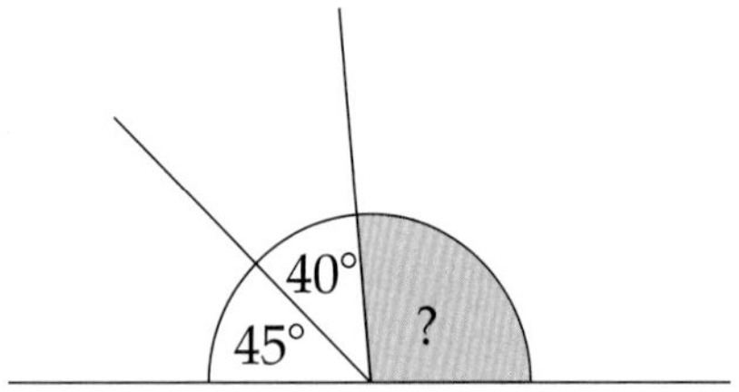

d

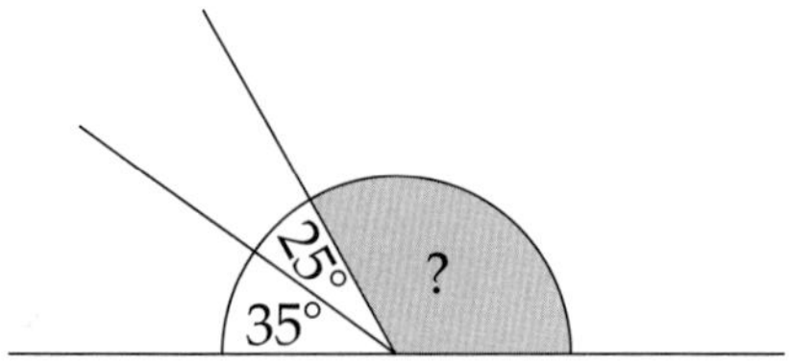

9b

2 Measure each of these angles.

a

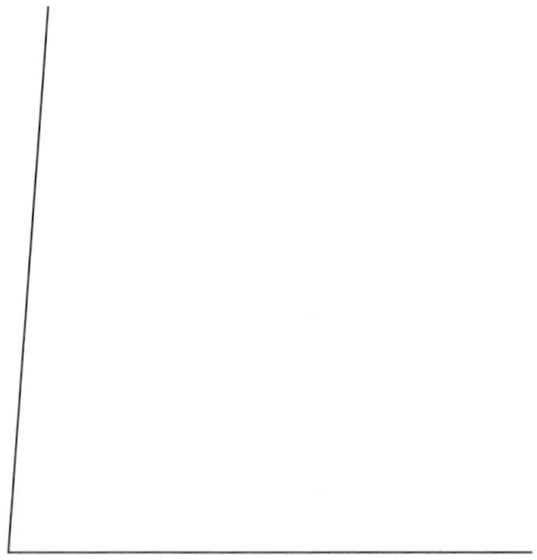

c

b

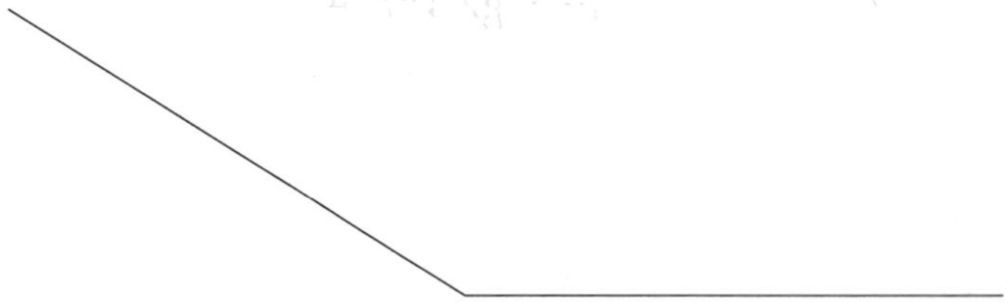

d

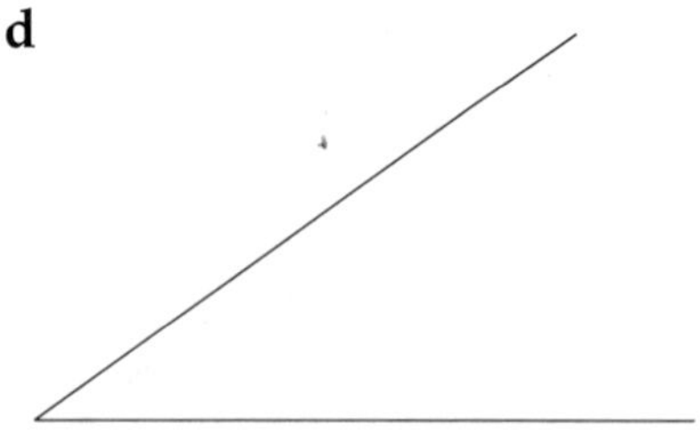

9b²

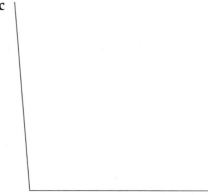

3 Draw these angles accurately.

a 65° **b** 110° **c** 90° **d** 40° **e** 150°

9c

4 Find the missing angle in each diagram.

a

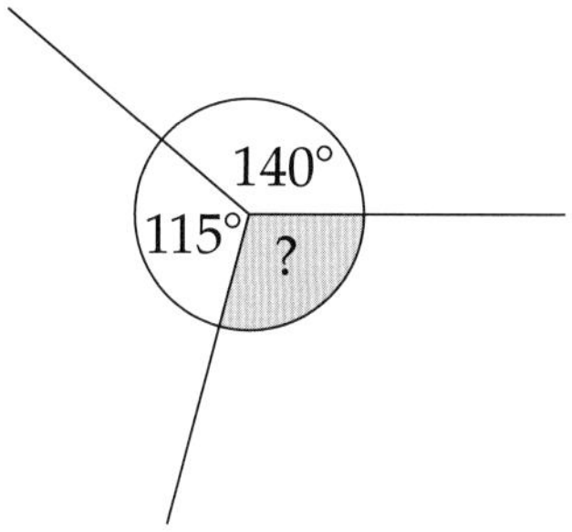

b

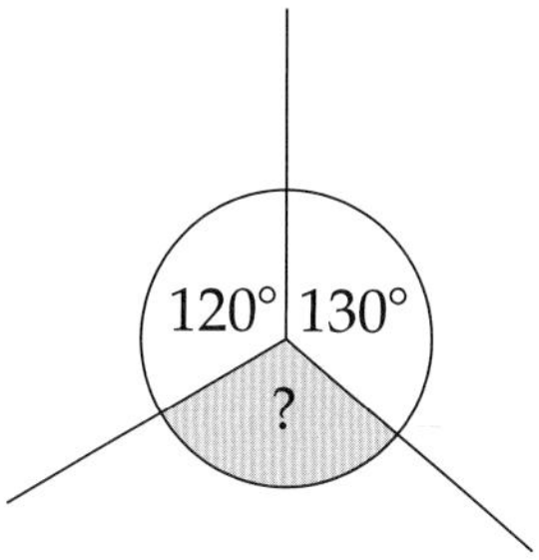

c

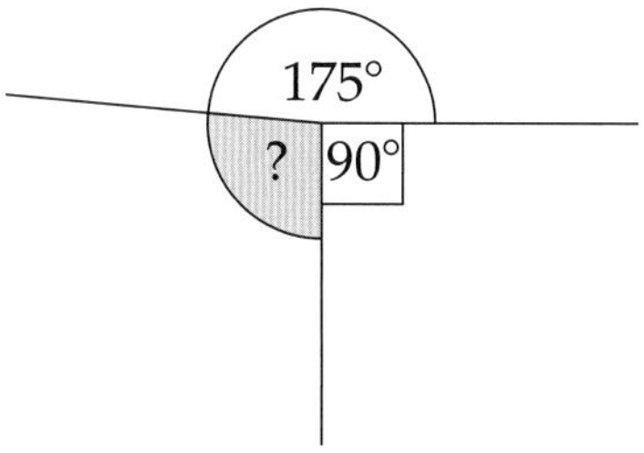

d

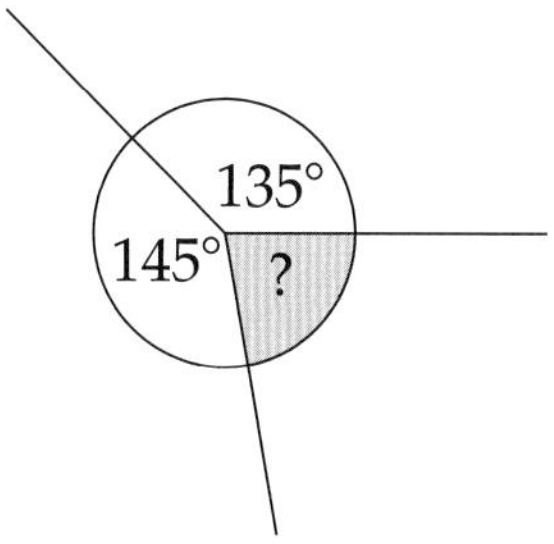

5 Match the triangle to its name and description.

Right-angled

Equilateral

Isosceles

Scalene

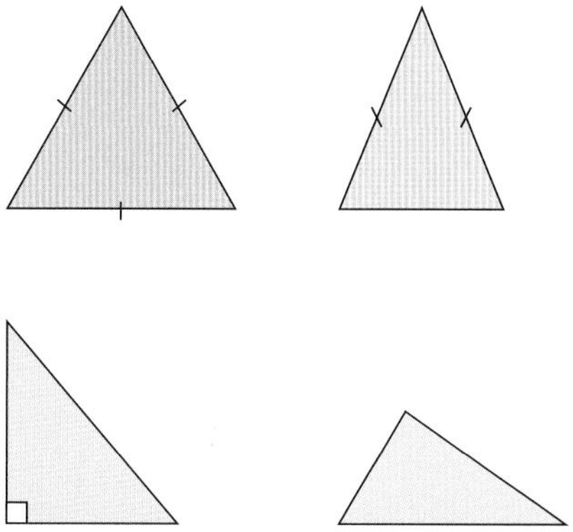

All sides different.
All angles different.

One angle is 90°

Two sides are equal.
Two angles are equal.

All sides are equal.
All angles are equal.

6 Name each 3-D shape.

a 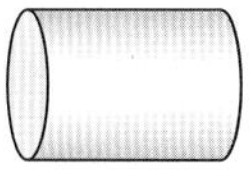

b 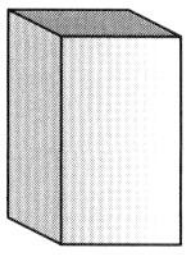

c 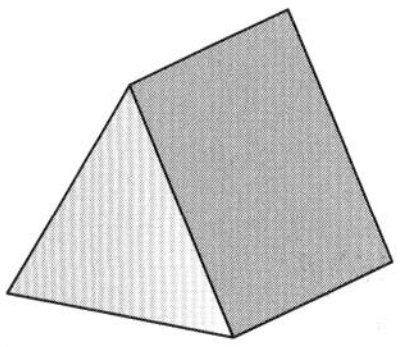

d 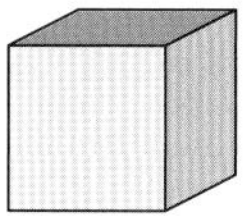

e 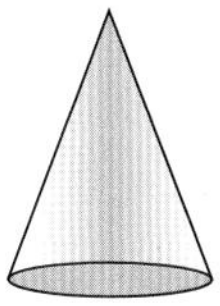

f 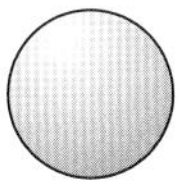

g 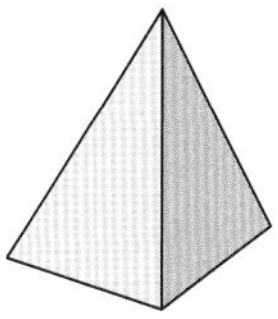

9 Summary

Key indicators

- Sort 2-D shapes **Level 3**
- Understand angles **Level 3**

Level 3

1 a Write the name of each shape.

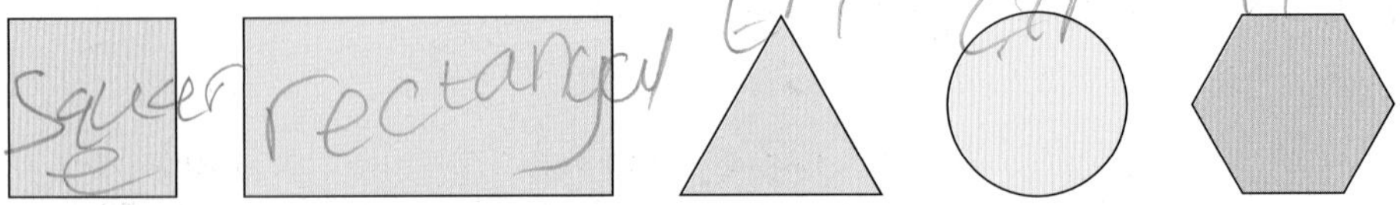

A B C D E

b List the shapes that are regular.

Samir's answer ✓

The triangle is equilateral as the 3 sides are equal.

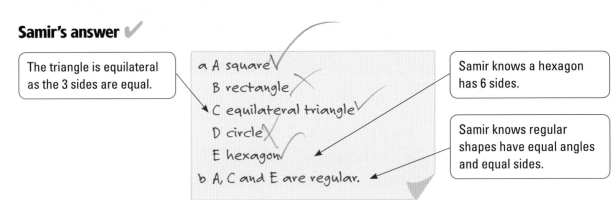

a A square
B rectangle
C equilateral triangle
D circle
E hexagon
b A, C and E are regular.

Samir knows a hexagon has 6 sides.

Samir knows regular shapes have equal angles and equal sides.

Level 3

2 a Look at the quadrilateral.
Which angle is biggest?

☐ Angle *a* ☐ Angle *b* ☐ Angle *c* ☐ Angle *d*

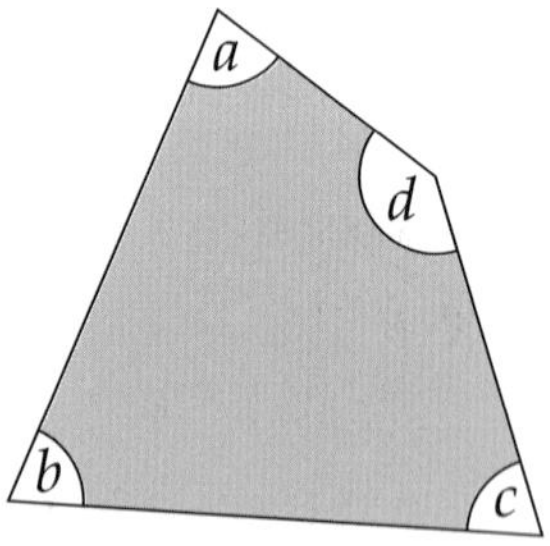

b Now look at this quadrilateral.
Angle *e* is marked with straight lines.
What does this tell you about the angle *e*?

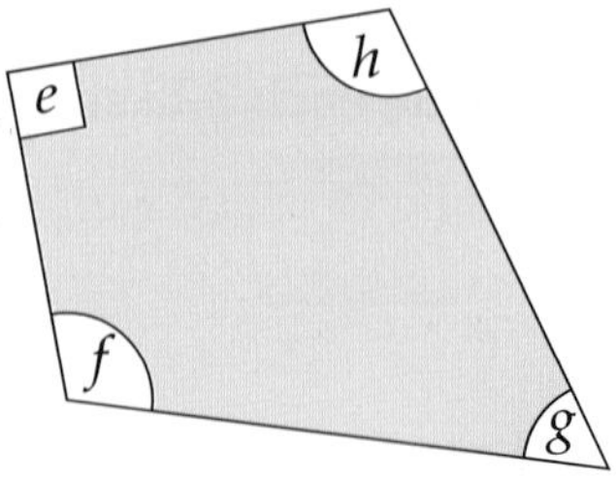

Key Stage 3 2006 3–5 Paper 2

10 Algebra

Integers and graphs

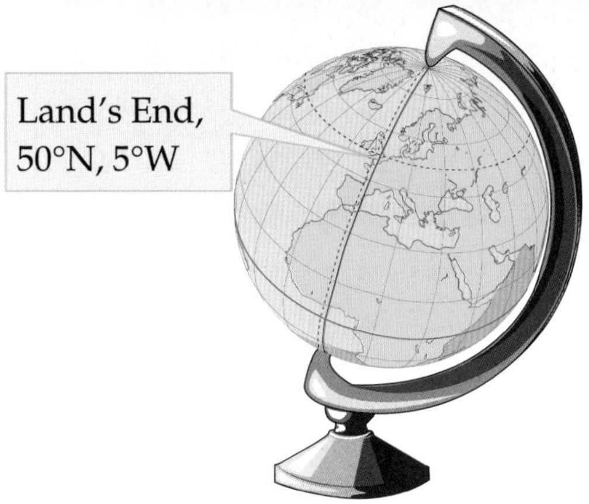

You can give the coordinates of a location on Earth using latitude and longitude. The coordinates of Land's End are (50°N, 5°W). This means 50 lines of latitude north of the equator and 5 lines of longitude west of the prime meridian which passes through London.

What's the point? Coordinates give the positions of a specific point on a graph, a map or even a planet!

Check in

Level 3

1

3	10	15	18	20
26	27	35		

Write all the numbers that are

a even **b** odd

c in the 3 times table **d** in the 5 times table

2 Send each input through the function ×4.

Input **Output**

a 3 □

b 5 □

c 9 □

d 10 □

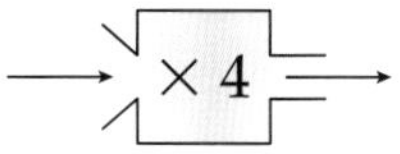

Level 4

3 Fill in the missing numbers in this mapping.

Input → **Output** (+8)

Input	Output
2	□
□	12
5	□
□	16

10a Factors

- Know how to find the factors of a number

Keywords
Factor *Pair*
Multiply

The number 8 appears four times in this table.

$8 = 1 \times 8$ $8 = 8 \times 1$

$8 = 2 \times 4$ $8 = 4 \times 2$

×	1	2	3	4	5	6	7	8	9	10
1	1	2	3	4	5	6	7	8	9	10
2	2	4	6	8	10	12	14	16	18	20
3	3	6	9	12	15	18	21	24	27	30
4	4	8	12	16	20	24	28	32	36	40
5	5	10	15	20	25	30	35	40	45	50
6	6	12	18	24	30	36	42	48	54	60
7	7	14	21	28	35	42	49	56	63	70
8	8	16	24	32	40	48	56	64	72	80
9	9	18	27	36	45	54	63	72	81	90
10	10	20	30	40	50	60	70	80	90	100

p. 232

- The numbers that **multiply** together to make 8 are **factors** of 8.
  1, 2, 4 and 8 are factors of 8.
  The factor **pairs** are 1 × 8 and 2 × 4.

1 × 8 and 2 × 4 are the same as 8 × 1 and 4 × 2.

You can think of factors like the number of counters in a row. Eight counters can be arranged in rows in four different ways:

The factors of 8 divide into 8 without leaving a remainder.

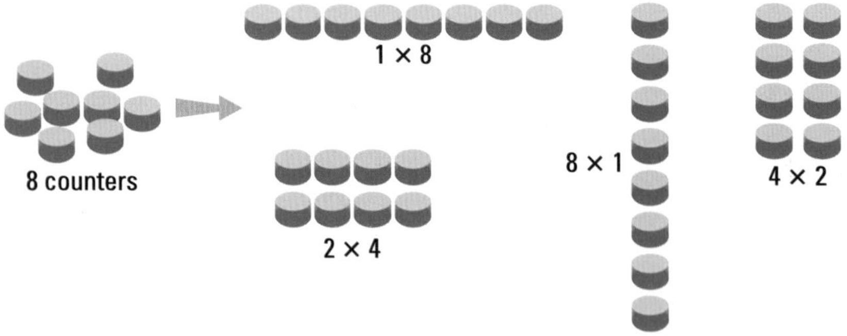

example

What are the factors of 6?

Arrange six counters in equal rows.

Write the multiplication for each arrangement.

6×1, 1×6, 2×3, 3×2

The factors of 6 are: 1, 2, 3 and 6.

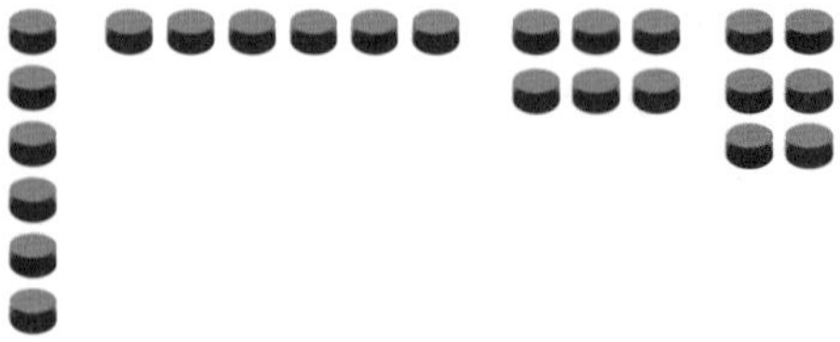

Exercise 10a

1 **a** Arrange these 12 counters into equal rows.
b Write a multiplication for each of your diagrams.
c Check your answers with the multiplication table.
d List all the factors of 12.

2 Here are 20 counters.
a Find six different ways to arrange them into equal rows.
b List **all** of the factors of 20.
c Which factors do not show in the multiplication table?

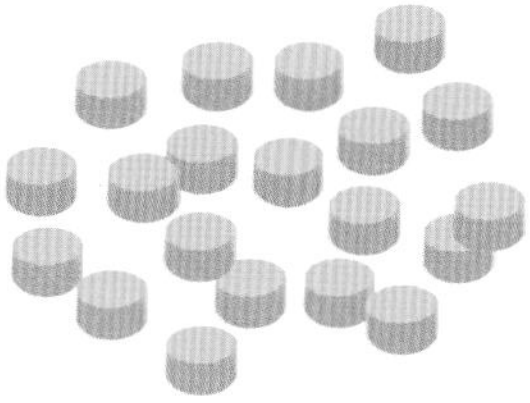

3

> Look at all your answers so far. You can see that
> - 1 is a factor of all numbers.
> - All numbers are factors of themselves.
>
> For example $20 = 20 \times 1$ $12 = 12 \times 1$ $6 = 6 \times 1$

Use these facts and the multiplication table to list the factors of these numbers.

a 9	**b** 12	**c** 15
d 16	**e** 18	**f** 21
g 24	**h** 27	**i** 25

4 Find which number has each set of factors.

a 1, 2, 4	**b** 1, 2, 4, 8, 16	**c** 1, 2, 3, 6, 9, 18
d 1, 3	**e** 1, 2, 4, 8, 16, 32	**f** 1, 2, 4, 5, 10, 20, 25, 50, 100

5 Match each number with its set of factors.
Be careful! Each set has a number that isn't a factor.
Write all the odd numbers out and find the mystery number they are all factors of.

13 **60** **30** **27**

a 3 2 30 1 10 15 1

b 27 9 3 1 3

c 1 2 12 60 3 20 4 15 30 5 6 10 13

d 39 13 1

challenge

Look at these shapes.
Which one has the greater area?

a

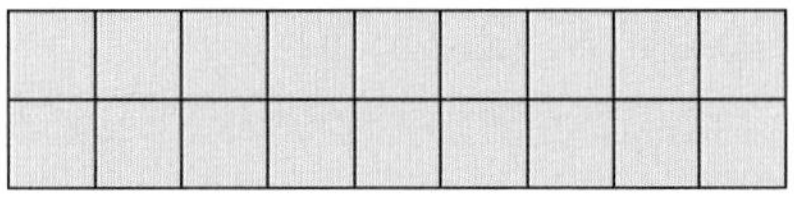

b

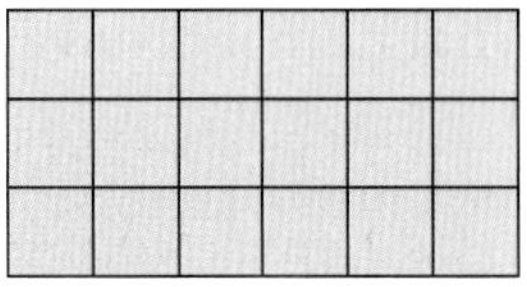

c

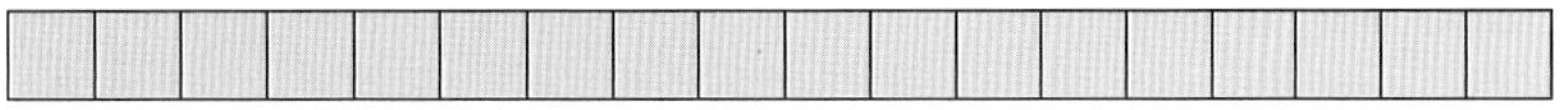

10b Multiples

- Know how to list the multiples of a number

Keywords
Factor
Multiple

- **Factors** show what a number is made of. $18 = 3 \times 6$
  You can divide to find factors. $18 \div 3 = 6$

- **Multiples** show how a number makes up other numbers.
  You multiply to find multiples. $2 \times 9 = 18$ $2 \times 10 = 20$

p. 232

2 is multiplied by each of the numbers in the arrow boxes.

The numbers in the circles are multiples of 2.

They appear in the 2 times table.

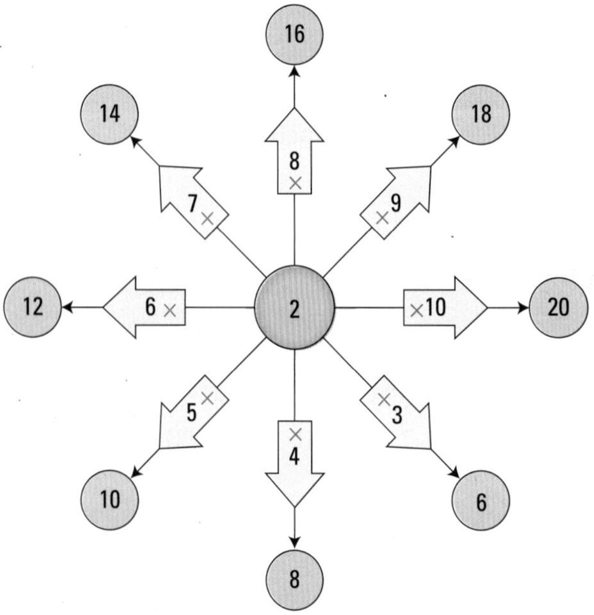

example

What are the multiples of 3 up to 20?

$3 \times 2 = 6$ $3 \times 3 = 9$ $3 \times 4 = 12$ $3 \times 5 = 15$ $3 \times 6 = 18$
6, 9, 12, 15 and 18 are multiples of 3.

example

What numbers have these multiples? 8, 12, 16, 20

Look at the factors:

$2 \times 4 = 8$	$2 \times 6 = 12$	$2 \times 8 = 16$	$2 \times 10 = 20$
	$3 \times 4 = 12$	$4 \times 4 = 16$	$4 \times 5 = 20$

2 and 4 have these numbers as multiples.

Exercise 10b

1 Copy the diagram to find multiples of 5. Fill in all of the circles.

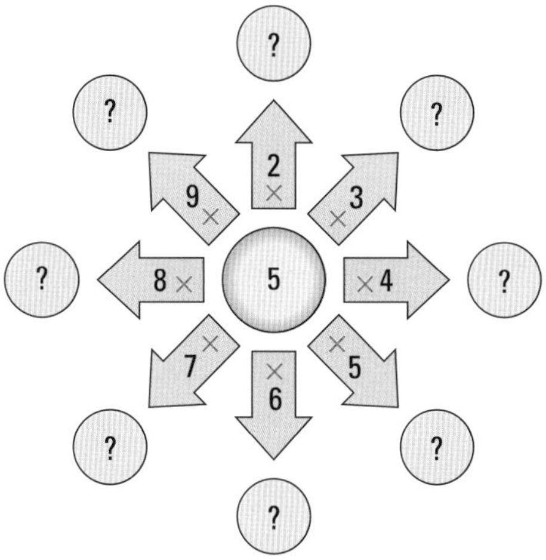

2 Repeat Question **1** for multiples of 3 by placing 3 at the centre.
Then repeat for multiples of 6.

3 **a** Write a list of multiples of 2 up to 30.
b Write a list of multiples of 3 up to 30.
c What numbers up to 30 are multiples of both 2 and 3?

4 24 is a multiple with eight factors. Find as many of these as you can.

5 How many factors does 36 have? List all the factors if it helps.

6 **a** Which numbers have all these multiples?

6, 12, 36,
18, 24

b What would be the next number in the ring?

challenge

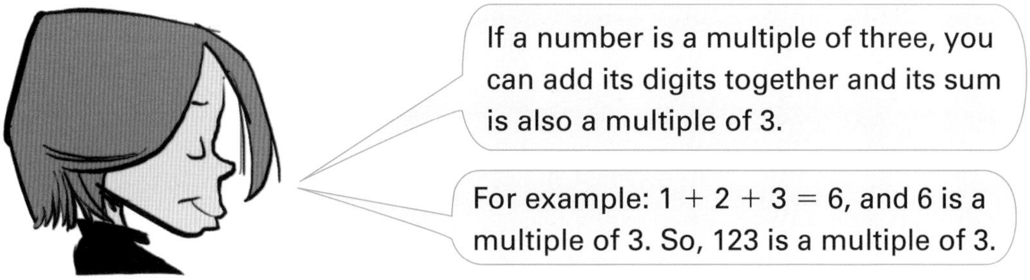

If a number is a multiple of three, you can add its digits together and its sum is also a multiple of 3.
For example: 1 + 2 + 3 = 6, and 6 is a multiple of 3. So, 123 is a multiple of 3.

Use Jenny's rule to check whether these numbers are multiples of 3.

a 69 **b** 175 **c** 174 **d** 711 **e** 253 **f** 2058

10c Square numbers

- Know what square numbers are and how to find them

Keywords
Square number
Symbol

Jack has a bag of counters.
He begins to arrange the counters in order.
Only certain numbers of counters can be made into a square.

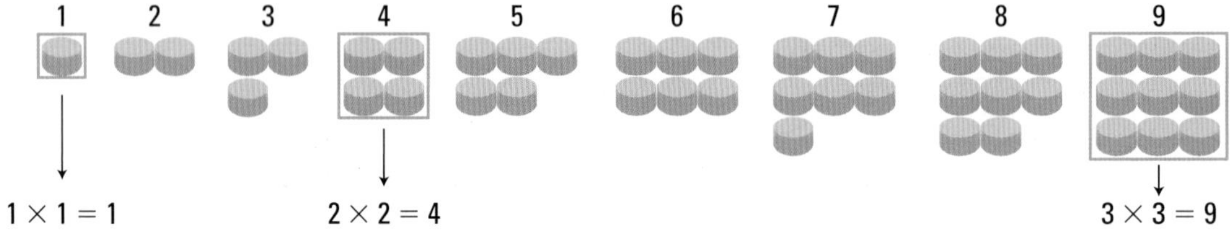

Jack has found the first three **square numbers**.

- A number multiplied by itself is a square number.
  $3 \times 3 = 9$ 9 is a square number.

- The **symbol** for square is a small figure 2 beside the number.
  3 squared is written 3^2 $3 \times 3 = 9$

A times table will help you identify square numbers up to 100.

$1 \times 1 = 1$
$2 \times 2 = 4$
$3 \times 3 = 9$
$4 \times 4 = 16$

Can you see a pattern?

×	1	2	3	4	5	6	7	8	9	10
1	1	2	3	4	5	6	7	8	9	10
2	2	4	6	8	10	12	14	16	18	20
3	3	6	9	12	15	18	21	24	27	30
4	4	8	12	16	20	24	28	32	36	40
5	5	10	15	20	25	30	35	40	45	50
6	6	12	18	24	30	36	42	48	54	60
7	7	14	21	28	35	42	49	56	63	70
8	8	16	24	32	40	48	56	64	72	80
9	9	18	27	36	45	54	63	72	81	90
10	10	20	30	40	50	60	70	80	90	100

example

What is missing in these calculations?

a $5 \times \square = 5^{\square} = 25$ **b** $6 \times 6 = \square^2 = \square$

a $5 \times 5 = 5^2 = 25$ **b** $6 \times 6 = 6^2 = 36$

Exercise 10c

1 Jack makes a sketch to find the first three square numbers.
Copy Jack's pattern and complete the next two square numbers.

$1 \times 1 = 1$ $2 \times 2 = 4$ $3 \times 3 = 9$

2 Here are the first 10 square numbers.
Copy and complete the list.

a $3^2 = 3 \times 3 = 9$ **b** $1^2 = 1 \times 1 = 1$ **c** 6^2 **d** 4^2
e 9^2 **f** 2^2 **g** 10^2 **h** 8^2
i 5^2 **j** 7^2

3 Follow the square numbers only through the maze.
As you arrive at each square number write the letter written in the box. At the end you should have spelled a word.

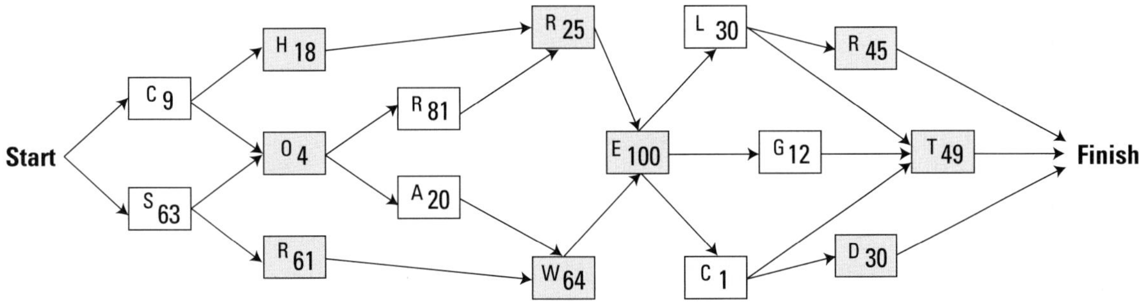

challenge

Kiran has a pile of 2p coins. She arranges them in squares.

The first square is worth 2p. The second square is worth 8p. The third square is worth 18p.

a What would the fourth square be worth?
b What would the tenth square be worth?
c Kiran has 40p worth of 2p coins.
What is the biggest square she can make with them?

10d Coordinates

- Know how to plot points using positive whole numbers

Keywords
Axes
Coordinates
Point
x-axis
y-axis

- A grid has two **axes**.

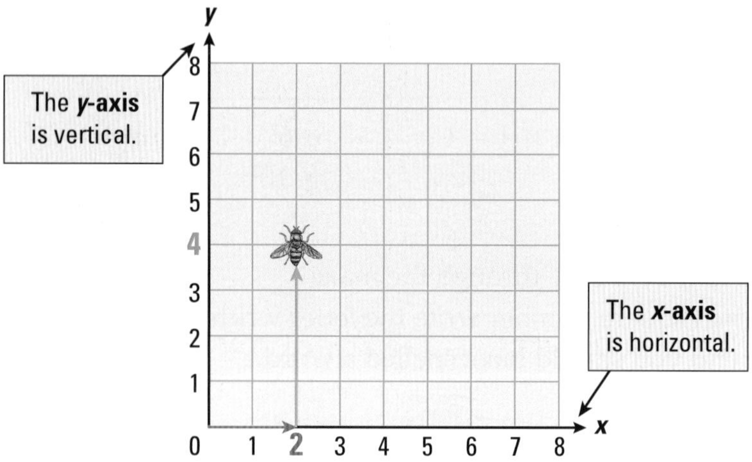

- **Coordinates** give the position of a **point** on the grid. The bee is at the coordinates (2, 4).

The brackets are important because they show that order matters.

- You read the x-axis first and the y-axis second to find a coordinate. (x, y)
  (2, 4) This means **2** across and **4** up.

example

a Give the coordinates for **A**, **B** and **C**.
b Point **D** is at (1, 5). Plot point **D**.

a **A** (2, 1) 2 across, 1 up
B (5, 4) 5 across, 4 up
C (3, 7) 3 across, 7 up

b Plot point **D** by going 1 across and 5 up.

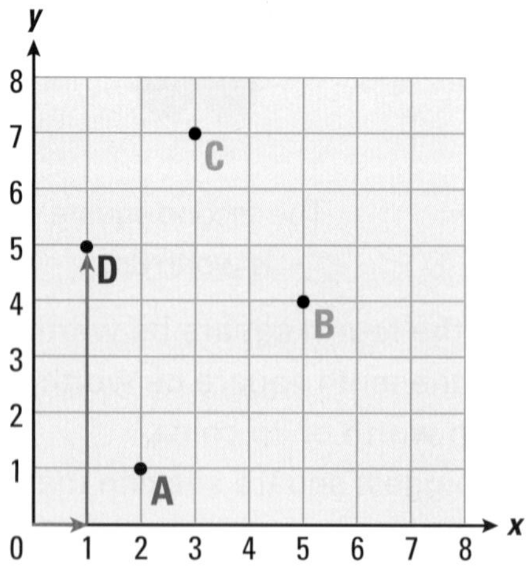

Exercise 10d

1 Write the coordinates for the things in this garden.

a rake
b flower
c spade
d tree
e chair
f rock

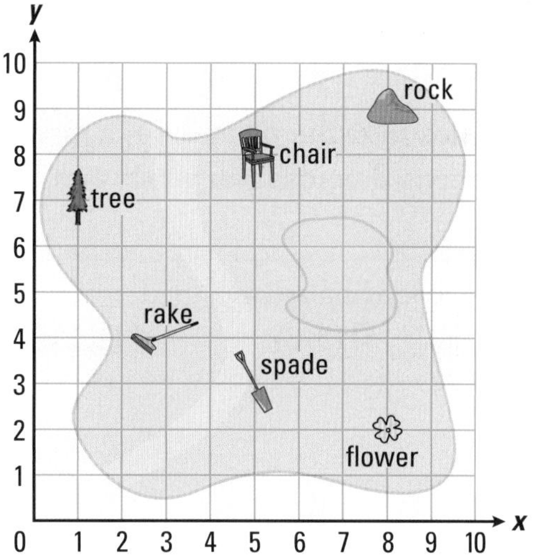

2 Write the coordinates of each point.

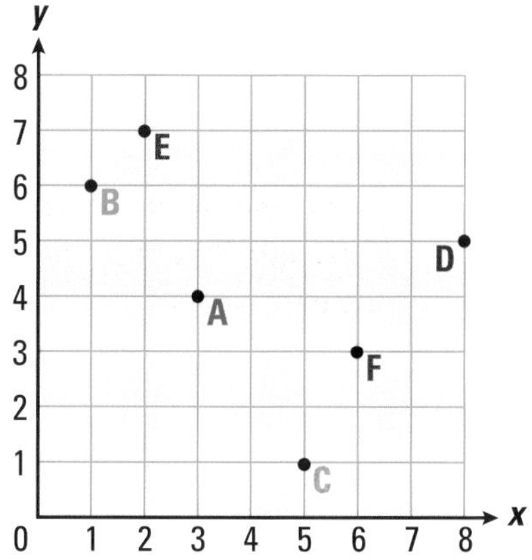

3 Copy the grid in question **2** without the points. Plot and label each of these points on your grid.

A (2, 3)
B (1, 1)
C (1, 6)
D (3, 6)
E (7, 8)
F (4, 1)
G (4, 4)
H (2, 8)

investigation

Write coordinates for each place on this map.

a Edinburgh
b Glasgow
c Uig
d Elgin
e Dundee

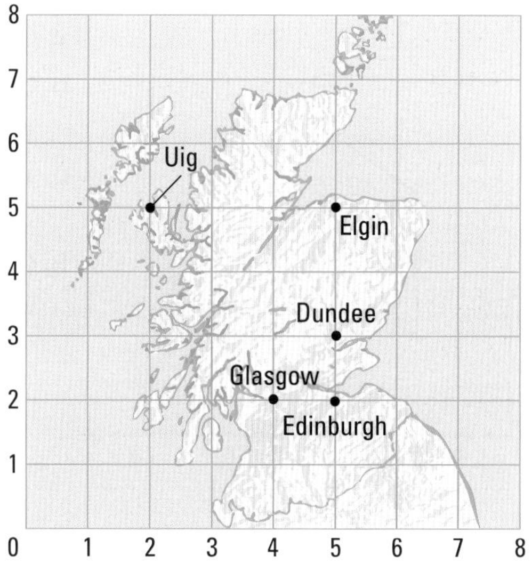

10e Coordinates and lines

- Plot points and connect them with straight lines.

Keywords
Coordinates
Plot
Straight line

- **Coordinates** give the position of a point on a gird.
  (3, 5) means **3** across the *x*-axis and **5** up the *y*-axis.

example

Plot these coordinates on a grid.
P (3, 5) **Q** (5, 3) **R** (2, 2)

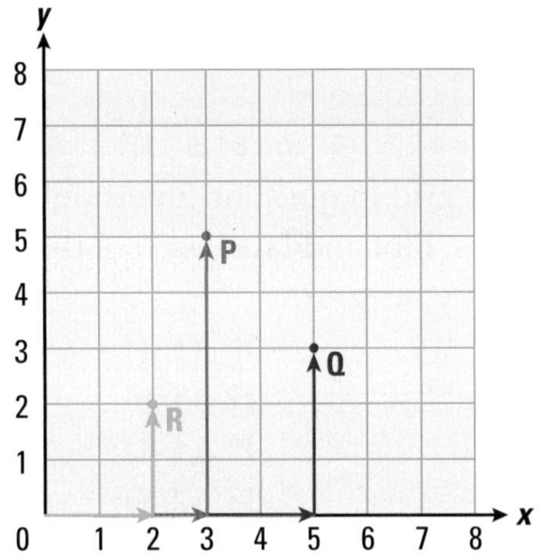

P go across 3, 5 up
Q go across 5, 3 up
R go across 2, 2 up

- You can connect plotted points with a **straight line.**

example

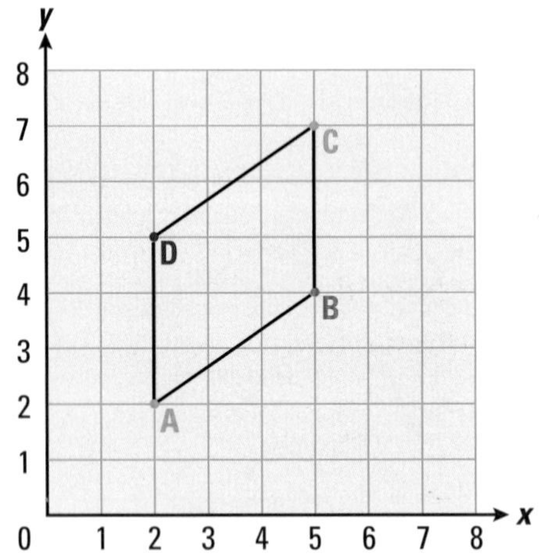

Plot these points on a grid.
A (2, 2) **B** (5, 4) **C** (5, 7) **D** (2, 5)

b Connect the coordinates, in order, with a straight line.
c What kind of shape have you drawn?

b Connect the points starting with **A**. Make sure your lines are straight!
c The shape is a parallelogram.

Exercise 10e

1 Copy this grid.
Plot and label each of these points.

A (2, 3) B (4, 1)
C (1, 2) D (3, 2)
E (6, 4) F (5, 7)

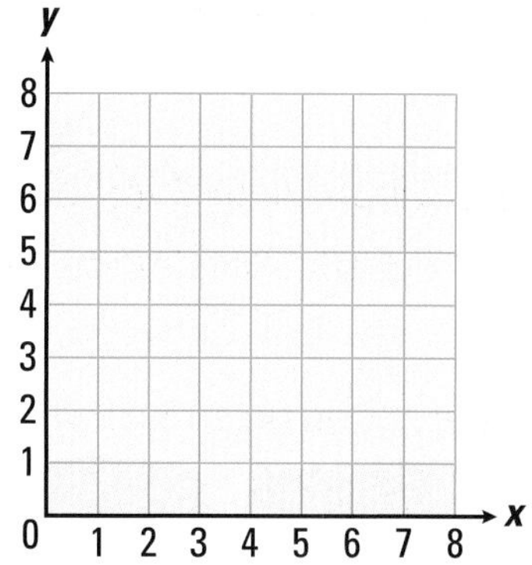

2 **a** Copy this grid. Plot and label each point.
A (1, 1)
B (1, 7)
C (5, 7)
D (9, 4)
E (5, 1)
b Join the coordinates in order to make a shape.
c What is the name of the shape?

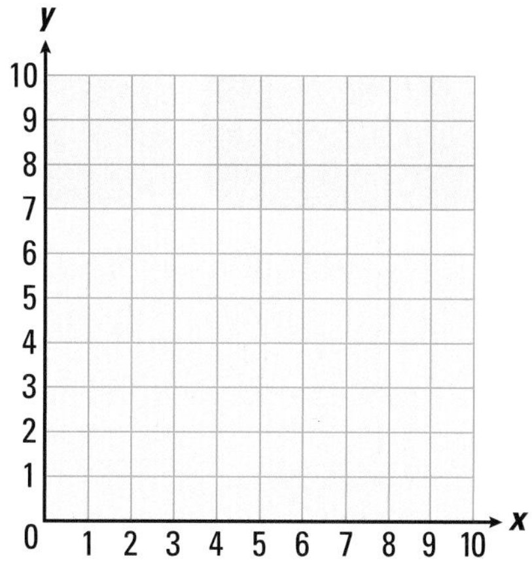

3 **a** Copy the grid from question **2** three times.
b Plot a set of these points on each grid.
c Connect the points in order with straight lines.
d Give the name of the shape you have drawn.
Set 1: A (4, 8), B (1, 6), C (4, 1), D (7, 6)
Set 2: E (4, 6), F (6, 1), G (1, 4), H (7, 4), I (2, 1), J (4, 6)
Set 3: K (2, 5), L (4, 6), M (6, 6), N (8, 5),
O (6, 2), P (4, 2), Q (2, 3), R (2, 5)

investigation

Data is plotted on line graphs as you have learned in Lesson 5d.
Look at the line graph for Question 1 on page 81 and write the data as a series of coordinates.

10f Reading graphs

- Understand line graphs for situations that change over time

Keywords
Graph
x-axis
y-axis

- You can often see a link between two things by looking at a **graph**.

This graph shows the link between time and the brightness of the firework.

When the firework is lit it starts to brighten slowly.

The firework is very bright for a short time.

It becomes dark again quickly.

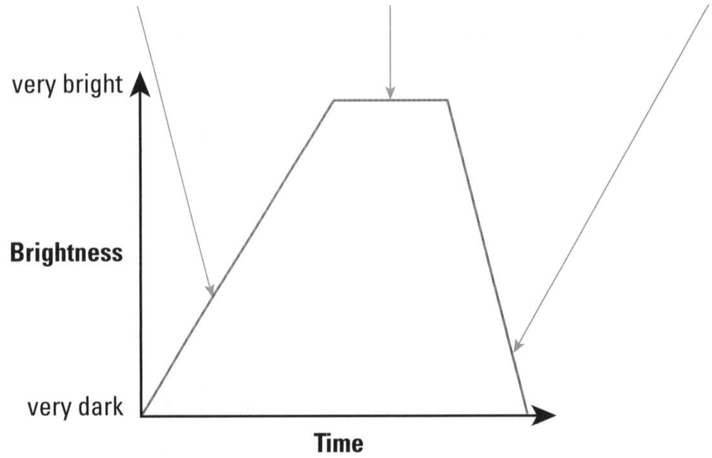

Time is on the ***x*-axis**.

Brightness is on the ***y*-axis**.

example

Match the graph with the correct description.

a A torch is turned on and it stays on.
b A torch flashes once.
c A torch flashes on/off and on/off.

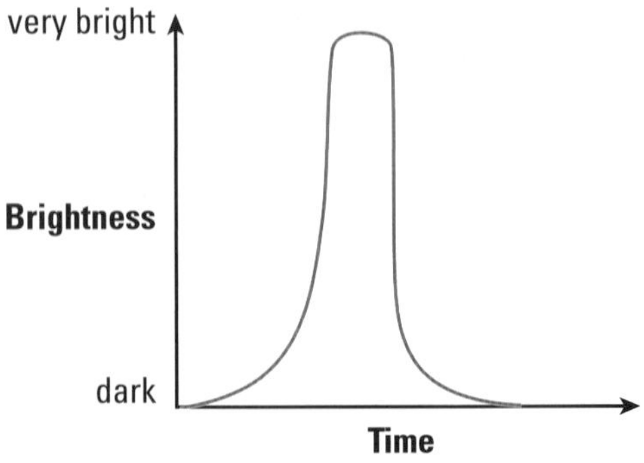

Answer **b** is correct because there is only one peak when the light is switched on.

Exercise 10f

1 Match each description with its correct graph.

a A car's indicator keeps flashing

b Cinema lights are dimmed quickly

c Cinema lights are dimmed slowly

d A light is turned on in a room

1

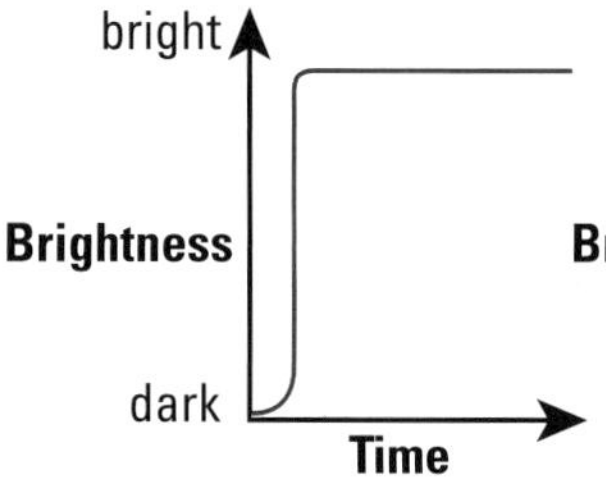

2

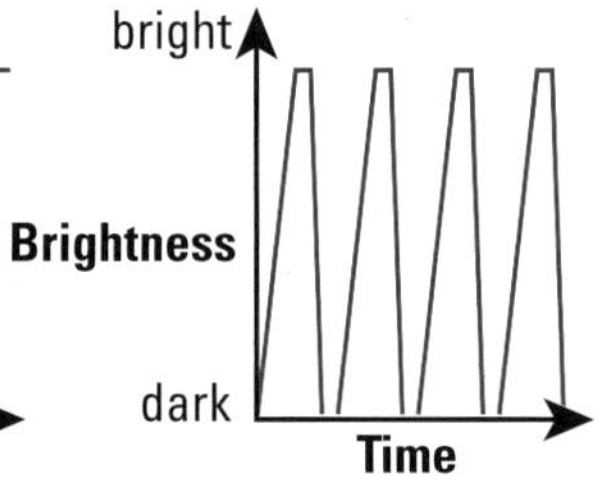

3

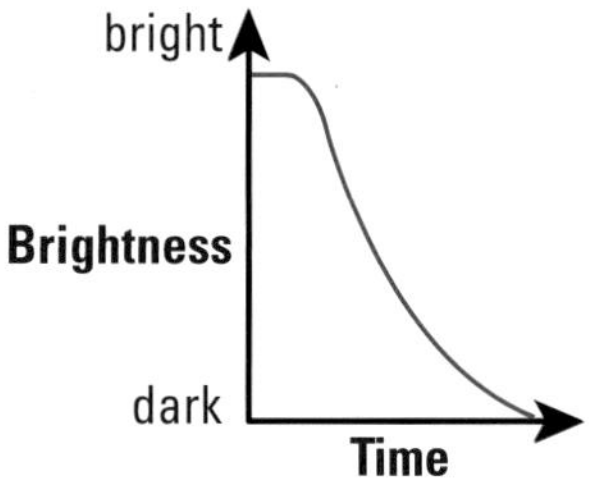

4

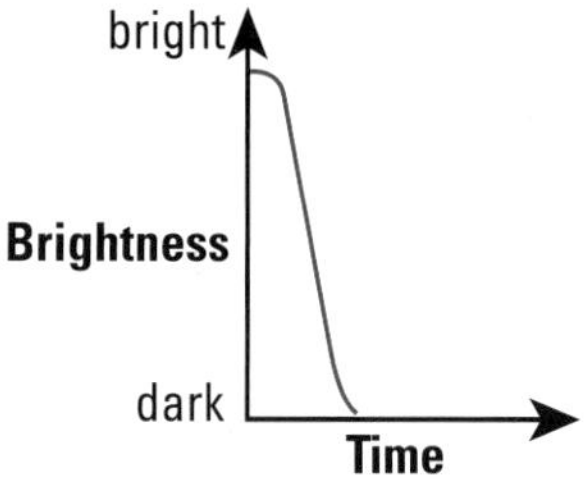

2 Match each description with a possible graph.

a The temperature slowly climbs from 0 °C

b The temperature rises and falls quickly

c The temperature starts high and falls very quickly

d The temperature climbs, stays the same for a while and climbs again

e The temperature starts above 0° and rises slowly.

f The temperature rises quickly, stays the same for a bit and then falls

1

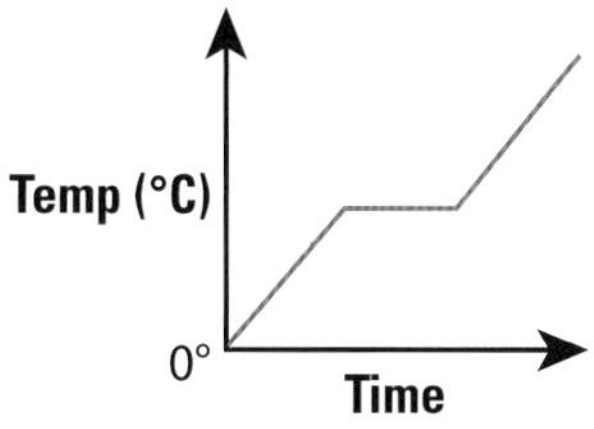

2

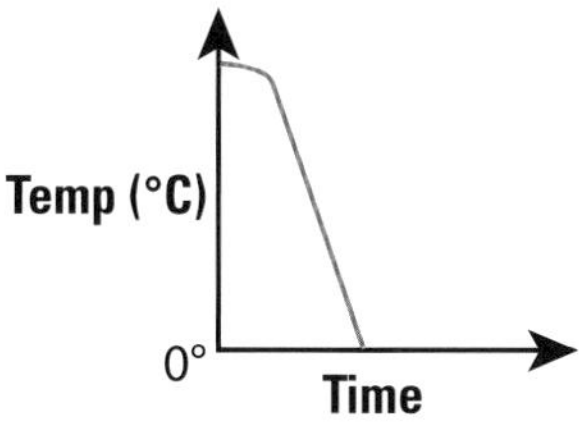

3

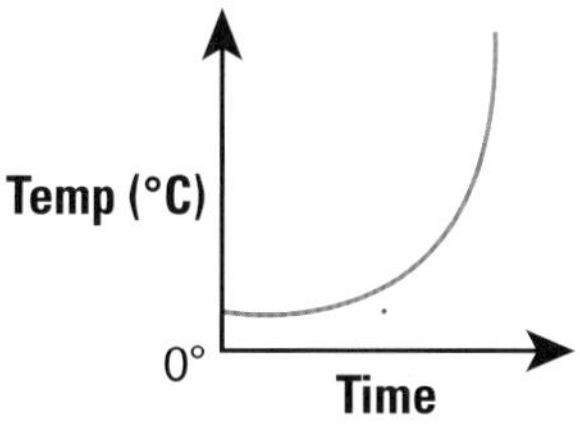

4

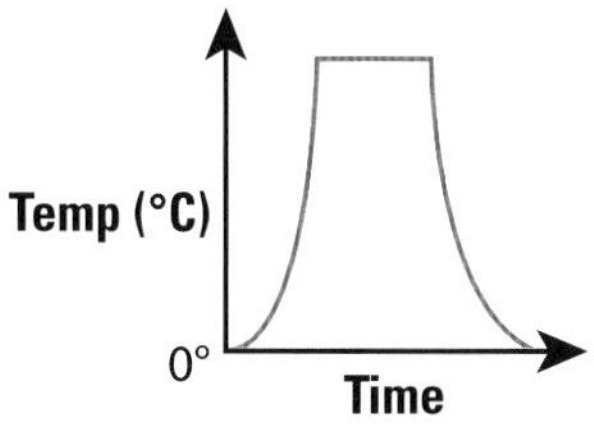

5

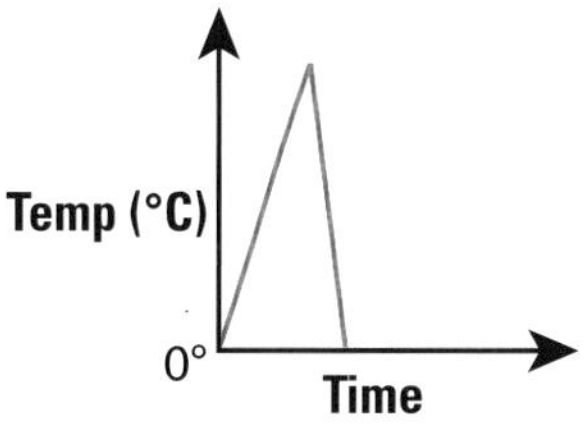

6

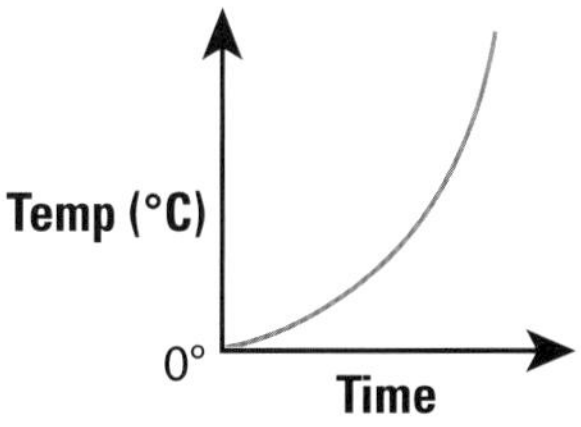

investigation

The graph shows a cyclist's journey to the park.

Write a short description of this journey.

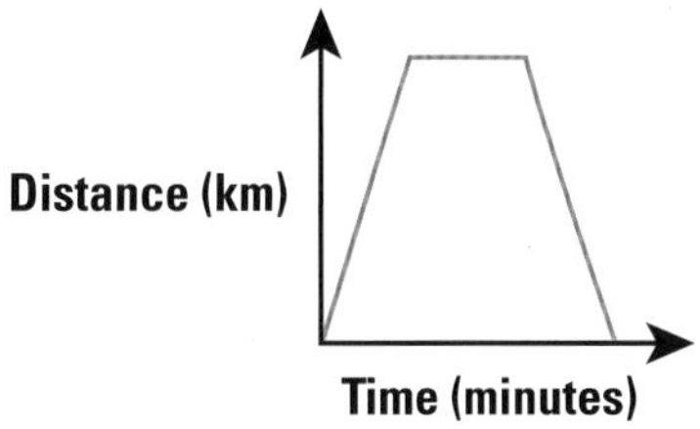

10a

1 Find the factors of each number.

a 28 b 30 c 42
d 32 e 50 f 56
g 40 h 48 i 54

10b

2 Copy the diagram to find these multiples.

a

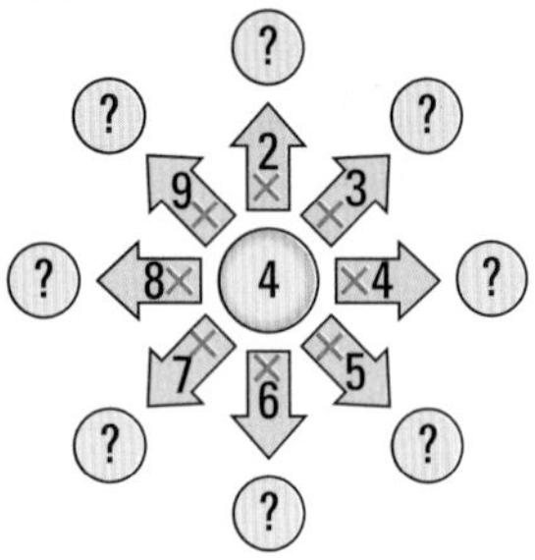

b

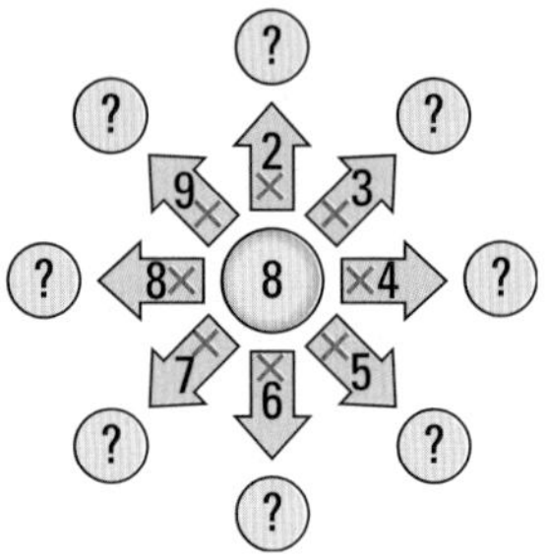

10c

3 Look at this list of numbers.
Which are square numbers and which are not?
What number is multiplied by itself to give the square numbers you have identified?

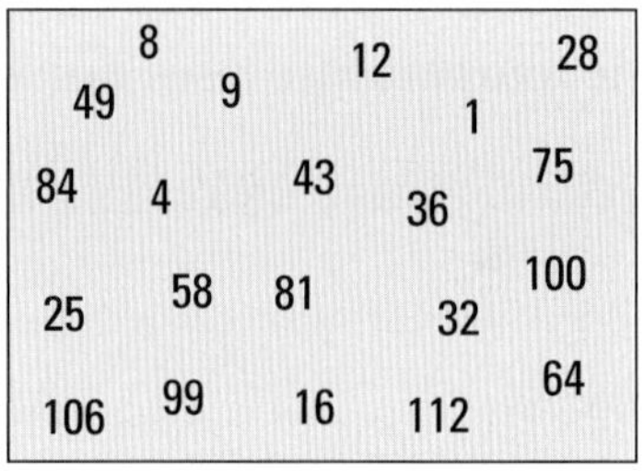

10d

4 Write the coordinates of each point.

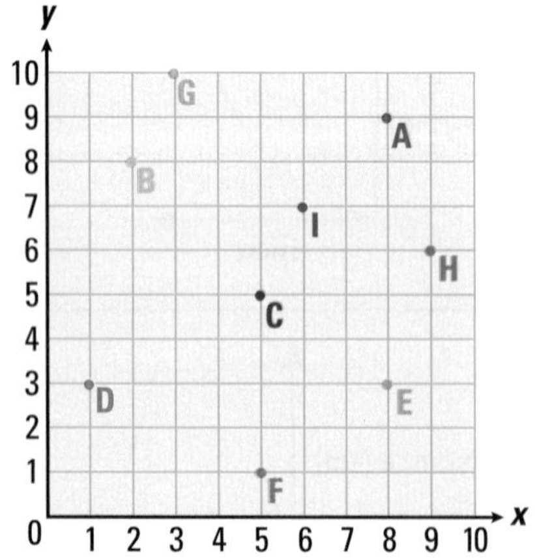

10e

5 For each part, plot the points given on a grid with axes labelled 1 to 10. Join each point to the next with a straight line and then suggest a name for the shape you have drawn.

a (5, 1), (5, 3), (0, 5), (0, 6), (5, 4), (5, 5), (10, 5), (10, 1), (5, 1)

b (1, 2), (1, 4), (0, 4), (0, 5), (7, 5), (8, 7), (9, 7), (10, 5), (10, 4), (9, 2), (8, 2), (7, 4), (3, 4), (3, 2), (1, 2)

10f

6 The graphs below show the relationship between time and the number of people in a theatre during a play. Match each of the descriptions with a possible graph.

a The play had no interval.

b Relatively few people went to the play and nearly all of them left the theatre during the interval. Most didn't come back.

c The second half of the play was much longer than the first half.

d Relatively few people left the theatre during the interval.

1

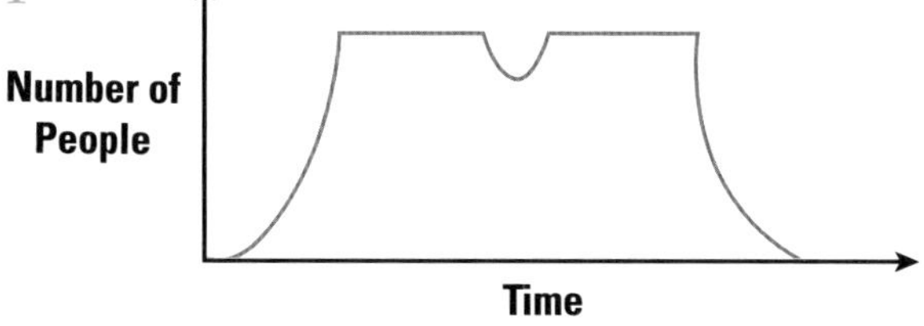

2

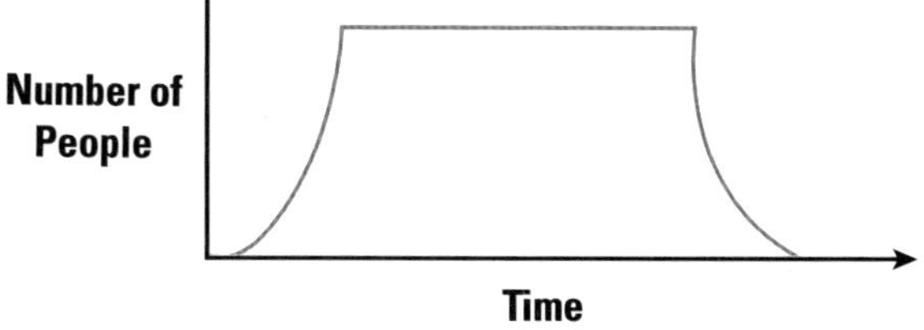

3

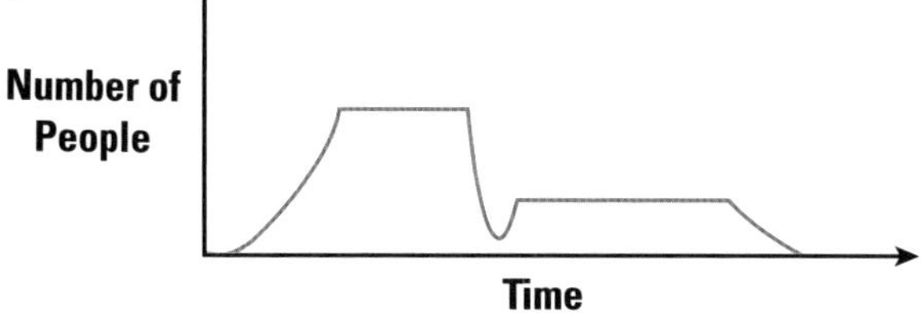

4

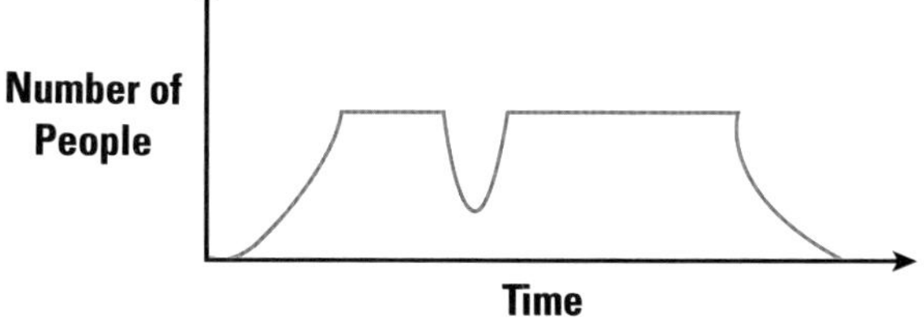

10 Summary

Key indicators

- Recognise multiples and factors Level 4
- Read and plot coordinates in the first quadrant Level 4

Level 4

1

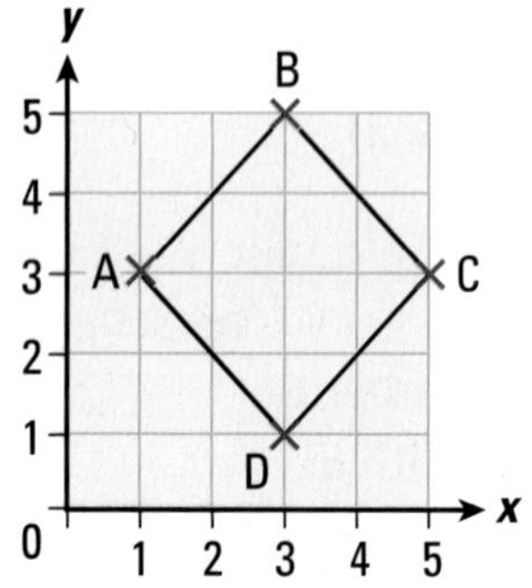

a Write down the coordinates of the points A, B, C and D.

b What is the name of shape ABCD?

Connor's answer ✔

Connor remembers *x* first, then *y*.

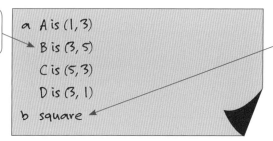

a A is (1, 3)
B is (3, 5)
C is (5, 3)
D is (3, 1)
b square

Connor recognises the shape because a square has 4 equal sides and 4 right angles.

Level 3

2 **a** A three-digit number is a multiple of 4.
What could the number be?
Give an example.
Now give a different example.

b A two-digit number is a factor of 100.
What could the number be?
Give an example.
Now give a different example.

Key Stage 3 2007 3–5 Paper 1

11 Number

Fractions, ratio and proportion

Baked beans are one of the healthiest foods you can eat. One serving can contain 5% of your daily fibre, 23 % of your daily protein and 13 % of your daily calcium intake. They also have a high proportion of healthy carbohydrates.

What's the point? Food products must contain nutritional guidance on their label. You need to understand percentages to make informed choices about your diet.

Check in

Level 3

1 What fraction of these beads is pink?

a 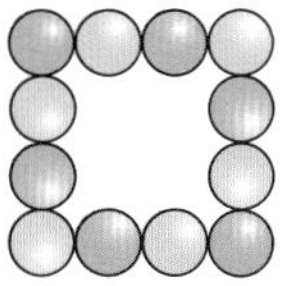

b 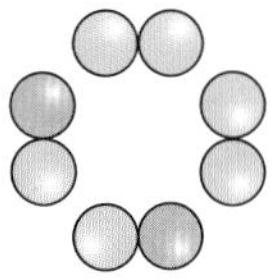

c 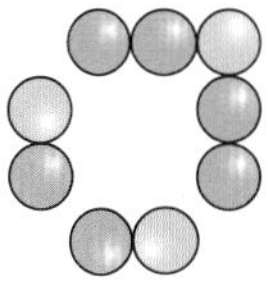

Level 4

2 Copy these boxes and match each mixed numbers with its improper fraction. The first one has been done for you.

$\frac{3}{2}$	$\frac{7}{4}$	$\frac{7}{2}$	$\frac{11}{3}$	$\frac{12}{5}$

$3\frac{1}{2}$	$3\frac{2}{3}$	$1\frac{1}{2}$	$1\frac{3}{4}$	$2\frac{2}{5}$

($\frac{3}{2}$ ↔ $1\frac{1}{2}$)

3 Use multiplication to complete these equivalent fractions.

a $\frac{1}{2} = \frac{\square}{100}$ **b** $\frac{1}{4} = \frac{\square}{100}$ **c** $\frac{1}{\square} = \frac{10}{100}$ **d** $\frac{\square}{4} = \frac{75}{100}$ **e** $\frac{4}{5} = \frac{\square}{100}$

Fractions and division

- Use simple division to find a fraction of a quantity

Keywords
Denominator Share
Divide
Numerator

When you find $\frac{1}{3}$ of something, you **share** it three ways.
This is the same as **dividing** by 3.

p. 58

$\frac{1}{3}$ of six sweets | a cake shared into thirds | $\frac{1}{3}$ of 15

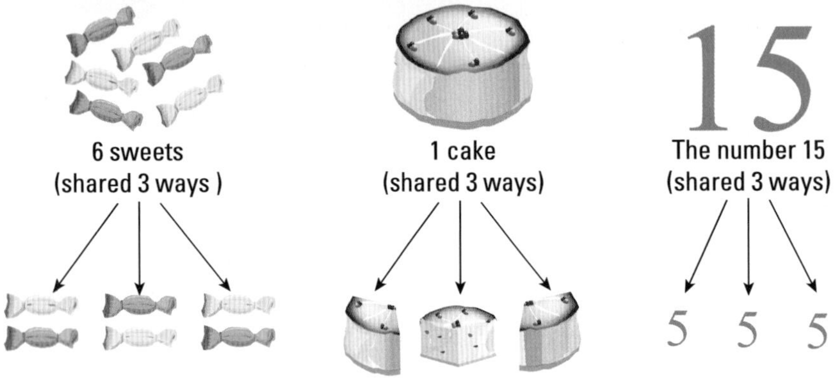

$6 \div 3 = 2$ | $1 \div 3 = \frac{1}{3}$ | $15 \div 3 = 5$

- When you find a fraction of an amount, you divide the amount by the **denominator**.

  $\frac{1}{5}$ of $25 = \frac{25}{5} = 25 \div 5 = 5$

example

Find $\frac{1}{3}$ of

a 9 kg

b 21 stamps

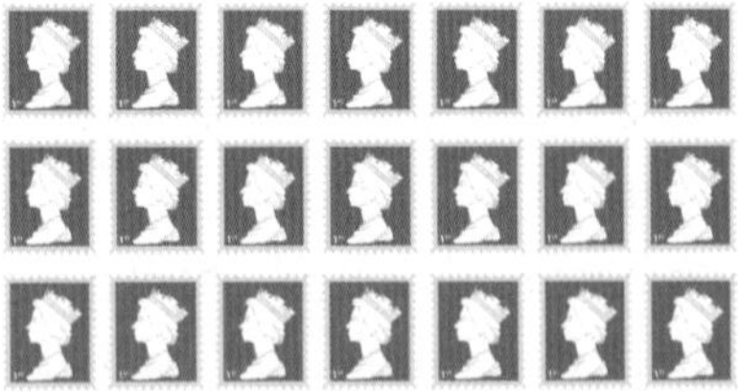

c 12 m

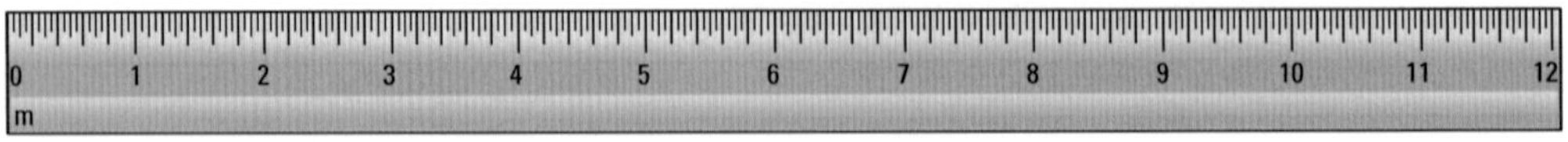

a 9 kg shared 3 ways is:
$9 \div 3 = 3$ kg
$\frac{1}{3}$ of 9 kg = 3 kg

b 21 stamps shared 3 ways is:
$21 \div 3 = 7$ stamps
$\frac{1}{3}$ of 21 stamps = 7 stamps

c 12 m shared 3 ways is:
$12 \div 3 = 4$ m
$\frac{1}{3}$ of 12 m = 4 m

Exercise 11a

1 Divide.

a $8 \div 2 = \square$ **b** $9 \div 3 = \square$ **c** $10 \div 5 = \square$ **d** $12 \div 4 = \square$ **e** $15 \div 3 = \square$

2 Copy and complete these statements.

a To find $\frac{1}{5}$ of an amount, divide by ____.

b To find $\frac{1}{10}$ of an amount, divide by ____.

c To find $\frac{1}{2}$ of an amount, divide by ____.

d To find $\frac{1}{8}$ of an amount, divide by ____.

e To find $\frac{1}{4}$ of an amount, divide by ____.

3 Here are groups of sweets.

a Find $\frac{1}{3}$

b Find $\frac{1}{4}$

c Find $\frac{1}{5}$

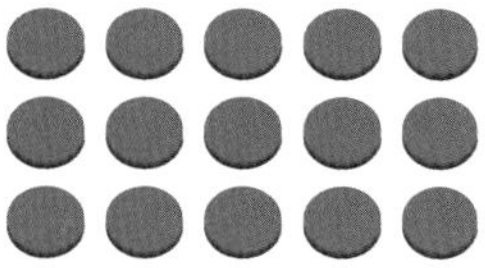

d Find $\frac{1}{2}$

e Find $\frac{1}{3}$

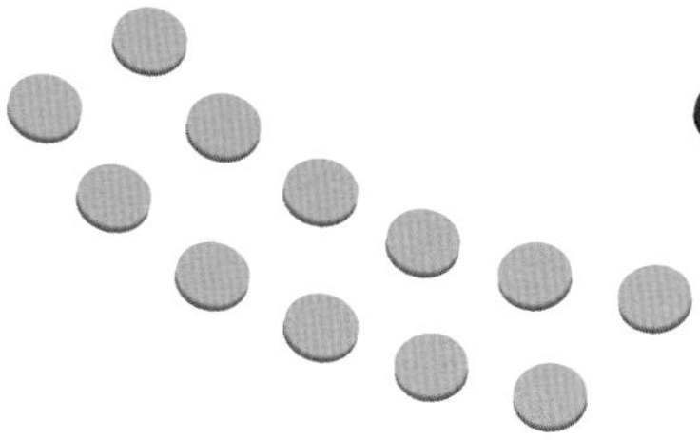

f Find $\frac{1}{4}$

4 Tracey is selling lemonade at the school fete.

a If one jug of lemonade fills eight glasses, what fraction of the lemonade does each glass hold?

b How many jugs of lemonade will Tracey need to make in total if she sells 64 glasses of lemonade?

problem

Harry has a new job as a cake tester!
Each time he 'tests' a cake he has to eat a slice that is $\frac{1}{5}$ of a cake.
At the end of the day Harry has tested 40 cakes.
How many whole cakes has he eaten?

11b Fractions of a quantity

- Use division to find multiple fractions of a quantity

Keywords
Fraction
Numerator

- Some fractions have 1 as a **numerator.**

  $\frac{1}{3}, \frac{1}{6}, \frac{1}{10}$

Find $\frac{1}{4}$ of 12 eggs.

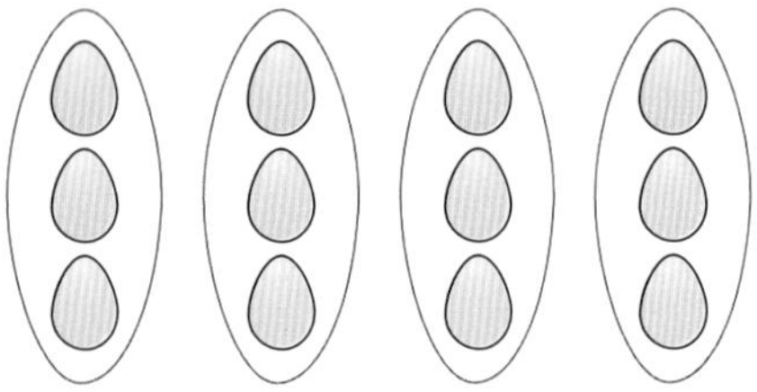

12 shared 4 ways is

$12 \div 4 = \frac{12}{4} = 3$

$\frac{1}{4}$ of 12 is 3.

example

What is $\frac{1}{3}$ of 15 eggs?

$\frac{1}{3}$ of $15 = \frac{15}{3}$

$15 \div 3 = 5$ $\qquad$ $\frac{1}{3}$ of 15 eggs is 5 eggs.

- Some fractions have a numerator greater than 1.

  $\frac{2}{3}, \frac{5}{6}, \frac{7}{10}$

Find $\frac{3}{4}$ of 12 eggs.

$\frac{1}{4}$ of 12 eggs $= 12 \div 4 = 3$ eggs

So $\frac{3}{4}$ will be 9 eggs.

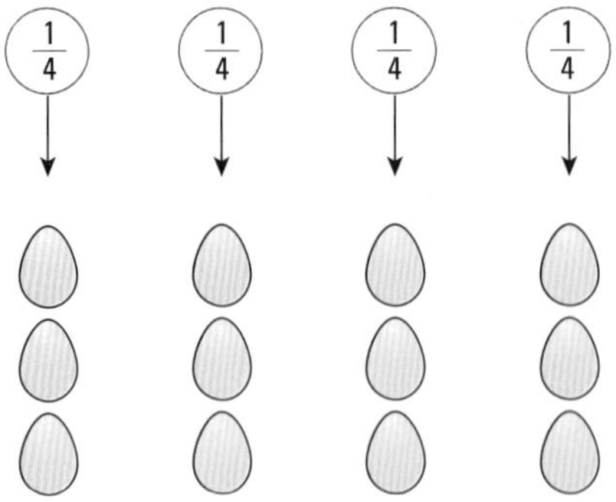

example

What is $\frac{2}{3}$ of 15 eggs?

$\frac{1}{3}$ of $15 = \frac{15}{3}$ $\quad$ $15 \div 3 = 5$ $\quad$ $\frac{1}{3}$ of 15 eggs $= 5$ eggs

$\frac{2}{3}$ of $15 = \frac{1}{3}$ of $15 + \frac{1}{3}$ of 15

$= 5 + 5 = 10$ eggs

Exercise 11b

1 Find $\frac{1}{2}$ of each amount.

a 6 **b** 12 **c** 20 **d** 100 **e** 30

2 Find $\frac{1}{3}$ of each amount.

a 9 **b** 12 **c** 21 **d** 30 **e** 36

3 Find $\frac{1}{4}$ of each amount.

a 12 **b** 24 **c** 16 **d** 40 **e** 36

4 Find $\frac{1}{5}$ of each amount.

a 15 **b** 25 **c** 50 **d** 40 **e** 100

5 Twenty people get onto a bus.

a $\frac{1}{4}$ of them support City.
How many support City?

b $\frac{1}{5}$ of them support Rovers.
How many support Rovers?

c How many of the people support neither City nor Rovers?

6 Here is a collection of buttons.

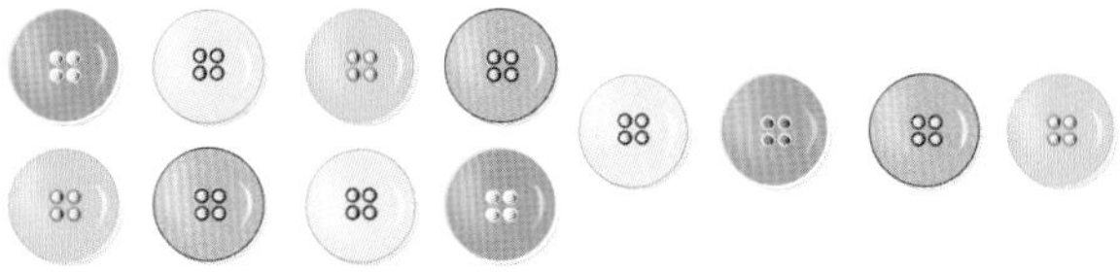

a Find $\frac{2}{3}$ of this group.

b Find $\frac{3}{4}$ of this group.

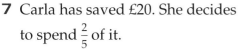

7 Carla has saved £20. She decides to spend $\frac{2}{5}$ of it.
How much does Carla spend?

8 In a class of 21 students, seven have a pet cat.
What is this as a fraction of the group?

task

There are 21 people in this group.

$\frac{2}{7}$ of this group voted 'Yes'.

$\frac{2}{3}$ of this group voted 'No'.

How many voted 'Don't know'?

Percentages

- Use number lines and fractions to find percentages of quantities

Keywords
Equivalent
Fraction
Percentage

- A **percentage** is a **fraction** out of 100.

  10% means $\frac{10}{100} = \frac{1}{10}$

p. 240

You can divide 20 marbles equally into 10 sections.

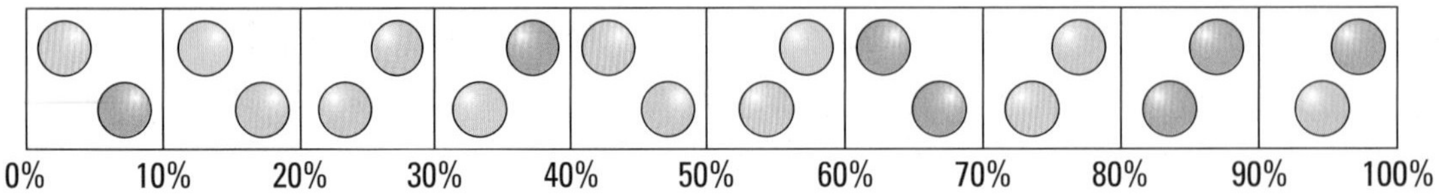

Each section is 10% or $\frac{1}{10}$ of the strip.

10% is **equivalent** to $\frac{1}{10}$.

There are two counters in each section.

10% of 20 counters = 2 counters $\quad \frac{1}{10}$ of 20 counters = 2 counters

20% of 20 counters = 4 counters $\quad \frac{2}{10}$ of 20 counters = 4 counters

50% of 20 counters = 10 counters $\quad \frac{1}{2}$ of 20 counters = 10 counters

50% is 5 sections out of 10. You can say that 50% = $\frac{1}{2}$.

This square is made from 100 squares.
Each square is 1% or $\frac{1}{100}$ of the whole.
The part shaded purple is 20% or $\frac{20}{100}$.
The part shaded orange is 5% or $\frac{5}{100}$.
The part left unshaded is

$100 - 20 - 5 = 75$ squares.

75 squares is 75% or $\frac{75}{100}$.

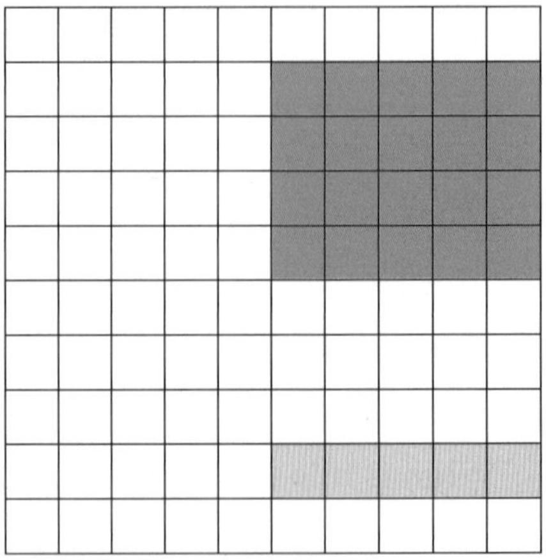

example

Find 50% of each amount.

a 100 litres **b** 60 kg **c** 24 students

50% is the same as $\frac{1}{2}$. So you need to find half of the amount.

a $\frac{1}{2}$ of 100 litres
$= 100 \div 2$
$= 50$ litres

b $\frac{1}{2}$ of 60 kg
$= 60 \div 2$
$= 30$ kg

c $\frac{1}{2}$ of 24 students
$= 24 \div 2$
$= 12$ students

Exercise 11c

1 Ravi surveyed his classmates and found that

a 40% of students in the class are boys.
What percentage are girls?

b 35% of students use cars to get to school.
What percentage does not use cars?

c 75% of students own a bicycle.
What percentage does not own a bicycle?

2 What percentage of each rod is painted red, and what percentage is blue?

a
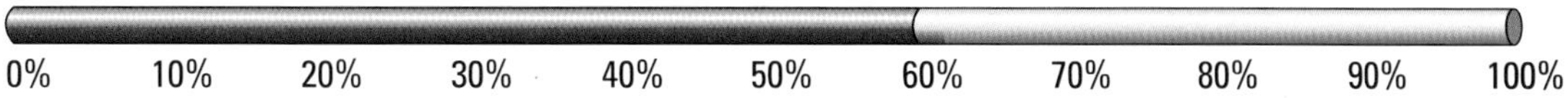

b
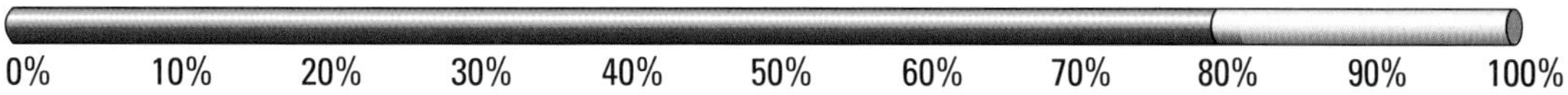

c
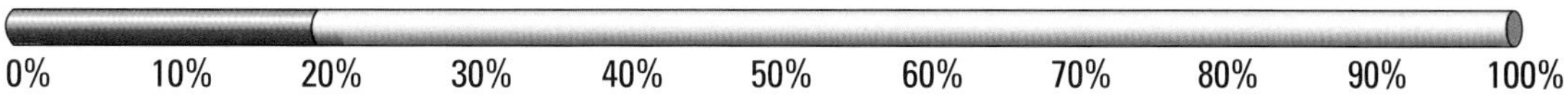

3 Thirty marbles are divided equally onto a percent strip.

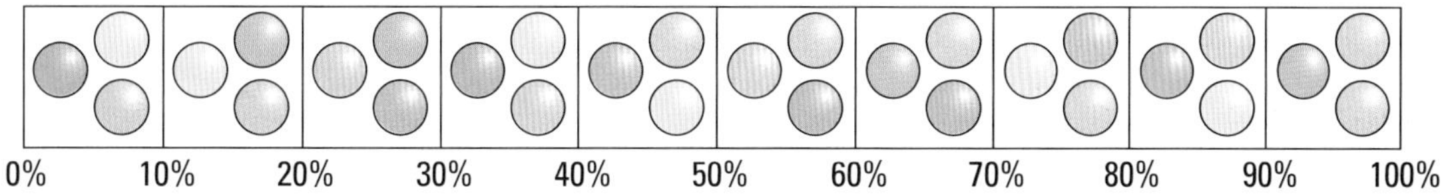

Copy and complete these percentage calculations.
Use the percent strip to help you.

100% = 1 whole

a 10% of 30   b 30% of 30   c 50% of 30
d 80% of 30   e 60% of 30   f 100% of 30

4 Find 50% of these amounts.

a £12   b 30 kg   c 90 days
d 50p   e 22 minutes   f 120 litres

5 Find 10% of these amounts.

a 100 litres   b 50 m   c 30 hours
d 90 kg   e £150   f 250 votes

problem

The small print on the carton says, 13% of the drink is juice.
What percentage is water?

11d Ratio and proportion

- Find and use simple ratios

Keywords
Proportion
Ratio
Whole

Ratio

Laura is making a necklace.
a **ratio** of two red beads to one gold bead.

2 : 1

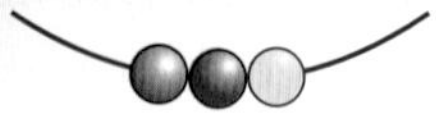

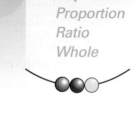

Laura continues...
a ratio of four red beads to two gold beads.

4 : 2

and again...
a ratio of six red beads to three gold beads.

6 : 3

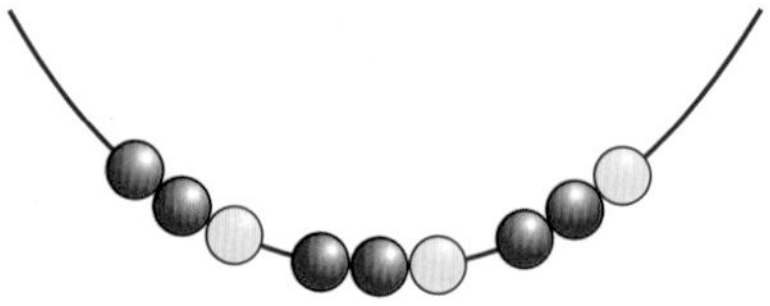

- The ratio tells you how many red beads you have for every gold bead.

Proportion

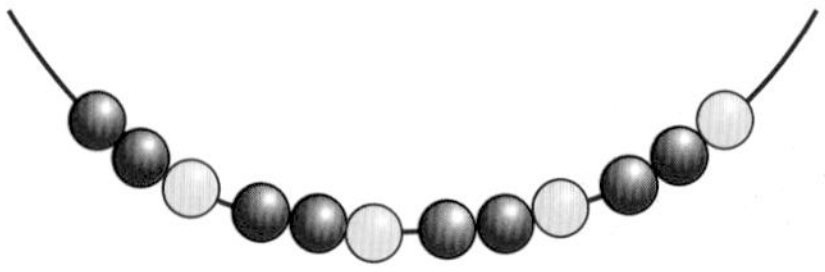

Laura looks at the finished necklace.

There are 12 beads in total:
eight red beads and four gold beads.

The **proportion** of gold beads is 4 out of 12. $\frac{4}{12}$ or $\frac{1}{3}$

The proportion of red beads is 8 out of 12. $\frac{8}{12}$ or $\frac{3}{4}$

- A proportion tells what part of a **whole** something is.
  It can be written as a fraction, a decimal or a percentage.

example

a What is the ratio of blue beads to green beads?
b What proportion of the beads are green?

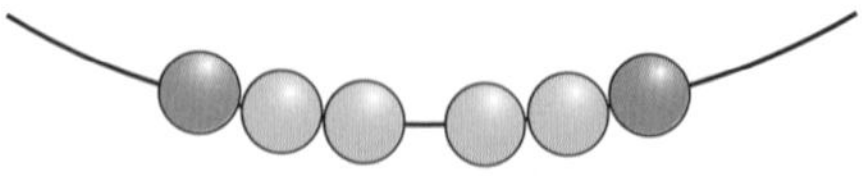

a There are 2 blue beads and 4 green beads.
The ratio of blue beads to green beads is:

$$2 : 4 \xrightarrow{\div 2 \quad \div 2} 1 : 2$$

b There are 4 green beads out of 6 total beads.
The proportion is 4 out of 6, which is $\frac{4}{6}$ or $\frac{2}{3}$.

Exercise 11d

1 For each of these drawings, give
 i the number of apples
 ii the number of oranges
 iii the ratio of apples to oranges.

apples : oranges

a 
b 
c 
d 
e 
f 
g 
h 

2 What proportion of the striped rod is painted green?
Give your answer as a fraction

3 Micah is mixing red and yellow paint to make orange.
To make orange, he mixes 3 tins of yellow to 1 tin of red.

a What is the ratio of red paint to yellow paint?

b Micah has two tins of red paint. How many tins of yellow paint will he use to mix orange?

4 Micah now mixes green.
For each tin of yellow paint he uses two tins of blue paint.

a What is the ratio of yellow paint to blue paint?

b Micah has three tins of yellow paint. How many tins of blue paint will he use to mix green?

c As a fraction, what proportion of the paint is yellow?

problem

There are 20 sweets in a box.
Give your answers as a fraction.
a What proportion of the sweet wrappers are red?
b What proportion of the sweet wrappers are green?
c What proportion of the sweet wrappers are gold?
Can you simplify any of your answers?

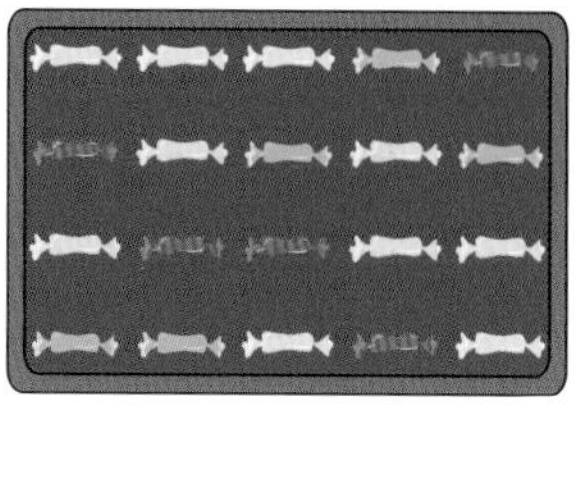

11d[2] Ratio and proportion problems

- Find and use simple proportions

Keywords
Diagram
Proportion
Ratio

Tom is making a necklace.
Two blue beads for every three red beads.
A **ratio** of 2 : 3

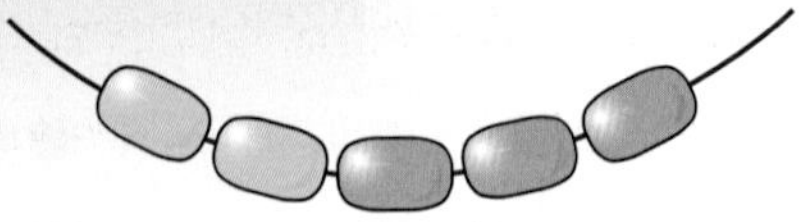

His necklace has 15 beads in total.

The **proportion** of **blue** beads is six out of 15.

$$\frac{6}{15} = \frac{2}{5} \quad (\div 3)$$

The proportion of **red** beads is nine out of 15.

$$\frac{9}{15} = \frac{3}{5} \quad (\div 3)$$

example

a If Tom's necklace continued, what colour would the 20th bead be?
b If the necklace had 25 beads, how many of them would be red?

?

a B B R R R   B B R R R   B B R R R   B B R R (R)
5 beads   5 beads   5 beads   5 beads

The 20th bead will be red.

b For each group of five beads, three are red.
25 beads make five groups.
5 groups × 3 red beads
= 15 beads.

Blue beads	Red beads	Number of beads
2	3	5
4	6	10
6	9	15
8	12	20
10	15	25

There will be 15 red beads in a necklace of 25 beads.

Exercise 11d^2

1 Sarah threads beads onto a string.
She records the number and colour of beads in a table.

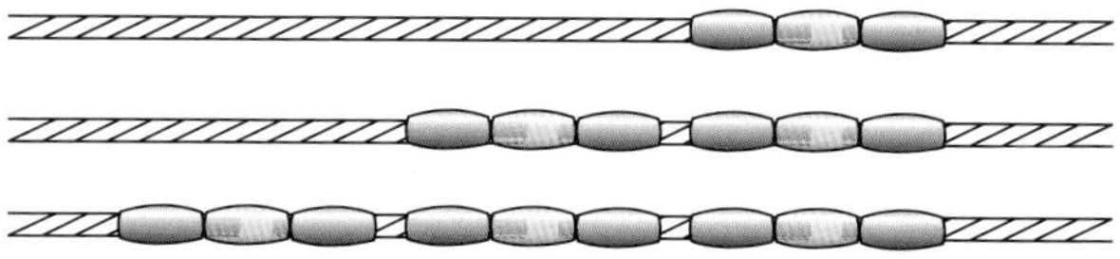

Gold	Green	Total number
1	2	3
2	4	6
3	6	9

a What is the ratio of gold beads to green beads?
b Copy and continue the table by adding three more rows.
c What colour will the 15th bead be?
d As a simple fraction, green beads are what proportion?

2 This is a recipe for salad dressing

6 parts vinegar
2 parts oil
1 part lemon juice
1 part chopped herbs

a When mixed, how many parts of dressing will there be in total?
b What proportion of the dressing is oil?
c What proportion of the dressing is vinegar?

Did you know?

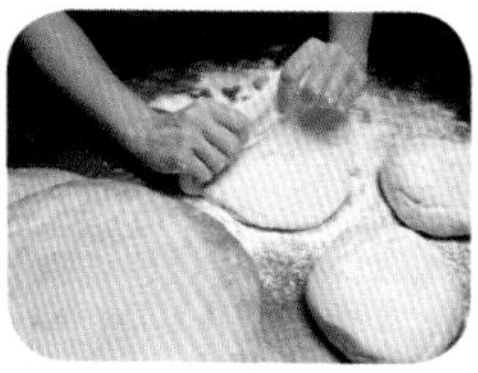

When you use a recipe the ingredients are mixed in **proportion.**

3 This is a recipe for short crust pastry

8 parts flour
5 parts butter
2 parts water
1 part sugar

a As a simple fraction, what proportion of the pastry is flour?
b As a simple fraction, what proportion of the pastry is water?
c Max needs to make a large amount of pastry.
He starts with 40 parts flour.
List how many parts butter, water and sugar he will add.

challenge

This is a stained glass window in the village hall.

a What is the ratio of colours, **blue** to **red** to **yellow**?
? : ? : ?

b As a fraction, what proportion of the whole pattern is blue?

11 Consolidation

11a

1 Share these counters into 2 groups.

a There are ___ counters in each group.

b As a fraction, each group is $\frac{?}{?}$ of the total.

2 What is

a $\frac{1}{10}$ of 30 **b** $\frac{1}{2}$ of 24 **c** $\frac{1}{5}$ of 30 **d** $\frac{1}{4}$ of 24 **e** $\frac{1}{8}$ of 24

3 Share these counters into 4 groups.

a There are ___ counters in each group.

b As a fraction, each group is $\frac{?}{?}$ of the total.

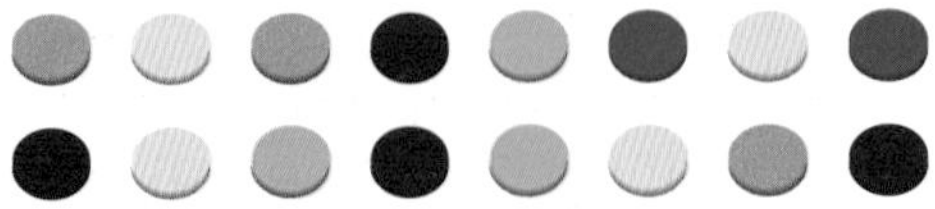

11b

4 25 counters are shared out onto this grid.

a How many counters are there in $\frac{1}{5}$ of the grid?

b How many counters are there in $\frac{3}{5}$ of the grid?

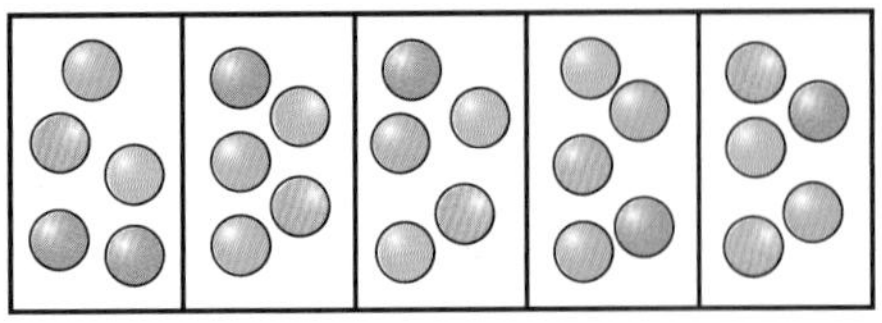

5 Find

a $\frac{2}{5}$ of 10 **b** $\frac{2}{3}$ of 15 **c** $\frac{3}{4}$ of 12 **d** $\frac{3}{10}$ of 20 **e** $\frac{3}{5}$ of 20

11c

6 40 teachers are surveyed about the time that school starts each morning. Use the percent strip below to help you.

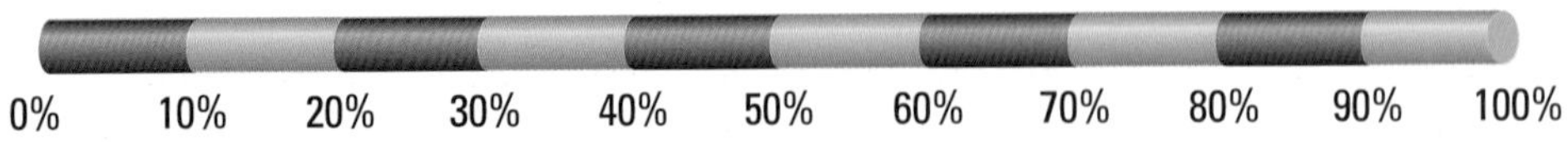

a 40% vote for an earlier start. How many vote for this?

b 30% vote to keep the same start time. How many vote for this?

c 20% vote for a later start. How many vote for this?

d 10% vote 'Don't Know'. How many vote for this?

7 100 students are surveyed about the time that school starts each morning.

a 7% vote for an earlier start. How many vote for this?

b 23% vote to keep the same start time. How many vote for this?

c 61% vote for a later start. How many vote for this?

d 9% vote 'Don't Know'. How many vote for this?

8 Give each of these ratios in its simplest form.

a 14:16 b 3:9 c 10:15 d 5:25 e 24:40 f 27:36

9 Coloured tiles are used to make a pattern.

a What is the ratio of yellow tiles to blue tiles?

b When the tiling is finished, what proportion of the tiles are blue? (Show as a simple fraction)

10 Coloured tiles are used to make another pattern.

a What is the ratio of red tiles to green tiles?

b As a fraction, what proportion of the finished tiling is red?

c As a fraction, what proportion of the finished tiling is green?

11 a Three sisters, Jean, Rita and Barbara, live near to each other. Then decide to take their families to see their brother George. During the journey Jean's car consumed 10 litres of petrol, Rita's consumed 12 litres and Barbara's consumed 14 litres. Express the figures as a ratio in its simplest form.

b The three sisters decide to take their families to see their other brother Tony, who lives further away than George. If Jean's car uses up 15 litres of petrol for this journey, how much is used up by **i** Rita's car **ii** Barbara's car?

11 Summary

Key indicators

- Multiply a fraction by a whole number Level 4
- Understand percentage as the number of parts in every 100 Level 4
- Find a simple percentage of small whole numbers Level 4

Level 3

1 calculate **a** $\frac{1}{2}$ of 30

b $\frac{1}{3}$ of 30

c $\frac{2}{3}$ of 30

Amal's answer ✔

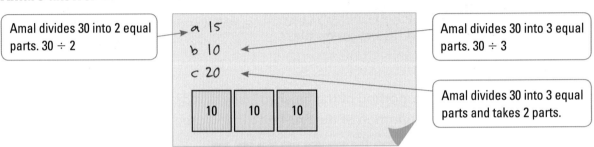

Amal divides 30 into 2 equal parts. 30 ÷ 2

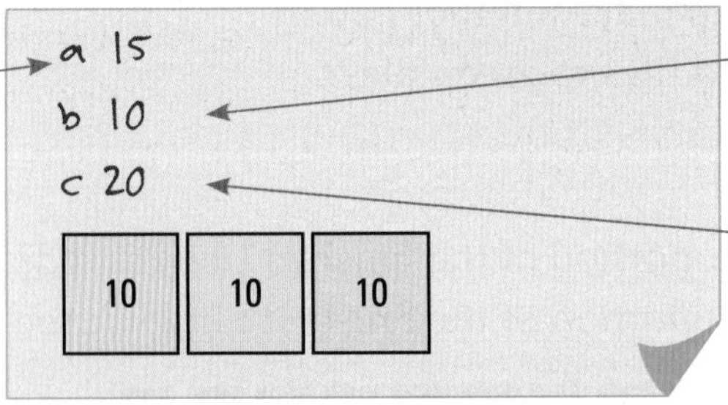

Amal divides 30 into 3 equal parts. 30 ÷ 3

Amal divides 30 into 3 equal parts and takes 2 parts.

Level 4

2 Molly asked the students in her class how many pets they had.
She recorded her results on a pie chart.

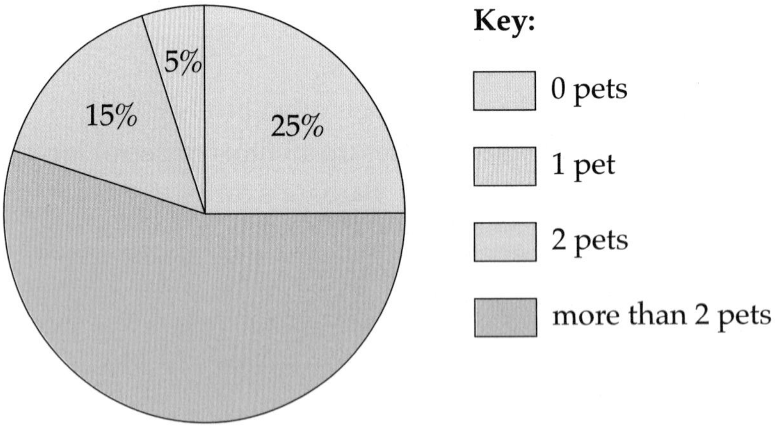

a What percentage of students had only one pet?

b There are 20 students in the class.
How many students had 0 pets?

Year 7 2007 3–4 Paper 1

12 Algebra

Symbols and expressions

Credit cards can be used as payment instead of cash. However, you are then in debt to the credit card company and must pay the money back to them. If you don't pay all of the debt you owe, you end up paying back more money.

What's the point? Credit card companies use complex expressions and equations to determine how much you owe.

Check in

Level 4

1 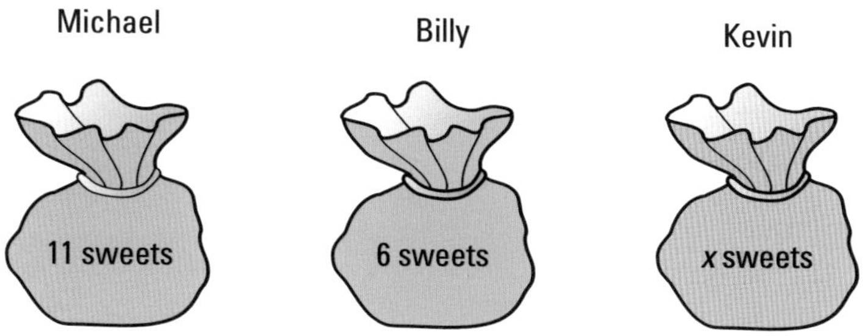

Three brothers each have a bag of sweets. Anne gives each brother 4 more sweets. Write a sum to work out the total number of sweets for each brother.

Level 5

2 A shelf can contain y books.

a How many books will there be in a cupboard containing 6 of these shelves?

b Kathleen removes 3 books from one shelf. How many books are left on that shelf?

3 Substitute and work out these expressions if $k = 8$.

a $k + 4$ **b** $k - 5$ **c** $10 - k$ **d** $3 \times k$ **e** $k \div 2$

12a Using symbols

- Use letters to stand for numbers

Keywords
Represent
Symbol

- Letters can be used as symbols for numbers.

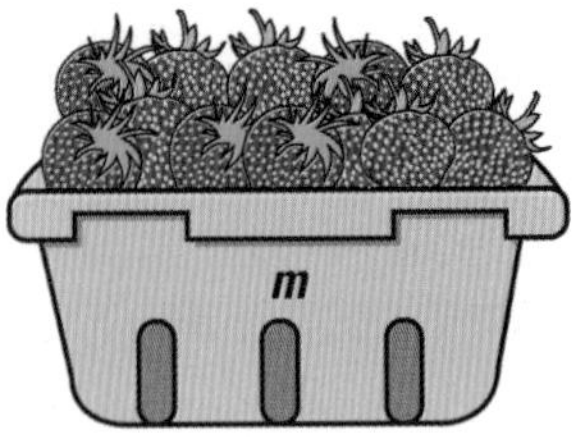

Sam doesn't know how many strawberries are in this box.
He uses the symbol m to represent the number of strawberries.

Take away four strawberries
$m - 4$ strawberries

Add 5 strawberries
$m + 5$ strawberries

Double the strawberries
$\mathbf{2} \times m$ strawberries
$\mathbf{2} \times m = 2m$

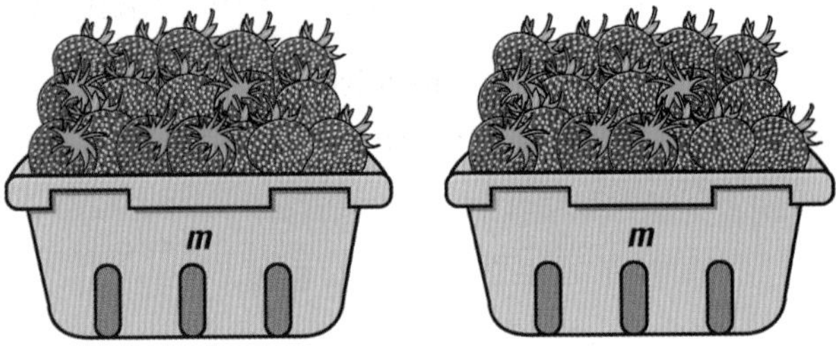

Jo has another box of strawberries.
She says, 'I have n strawberries in my box.'

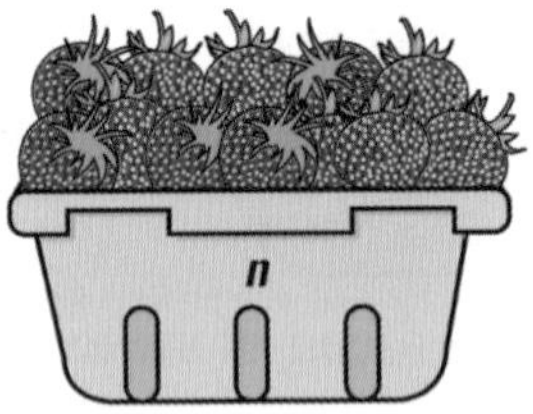

Sam and Jo add together their strawberries.

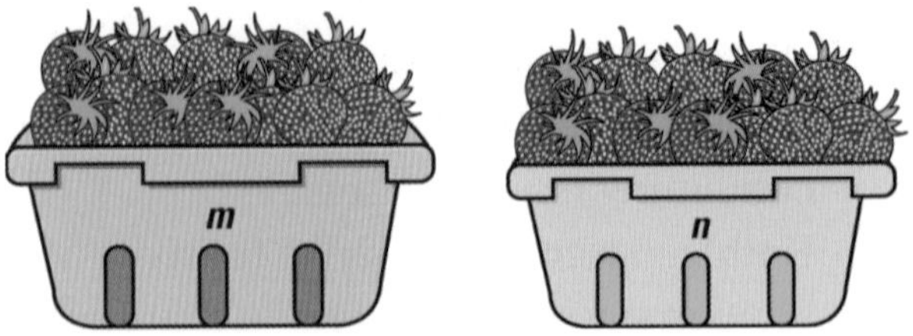

p. 248 They have $m + n$ strawberries altogether.

Exercise 12a

Start each question with *m* strawberries.

1 There are m strawberries in a box.
How many strawberries will there be in total if you

a add 1	**b** add 3	**c** take away 6
d take away 12	**e** add 50	**f** halve them
g multiply by 3	**h** add p strawberries	**i** take away s strawberries?

2 In each of these questions there are x cakes to start with.
Work out how many cakes there are after these questions.

a Susan takes six of the cakes. How many are left?

b Nick bakes 20 more cakes and adds them to the rest. How many are there now?

c Nina works very hard and makes three times the starting number of cakes. How many cakes has she made?

d If you add Nina's cakes to Nick's cakes, how many will there be altogether?

3 This piece of string is 30 cm long.

a If Sarah cuts off p cm from one end, what length is left?

b If she cuts another p cm, how much string is left?

4 **a** There are b soldiers in a row.
How many soldiers will there be in 12 rows?

b If each row is increased by three more soldiers, what is the new number of soldiers in each row?

5 **a** Jack picks x kg of apples. Derek picks y kg.
How much do they pick altogether?

b 10 kg of the apples are bruised and have to be thrown away. What weight of apples is left?

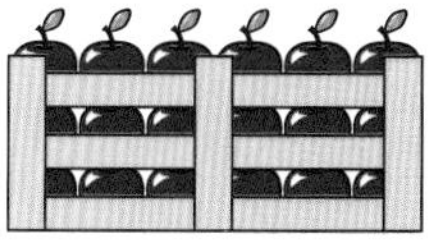

challenge

Each box holds 12 tea cups.
Each crate holds y saucers.
What should y be so each tea cup has a saucer?

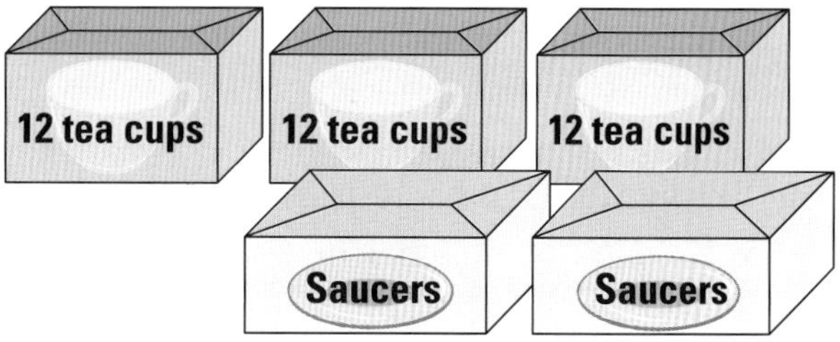

12b Adding with symbols

- Add 'like terms' together

Keywords
Like
Symbol
Unlike

If things are the same sort, they are **like.** If things are different, they are **unlike.**

These are both cows.

5 cows + 6 cows = 11 cows

The cow and farmer are different.

4 farmers + 3 cows = 4 farmers + 3 cows

These are all x's. They are like symbols.

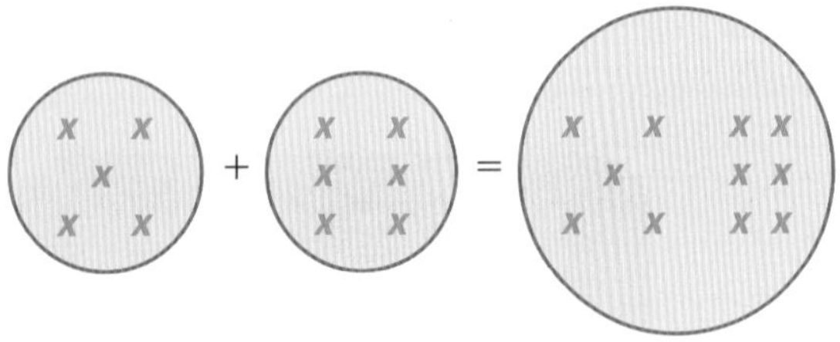

- You can add **like symbols** together.
  $5x + 6x = 11x$.

These are a mixture of x's and y's. They are unlike symbols.

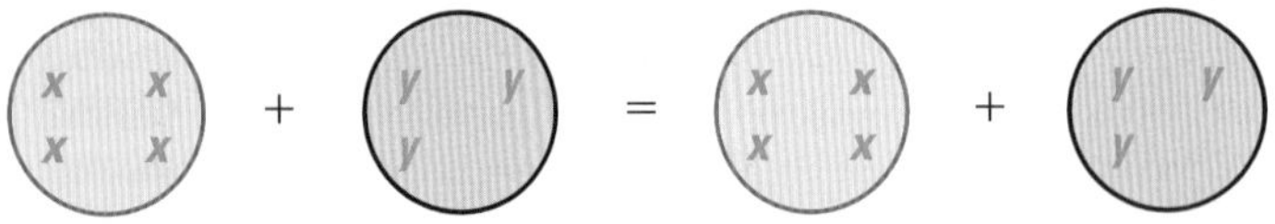

- You cannot add **unlike symbols** together.
  $4x + 3y = 4x + 3y$

example

Add the like symbols in each question.

a $5x + 7x$ **b** $15y + 4h$

a $5x + 7x = 12x$ Like symbols can be added.

b $15y + 4h$ Unlike symbols cannot be added.

Exercise 12b

1 Add these numbers together in your head.

a $3 + 1 + 4$ b $2 + 6 + 3$ c $4 + 5 + 6$

d $12 + 10 + 9$ e $15 + 3 + 20$ f $22 + 1 + 7$

g $19 + 12 + 1$ h $2 + 6 + 22$ i $29 + 3 + 15$

2 Add together the symbols in each ring.

a

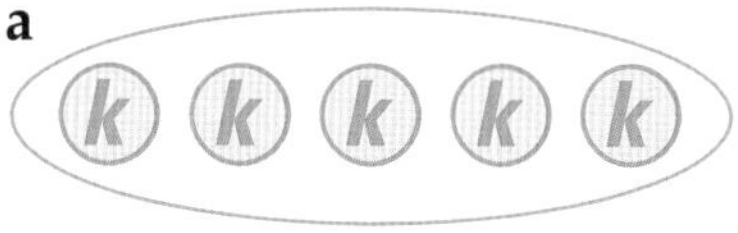

b

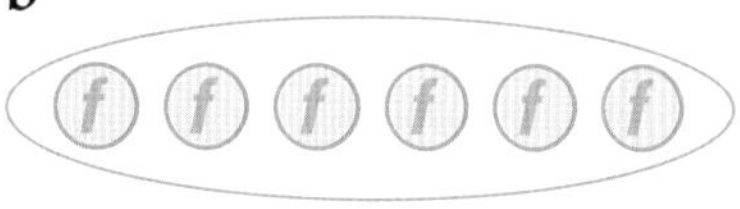

c

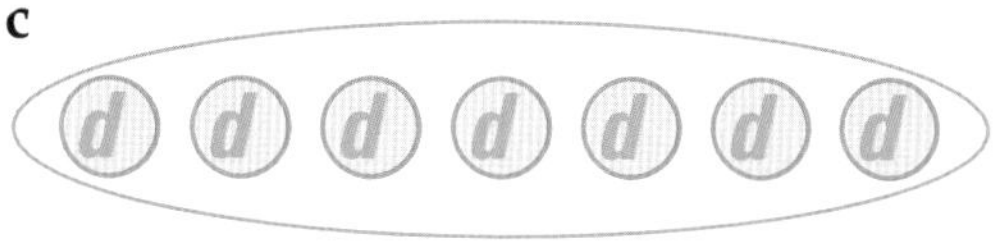

d

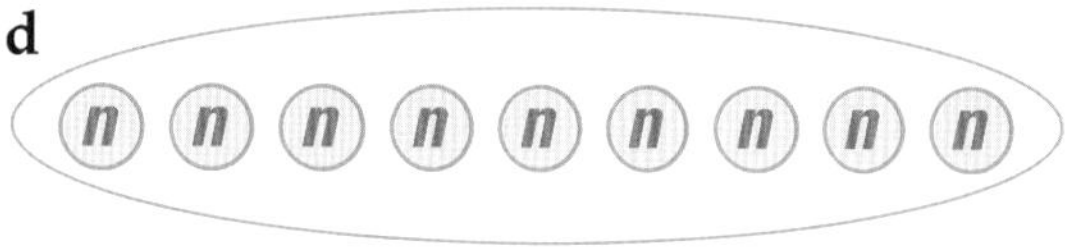

3 Find the weights shown on the scales by adding the like symbols together.

a

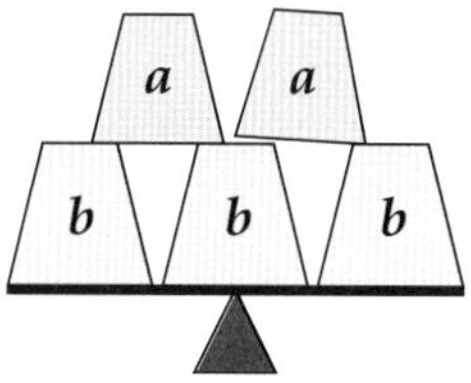

b

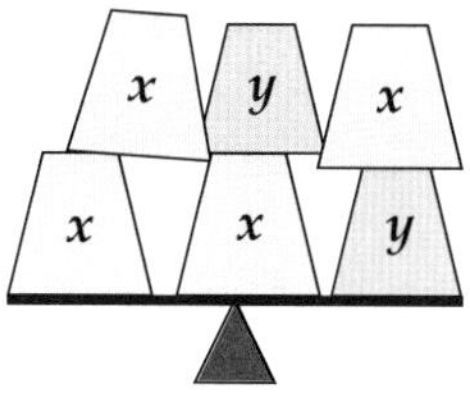

c

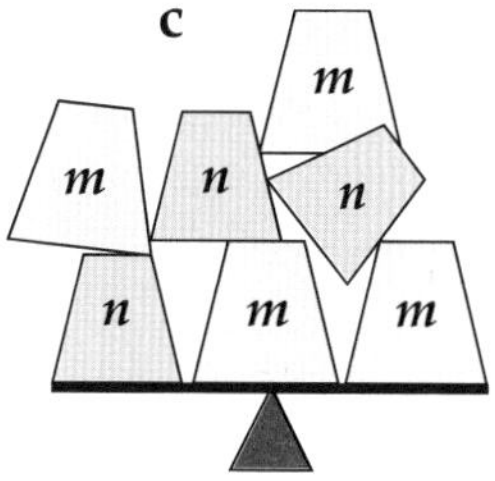

4 Add like symbols in each of these.

a $2m + 5m$ b $50f + 25f$ c $22d + 12d$

d $10k + 5k$ e $14y + 7y$ f $20z + 4z$

g $14g + 4g + 2g$ h $4q + 4q + 2q$ i $6y + 3y + 30y$

j $27w + 5w + 2w$ k $14b + 6b + 2b$ l $45j + 15j + 5j$

5 Write if each of these questions have like or unlike symbols. Add together the like symbols.

a $4m + 5m$ b $3s + p$ c $x + y$

d $x + 2x$ e $2s + 3s$ f $2p + 2r$

challenge

What is the perimeter of this rugby pitch?
What is the perimeter of a real life rugby pitch?
Use the Internet to find out.

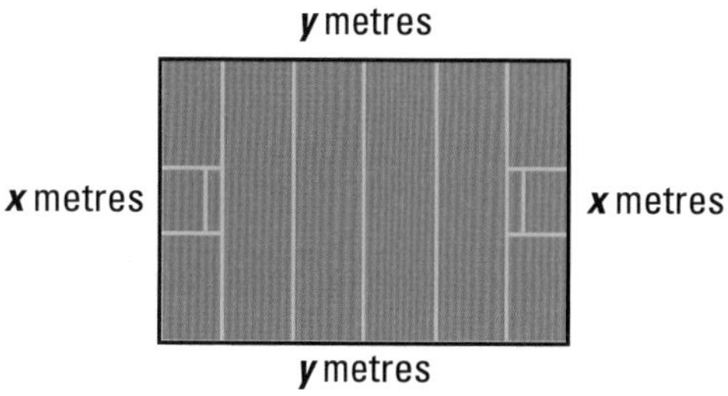

12c Simplifying symbols

- Add and subtract 'like terms'

Keywords
Like symbols
Simplify

- You can subtract **like symbols.**

  $6x - 2x = 4x$

Each of these packets contains ***x*** seeds.

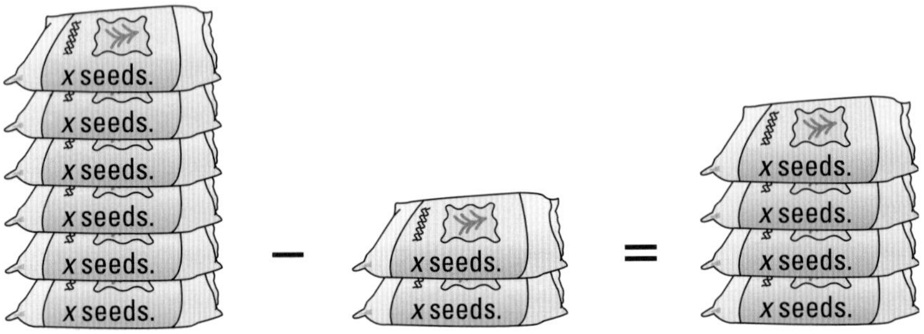

$6x \quad - \quad 2x \quad = \quad 4x$

example

Subtract like symbols.

a $5b - 2b$ **b** $10a - 6a$ **c** $3e + 6e - 5e$

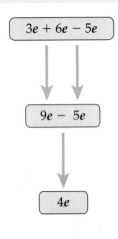

a $5b - 2b = 3b$ **b** $10a - 6a = 4a$ **c** $3e + 6e - 5e = 9e - 5e$
$= 4e$

- You can write like terms more easily by adding and subtracting.

  This makes the expression simpler.

This is called **simplifying**.

$3e + 6e - 5e$

↓

$9e - 5e$

↓

$4e$

You can also simplify larger expressions.

$4a + 2a + 5b - 3a + 2b$

$4a \quad 2a \quad -3a$ $5b \quad 2b$

Now you can simplify the '*a*' terms and the '*b*' terms separately.

$4a + 2a - 3a = 6a - 3a$
$= 3a$

$5b + 2b = 7b$

$3a + 7b$

Exercise 12c

1 Work out these calculations in your head.

a 12 − 3 + 2 **b** 32 − 3 + 15 **c** 26 + 6 − 3

d 47 − 39 + 9 **e** 63 + 12 − 23 **f** 100 − 93 + 13

2 Write the symbols in each ring as simply as you can.

a (m m m n n) **b** ($2s$ s s p p)

c ($4t$ t $2r$ $3r$ r) **d** ($2d$ $2d$ $3e$ $3d$)

3 Simplify these by subtracting like symbols.

a $7t - 4t$ **b** $15g - 10g$ **c** $12h - 7h$

d $16x - 7x$ **e** $21p - 8p$ **f** $13q - 4q$

g $15m - 2m - 4m$ **h** $19b - 12b - 2b$ **i** $21c - 7c + 9c$

j $18x - 5x - 12x$ **k** $14y - 3y - 7y$ **l** $30u - 17u + 6u$

4 **a** For each of these, gather like symbols together into boxes like these.

b Simplify symbols in each box.

c Add the simplified symbols together.

i $16a - 4a + 7b + 4b - 3a$ → [$16a$ .....] [$7b$ .....] =

ii $20x + 12y + 8x - 9y + 9y - 11x$ → [$20x$ .....] [$12y$ .....] =

iii $8f - 6h - 2h + 7f + 15h - 3h$ → [$8f$ .....] [$-6h$ .....] =

5 Add like symbols in each of these to simplify them.

a $2x + 4x + 3p$ **b** $15t + 5t + 6k$ **c** $22c + 4c + 2h$

d $40g + 20g + 3d + 10d$ **e** $5y + 2y + 4t + 2t$ **f** $8z + 12z + 20y + 4y$

challenge

James has $14\boldsymbol{x}$ songs on his mp3 player. He loses half his songs. He then downloads $4\boldsymbol{x}$ songs and $3\boldsymbol{y}$ games. Write symbols for the number of files James has.

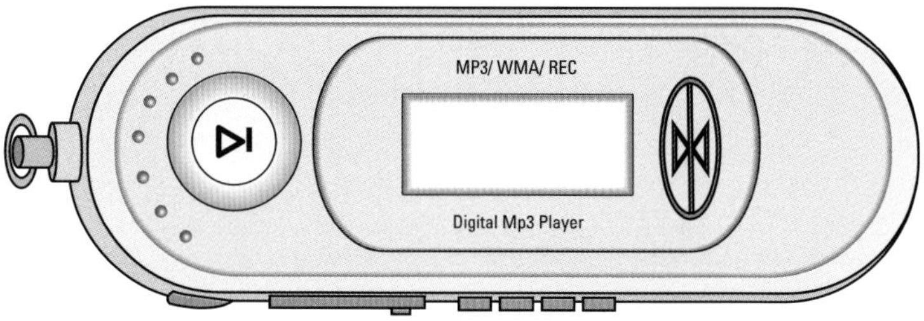

12d Substitution

- Substitute numbers for letters to work out the value of an expression

Keywords
Substitute

p. 96

When you change one player in for another in a football game, you use a **substitute**.

- When you swap a symbol for a number you are **substituting**.
  You can then work out the calculation with actual numbers.

Anna has a bag of pens.
She doesn't know how many she has.
She says, 'I have p pens in my bag.'

She decides to count them all.
There are 14 pens.

She now knows that $p = 14$.

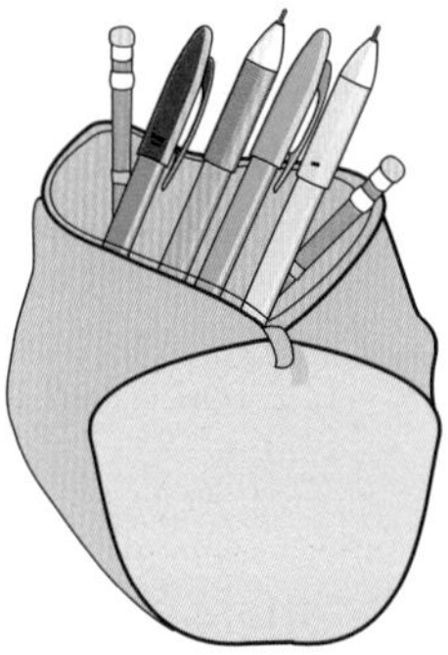

- To substitute, replace a symbol with a number.

  If $v = 10$ $\quad v + 6 = 10 + 6$
  $\quad = 16$

p. 248

example

In each question, substitute $h = 9$ and work out the answer.

a $h + 6$ **b** $3 \times h$

a $h + 6 = 9 + 6$
$= 15$

b $3 \times h = 3 \times 9$
$= 27$

You can write $3 \times h$ as $3h$.

Exercise 12d

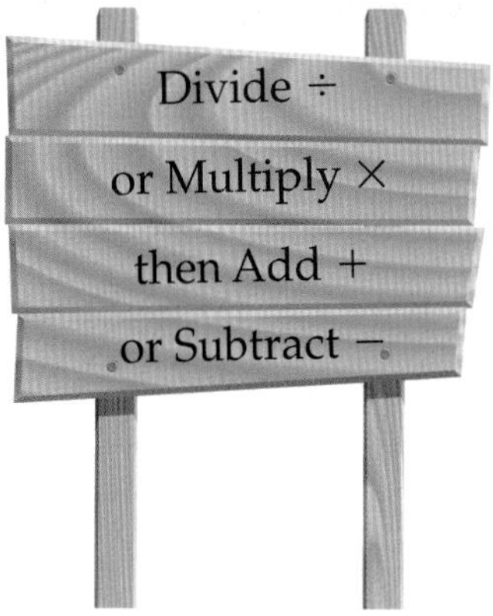

1 Simplify each expression.

a $4x + 9x - 2y$ b $5p - 2p + 6r$
c $7y - 2z + 9y$ d $2h + 10h + 20h$
e $8k - 6k - k$ f $15q + 7y - 2y$
g $6x - 2x + 8x$ h $14g + 7h - 5h$

2 If p is worth 8, work out these calculations.

a $p + 2$ b $p - 5$ c $p \div 2$
d $p + p$ e $p \div p$ f $2 \times p$

3 If f is worth 6, work out these calculations.

a $f + 8$ b $f + 5$ c $f \times 5$
d $f + f$ e $f \times f$ f $f \times 9$

4 If m is worth 8 and n is worth 6, work out these calculations.

a $m + n$ b $m - n$ c $n - m$

5 Work out the weight on each scale if $x = 5$ kg and $y = 2$ kg

a

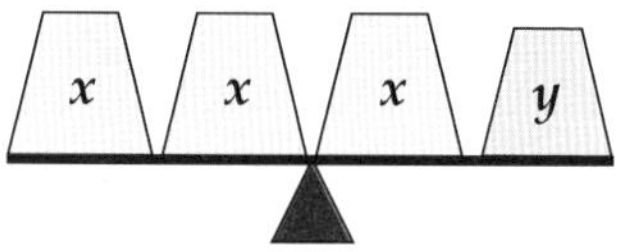

b

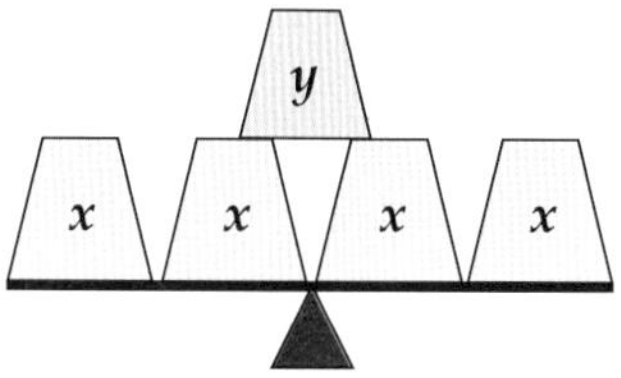

c

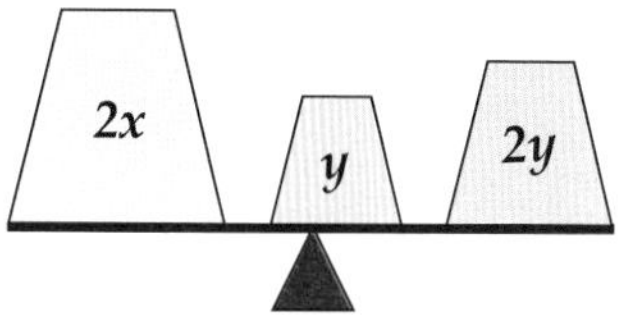

6 Substitute $x = 8$, $y = 12$, and $z = 15$ into each expression and evaluate.

a $x + 12$ b $y \div 2$ c $z \times 2$ d $y + z$
e $z + x + y$ f $z - y$ g $5 \times x$ h $3 \times z$
i $y \times 5$ j $z \div 3$ k $8 \times x$ l $60 \div z$

challenge

Evaluate these expressions when

$m = 10, n = 6, p = 7$

a $2m - 2n$ b $n \div 2 + 13$ c $8 - n \div 3$
d $3m - 4$ e $10n - 20$ f $25 - 2m$
g $5p + 5$ h $6m + 9$ i $m \times 2 + 9$

12 Consolidation

12a

1 Liam has m sweets.

a He gives y sweets to Sharon. How many does Liam have now?

b Then Ben gives Liam 10 sweets. How many does Liam have now?

2 Rebekah is cooking breakfast for herself, her parents and two brothers.

a She has bought q sausages, r eggs and s rashers of bacon. If everyone has one sausage, two eggs and three rashers of bacon, how many of each will she have left over?

b There were z slices of bread in the loaf and the loaf was finished after breakfast. Rebekah and her brothers each had two slices and Rebekah's parents each had one slice. What was z?

12b

3 Collect like terms in each of these expressions.

a $3u + 7v + 5u$

b $6x + 4y + x$

c $3p + 7q + 2p + 5q$

d $3a + 5b + 2a + 4b$

e $2a + 3b + 3a + 4b + 4a$

f $12m + 6n + 7m + n + 3m$

g $9x + 3y + 7x + 2y + 5x + y$

12c

4 Collect like terms in each of these expressions.

a $7x + 9y - 5x$

b $8u + 6v - 3u$

c $2d + 7e + 3d - 4e$

d $5q + 9r + 2q - r$

e $9p + 7q - 4p - 3q$

f $12m + 10n - 7m - 3n$

g $20c + 11d - 8c - 7d$

h $8p + 6q - 3p - 2q + 4p$

5 If $m = 6$ and $n = 2$, find the value of each of these.

a $m \div n$

b $(7 \times m) - (4 \times n)$

c $(15 \times n) - (2 \times m)$

d $(m \times n) + 15$

e $(10 - m) \times n$

f $(m \times n) \div 4$

g $(5 \times m) + (6 \times n)$

Maths Life

Media maths

Newspapers are full of maths. You can read the numbers as you would the words.

The Newspaper | Monday 20 April 2009

Couch Potatoes on the Rise

Only a third of men and a quarter of women meet government guidelines of 30 minutes of moderate exercise 5 times a week.

Young people and children are advised to take 60 minutes of moderate exercise 5 times a week, but new data shows only 65% do.

How much exercise should a man or woman take per week?

What about a young person?

APRIL 2009

Monday, 13 April
Walk to/from school - 20 minutes

Mandy - get CDs back?

Tuesday, 14 April
Walk to/from school - 20 minutes
PE - 40 minutes

Wednesday, 15 April
Take dog to park - 60 minutes

Call Sarah!!

APRIL 2009

Thursday, 16 April
Walk to/from school - 20 minutes
PE - 40 minutes

Friday, 17 April
Cycle to/from school - 10 minutes

Saturday, 18 April
Swim - 45 minutes

Sunday, 19 April
Cycle to/from the shops - 30 minutes

Total active time

Arrange my activities each week so that I will be active for

a 300 minutes
b 400 minutes
c 460 minutes
d 495 minutes

Record and time your activities for a week. Do you meet the target?

12 Summary

Key indicators

- Use letters to represent numbers Level 4

Level 4

1 Work out the values of a, b and c in

a $2 \times 5 + 3 = a$

b $2 \times 5 + b = 17$

c $c \times 5 + 8 = 23$

Mireya's answer ✓

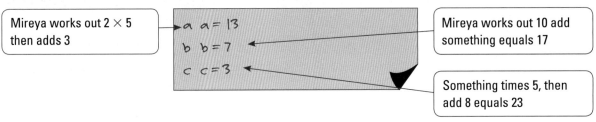

Mireya works out 2×5 then adds 3

a $a = 13$

b $b = 7$

c $c = 3$

Mireya works out 10 add something equals 17

Something times 5, then add 8 equals 23

Level 4

2 Here is information about some bags of marbles.

> Altogether, there are 10 bags
> Each bag contains 12 marbles
> Each marble weighs 7 grams

Use the information to match each question with the correct calculation. The first one is done for you.

Question	Calculation
How many bags are there altogether? →	10
How many marbles are there altogether?	10×7
How much does each bag of marbles weigh?	10×12
	12×7
How much do all 10 bags of marbles weigh altogether?	$10 \times 12 \times 7$
	$10 + 12 + 7$

Key Stage 3 2007 3–5 Paper 2

13 Shape

Transformations and symmetry

This butterfly is symmetrical. You can imagine a line running down its middle which makes its right side exactly the same as its left side. Other examples of symmetry in nature include leaves, crabs, starfish and people's faces.

What's the point? Shapes can be described by the kind of symmetry they do or do not have.

Check in

Level 3

1 Jason is looking at photographs on a computer. He must click either 'rotate clockwise' or 'rotate anticlockwise' to see the photographs the correct way up. Write the correct instruction for these.

a 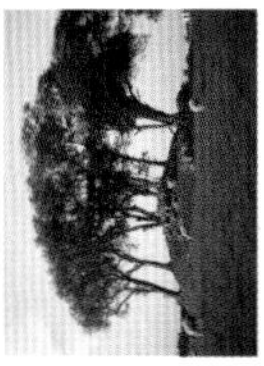

b 

c 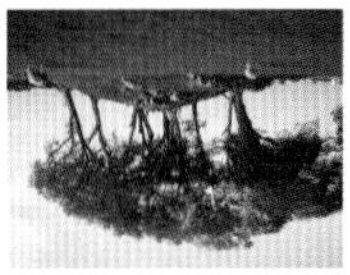

2 Follow these instructions in order.

① Face North ② Turn 90° clockwise

③ Turn 180° ④ Turn 270° anticlockwise

Write the direction that you are now facing.

Level 4

3 Write the coordinates for the corners of each of these shapes.

a 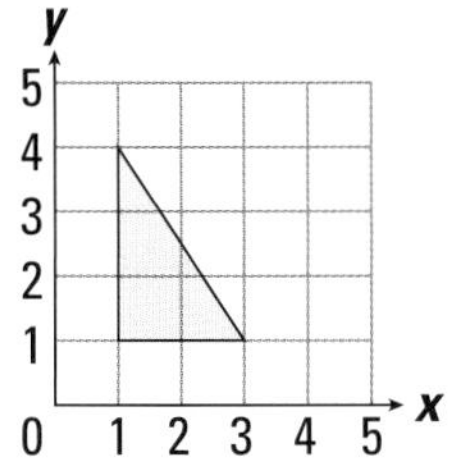

b 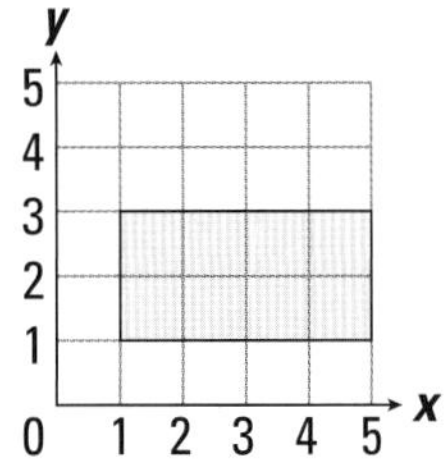

c 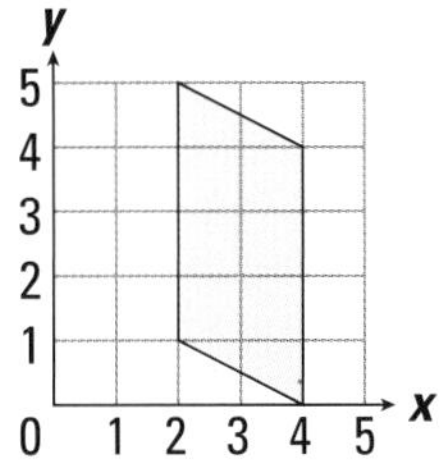

Lines of symmetry

- Find lines of symmetry

Keywords
Line of symmetry
Reflection
Symmetry

Ruby folds a piece of card. She cuts a shape along the folded edge … … then unfolds it.

The fold line is the **line of symmetry**.

- A shape has reflective **symmetry** if it folds exactly onto itself.

These shapes have one line of symmetry.

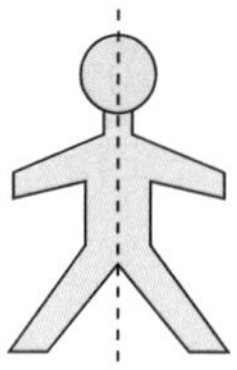

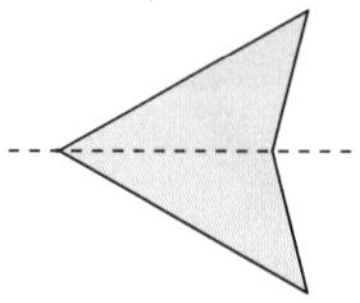

The dashed line shows the line of symmetry.

These shapes have more than one line of symmetry.

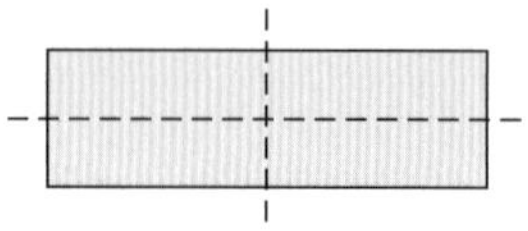
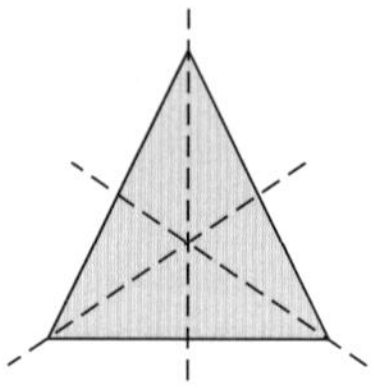
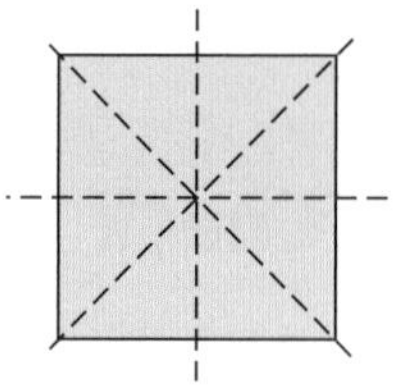

These shapes have no lines of symmetry.

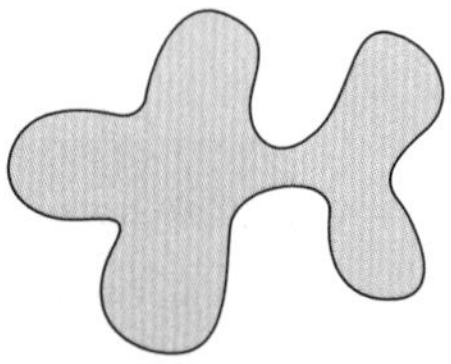
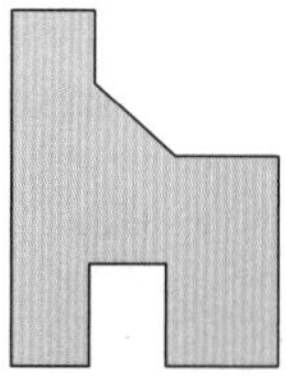

- Hold a mirror on a line of symmetry to see the whole shape.
  This is a **reflection**.

example

State if these shapes have one line of symmetry, more than one line of symmetry or no lines of symmetry.

a

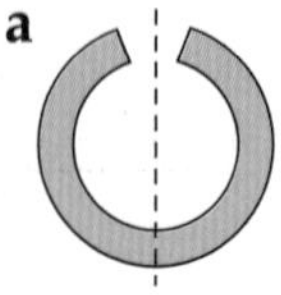

One

b

None

c

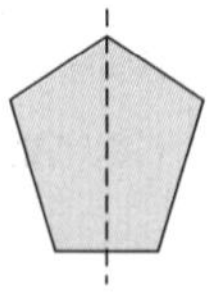

One

d

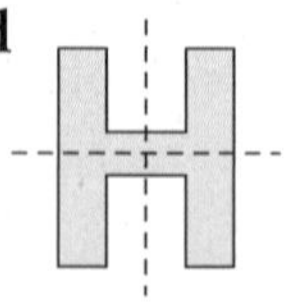

Two

Exercise 13a

1 How many lines of symmetry does each shape have?

a 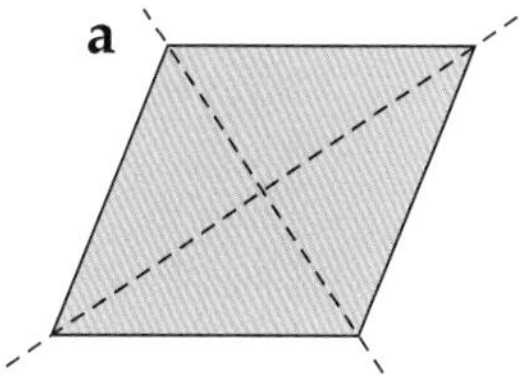
b 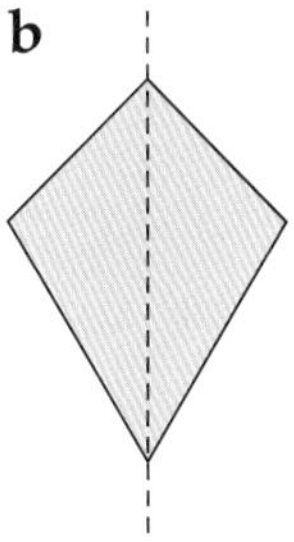
c 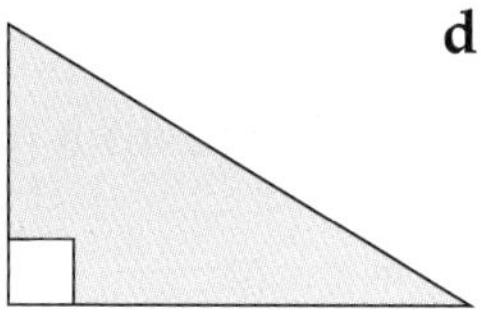
d 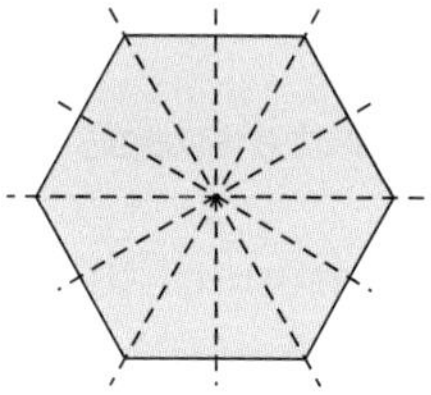

2 These shapes have only one line of symmetry.
Copy or trace them and draw the line of symmetry.

a 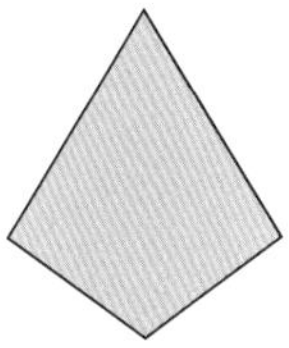
b 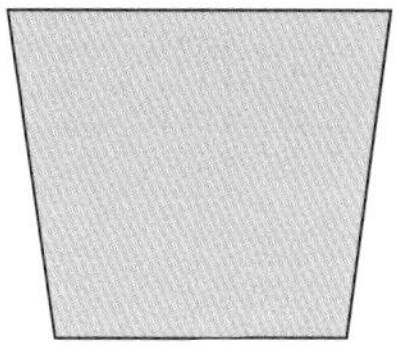
c 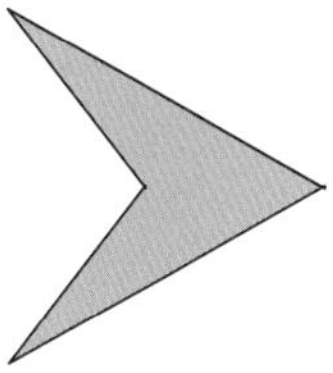
d 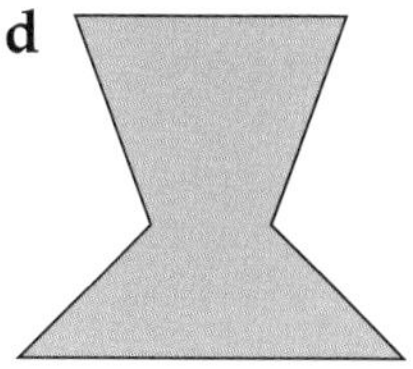
e 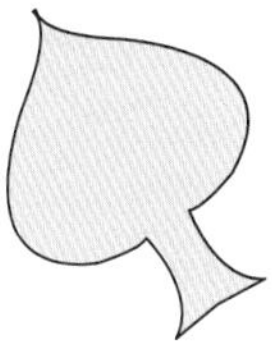

3 These shapes have more than one line of symmetry.
Copy or trace them and draw the lines of symmetry.

a 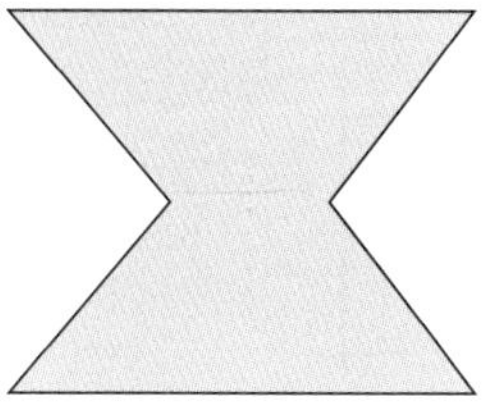
b 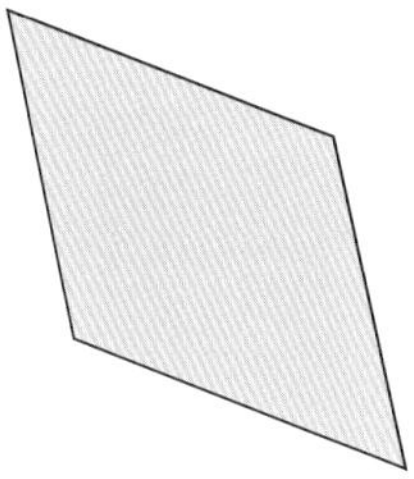
c 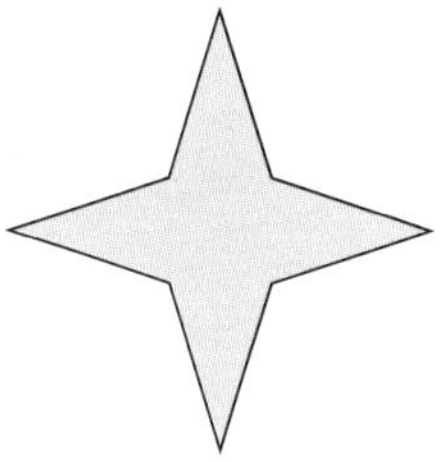

challenge

Kiran is looking at car badges. How many lines of symmetry does each badge have?

a 
b 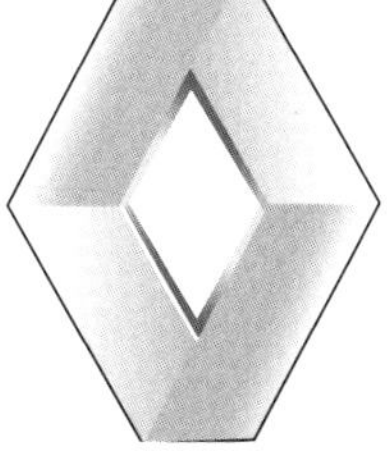
c 
d 
e 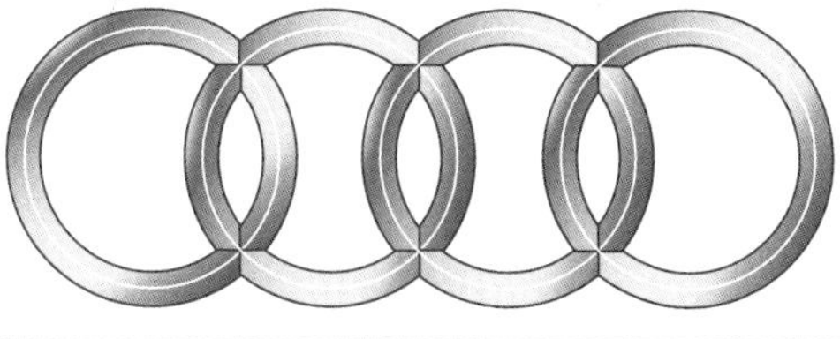

Reflection

- Reflect a shape in a mirror line

Keywords
Image *Reflection*
Mirror line *Object*

- You can **reflect** a shape in a **mirror line** on a grid.

The **object** is in front of the mirror
You can see the **image** in the mirror.

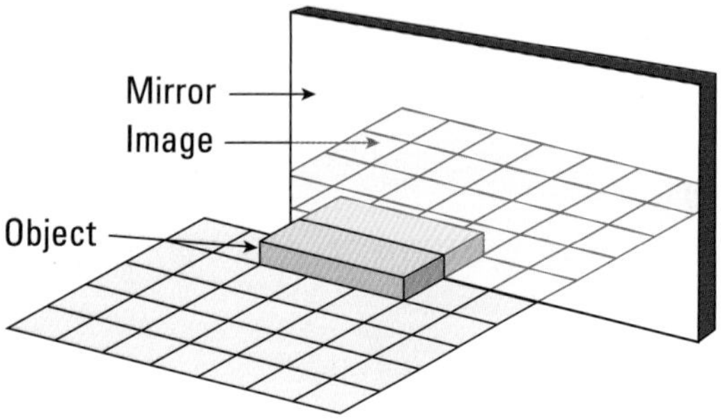

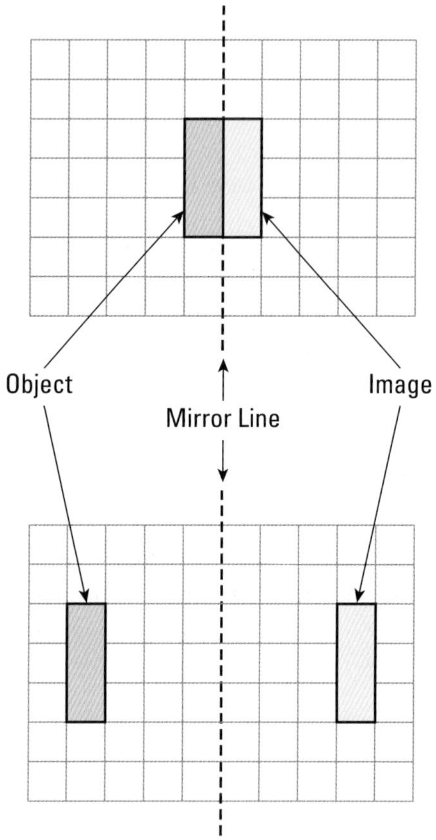

The object is moved further away.
The image is further away too.

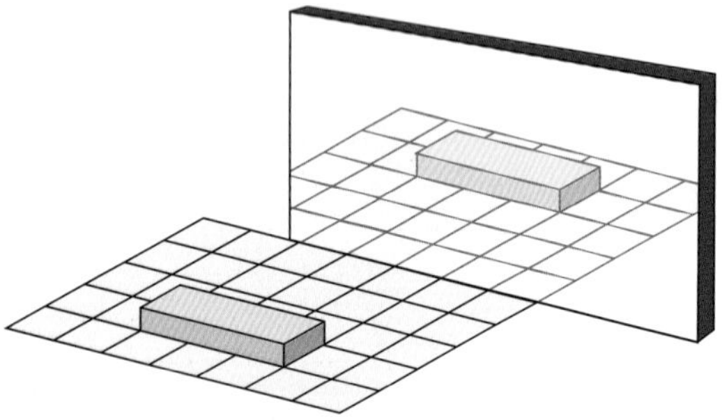

example

Reflect shape A in the mirror line.

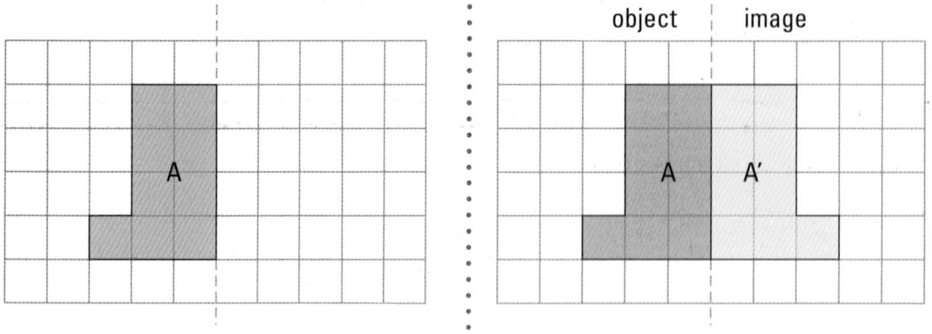

Exercise 13b

1 Kiko looks into a mirror. Which image is her true reflection?

a

b

c

2 Copy these shapes onto squared paper.
Complete the reflection and name the finished shape.

You can use a mirror to help.

a

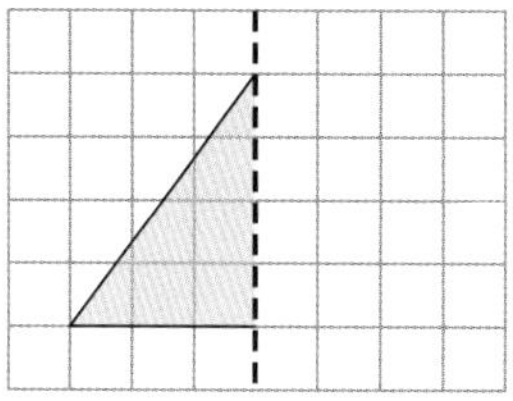

b

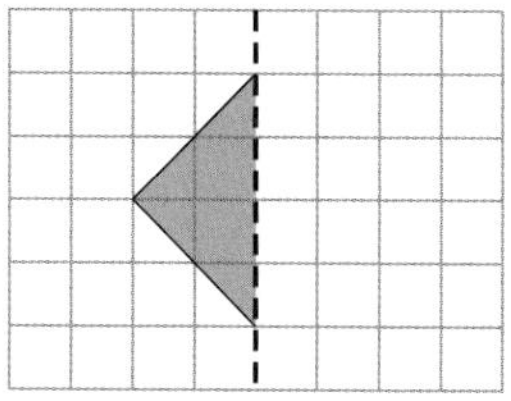

c

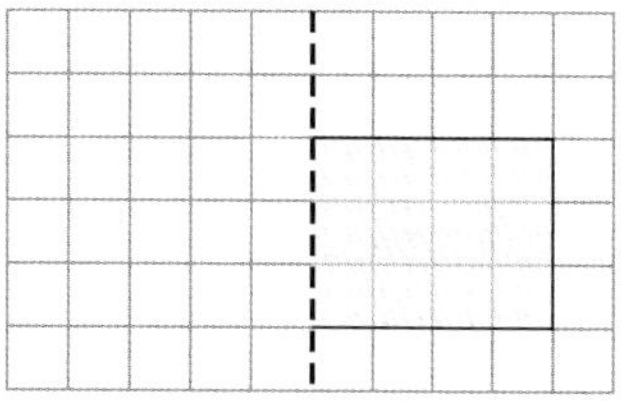

3 Copy each shape and mirror line onto squared paper.
Draw the reflection of the shape in the mirror line.

a

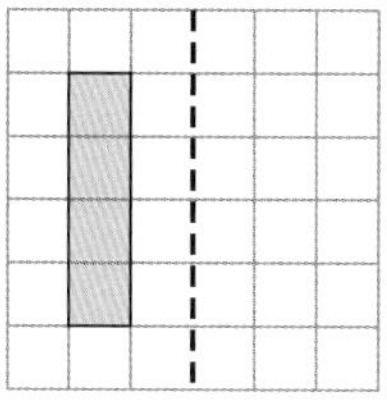

b

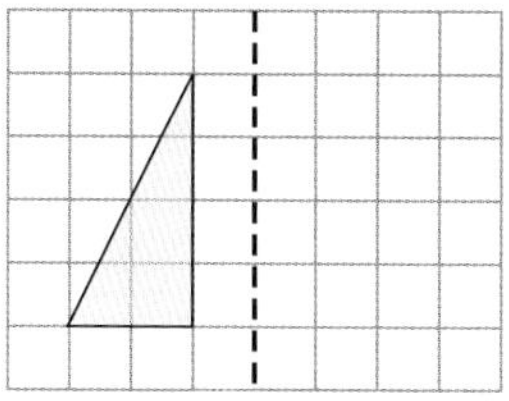

c

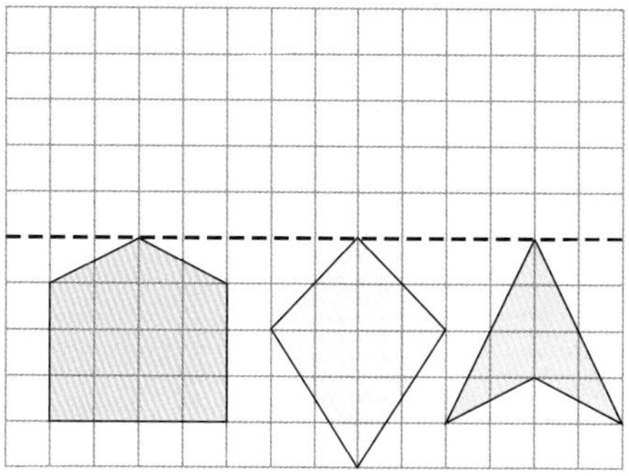

challenge

These shapes are reflected in a horizontal mirror line.
Trace or copy the shapes into your book. Reflect them.
What words do they make?

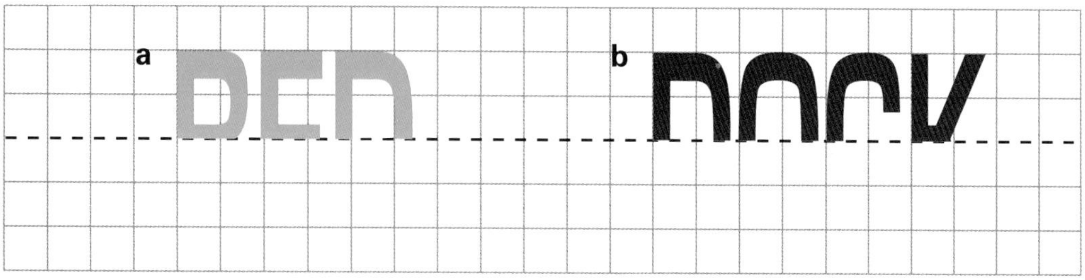

13c Translation

- Slide a shape and carry out a translation

Keywords
Diagram
Reflection
Translation

Members of class 7G are practising dance steps for the end of term show.
They are meant to move around the stage together . . . . but

Their teacher decides to draw **diagrams** of the steps so that the dancers have a clear plan of the moves.

When you **reflect** a shape you 'flip' it over.
If you slide a shape along you **translate** it.

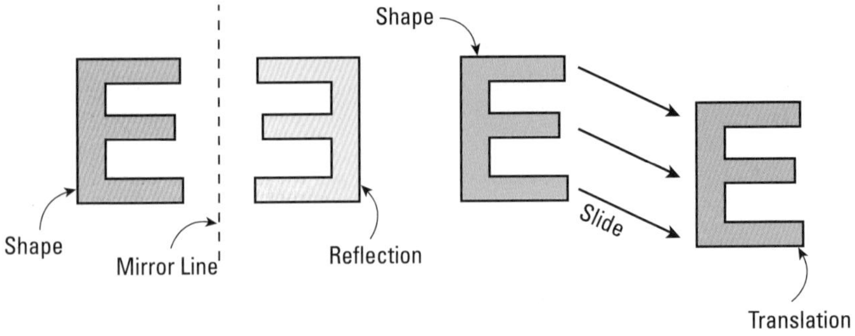

- In a **translation**, a shape moves:
  First, right or left   Second, up or down

example

Describe these translations.

a

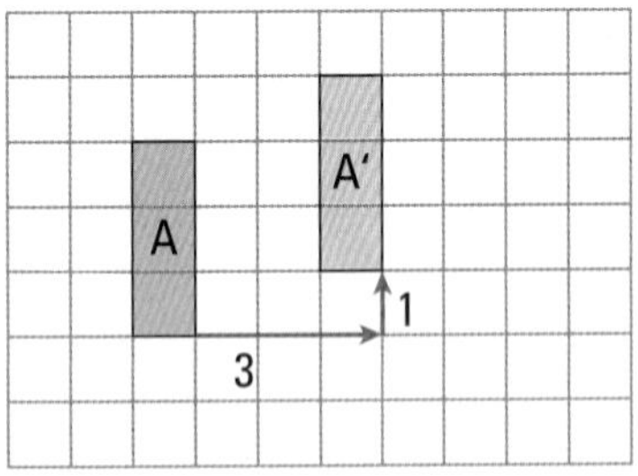

b

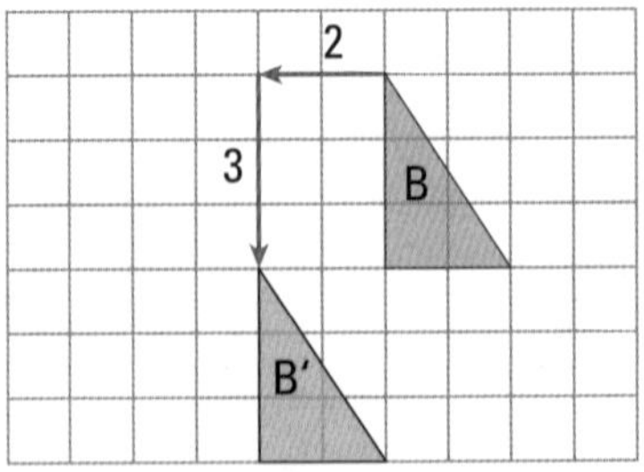

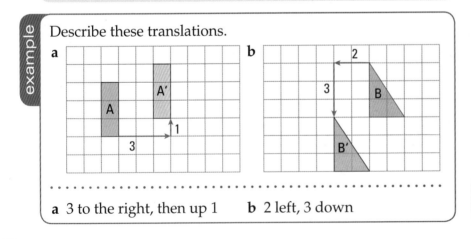

a 3 to the right, then up 1   **b** 2 left, 3 down

Count across first, then up or down

Exercise 13c

1 Which letter will the dancer reach if she follows each of these directions? Always start from the dancer. The first is done for you.

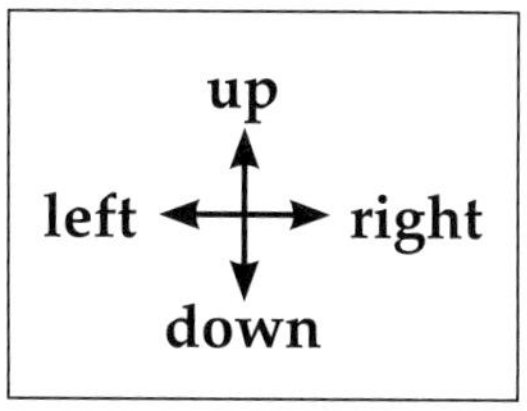

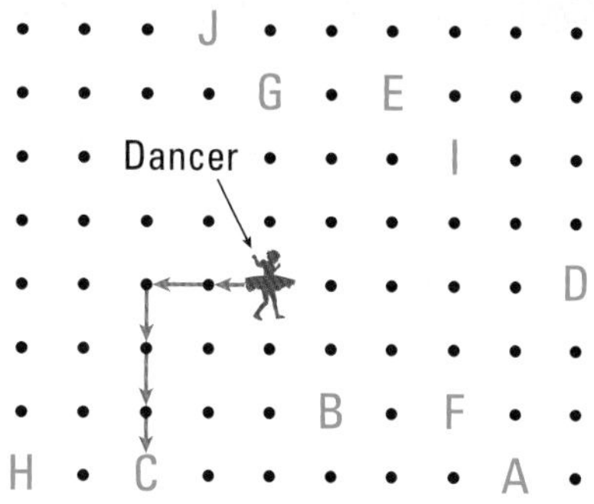

a 2 steps left, 3 steps down = C
b 3 steps right, 2 steps up
c 4 steps right, 3 steps down
d 1 step left, 4 steps up
e 4 steps left, 3 steps down
f 5 steps right, 0 steps up or down
g 0 steps right or left, 3 steps up
h 1 step right, 2 steps down
i 2 steps right, 3 steps up
j 3 steps right, 2 steps down

2 Copy and complete these statements to describe each translation.

a

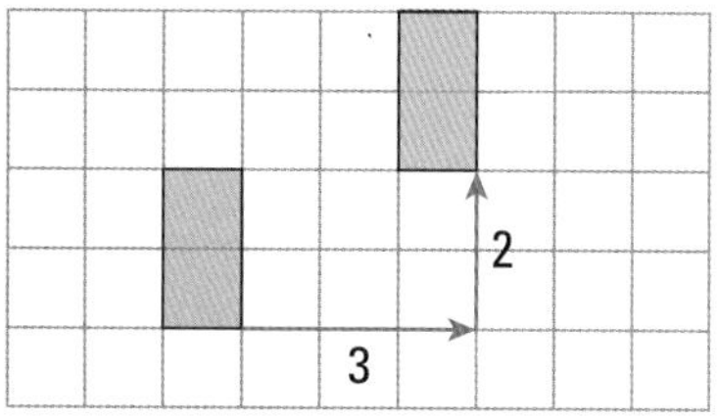

____ to the right, ____ up

b

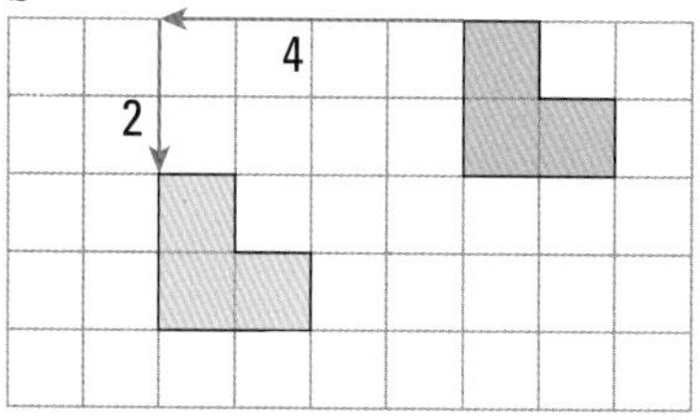

____ to the left, ____ down

c

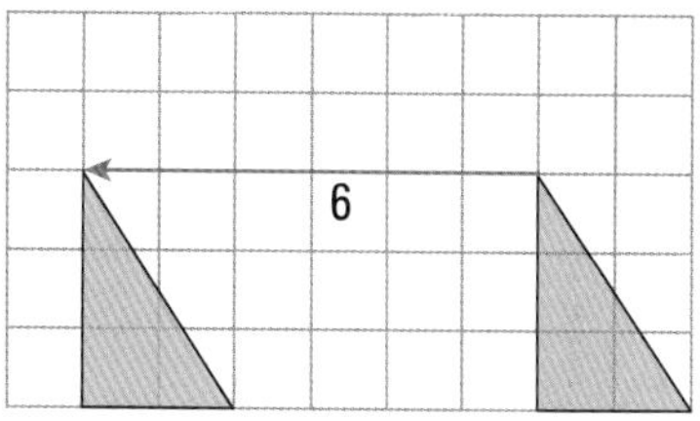

____ to the left, ____ down

challenge

1 Each translation moves triangle A to another position. Give the number of the position it moves to.
- a 1 to the right, 4 up
- b 4 to the left, 3 down
- c 5 to the right, 6 down
- d 5 to the left, 0 up or down

2 Describe how triangle A translates to these positions.
- a A to B
- b A to C
- c A to D
- d A to E

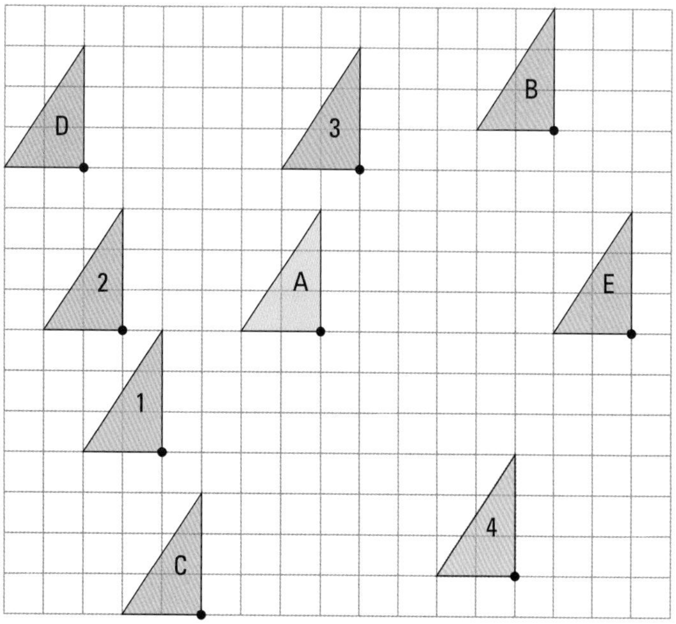

Rotation

- Rotate a shape about a fixed point

Keywords
Anticlockwise
Clockwise
Rotation

The blades on a wind turbine rotate around a fixed point.

- A **rotation** is a turn.

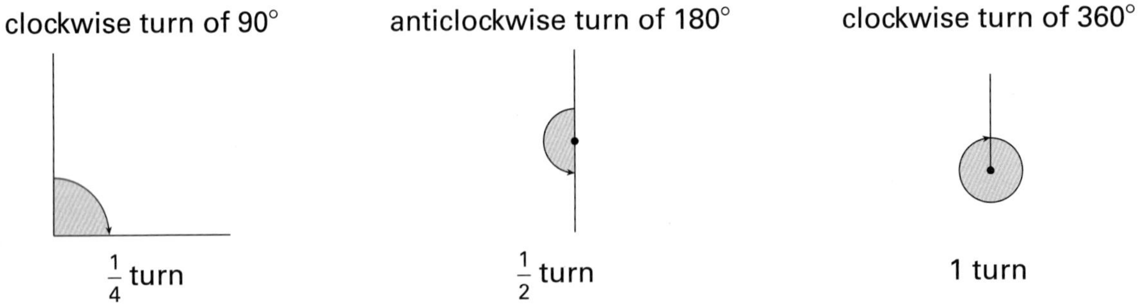

- You can rotate a shape about a point to make a pattern.

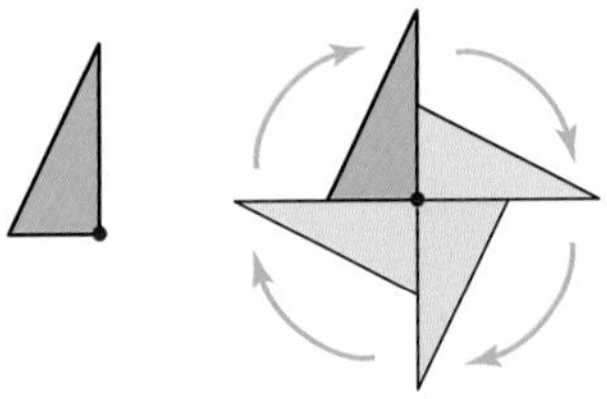

example

a Sketch this shape after it rotates 90° clockwise about the point.
b Sketch this shape after it rotates 90° anticlockwise about the point.

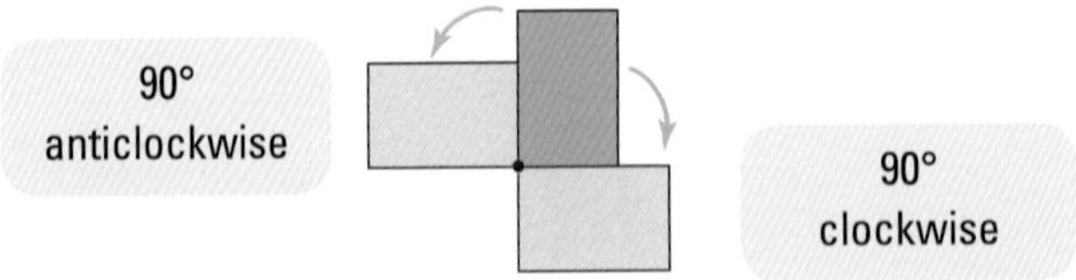

Exercise 13d

1 Choose the direction and angle from the boxes to describe each turn.

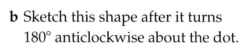

clockwise	anticlockwise

90°	180°	360°

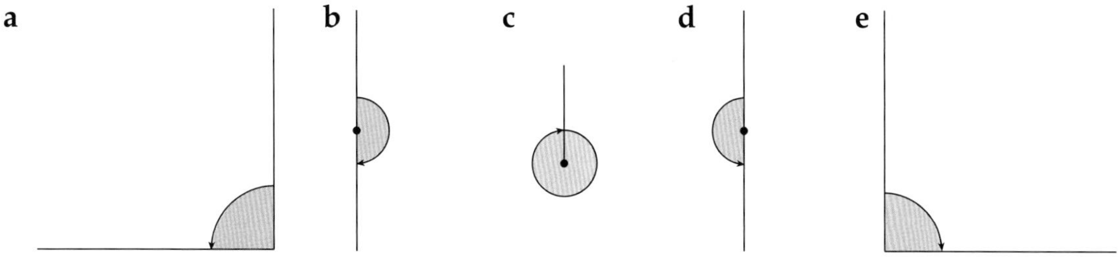

2 **a** Sketch this shape after it turns 90° anticlockwise about the dot.

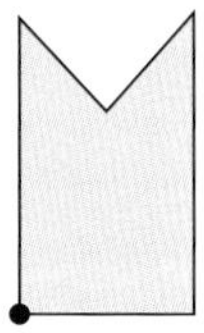

b Sketch this shape after it turns 180° anticlockwise about the dot.

3 **a** Copy this shape on squared paper.
b Rotate the shape about the dot clockwise through 90°.
c Draw the rotated shape.
d Rotate the shape through 90° again.
Draw the rotated shape.
e Repeat until the shape is back at the start.

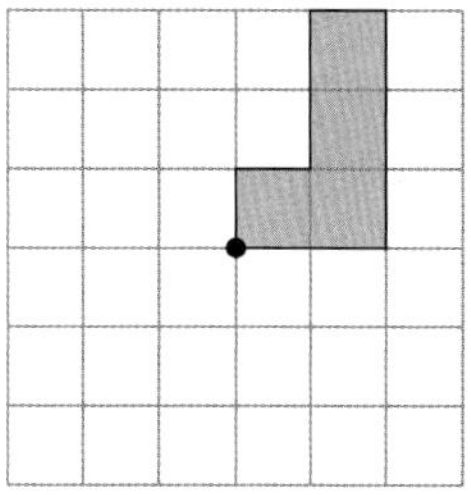

You should have four shapes in your pattern.

challenge

Sketch these letters after a rotation of 180° clockwise about the cross.

You can turn the page upside down to see a 180° turn.

13e Reflection, translation, rotation

- Move a shape into a new position by reflection, rotation and translation

Key words

Image
Mirror line
Object
Reflection
Rotation
Translation

- A **reflection** is a mirror image.

The **object** is reflected in the **mirror line**.
The reflection is called the **image**.
The object and image are the same distance from the mirror line.

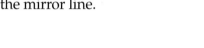

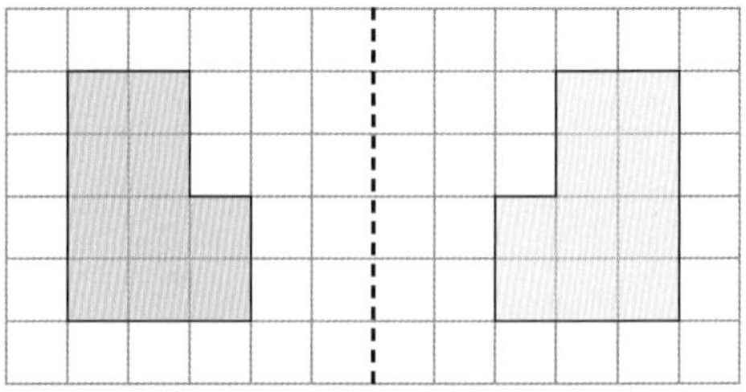

- A **translation** is a 'slide'.

In a translation, the object slides left or right first, then up or down.
The green shape has moved 4 to the right and 3 down.

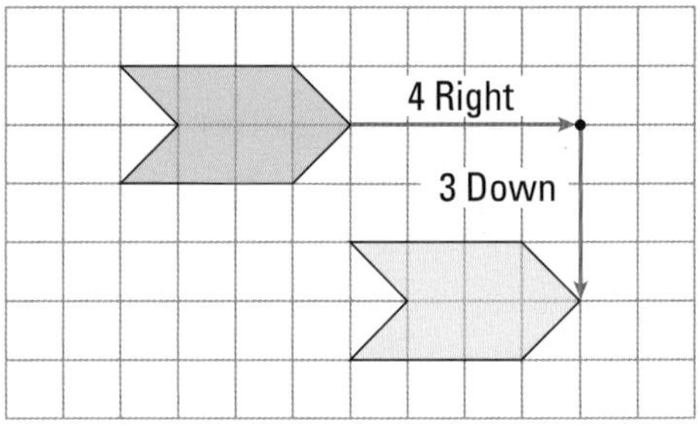

- A **rotation** is a turn.

When you rotate a shape you need to know three things.

1 The direction of turn
2 The angle of turn
3 The centre of rotation, the point about which the shape rotates, ×

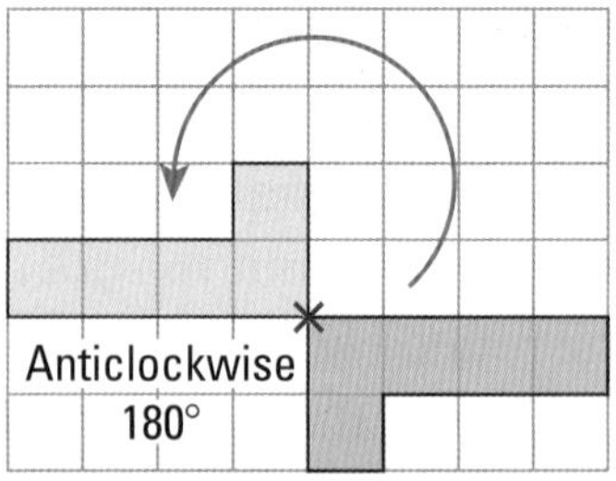

example

Rotate this shape clockwise through 90° (a $\frac{1}{4}$ turn).

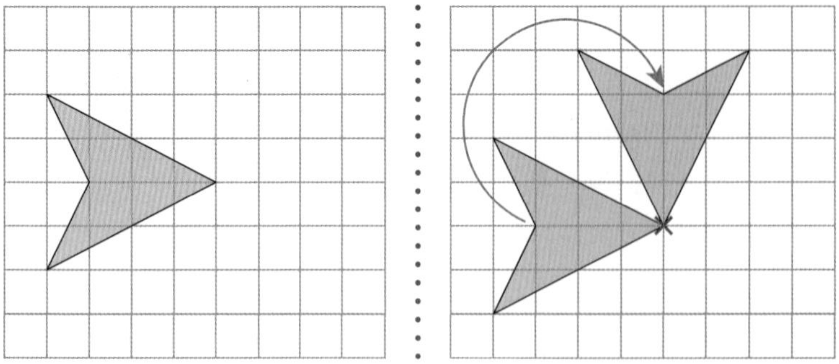

Exercise 13e

1 Reflect this shape in the mirror line.

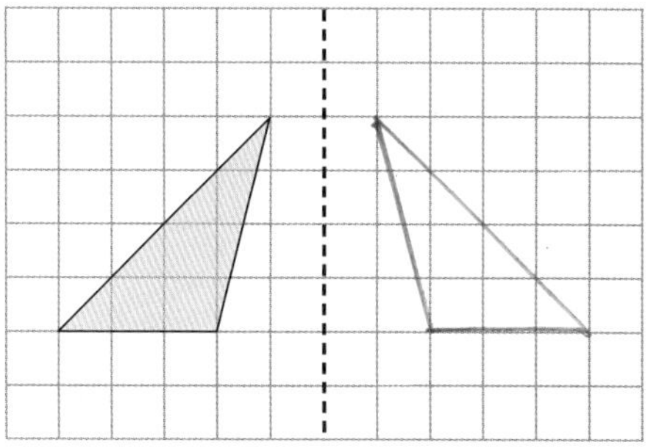

2 Translate this shape 6 left, 4 down.

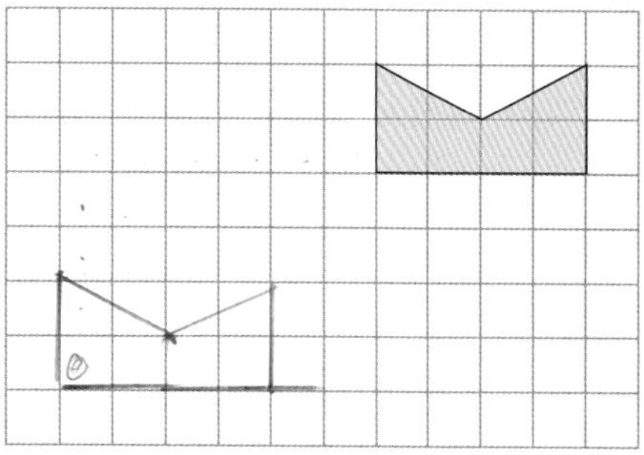

3 Copy each shape on squared paper. Follow the instructions below to rotate each shape.

The centre of rotation is marked with a red cross.

Shape **a** Clockwise, 90°
Shape **b** Anticlockwise 180°
Shape **c** Anticlockwise 90°
Shape **d** Clockwise 180°
Shape **e** Anticlockwise 270°
($270° = \frac{3}{4}$ of a turn.)

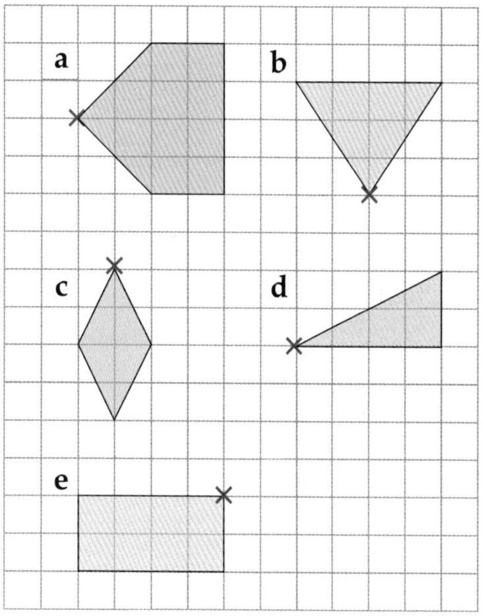

challenge

Decide if each shape has been reflected, transformed or rotated.

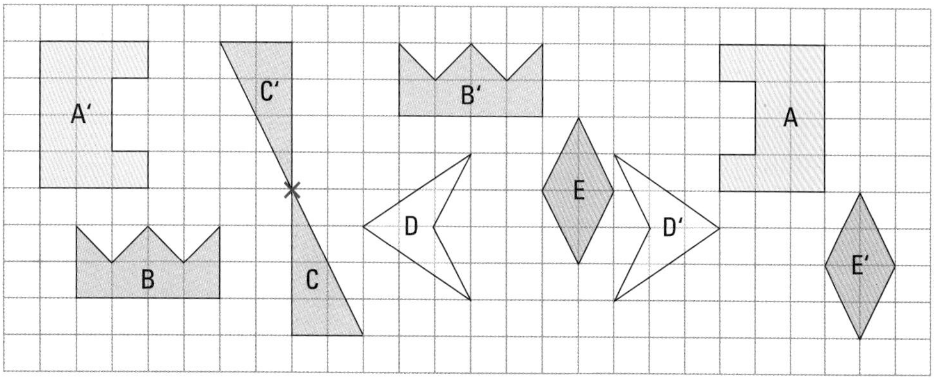

13f Tessellations

- Make tessellating patterns the same shape

Keywords
Reflect *Tessellation*
Rotate *Translate*

This shape repeats itself across the wall.

Different colours are used, but it's the same shape.

There are no gaps or overlaps. This is a **tessellation**.

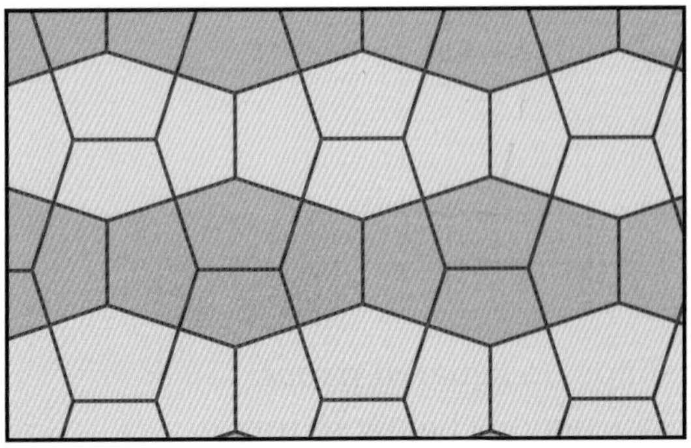

The shape has been reflected and rotated.

- You can **reflect, translate** or **rotate** some shapes to make them tessellate.

This tessellation uses translation.

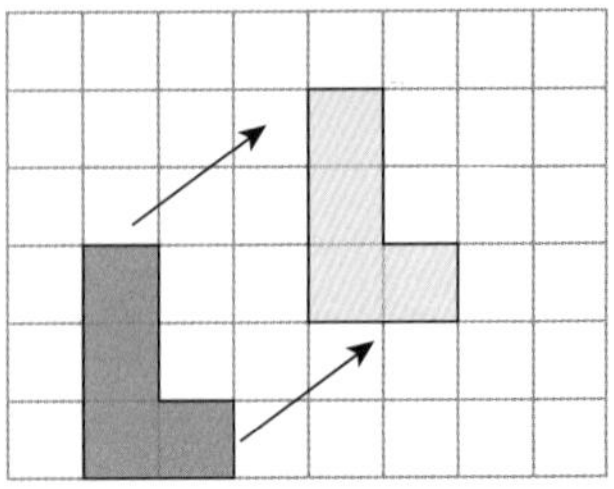

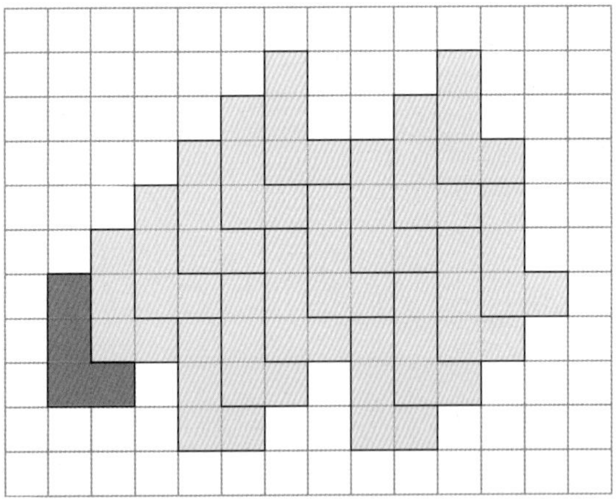

example

Use reflection and translation to complete this tessellation.

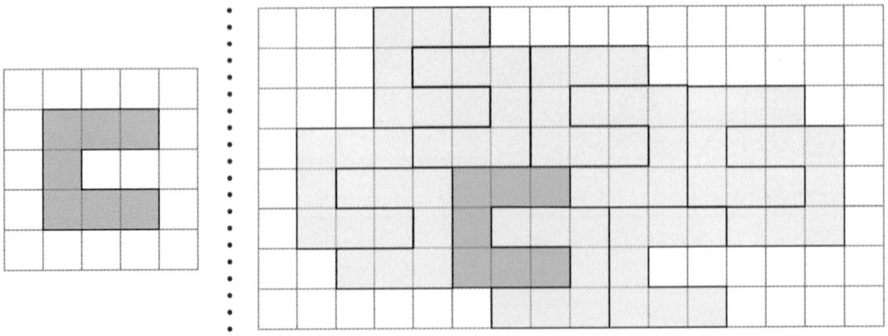

Exercise 13f

1 Draw these shapes on squared paper.
Use translations to make a tessellation.
The first has been started for you.

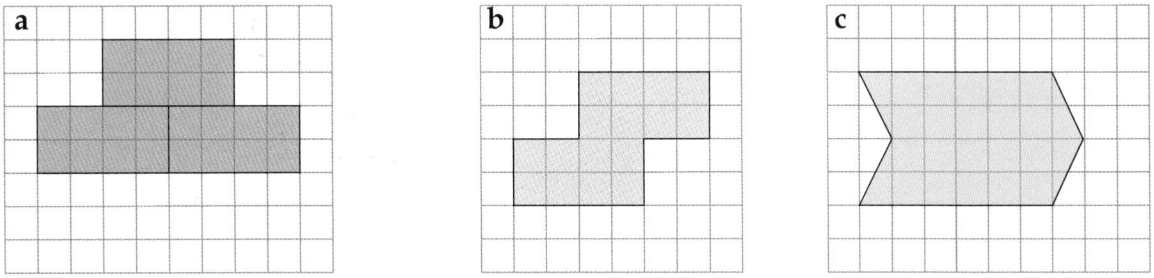

2 Draw these shapes on squared paper.
Use reflection to make a tessellation.
The first has been started for you.

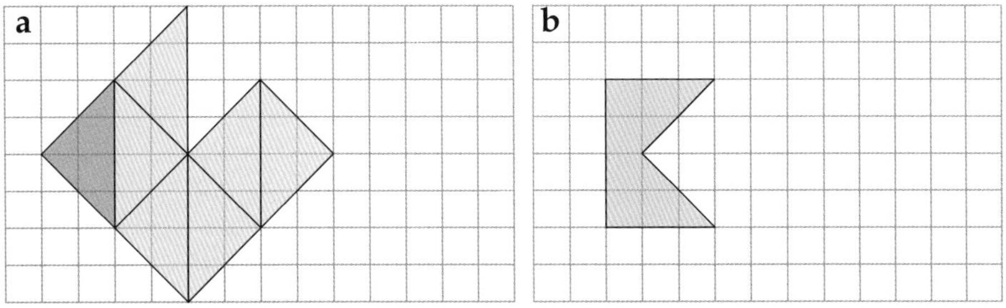

3 Copy each shape onto squared paper.
Repeat each shape 10 times to show how they tessellate.

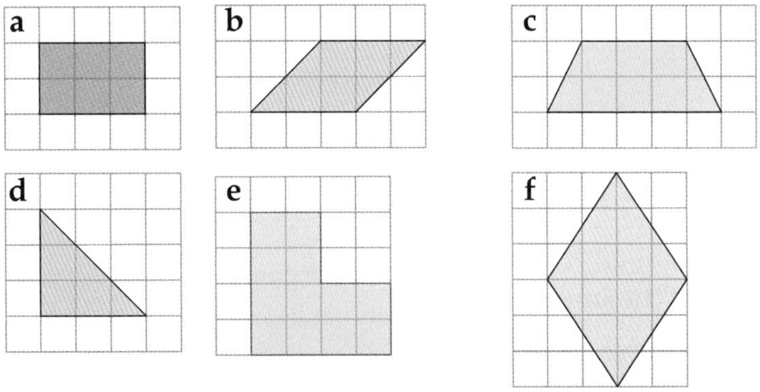

challenge

Bees construct honeycombs from wax.
They build hexagonal cells in which
to rear their young and store honey.
On square paper, tessellate a hexagon
to show what the comb might look like.

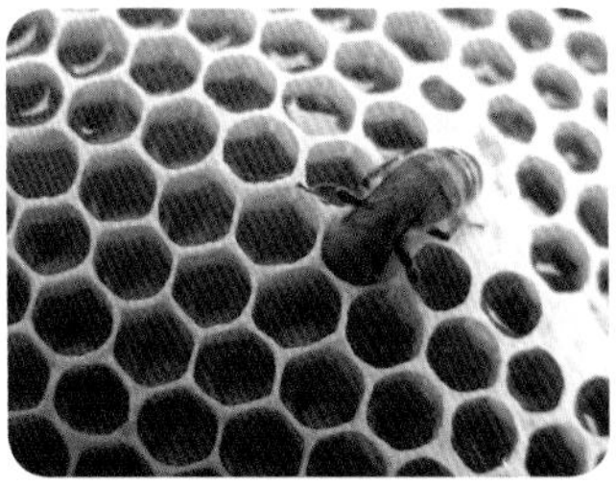

13 Consolidation

13a

1 These shapes have only one line of symmetry.
Copy each shape and draw the line of symmetry on your copy.

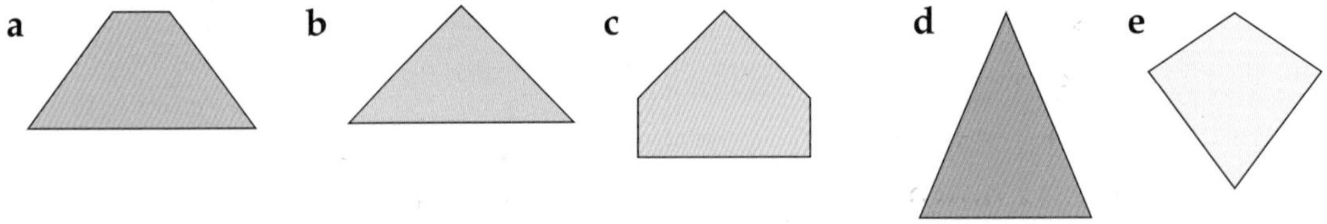

2 These shapes have more than one line of symmetry. Copy each shape and draw the lines of symmetry on your copy.

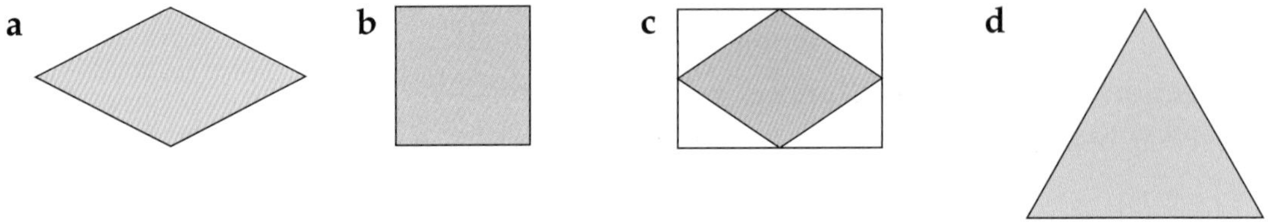

13b

3 Copy each shape onto square grid paper and reflect the images in the mirror line.

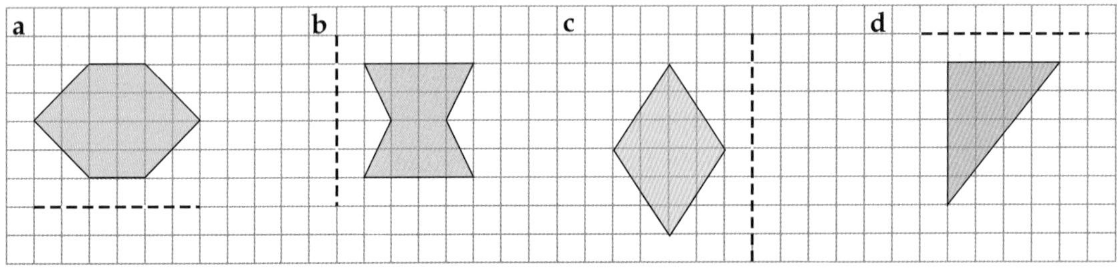

13c

4 **a** Copy this shape onto square grid paper and reflect the image in the mirror line.
b Give coordinates for the corners of the image.

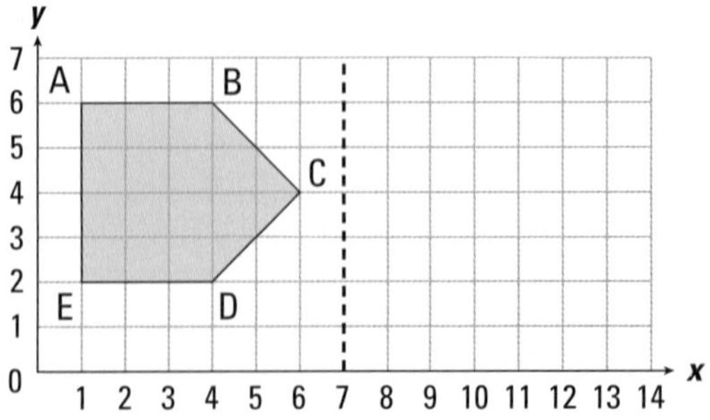

5 Copy this shape onto squared paper. Complete these four translations of the shape.

Translation A: 4 left, 3 up
Translation B: 3 right, 3 down
Translation C: 5 left, 2 down
Translation D: 1 right, 4 up

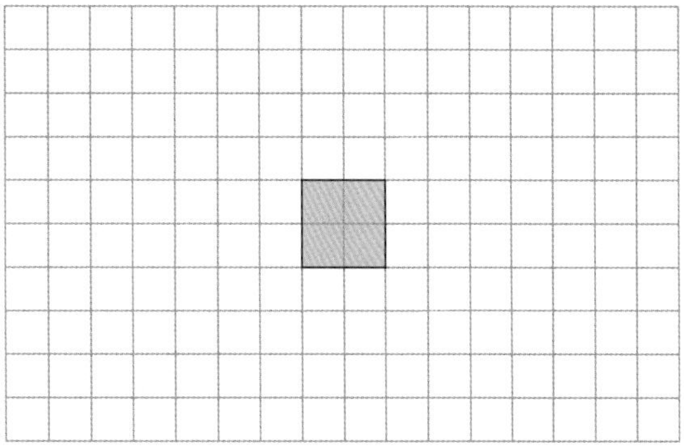

6 Copy the diagram onto square grid paper. Draw the image of the object after following each of these instructions.

a A reflection in the mirror line.
b A translation by 4 to the right and 4 down.
c A clockwise rotation of
  i 90 degrees
  ii 180 degrees and
  iii 270 degrees about the point, ×.

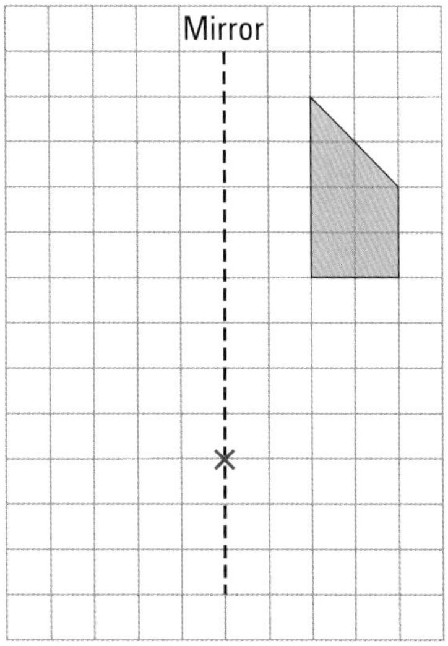

7 Test each shape to see if it will tessellate.
(Remember there must be no gaps or overlaps.)

a
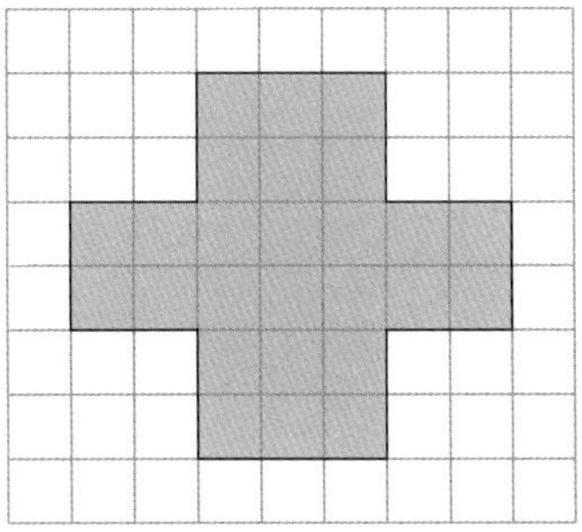

b
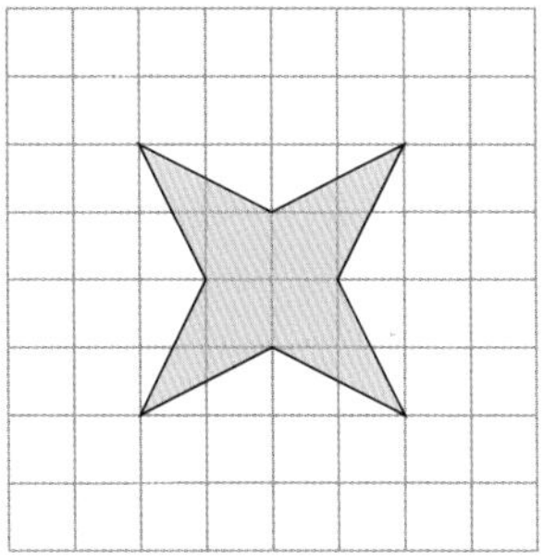

c
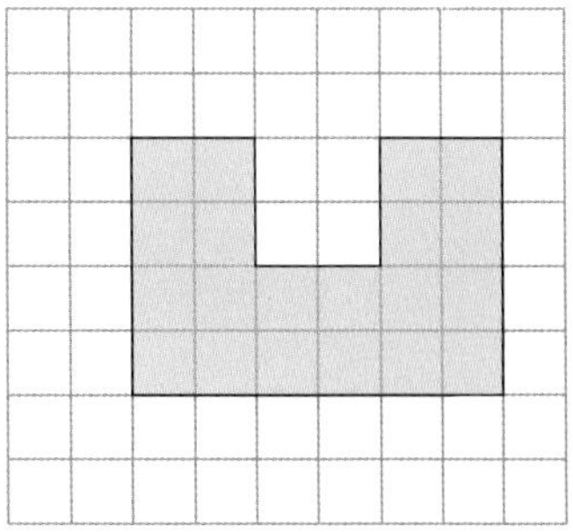

13 Summary

Key indicators

- Recognise line symmetry of 2-D shapes **Level 3**
- Recognise reflection in mirror lines Level 4
- Recognise rotation about a given point Level 4

Level 3

1 Each shape has one line of symmetry.
Draw the line of symmetry on each shape.

a

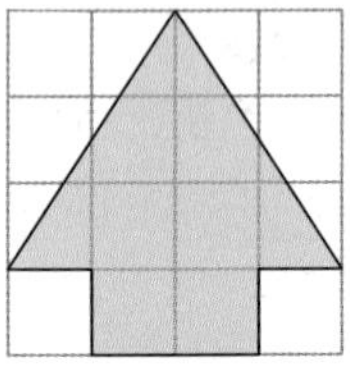

b

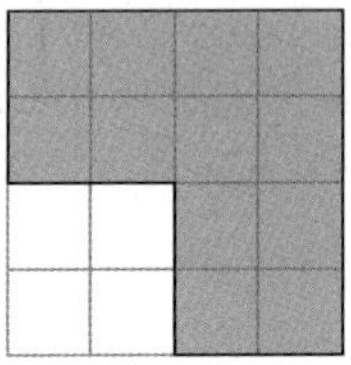

Rose's answer ✔

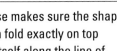

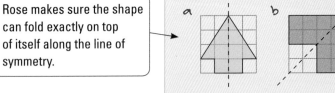

Rose makes sure the shape can fold exactly on top of itself along the line of symmetry.

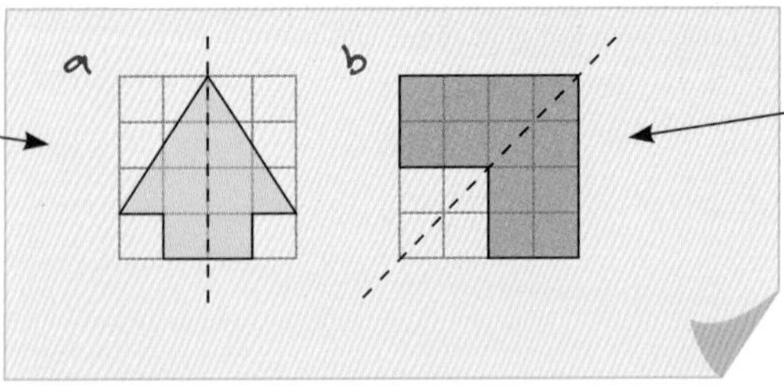

Rose can rotate the page to make the line of symmetry vertical.

Level 3

2 The directions to move from A to B on the square grid are move East 2 then North 1

The arrowed lines form two sides of a rectangle.

Starting at B, write down two more directions to complete the rectangle.

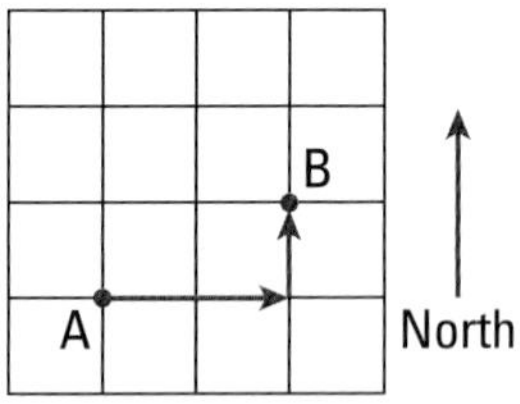

14 Data

Averages

In the 2006–2007 Premiership season, Manchester United scored a total of 83 goals in 38 games. Their highest score was 5 goals and their lowest score was 0 goals, so there was a goal range of 5 goals.

What's the point? Statistics are used throughout sports to keep track of achievements. You can compare the data to compare the teams.

Check in

Level 2

1 Put these numbers in order from smallest to largest.

a 3, 5, 9, 2, 6, 4, 12

b 14, 8, 18, 11, 15

c 96, 94, 102, 90, 89, 93

Level 3

2 Work out these calculations without using a calculator.

a $\frac{15 + 3}{2}$ b $\frac{2 + 3 + 4}{3}$ c $\frac{8 + 10 + 12 + 18}{4}$

3 This bar chart shows the favourite newspaper of each member of staff at Claremont School.

a How many staff said that they prefer *The Times*.

b Which is the most popular newspaper?

c How many staff are there at Claremont School?

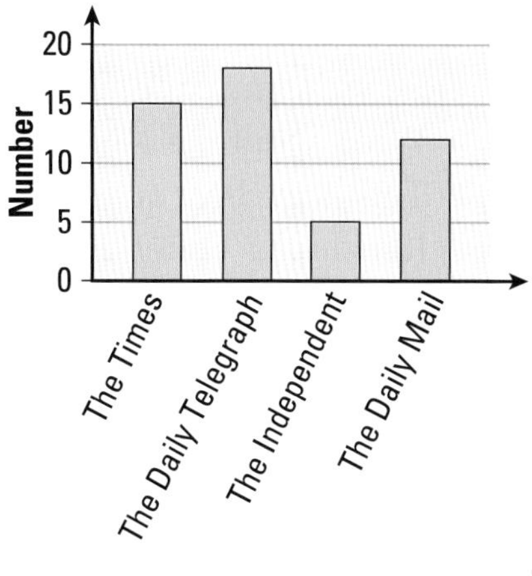

14a Planning and collecting data

- Solve problems by collecting and selecting data

Keywords
Collect *Select*
Interpret *Survey*
Questionnaire

Tracy wants to find out how students get to school.

She **collects** data by **surveying** students.

She writes a **questionnaire.**

1) How old are you? ________

2) How do you get to school each day?
Car ☐ Bus ☐ Walk ☐ Cycle ☐ 4 × 4 ☐ Other ☐

3) When do you get to school?
Before 8.00 am ☐ 8.00 to 8.30 am ☐ After 8.30 am ☐

She has collected a lot of data but only **selects** to look at Question 2.
Question 2 gives her the data she wants to **interpret.**

example

Tracy wants to find out what subject students prefer.
Which question would be best to ask?

a) Do you like Maths?

b) Which subject is your favourite?
English ☐ Maths ☐ PE ☐ Geography ☐ French ☐ Other ☐

c) What is your favourite subject? ________

Here are some comments on the questions.

a What about the other subjects?

b This is the best question. It gives a choice of subjects.
It includes 'Other' in case the students' answer isn't a choice.

c There could be any answer! It would be too hard to keep track of answers.

Exercise 14a

1 Anna wants to know students' favourite kind of music.
Which question would be best to ask? Explain your choice.

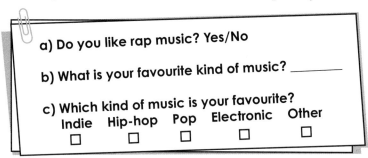

a) Do you like rap music? Yes/No

b) What is your favourite kind of music? ________

c) Which kind of music is your favourite?

Indie	Hip-hop	Pop	Electronic	Other
☐	☐	☐	☐	☐

2 Anna now wants to know how students listen to music.
Write a question for her questionnaire.

3 Anna wants to know which DJs students listen to most.
She wrote these questions. Explain how she could improve each question.

a

Do you like DJ Backbeat?

b

Which DJ is your favourite?

Dj Gusto ☐

Grooverider ☐

Elektra ☐

c

Do you want to be a DJ when you grow up?

discussion

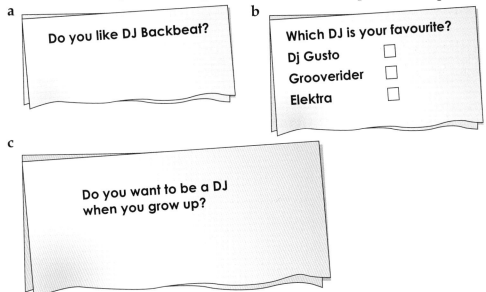

Journalists need to write good questions to get correct data.
What question do you think the journalist asked to get these responses?

I like the holidays!

Springtime is best.

I live for Football season!

Summer is wonderful!

14b Organising data

- Make a tally chart
- Make and use frequency tables

Keywords
Frequency table
Tally chart

p. 74

- You can organise data in a **frequency table.**

example

Sammi wanted to find out the most popular mobile phone colour.
She recorded the colours of 12 friends' phones.

Red	Black	Black	Brown	Black	White
Pink	Black	Black	Silver	Red	Silver

Organise this set of data into a table.

The table shows the **frequency** for each colour.

Colour	Red	Black	Brown	White	Silver	Pink
Frequency	2	5	1	1	2	1

Frequency answers the question, 'How many?'

- If you have a large set of data, it is easier to make a frequency table using a **tally chart.**

example

Ben recorded the number of boys and girls attending a school club using a tally chart. Draw a frequency table for this set of data.

Boys	卌 卌 卌 II
Girls	卌 卌 III

The table shows the frequencies.

	Boys	Girls
Frequency	17	13

The symbol 卌 is used to represent a group of 5.

A tally chart can also include the frequency.

Favourite vegetable	Tally	Frequency
Carrot	卌 I	6
Beetroot	卌	5
Tomato	II	2
Sweetcorn	III	3
Peas	卌 III	8

Exercise 14b

1 The children in class 7F ate these fruits one lunchtime.
Draw a frequency table for this set of data.

2 The tally chart shows the numbers of people attending three school clubs one evening.
Make a frequency table for this set of data.

Club	Tally
Art Club	𝍸 𝍸 𝍸 I
Netball Club	𝍸 𝍸 𝍸 𝍸 II
Computer Club	𝍸 𝍸 III

3 Heather took part in a bird watching project.
The diagram shows the number of birds that she saw in one hour.
a Make a tally chart for this set of data.
b Use your tally chart to produce a frequency table.

challenge

Ronnie and Johnny recorded their dart scores differently. Who won?

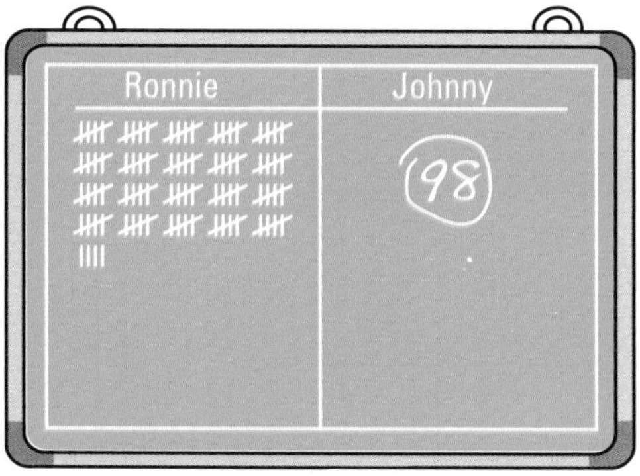

14c More bar charts

- Draw and use pictograms and bar charts

Keywords
Bar chart
Frequency table
Tally chart

p. 78

- With a set of data, you can:
  - Draw a **tally chart** to organise the data.
  - Use the tally chart to produce a **frequency table**.
  - Use the frequency table to draw a **bar chart**.

example

Astrid was asked by the school council to find out how students in her tutor group travelled to school.

She wrote down their answers.

Bus	Bus	Walk	Bike	Bus	Walk	Bus	Car	Bus	Bus
Bus	Bike	Car	Bus	Bus	Car	Bus	Bus	Bus	Walk
Car	Car	Bus	Bus	Walk	Bus	Walk	Bike	Bus	Bus

Produce a bar chart to represent this set of data.

First, make a tally chart.

Travel	Tally	Frequency
Bus	~~IIII~~ ~~IIII~~ ~~IIII~~ II	17
Walk	~~IIII~~	5
Bike	III	3
Car	~~IIII~~	5

Frequencies can be included in the tally chart.

Now draw the bar chart.

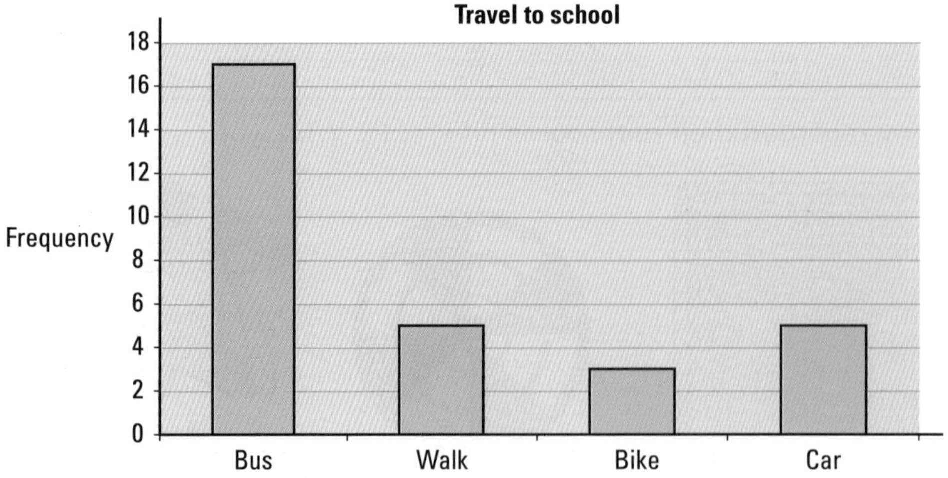

Exercise 14c

1 Draw a bar chart for the data in this pictogram.

Number of books read during Year 7 Reading Marathon

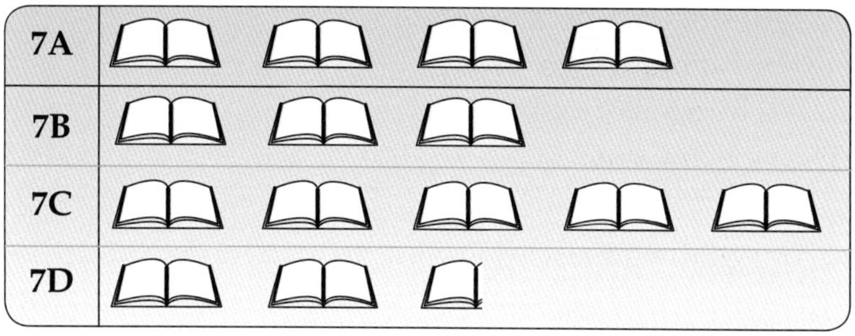

Key: [book] = 10 Books

2 Draw a bar chart for the data in this frequency table.

Packs of cat food eaten by Cheryl's cat in one week

Flavour	Lamb	Tuna	Cod	Beef
Frequency	4	1	5	2

3 Draw a bar chart for this set of data.

Vehicles recorded in a traffic survey

Vehicle	Car	Van	Lorry	Bus
Frequency	48	7	3	4

4 Here are the sports options chosen during Year 7 Activity Week at Speedwell Middle School.

a Draw a tally chart for this set of data.

b Use your tally chart to draw a frequency table.

c Use your frequency table to draw a bar chart.

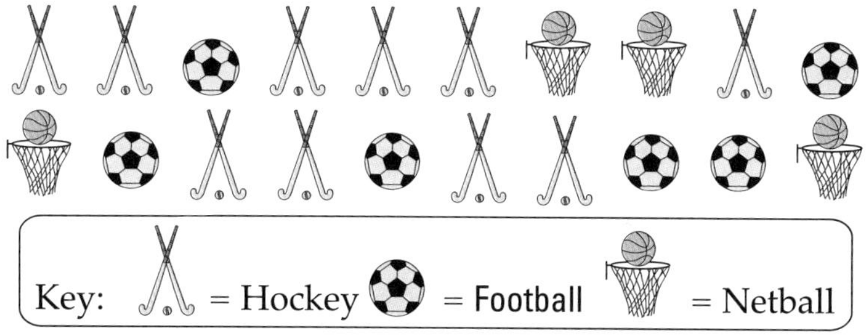

challenge

The Head of Year 7 at Fairview High School noted the tutor groups of the 50 students taking part in a school trip.

7W	7W	7Z	7W	7Y	7Z	7W	7X	7Y	7W
7Y	7X	7W	7Y	7W	7X	7Z	7Z	7W	7W
7W	7W	7Z	7Z	7W	7W	7W	7W	7X	7Z
7Z	7Y	7W	7X	7W	7Y	7Y	7W	7Y	7W
7X	7W	7W	7W	7Z	7W	7W	7X	7X	7X

Draw a bar chart to represent this set of data.

14c² More line graphs

- Use line graphs for changes over time

Keywords
Series

p. 80

- You can draw more than one **series** of data on a graph to compare the main features of the different data series.
  A graph is much clearer than a table of data.

example

Mark drew a graph to show the water level in Grey's Reservoir over two years.
Describe the main features of the graph.

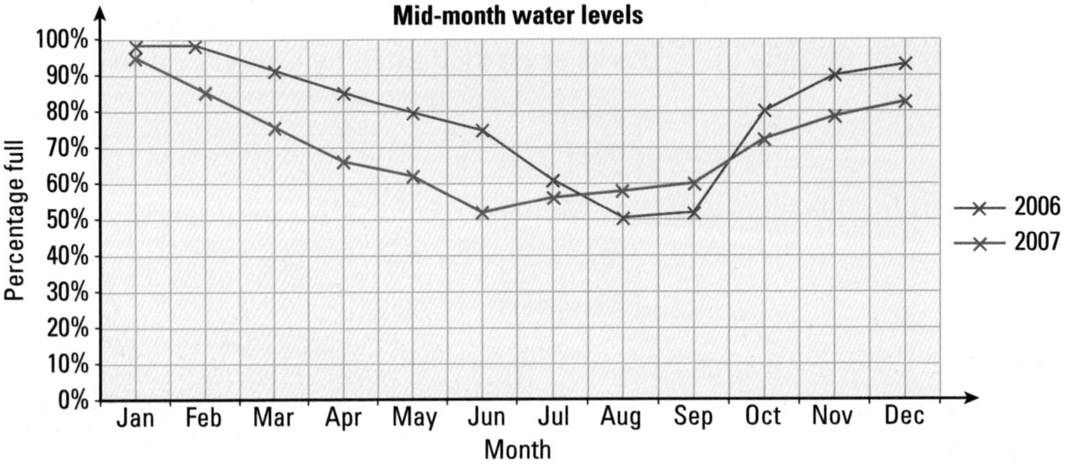

- In both years, the reservoir is highest during the winter months, and lowest during the summer months.
- The water levels were generally higher in 2006 than in 2007.
- The minimum level was just over 50% in both years.
- This level was achieved in June for 2007, and in August for 2006.

example

Mark drew this table as well.
Describe the main features of the data

Mid-month water levels (percentage full)

	Jan	Feb	Mar	Apr	May	Jun	Jul	Aug	Sep	Oct	Nov	Dec
2006	98	98	91	86	80	75	61	51	52	80	90	93
2007	95	85	76	67	62	52	57	58	60	72	79	82

This is actually the same data that was used in the previous example.
However, it is far easier to describe the data using the graph.

Exercise 14c^2

1 This line graph shows how the grass height of a lawn changed.

 a What was the grass height on day 1?

 b What was the greatest height the grass reached?

 c On which day was the grass cut?

 d Estimate the height of the grass on day 15.

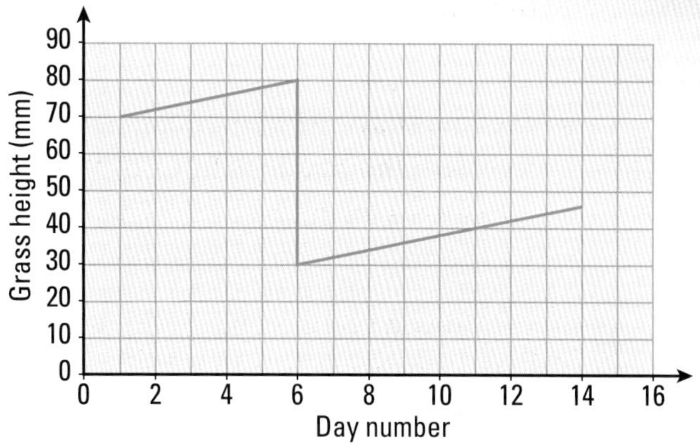

2 This line graph shows how the tide level at Dewey Harbour changed one day.

 a There were two low tides. When did these happen?

 b What were the times of the two high tides?

 c What was the height of the tide at 10 a.m.?

 d Captain Sparrow needs the height of the tide to be at least 8 m, so that he can sail his ship into the harbour. Between which times can he enter the harbour?

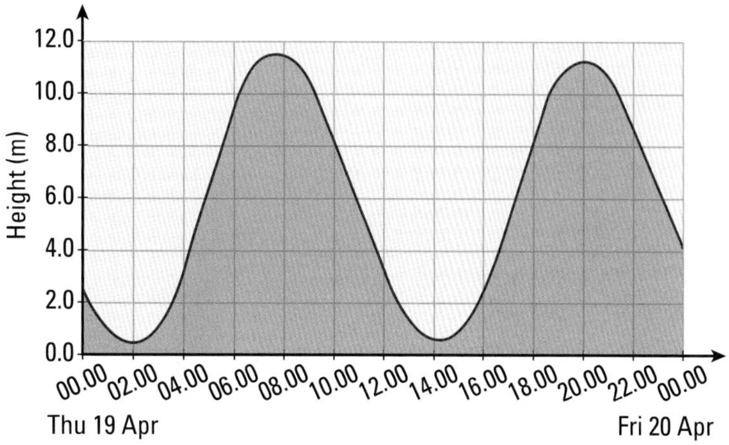

3 This line graph shows the average monthly temperatures in two cities.

 a Estimate the maximum temperature in each city in January.

 b During which months would you expect the temperature in Moscow to be higher than it is in Sydney?

 c For how many months of the year would you expect the temperature in Moscow to be below freezing?

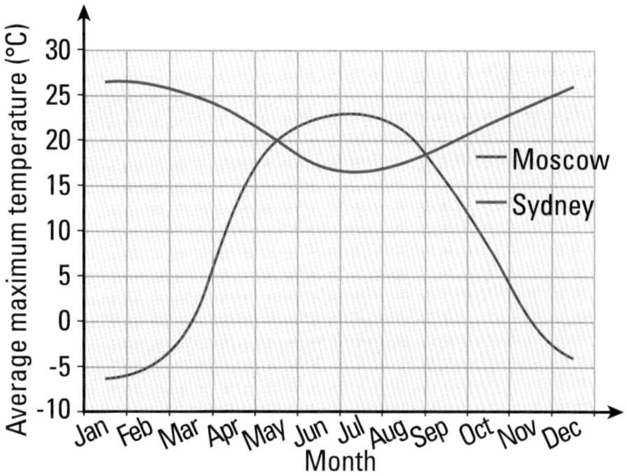

discussion

Find some examples of line graphs from newspapers or magazines, and describe their main features.

14d Averages – the mode

- Use the mode as an average

Keywords
Average
Frequency table
Mode

- An **average** is one value that represents a whole set of values. The mode is one type of average.

- The **mode** is the most common value in a set of data.

example

Twelve people wrote down their shoe sizes. Find the mode of this set of data.

The data can be written as a **frequency table**.

Shoe size	3	4	5	6
Frequency	2	5	4	1

The most common shoe size was 4.
The mode of this set of data is Size 4.

The mode is the size with the highest frequency.

The mode does not have to be a number.
This table shows the eye colour of 25 students

Eye colour	Blue	Green	Brown	Black
Frequency	7	5	12	1

Brown is the mode.

- A set of data might have two (or more) modes.

- A set of data might have no mode.

example

Find the mode of each set of data.

a 3 6 6 6 7 8
b 4 4 5 8 9 9 10
c 2 5 7 8 11

a The mode is 6.
b This set of data has two modes. The modes are 4 and 9.
c All of the values have a frequency of 1. There is no mode.

It helps to put data in order to find the mode.

Exercise 14d

1 Find the mode of each set of data.

a	3	5	5	8						
b	1	4	4	6	6	6	7	8	8	10
c	2	3	3	5	6	7	7	7	9	
d	14	17	17	19	22					

These sets of data are already in order.

2 Find the mode of each set of data.

a	3	4	2	4						
b	5	7	8	5	8	4	6	8	3	8
c	19	17	18	19	15	18	16	18		
d	3.1	3.5	3.4	3.3	3.4	3.4				

These sets of data are not in order.

3 Pat recorded the number of people travelling in each car going past a check point.

a Make a **tally chart**.

b Draw a frequency table.

c Use your frequency table to find the mode of the set of data.

4 Suresh asked 50 people to keep a record of how many telephone calls they received in a week.

a Make a tally chart and a frequency table for this set of data.

b Use your frequency table to produce a **bar chart** for the data.

c Find the mode of the number of calls received.

Phone Calls

File Edit View Insert Format Tools Data Window Help Acrobat

	A	B	C	D	E	F	G	H	I	J
1	4	9	11	7	8	15	12	6	4	8
2	8	8	9	6	10	9	9	8	5	2
3	9	6	5	12	9	7	9	8	6	9
4	9	9	9	9	6	4	7	7	10	8
5	6	4	5	8	9	11	7	10	7	11

challenge

You say something is 'the mode' if it is fashionable. What do you think is 'the mode' in this picture?

14d² Averages – the median

- Use the median as an average

Keywords
Median
Order

The **median** is another type of average.

p. 2

- To find the median, put the data in order, and then find the middle value.
  3 3 4 (5) 5 6 7   5 is the median.

example

Jules asked nine people their ages.

	12	34	56	21	13	9	4	17	34

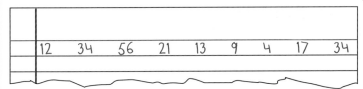

Find the median age for this group of people.

Put the data in **order**.

4   9   12   13   17   21   34   34   56

The middle number is 17, so the median age is 17.

It is easy to find the 'middle number' when you have an odd number of data values.
If you have an even number of data values, there will be no 'middle number', but you can still find the median.

example

Find the median age.
26   81   45   53

First, put the values in order:

26   (45   53)   81

There is no 'middle number'.
Take the two numbers nearest the middle.   45 and 53
Add them together,   45 + 53 = 98
and divide the total by 2.   98 ÷ 2 = 49
The median age is 49.

Exercise 14d²

1 Find the median of each set of data.

These sets of data are already in order.

a 2 3 4 4 7

b 4 9 12

c 3 6 8 11 12

2 Find the median of each set of data.

These will need to be ordered before finding the median.

a 5 7 4

b 2 9 8 3 4

c 1 9 6 8

3 At the Athens Olympics, the men's 100 m final times were

Place	1	2	3	4	5	6	7
Time (s)	9.85	9.86	9.87	9.89	9.94	10.00	10.10

Find the median finishing time for the race.

4 Arrange each set of data in order.
Find the median of each.

a Nine children's shoe sizes: 3, 6, 4, 6, 6, 5, 4, 7, 6

b Ten people's ages: 21, 18, 35, 48, 16, 26, 30, 18, 14, 10

c Lengths (in cm) of six worms: 11, 9, 12, 10, 12, 13

d Number of people in ten families: 4, 5, 3, 2, 4, 3, 4, 3, 2, 6

5 The populations of five cities are

Leicester	280 000
Brighton & Hove	248 000
Manchester	422 000
Cardiff	305 000
Edinburgh	449 000

a Write this list of populations in order of size.

b Find the median population of the five cities.

Edinburgh

discussion

Find the median of these data sets.

a 4, 5, 6, 100, 100

b 1, 3, 4, 5, 8, 9

c 10, 11, 15, 205, 318, 906

Is the median a good representation of the data?

14e The range

- Use the range to measure the spread of data

Keywords
Difference *Minimum*
Maximum *Range*

- You can measure how 'spread apart' a set of data is by finding the **range**.

- The range is the **difference** between the largest and smallest values.
  Shoe sizes: (3) 3 4 4 5 7 (9)
  Subtract: $9 - 3 = 6$ The range is 6 shoe sizes.

The largest and smallest values are called the **maximum** and **minimum.**

example

Debbie asks eight people how many cups of coffee they had drunk today.
Find the range of this set of data.

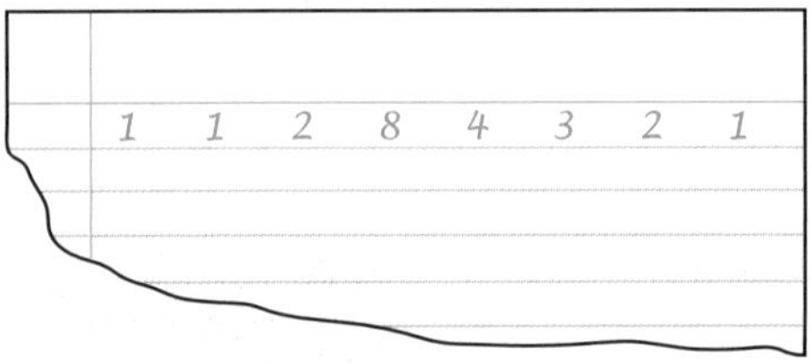

In order: (1) 1 1 2 2 3 4 (8)
The range = maximum − minimum
$= 8 - 1$
The range is 7.

- You can work out the range and the median of a set of data at the same time.

example

The guide lists the heights of the players in two basketball teams.
Find the range of the heights for each team.

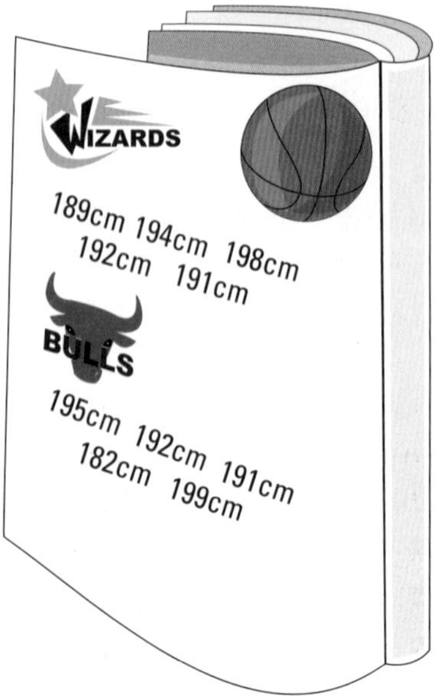

First, write the data in order.

Wizards	189	191	192	194	198
Bulls	182	191	192	195	199

The range for the Wizards is 198 cm − 189 cm = 9 cm
The range for the Bulls is 199 cm − 182 cm = 17 cm
The heights of the Bulls are much more varied than the heights of the Wizards.

Exercise 14e

1 Find the range for each set of data.

a	3	9	14		
b	4	5	9	22	25
c	3	7	7	9	
d	4	8	9	12	

2 Write each set of data in order. Then find the range of each set.

a	4	11	6		
b	3	8	6	7	9
c	5	5	1	9	
d	6	12	5	8	

3 Alex weighed six cats. The heaviest cat weighed 4.8 kg, and the lightest one weighed 3.1 kg.
What was the range of the weight of the cats?

4 Calculate the range of the heights of the buildings shown in the table.

Building	Height (m)
Taipei 101, Taipei, Taiwan	508
Petronas Tower 1, Kuala Lumpur, Malaysia	452
Petronas Tower 2, Kuala Lumpur, Malaysia	452
Sears Tower, Chicago	442
Jin Mao Building, Shanghai	421

Petronas Towers

5 The range of the lengths of four motorways was 51 km.
The shortest motorway was 104 km.
How long was the longest motorway?

discussion

Find the range of each of these sets of data.

a	£19	£10	£16	£13	£12	£20
b	£5	£25	£5	£5	£5	
c	7p	5p	26p	18p	£20.05	

Does the range give you a good picture of how the data in each set are spread out?

14f Comparing data sets

- Compare two sets of data using the mode and range

Keywords
Average *Median* *Mode* *Range* *Spread* *Size* *Varied*

You often need to compare two sets of data.

- An **average** can be used to compare the **size** of the values.
  mode = most common
  The modal score is the most common score.

Another average is the **median**, or middle number.

- The **range** can be used to compare the **spread** of the values.
  range = maximum − minimum

example

For a science experiment, Mandy measured leaves (in millimetres) from two different trees.
Compare the two sets of data.

Oak	42	42	44	45	47	47	47	47	50	50	51
Birch	24	27	32	34	38	38	38	43	44	47	48

The Oak has a modal leaf length of 47 mm.
The range is 51 mm − 42 mm = 9 mm.

The Birch has a modal leaf length of 38 mm.
The range is 48 mm − 24 mm = 24 mm.

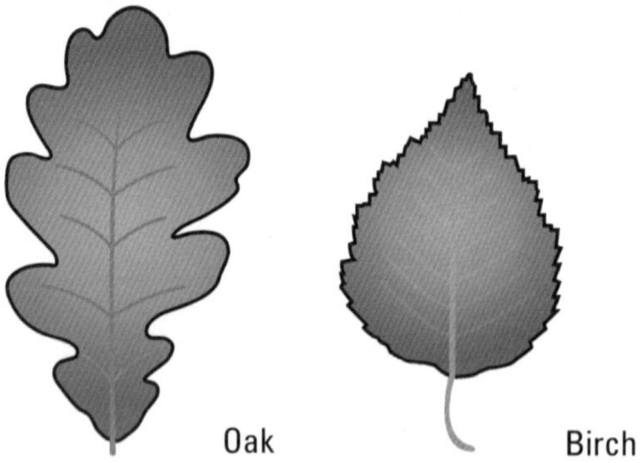

On these trees, it is more common for the Oak leaves to be longer than the Birch leaves.

However, the Birch leaf lengths are much more **varied** than the Oak leaf lengths.

Varied means differing.

Exercise 14f

1 Mrs Jones recorded the tests scores for five students in Class 7A and five students in Class 7B.

7A test scores	4	8	9	9	10
7B test scores	2	3	5	10	10

a Find the modal score for each class.
b Find the range of the scores from each class.
c Which class did best on the test? Explain your answer.
d Which class had the most varied scores? Explain your answer.

2 Class 7M recorded the number of pieces of homework they handed in last week.

Boys	8	7	7	6	8	7	6	8	8	7
Girls	4	11	9	11	7	9	10	11	2	5

a Calculate the mode for the boys.
b Calculate the mode for the girls.
c Which group usually hands in the most homework? Explain your answer.
d Find the range for the boys.
e Find the range for the girls.
f Was the boys' or the girls' homework more varied? Explain your answer.

3 The students in Class 7W did two sports assessments.
Each student was given a mark out of 10.
The table shows the results

Run	9	8	8	9	7	8	9	8	7	9	9	9	8	7	10
	9	9	8	8	7	8	9	8	9	8	7	5	9	8	9
Stretch	7	9	4	7	5	7	7	9	5	6	7	3	7	7	2
	7	4	7	5	9	6	2	7	3	6	7	2	6	7	7

a Calculate the mode for each assessment.
b Calculate the range of the scores for each assessment.
c How would you compare the class' performance on the two tests?

task

Look up the end of season results for your local football team.
a Find the modal number of goals scored.
b Find the range of goals scored.
c Does the mode or the range give a better idea of how the team did?

14 Consolidation

14a

1 Eva decides to ask all of the students in her group at college which method of energy conservation they each think is the most important.

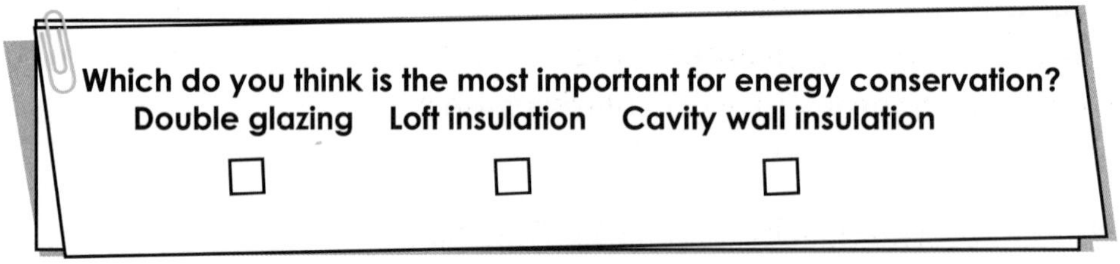

Which do you think is the most important for energy conservation?
Double glazing
Loft insulation
Cavity wall insulation

Suggest any improvements that might be made to Eva's questionnaire.

14b

2 A dice was rolled 30 times. The scores were:

2	5	1	3	1	3	4	1	6	4	4	4	4	2	5
5	5	3	5	4	3	5	2	3	4	2	3	2	6	6

a Make a tally chart for this set of data.

b Use your tally chart to produce a frequency table.

14c

3 The table shows details of the weights of the 30 children in Class 7D.

Weight (kg)	40	41	42	43	44	45	46
Frequency (number of children)	2	3	5	8	7	4	1

Display the data on a bar chart.

14c²

4 A group of hikers walked 20 km between 10 a.m. and 2.30 p.m. The line graph shows details of their progress.

a What distance had they walked by **i** 11.15 a.m. **ii** 12.15 p.m. **iii** 10.45 a.m. and **iv** 12.45 p.m.?

b During which half hour interval did they walk the furthest? How far was this?

c Between which times did they stop for lunch?

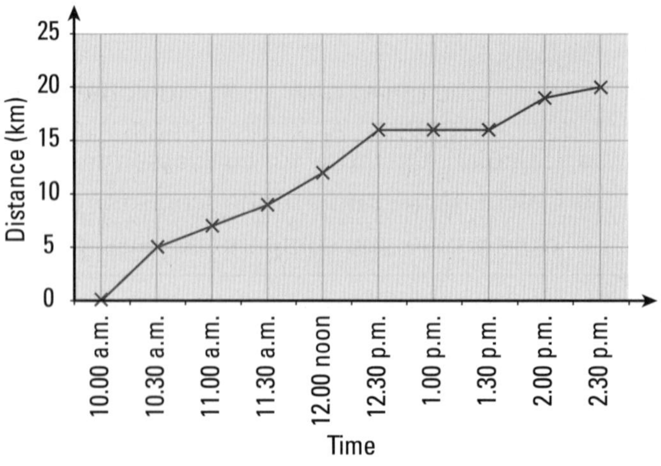

14d

5 Find the mode of each set.

a	5	7	6	5	8	5	4	5
b	6	7	7	4	7	5	7	7
c	cat	dog	cat	hamster	dog	cat		
d	blue	red	green	blue	black	blue		

14d²

6 Arrange these sets of data in order and find the median.

a One day a lifting bridge had to be raised eight times and the delays to traffic were
12, 18, 21, 23, 13, 9, 11 and 17 minutes.

b The distances between successive roundabouts along a road are
500, 300, 1000, 900, 650, 600, 400, 1100, 750, 450, 950 and 800 metres.

c In a cricket match all eleven players batted and their scores were,
65, 43, 35, 8, 21, 0, 6, 17, 32, 13 and 10 runs.

14e

7 Two village football teams met in a local cup final after a four round contest. Their match attendances were as shown. Find the range for both sets of figures and comment on your results.

	1st Round	2nd Round	3rd Round	Semi Final
Team A	1370	1410	1840	2360
Team B	560	1040	2130	3250

14f

8 Near to where Shani works there are two cafes that she can go to at lunch time. She timed how long it took the waitress on duty to bring her lunch on ten different occasions at both cafes.

Cafe A 5, 3, 3, 6, 6, 8, 3, 5, 3 and 8 minutes

Cafe B 8, 8, 6, 4, 6, 3, 8, 8, 5 and 4 minutes

Find the mode and range for each of the two sets of data.
Comment on your results in as many ways as possible.

14 Summary

Key indicators

- Construct graphs and charts **Level 3**
- Find the mode and median Level 4
- Calculate the range Level 4

Level 3

1 The eye colours of the students in Reece's class are shown in the table.

Construct a bar chart to show the information.

Eye colour	Tally
Brown	𝍸 II
Blue	𝍸 𝍸
Green	IIII
Grey	III
Black	II

Kelly's answer ✔

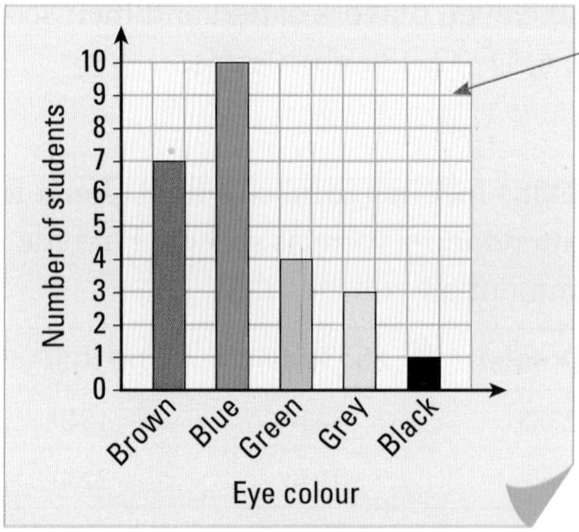

Kelly writes down the totals for each colour.

Brown	7
Blue	10
Green	4
Grey	3
Black	1

Level 4

2 These are the names of the twelve people who work for a company.

Ali	Claire	Kiki	Suki
Brian	Claire	Lucy	Tom
Claire	James	Ryan	Tom

a What name is the mode?

b One person leaves the company.
A different person joins the company.
Now the name that is the mode is Tom.
Write the missing names in the sentences below.

The name of the person who leaves is __________

The name of the person who joins is __________

Key Stage 3 2007 3–5 Paper 2

15 Number

Calculations

In 1843, Lady Ada Lovelace wrote what would become the first computer program when she wrote a series of instructions for one of the first 'computers', the Analytical engine.

What's the point? Computers and calculators aren't as modern as we think. People have been using these tools for generations.

Check in

Level 2

1 Copy and complete these two digit additions and subtractions.

a $\begin{array}{r} 3\ 3 \\ +\ 1\ 6 \\ \hline \square\square \end{array}$ **b** $\begin{array}{r} 2\ 8 \\ -\ 1\ 2 \\ \hline \square\square \end{array}$ **c** $\begin{array}{r} 5\ 6 \\ +\ 2\ \square \\ \hline \square\ 9 \end{array}$ **d** $\begin{array}{r} 1\ 6\ \square \\ -\ \ \square\ 2 \\ \hline \square\ 1\ 2 \end{array}$ **e** $\begin{array}{r} \square\ 1\ 5 \\ +\ 3\ \square\ 2 \\ \hline 9\ 5\ \square \end{array}$

Level 3

2 Copy and complete this grid to work out this multiplication.

×	200	10	4
5			

$214 \times 5 =$

Level 4

3 Copy and complete these equivalences.

a $50\% = \frac{50}{100} = \frac{1}{\square}$ **b** $25\% = \frac{25}{100} = \frac{\square}{4}$ **c** $10\% = \frac{10}{100} = \frac{\square}{\square}$

15a Mental methods of addition

- Use a number line to help to add numbers mentally

Keywords
Jottings
Lots of

Remember, using mental methods to add can make your work easier.

Adding in 10s

p. 8

31 + 40 . . . (40 is 10 + 10 + 10 + 10)

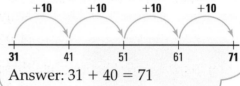

Start at 31 and add four **lots of** 10.

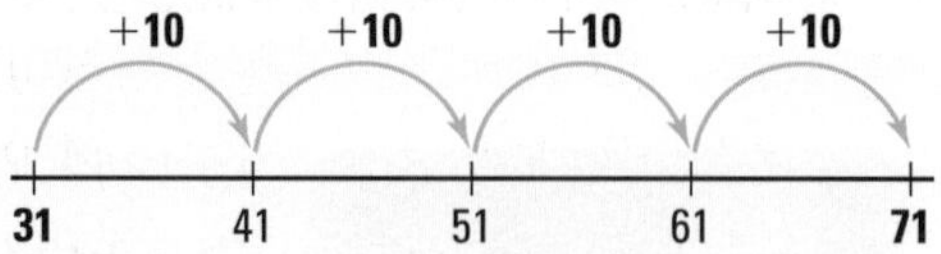

Answer: 31 + 40 = 71

Adding in 10s and units

34 + 23 . . . (23 is 10 + 10 + 1 + 1 + 1)

Start at 34 and add two **lots of** 10 and then 3 units.

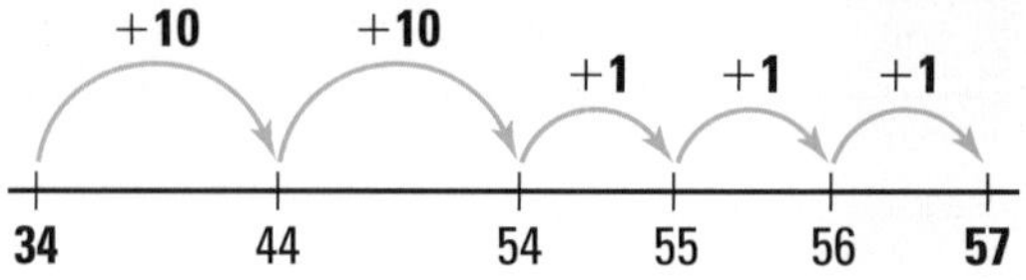

Answer: 34 + 23 = 57

Using jottings

511 + 2380

Start with the bigger number, 2380 and then add on 511 (5 hundreds, 1 ten and 1 unit).

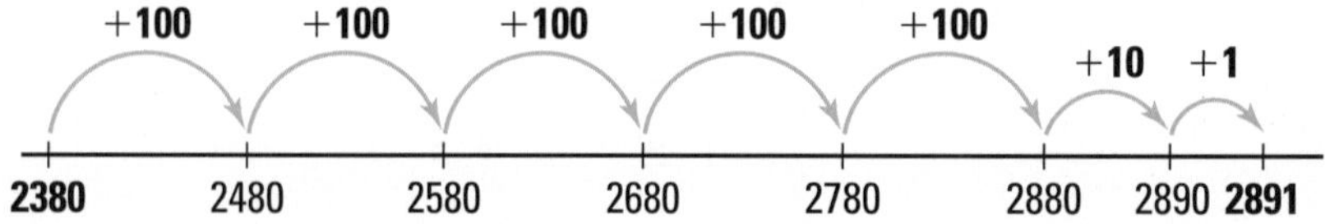

Answer: 511 + 2380 = 2891

example

Use jottings to add 36 and 142.

Count on from the larger number.

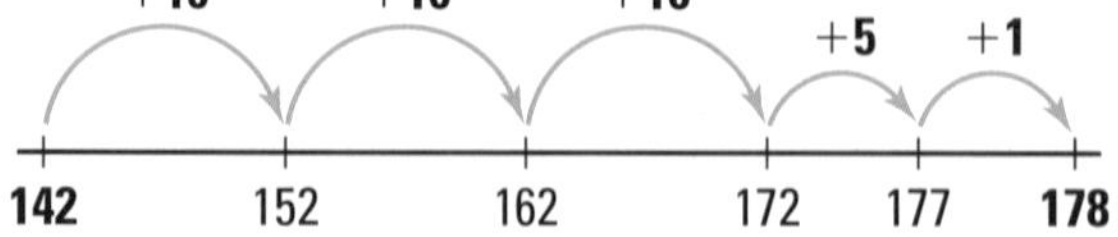

Answer: 142 + 36 = 178

Exercise 15a

1 Work these problems out in your head.

a 5 + 4	**b** 10 + 6	**c** 9 + 6	**d** 5 + 13
e 0 + 12	**f** 15 + 4	**g** 8 + 9	**h** 6 + 11
i 16 + 3	**j** 7 + 13	**k** 7 + 8	**l** 14 + 6

2 By counting on in jumps of 10, complete these number patterns.

a 21, 31, □, □, 61 **b** 47, □, □, □, 87, □

c 84, □, □, □, □, 134 **d** 99, □, □, □, □, □

3 By counting on in jumps of 100, complete these number patterns.

a 110, 210, □, □, □, 610 **b** 243, □, □, □, 643, □

c 76, □, □, □, 476, □ **d** 3, □, □, 303, □, □

4 Calculate these additions in your head.
Only write down your final answer.

a 25 + 20	**b** 33 + 40	**c** 17 + 30	**d** 39 + 50
e 25 + 21	**f** 34 + 41	**g** 27 + 32	**h** 56 + 33

5 These problems are more difficult.
Use jottings to help you.
The first one is started for you.

a 34 + 23 =

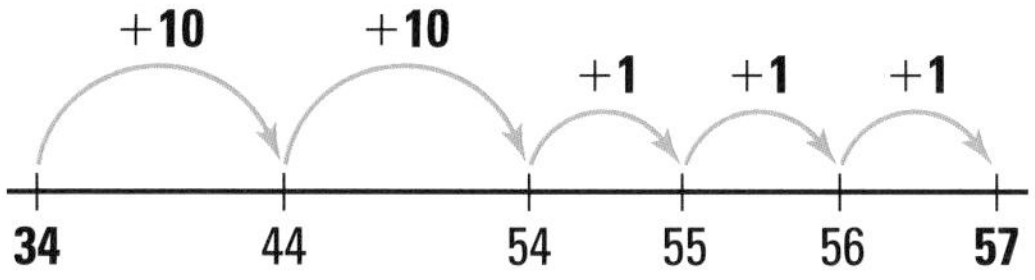

b 44 + 32 **c** 28 + 24

d 94 + 13 **e** 144 + 23

f 262 + 115 **g** 25 + 188

challenge

What addition sums are shown by these jottings?

a

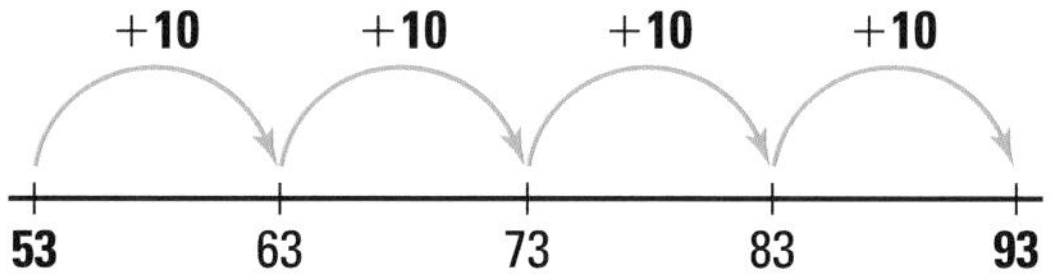

→ ? + ? = ?

b

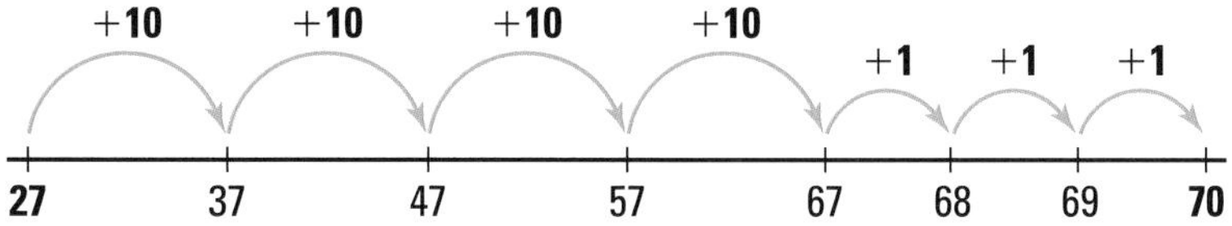

→ ? + ? = ?

15b Mental methods of subtraction

- Use a number line to help to subtract numbers mentally

Keywords
Jottings
Subtract
Take away

Remember, using mental methods to subtract can make your work easier.

p. 10

Subtracting in 10s

51 − 30 . . . (−30 is −10 − 10 − 10)

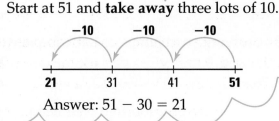

Start at 51 and **take away** three lots of 10.

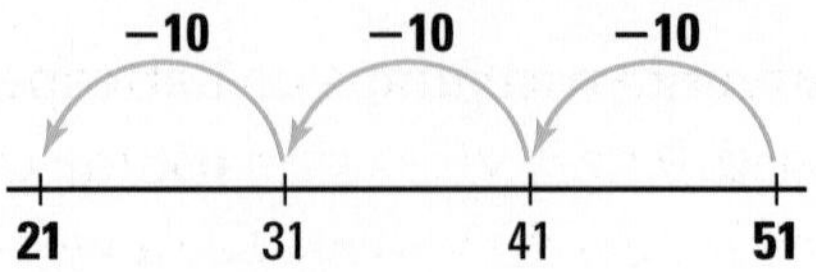

Answer: 51 − 30 = 21

Subtracting in 10s and units

45 − 23 . . . (−23 is −10 −10 − 1 − 1 − 1)

Start at 45 and take away two lots of 10 and then 3 units.

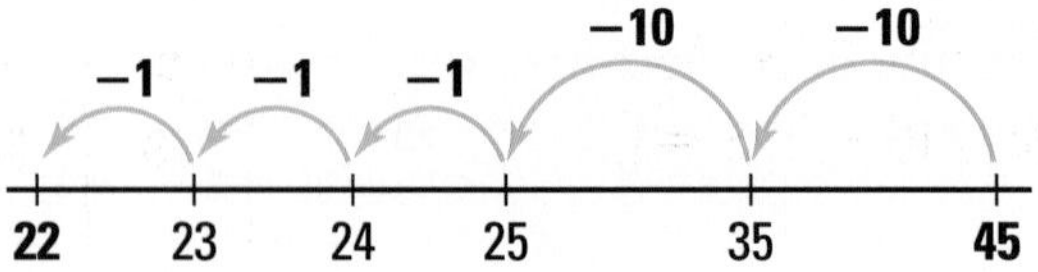

Answer: 45 − 23 = 22

Using jottings

453 − 36 . . . (−36 is −10 − 10 − 10 − 5 − 1)

Start at 453 and take away three lots of 10, one 5 and one unit.

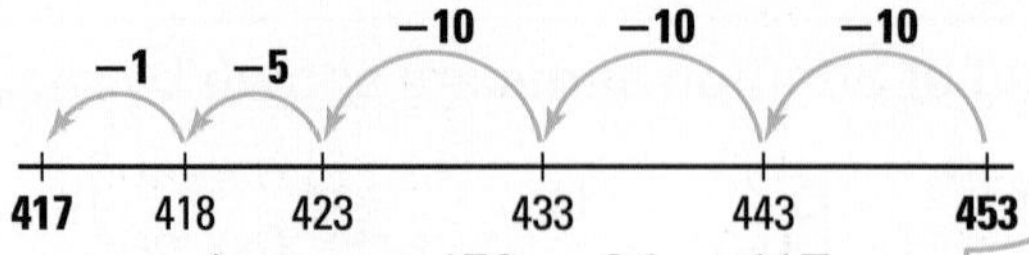

Answer: 453 − 36 = 417

example

Take 42 from 182.

Subtract in 10s and units. Start from the larger number.

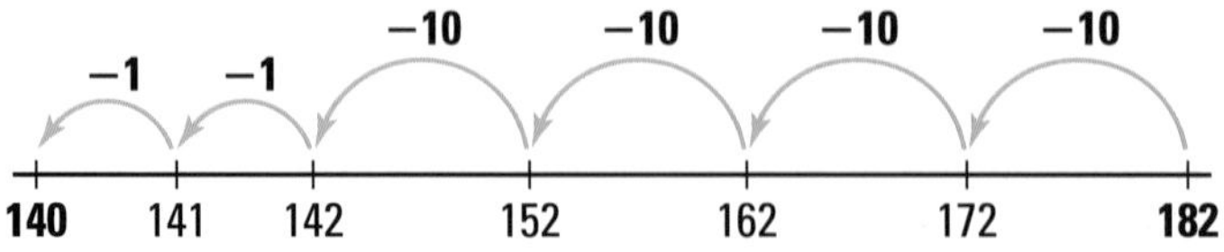

Answer: 182 − 42 = 140

Exercise 15b

1 Work these problems out in your head.

a 8 − 3 **b** 10 − 7 **c** 9 − 7 **d** 12 − 9

e 16 − 6 **f** 15 − 4 **g** 20 − 9 **h** 11 − 0

i 17 − 8 **j** 19 − 15 **k** 16 − 11 **l** 18 − 18

2 By counting back in jumps of 10, complete these number patterns.

a 92, 82, □, □, □, 42 **b** 57, □, □, □, 17, □

c 120, □, □, □, □, 70 **d** 157, □, □, □, □, □

3 The answer to each question corresponds to a letter in the grid. When you complete the questions, write the letters down to make a word.

You can do the problems in your head, or use jottings.

Letter 1: 79 − 44 = □

Letter 2: 60 − 41 = □

Letter 3: 107 − 62 = □

Letter 4: 71 − 45 = □

Letter 5: 134 − 88 = □

Letter 6: 146 − 118 = □

9	10	11	12	13	14	15	16
w	h	p	c	r	z	f	m
17	18	19	20	21	22	23	24
a	j	e	l	y	n	t	q
25	26	27	28	29	30	31	32
o	i	b	s	u	v	d	x
33	34	35	36	37	38	39	40
k	a	g	t	r	m	e	l
41	42	43	44	45	46	47	48
h	p	o	k	n	u	s	b

4 Work out these subtractions in your head. The first one is done for you.

a 5110 − 110

Answer: 5110 − 110 = 5000

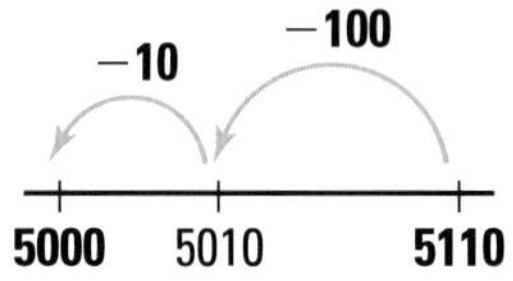

b 4800 − 400 **c** 2300 − 400 **d** 6500 – 450

e 4150 − 150 **f** 1100 − 200 **g** 1660 – 655

challenge

What subtractions are shown by these jottings?

a

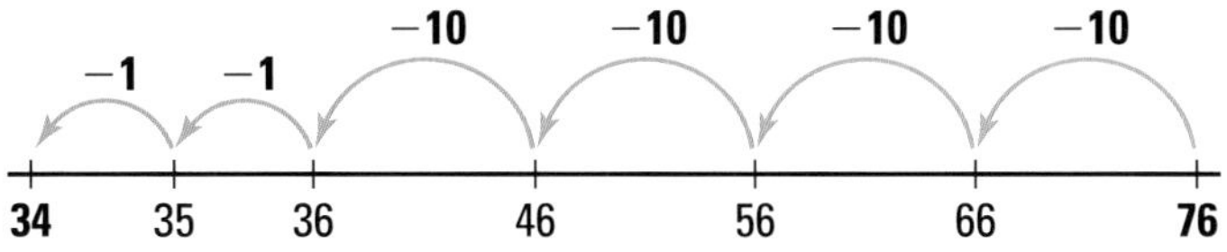

→ □ − □ = □

b

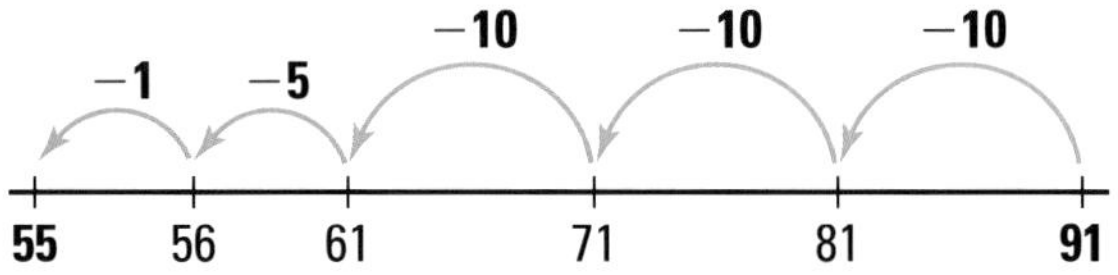

→ □ − □ = □

15c Written methods of + and −

- Use written methods with columns to add and subtract

Keywords
Carrying HTU
Column Vertical
Decomposition

Adding in columns

p. 12

H	T	U
4	2	6
+ 3	3	2
7	5	8

Add digits vertically down each column.

Carrying over

T	U
5	**8**
+ 2	**5**
	3
1	

8 add 5 makes 13 (1 ten and 3 units). The single 10 has to be carried over to the 10s column.

T	U
5	8
+ **2**	5
8	3
1	

Remember to include the 'carried-over' 10 when you add the 10s column. 58 + 25 = 83

Subtracting in columns

H	T	U
6	4	7
− 2	1	5
4	3	2

Subtract the bottom number from the top number in each column.

Decomposition

H	T	U
1	⁵~~6~~	¹**1**
+	2	**5**
		6

You cannot take 5 away from 1. Take 1 ten from the 6 tens, to make 11 in the units column. Take 5 from 11.

H	T	U
1	⁵~~6~~	¹1
+	**2**	5
1	**3**	6

Take the 2 tens from the 5 tens to leave you 3 tens. Now subtract the hundreds. 161 − 25 = 136

example

a Use column addition to work out 437 + 181

4	3	7
+ 1	8	1
6	1	8
1		

437 + 181 = 618

b Use column subtraction to work out 627 − 282

⁵~~6~~	¹2	7
− 2	8	2
3	4	5
1		

627 − 282 = 345

Decimal additions and subtractions can be done in the same way – but don't forget the decimal point.

54.2 – 23.6

T	U · t
5	³~~4~~·¹2
− 2	3·6
3	0·6

Exercise 15c

1 Use columns to work out the problems.

a 251 + 427 b 106 + 371 c 544 + 352 d 262 + 533

2 Use columns to work out the problems.

a 357 − 143 b 584 − 252 c 298 − 160 d 871 − 551

3 Work out these problems involving 'carrying' and decomposition.

Workcard 1
Addition

a 417 + 255	**b** 309 + 263	**c** 291 + 340
d 365 + 164	**e** 120 + 585	**f** 759 + 168

Workcard 2
Subtraction

a 580 − 155	**b** 762 − 435	**c** 918 − 452
d 707 − 237	**e** 419 − 290	**f** 635 − 365

4 Work out these problems. Remember to use the decimal point.

Workcard 3
Addition of decimals

a 35·4 + 53·5	**b** 56·2 + 20·3	**c** 24·8 + 33·4
d 33·5 + 15·5	**e** 10·9 + 55·5	**f** 29·8 + 30·8

Workcard 4
Subtraction of decimals

a 68·7 − 25·4	**b** 49·7 − 10·5	**c** 98·0 − 41·2
d 54·2 − 21·6	**e** 65·8 − 39·0	**f** 87·4 − 56·8

challenge

Here are some major problems!

a 12345678901234567890 + 98765432109876543210

b 8640864086408640 − 1234123412341234

15d Multiples and factors

- Know what multiples and factors are and find them

Keywords
Divide
Factor
Multiple

p. 154

Multiples

- Numbers in a multiplication table are called **multiples.**

Multiples of **5** are:
5, 10, 15, 20, 25 . . . . .

Is 21 a multiple of 7?
Yes, it is in the 7 times table.

Is 18 a multiple of 4?
No, it is not in the 4 times table.

×	1	2	3	4	5	6	7	8	9	10
1	1	2	3	4	5	6	7	8	9	10
2	2	4	6	8	10	12	14	16	18	20
3	3	6	9	12	15	18	21	24	27	30
4	4	8	12	16	20	24	28	32	36	40
5	5	10	15	20	25	30	35	40	45	50
6	6	12	18	24	30	36	42	48	54	60
7	7	14	21	28	35	42	49	56	63	70
8	8	16	24	32	40	48	56	64	72	80
9	9	18	27	36	45	54	63	72	81	90
10	10	20	30	40	50	60	70	80	90	100

p. 152

Factors

- A **factor** is a number that **divides** exactly into another number.

Factors of **8** are:

1, 2, 4, and 8

$8 \div \mathbf{1} = 8$
$8 \div \mathbf{2} = 4$
$8 \div \mathbf{4} = 2$
$8 \div \mathbf{8} = 1$

×	1	2	3	4	5	6	7	8	9	10
1	1	2	3	4	5	6	7	8	9	10
2	2	4	6	8	10	12	14	16	18	20
3	3	6	9	12	15	18	21	24	27	30
4	4	8	12	16	20	24	28	32	36	40
5	5	10	15	20	25	30	35	40	45	50
6	6	12	18	24	30	36	42	48	54	60
7	7	14	21	28	35	42	49	56	63	70
8	8	16	24	32	40	48	56	64	72	80
9	9	18	27	36	45	54	63	72	81	90
10	10	20	30	40	50	60	70	80	90	100

4 is a factor of all of these numbers – it divides into each one exactly.

4 ⟷ 4 , 8 , 12 , 16 , 20

All of these numbers are multiples of 4 – they are all in the 4 times table.

example

a Give three factors of 15. **b** Give three multiples of 8.

a $15 \div 1 = 15$
$15 \div 3 = 5$
$15 \div 5 = 3$
1, 3 and 5 are factors of 15.

b $8 \times 1 = 8$
$8 \times 2 = 16$
$8 \times 3 = 24$
8, 16 and 24 are multiples of 8.

Exercise 15d

1 Copy and complete these number patterns.

a Multiples of 3 → 3, 6, 9, □, □, 18

b Multiples of 6 → 6, 12, □, □, 30, 36

c Multiples of 10 → 30, 40, □, □, 70

d Multiples of 9 → 9, □, 27, □, 45, 54

2 Starting with each of the numbers in the green box, follow their multiples to one of the capital letters. Which number matches with which capital letter?

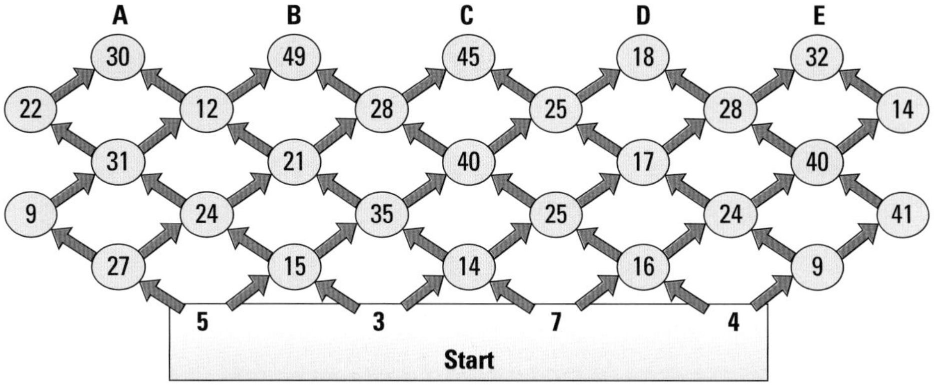

3 Copy and complete these statements about numbers and their factors. The first statement is done for you.

a 3 and 5 are factors of 15 → 15 ÷ 5 = 3 and 15 ÷ 3 = 5 and 3 × 5 = 15

b 4 and 5 are factors of 20 → 20 ÷ □ = 5 and 20 ÷ □ = 4 and □ × 5 = 20

c 9 and 2 are factors of 18 → □ ÷ 2 = 9 and 18 ÷ □ = 2 and 9 × □ = 18

d 4 and 3 are factors of 12 → □ ÷ 4 = □ and 12 ÷ □ = □ and □ × □ = □

4 List as many factors as you can for each of these numbers. The first is done for you.

a

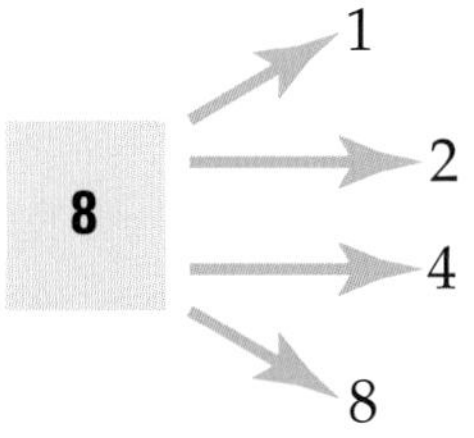

b

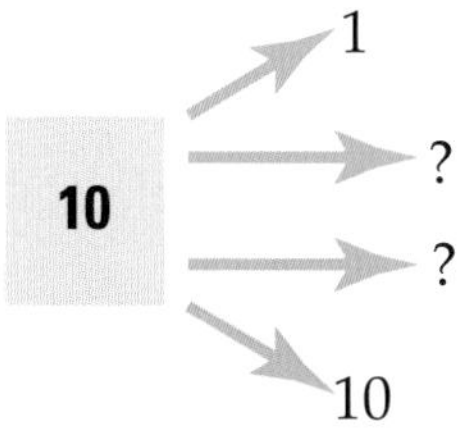

c

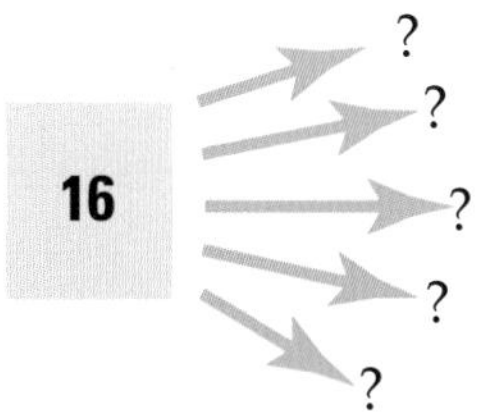

challenge

Some numbers have only two factors.
The factors of 5 are 1 and 5. It has no other factors.

Which of these numbers has only two factors?

12 9 7 14 13

Can you find a number that has just three factors?

15e Tests of divisibility

- Use tests of divisibility

Keywords
Digit Even
Divisibility Multiple

p. 110

Here are some quick and easy checks to see if your number will divide exactly.

÷ 2

If the number you are dividing into ends with an **even digit** (2, 4, 6, 8, 0), 2 will divide into it exactly.

28 → $28 \div 2 = 14$ ✓

23 → $23 \div 2 = 11\frac{1}{2}$ ✗

÷ 10

If the number you are dividing into ends with 0, 10 will divide into it exactly.

350 → $350 \div 10 = 35$ ✓

238 → $238 \div 10 = 23\frac{4}{5}$ ✗

÷ 5

If the number you are dividing into ends with 0 or 5, 5 will divide into it exactly.

45 → $45 \div 5 = 9$ ✓

37 → $37 \div 5 = 7\frac{2}{5}$ ✗

- **If a number can be divided by 5, it is a multiple of 5.**
  This is the same for all numbers.

example

Which two numbers in this list are not **multiples** of 5?

25, 57, 60, 205, 208, 325

Multiples of 5 end in 5 or 0.
57 and 208 do not follow this rule. They are not multiples of 5.

÷ 3

If the digits of the number you are dividing into add up to a multiple of 3 (3, 6, 9, 12 ...) then 3 will divide into it exactly.

Will 3 divide into 216 exactly? 2 + 1 + 6 = **9** (9 **is** a multiple of 3) ✓

Will 3 divide into 217 exactly? 2 + 1 + 7 = **10** (10 **is not** a multiple of 3) ✗

÷ 4

If the last two digits of the number you are dividing into is **divisible** by 4, then 4 will divide into it exactly.

Will 4 divide into 4**20** exactly? 4 divides into 20 exactly 5 times ✓

Will 4 divide into 3**27** exactly? 4 does not divide into 27 ✗

Exercise 15e

1 **a** Will 2, 5 and 10 all divide exactly into 20?
b Will 2, 5 and 10 all divide exactly into 40?
c Will 2, 5 and 10 all divide exactly into 35?
d What do you notice about the numbers that 2, 5 and 10 **will** all divide into exactly?

2 Which three numbers from the list cannot be exactly divided by 2?

26	44	31	68
180	109	15	662

3 Which two numbers from the list cannot be exactly divided by 10?

60	45	90	70
350	230	110	305

4 Which two numbers from the list cannot be exactly divided by 5?

30	85	55	58
125	103	160	105

5 Carlos has £216.
a Can he share it exactly 3 ways?
b Can he share it exactly 4 ways?
c Can he share it exactly 5 ways?

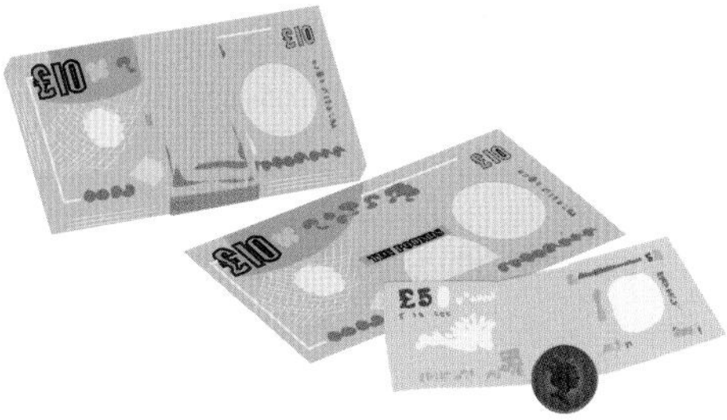

6 Cassie has £225.
a Can she share it exactly 3 ways?
b Can she share it exactly 4 ways?
c Can she share it exactly 5 ways?

7 Answer **yes** or **no** to each question.
a Can 5 divide into 47 860 exactly?
b Can 2 divide into 63 657 exactly?
c Can 4 divide into 31 724 exactly?
d Can 3 divide into 3141 exactly?
e Can 10 divide into 16 145 exactly?
f Can 3 divide into 3521 exactly?
g Can 2 divide into 84 130 exactly?
h Can 4 divide into 53 214 exactly?
i Can 5 divide into 15 151 exactly?
j Can 10 divide into 45 040 exactly?

challenge

Which number from this group **cannot** be divided exactly by at least one of these numbers: 2, 3, 4, 5 or 10?

135	340	229	312

Use tests for divisibility to find the correct answer.

15f Written methods of multiplication

- Multiply a large number by a single-digit number using a grid

Keywords
Grid *Multiply*
HTU *Partition*

p. 106

- The grid method helps you to work out harder multipications.

Multiply 6 × 35

Partition 35 into tens and units (30 + 5).
Lay the number out in a **grid**.

×	30	5
6		

Multiply the numbers together and write the answers into the grid.

×	30	5
6	180	30

Add the two answers from the grid

$$\begin{array}{r} 180 \\ +\ 30 \\ \hline 210 \end{array}$$

6 × 35 = 210

- For bigger multiplications, add a column for hundreds.

Multiply 6 × 245
Partition 245.
245 is 200 + 40 + 5

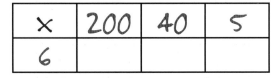

×	200	40	5
6			

Multiply the numbers together and write the answers into the grid.

×	200	40	5
6	1200	240	30

Add the four answers from the grid.

$$\begin{array}{r} 1200 \\ 240 \\ +\ 30 \\ \hline 1470 \end{array}$$

6 × 245 = 1470

example

Using the grid method, multiply 5 by 432.

×	400	30	2
5			

×	400	30	2
5	2000	150	10

$$\begin{array}{r} 2000 \\ 150 \\ +\ 10 \\ \hline 2160 \end{array}$$

5 × 432 = 2160

Exercise 15f

1 Partition these numbers into 100s, 10s and 1s.
The first is done for you.

a 264 = 200 + 60 + 4

b 357 **c** 158 **d** 333

e 796 **f** 609 **g** 850

2 Answer these problems.

a 200×4 **b** 4×300 **c** 400×5

d 20×30 **e** 30×30 **f** 40×50

g 50×200 **h** 30×500 **i** 600×40

3 Copy these grids. Complete each multiplication.

a 32×4

×	30	5
4		

b 53×5

×	50	3
5		

c 27×4

×	20	7
4		

d 213×6

×	200	10	3
6			

e 251×5

×	200	50	1
5			

f 468×4

×	400	60	8
4			

4 Use the grid method to complete these multiplications.

a 124×3 **b** 213×2 **c** 325×3

d 145×3 **e** 362×3 **f** 217×2

g 324×5 **h** 253×6 **i** 375×4

Make an estimate of what you think each answer will be.

challenge

Johnny is planning two parties.
Work out what he should charge for each.

a 213 guests × £6 each

×	200	10	3
6			

b 352 guests × £8 each

×	300	50	2
8			

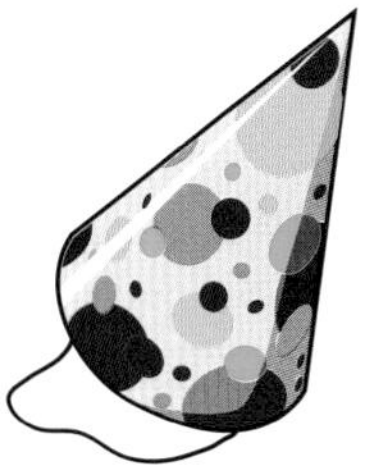

15g Written methods of division

- Divide a large number by a single-digit number using subtraction on a number line and in a written method

Keywords
Divide
Remainder
Subtraction

p. 108

- For some division problems you can use a number line.

example

Use subtraction on a number line to solve $27 \div 5$.

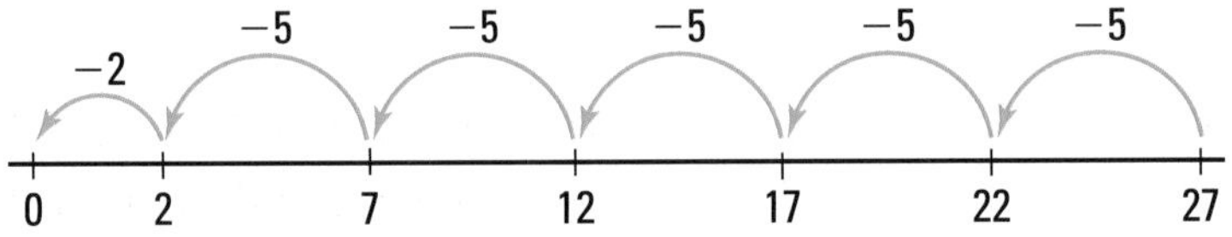

There are five jumps of 5 in 27 and a **remainder** of 2.
So … $27 \div 5 = 5$ r2

- For divisions involving bigger numbers you can use repeated subtraction.

Use repeated subtraction to solve $188 \div 6$.

You know that $10 \times 6 = 60$
Subtract as many groups of 60 (10×6) as you can.

$6\overline{)188}$ means $188 \div 6$.

```
6)188
 −60  ←  6 × 10
 128
 −60  ←  6 × 10
  68
 −60  ←  6 × 10
   8
  −6  ←  6 × 1
   2  →  remainder 2
```

10 + 10 + 10 + 1 = 31 groups of 6 in 188, with a remainder of 2.

Answer: $186 \div 6 = 31$ r2

You could make this working shorter.

```
6)188
−180      6 × 30
   8
  −6      6 × 1
   2      Answer: 31 r2
```

Exercise 15g

1 Copy and complete these multiplications.

a 6×10 **b** 3×10 **c** 7×10
d 4×10 **e** 9×10 **f** 5×10
g 12×10 **h** 18×10 **i** 23×10

2 Using your knowledge of the times tables, answer these division problems.

a $12 \div 2$ **b** $9 \div 3$ **c** $12 \div 4$
d $20 \div 5$ **e** $16 \div 2$ **f** $24 \div 6$
g $18 \div 9$ **h** $28 \div 4$ **i** $21 \div 7$

3 Use a times table to answer these.

a How many fives are there in 40? **b** How many threes are there in 27?
c How many fours are there in 36? **d** How many eights are there in 56?
e How many sevens are there in 63? **f** How many nines are there in 72?

4 Use a number line and repeated subtraction to answer these.

There will be a remainder to each answer.

a $35 \div 4$ **b** $43 \div 5$ **c** $45 \div 6$
d $66 \div 10$ **e** $53 \div 7$ **f** $67 \div 8$

5 Use repeated subtraction to solve these divisions. The first has been done for you.

a $4\overline{)98}$

$$\begin{array}{rl} 4\overline{)98} & \\ -40 & 4 \times 10 \\ \hline 58 & \\ -40 & 4 \times 10 \\ \hline 18 & \\ -16 & 4 \times 4 \\ \hline 2 & \end{array} \quad = 24 \text{ r}2$$

b $5\overline{)75}$ **c** $3\overline{)96}$ **d** $6\overline{)84}$ **e** $5\overline{)225}$
f $4\overline{)98}$ **g** $5\overline{)123}$ **h** $6\overline{)374}$ **i** $8\overline{)544}$

problem

a If there are 40 sweets total in five jars, how many sweets are there in one jar?
b If there are 80 sweets total in five jars, how many sweets are there in one jar?
c If there are 160 sweets total in five jars, how many sweets are there in one jar?

15h Finding percentages

- Find a percentage of a quantity using division

Keywords
Divide *Fraction*
Equivalent *Percentage*

p. 172

- A **percentage** is a **fraction** out of 100. $30\% = \frac{30}{100} = \frac{3}{10}$

$50\% = \frac{1}{2}$ $20\% = \frac{2}{10} = \frac{1}{5}$ $10\% = \frac{1}{10}$

- To find the percentage of an amount, find the **equivalent** fraction and **divide** by the denominator.
  To find 10% or $\frac{1}{10}$, divide by 10.
  To find 20% or $\frac{1}{5}$, divide by 5.
  To find 25% or $\frac{1}{4}$, divide by 4.
  To find 50% or $\frac{1}{2}$, divide by 2.

example

How much would you save in these sales?

a 10% off £80 **b** 25% off £120

a $10\% = \frac{1}{10}$

$\frac{1}{10}$ of £80 $= \frac{80}{10}$

$\frac{80}{10} = £8$

Save £8!

b $25\% = \frac{1}{4}$

$\frac{1}{4}$ of £120 $= \frac{120}{4}$

$\frac{120}{4} = £30$

Save £30!

50% is $\frac{1}{2}$

$\frac{1}{2}$ of £10 $= \frac{10}{2} = £5$ off

The old price − the amount off = the new price

£10 − £5 = £5

Exercise 15h

1 Find 50% of these amounts.

a £12 **b** 30 kg **c** 90 days
d 50p **e** 22 minutes **f** 64 people

2 Find 10% of these amounts.

a 50 m **b** 30 hours **c** 90 kg
d £150 **e** 250 votes **f** 110 litres

3 Find

a 20% of 40 **b** 60% of 80 **c** 30% of 60
d 40% of 70 **e** 70% of 30 **f** 20% of 25

4 How much would you save in these sales?

a

b

c

5 What is the new price of each item?
Use old price − amount off = new price.

a

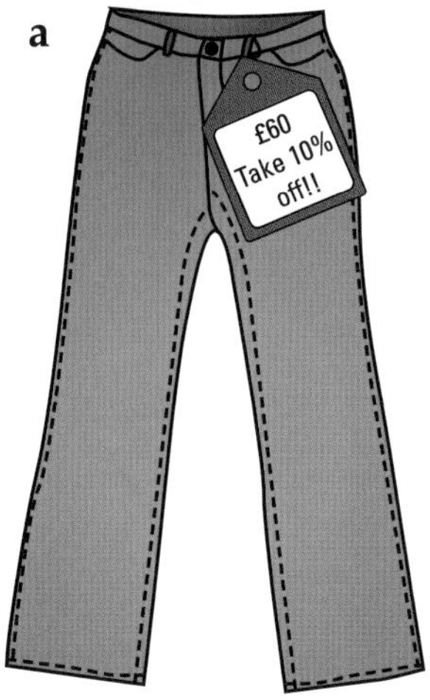

b

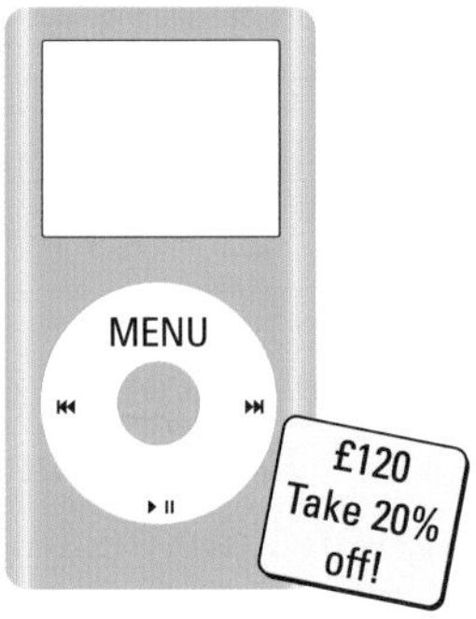

c

d

challenge

When you increase an amount by a percentage, you find the percentage and add it to the original amount. Use old price + amount increase = new price to find the new price of each item. Which pair of sunglasses costs more?

a

b

15i Solving problems

- Develop your own ways of solving number problems in different situations

Keywords
Calculation
Number operation

When solving a problem:

- make sure you understand the problem ☑
- make sure you understand the question ☑
- decide which numbers are important ☑
- decide which operations to use (+, −, ×, ÷) ☑
- plan how to work out the answer ☑
- work out the answer ☑
- check that the answer is sensible. ☑

example

In a bag of sweets there are nine toffee sweets, five fruit cream sweets and 13 hazelnut sweets.

I understand the problem.

a How many sweets are there in one bag?

I'll use addition to solve this.
$9 + 5 + 13 = 27$

b If all the hazelnut sweets are removed, how many sweets are left?

This is a subtraction sum.
$27 - 13 = 14$

c If each bag costs £1.20, how much will six bags cost?

This is a multiplication problem.
$6 \times £1.20 = £7.20$ – don't forget the £ sign and the decimal point!

d If three friends share a bag of sweets, how many sweets does each person have?

This is a division problem.
$27 \div 3 = 9$.

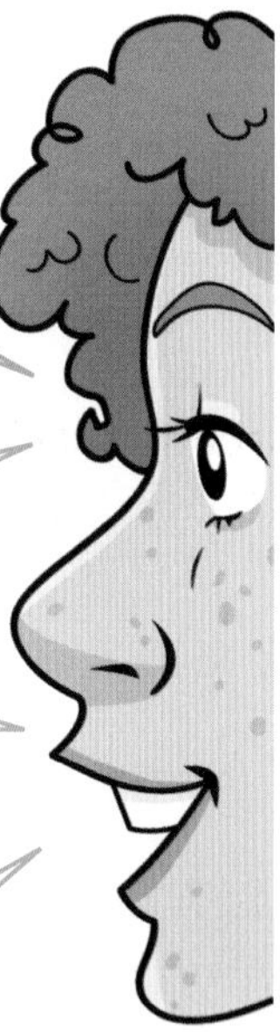

a There are 27 sweets in each bag.

b There are 14 sweets left.

c Six bags would cost £7.20.

d They would each have nine sweets.

Exercise 15i

1 Shiva is standing in a swimming pool.
The water is 125 cm deep
Shiva is 158 cm tall.
How many centimetres of Shiva's body are above the surface?

2 After their holiday Laura had £228 and \$164 in her purse.
Roy had £108 and \$88 in his wallet.

a How many dollars (\$) did they have between them?

b How many pounds (£) did they have between them?

3 Pears cost £1.55 a kilogram.
Apples cost 98p a kilogram.
Oranges are 35p each.
Charlotte buys 2 kg of pears and four oranges.
How much does she pay altogether?

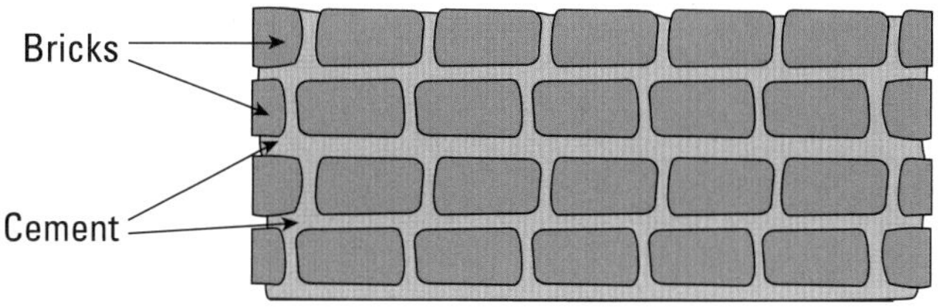

4 Each whole brick is 22 cm wide and 8.5 cm high.
The cement is 2 cm thick.

a How high is this wall?

b How wide is this wall?

5 The adult price for entry into the cinema is £6.00.
Children are half-price. 40 people visit the cinema and half of this number are children.

a How much money does the cinema take that day for child visitors?

b How much money does the cinema take that day for adult visitors?

task

What operation sign and number is missing from each circle?
Choose from the red list of numbers and operation signs to make sense of this 'number chain'.

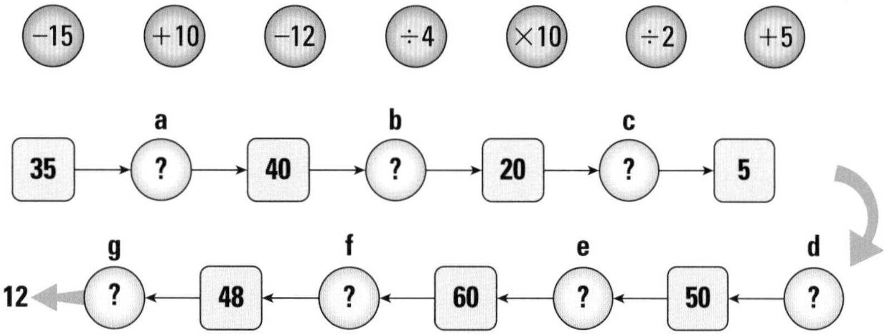

15 Consolidation

15a

1 Use the method of 'adding tens and then units' to find each answer.

a 54 + 31 **b** 70 + 14 **c** 62 + 22

2 Use a number line to find the answer if you need to.

a 77 + 35 **b** 88 + 26 **c** 60 + 54

15a²

3 Use the method of 'subtracting tens and then units' to find each answer.

a 89 − 43 **b** 68 − 22 **c** 96 − 51

4 Use a number line to find the answer if you need to.

a 102 − 57 **b** 110 − 65 **c** 91 − 48

15b

5 Complete these column additions and subtractions.

$$\begin{array}{r} 464 \\ +318 \\ \hline \\ \hline \end{array} \qquad \begin{array}{r} 218 \\ +302 \\ \hline \\ \hline \end{array} \qquad \begin{array}{r} 584 \\ -380 \\ \hline \\ \hline \end{array} \qquad \begin{array}{r} 670 \\ -235 \\ \hline \\ \hline \end{array}$$

15c

6 Write out the first five multiples of:

a 4 ➡ 4, ☐, ☐, ☐, ☐

b 7 ➡ 7, ☐, ☐, ☐, ☐

7 **a** One of these numbers is **not** a multiple of 3; which is it? **3** ➡ 6, 12, 18, 20, 24

b One of these numbers is **not** a multiple of 6; which is it? **6** ➡ 12, 18, 24, 26, 30

8 From the box below, write out all the factors of

a 12

b 15

c 20

d 30

2	3	5	8
4	10	6	

9 Copy and complete the table.
Write *yes* or *no* in all the spaces on your copy.

Number	Divides by 2?	Divides by 3?	Divides by 4?	Divides by 5?	Divides by 10?
154					
315					
364					
990					
1008					

10 Use grid multiplication to solve these:

a 5 × 23

×	20	3
5		

b 4 × 36 =

c 5 × 47 =

d 3 × 143

×	100	40	3
3			

e 3 × 465 =

f 6 × 254 =

11 Use repeated subtraction to solve these. (There are no remainders.)

a 3)105 **b** 4)124 **c** 6)168

These divisions have remainders.

d 5)187 **e** 4)143 **f** 6)172

12 For the following, find the discount and the price paid by the purchaser.

	Item	Marked price	Discount	Price paid
a Kettle	£40	5%		
b Refrigerator	£180	20%		
c Portable TV	£140	5%		
d Electric cooker	£270	20%		
e Vacuum cleaner	£105	20%		

15 Summary

Key Indicators

- Multiply and divide a HTU number by a U number Level 4
- Find a simple percentage of small whole numbers Level 4

Level 3

1 Work out

a 38 + 37
b 75 ÷ 5
c 362 − 87

Kamil's answer ✔

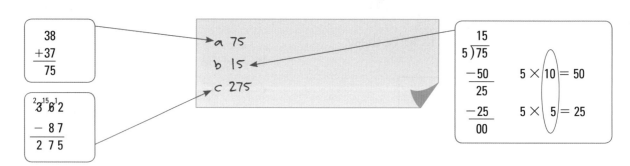

$$\begin{array}{r} 38 \\ +37 \\ \hline 75 \end{array}$$

$$\begin{array}{r} {}^{2}\not{3}\,{}^{15}\not{6}\,{}^{1}2 \\ -\ 87 \\ \hline 275 \end{array}$$

a 75
b 15
c 275

$$\begin{array}{r} 15 \\ 5\overline{)75} \\ -50 \\ \hline 25 \\ -25 \\ \hline 00 \end{array}$$

5 × 10 = 50
5 × 5 = 25

Level 4

2 A coach carries 45 people when full.
What is the most number of people that can travel on seven coaches?

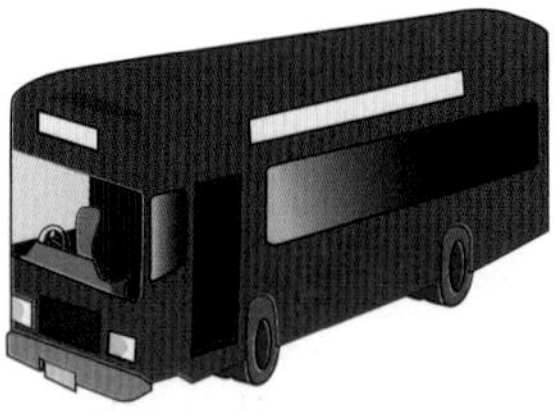

16 Algebra

Equations and formulas

During World War II, a team of codebreakers worked at Bletchley Park, Buckinghamshire, to break the codes used by the Axis forces. Mathematicians, chess champions and crossword puzzle fanatics used their problem-solving skills and a huge computer named Colossus to read the coded messages.

What's the point? The codes were set using functions. When the input and function were known, the output, or message, could be read.

Check in

Level 3

1 Find the output for each of these function machines.

a 3 → [+6] → ? **b** 10 → [−4] → ? **c** 5 → [×10] → ? **d** 8 → [÷7] → ?

Level 4

2 Find the input for each of these function machines.

a ? → [+9] → 12 **b** ? → [−4] → 3 **c** ? → [×5] → 20 **d** ? → [÷3] → 2

Level 5

3 Write an expression for each of these.

a Adam has p CDs. He buys 5 more CDs. How many CDs does Adam have now?

b Noah has a tree that is k cm tall. He cuts 100 cm from the top of the tree. How tall is the tree now?

c Levi buys 4 tickets to see his favourite band. Each ticket costs x pounds. How much does Levi pay?

16a Creating formulas

- Write a simple formula in words

Keywords
Formula
Input
Output

p. 180

Ellie works in a café.
She puts two teabags in every pot of tea.
She creates a **formula** to tell her how many teabags she needs in a day.

number of pots of tea × 2 teabags = number of teabags needed

p. 186

If Ellie makes 5 pots, she puts 5 in her formula.

5 pots of tea × 2 teabags = number of teabags needed
5 × 2 = 10 teabags needed

example

Ellie uses 3 eggs per fry-up.

a Write a formula for how many eggs she uses in a day.
b 5 people order fry-ups. How many eggs does she use?

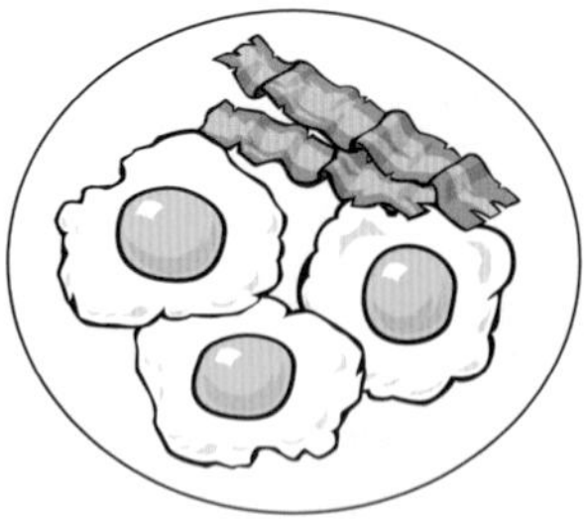

a number of fry-up orders × 3 eggs each = total number of eggs
b The formula gives
5 orders × 3 eggs each = total number of eggs
5 × 3 = 15
She uses 15 eggs in total.

Exercise 16a

1 Ellie uses 3 tomato slices for each sandwich.
Create a formula for how many tomato slices she uses each day.

number of sandwiches × □ = number of tomato slices

2 Use your formula from question **1** to calculate the number of tomato slices that Ellie will need for each order.

a 4 sandwiches
b 3 sandwiches
c 7 sandwiches
d 9 sandwiches
e 10 sandwiches
f 15 sandwiches

3 Ellie washes up 2 plates for every customer.

a Create a formula to show how many plates she washes up each day.
b Use your formula to find how many plates she washes up if there are

i 3 customers
ii 4 customers
iii 8 customers
iv 10 customers
v 7 customers
vi 9 customers
vii 20 customers
viii 13 customers

4 Ellie also washes up 1 cup per customer.
Write a new formula to show how many plates and cups she now washes up in total.

5 In question **4**, you wrote a formula for Ellie's washing up if she washes 2 plates and 1 cup per customer.
Use your formula to find how many items she washes up if there are

a 3 customers
b 4 customers
c 12 customers
d 14 customers
e 25 customers
f 30 customers
g 50 customers
h 0 customers

challenge

Use your formula from question **1**.
Ellie has orders for 18 sandwiches.
She has 53 tomato slices left in the fridge.

a Will she have enough tomato slices?
b How many extra or short does she have?

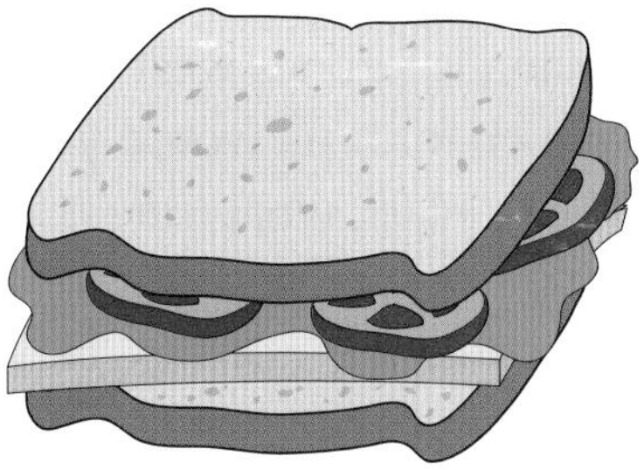

16a² Using formulas

- Use a simple formula written in words

Keywords
Formula
Problem
Substitute

- You can create a **formula** to help you solve a **problem**.

Problem
How can you quickly tell what time it is in other cities?

Earth is divided into 24 time zones.
Time zones begin at Greenwich, London.
As you move **east, add** 1 hour to London time.
As you move **west, subtract** 1 hour from London time.

- You can use symbols to help write a formula.

Create a formula!
Use g for London time
Use z for the number of zones difference between London and other cities.
The formulas for time in another city are:
time = $g + z$ (going east) or time = $g - z$ (going west)

- To use your formula, **substitute** real values for the symbols.

example

Athens is 2 zones east of London.
a Which formula would you use to find the time in Athens?
b If g is 17.00, what time is it in Athens?

Athens is in Greece.

a Use time = $g + z$ Athens is east.
b time = $g + 2$ Substitute 2 for z.
time = 17.00 + 2 Substitute 17.00 for g.
time = 19.00 (7 p.m.) in Athens.

Athens is 2 zones ahead.

example

Havana is 5 zones west of London.
a Which formula would you use to find the time in Havana?
b If g = 14.00, what time is it in Havana?

Havana is in Cuba.

a Use time = $g - z$ Havana is west.
b time = $g - 5$ Substitute 5 for z.
time = 14.00 − 5 Substitute 14.00 for g.
time = 9.00 (9 a.m.) in Havana

Havana is 5 zones behind.

Exercise 16a[2]

1 This table shows the number of zones difference from London.
Use the table to calculate city times using these formulas:

time = $g + z$ (going east) or time = $g - z$ (going west)

g = time in London It is 12.00 in London.

z = the number of zones difference

	City	Direction	Number of Zones Difference
a	Madrid	East	1
b	Los Angeles	West	8
c	Rome	East	2
d	Denver	West	7
e	Islamabad	East	5
f	Mexico City	West	6
g	Rio De Janeiro	West	4
h	Sydney	East	10
i	Honolulu	West	10
j	Hanoi	East	7

Time in London 12:00 p.m.

2 If the time is 6 p.m. (18:00) in London, work out the time in the cities in question **1**.

3 The time in London is 12:00 p.m.
Use the formulas backwards to find the time in London if it is

a 13:00 in Madrid

Madrid is east.
Madrid time = London time + 1
13:00 = London time + 1
12:00 = London time

b 16:00 in Madrid **c** 22:00 in Sydney **d** 09:00 in Denver

e 11:00 in Hanoi **f** 21:30 in Rome **g** 16:00 in Honolulu

challenge

$E = m \times c^2$ is a famous formula written by Einstein.
Substitute $m = 2$ and $c = 300\,000\,000$ into the formula to find E.
Use your calculator!

Functions

- Use a function machine to find outputs

Keywords
Function
Inverse
Operation

p. 32

- A **function** connects two numbers using operations.

input	operation	output
6	→ $+6$ →	12
6	→ $\times 2$ →	12

Both functions map 6 onto 12.

example

What functions could connect these inputs to the outputs?

a input output
3 → 9

b input output
5 → 12

c input output
16 → 4

a $3 \boxed{+6} = 9$
or
$3 \boxed{\times 3} = 9$

b $5 \boxed{+7} = 12$

c $16 \boxed{-12} = 4$
or
$16 \boxed{\div 4} = 4$

- You can use more than one operation in a function.

Multiply each input by 2 and then add 3 to get the output.

1 → $\times 2$ → $+3$ → 5

First, $1 \times 2 = 2$
Then, $2 + 3 = 5$
so, 1 → 5

example

What is the second operation needed to change each input to its output?

4, 5 → $\times 3$ → ? → 14, 17

$4 \times 3 = 12$ $5 \times 3 = 15$
$12 \boxed{} = 14$ $15 \boxed{} = 17$

$12 \boxed{+2} = 14$ $15 \boxed{+2} = 17$

The second operation is +2.

Exercise 16b

1 Find the output for each of these function machines.

a 3 → [+4] → ?

b 4 → [×3] → ?

c 7 → [+9] → ?

d 3 → [×10] → ?

2 Find the output for each machine when the input is 6.

a 6 → [+3] → ?

b 6 → [−4] → ?

c 6 → [×3] → ?

d 6 → [÷2] → ?

3 Work out the single function which changes each input to its output.

There may be more than one answer.

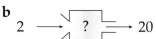

a 18 → [?] → 20

b 2 → [?] → 20

c 9 → [?] → 15

d 18 → [?] → 9

e 4 → [?] → 24

f 21 → [?] → 7

g 3 → [?] → 36

h 24 → [?] → 8

i 45 → [?] → 15

4 Work out the outputs for this function.

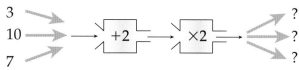

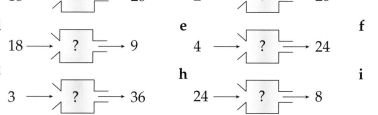

3, 10, 7 → [+2] → [×2] → ?, ?, ?

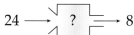

5 What is the second operation of this function?

a 1, 4, 10 → [×5] → [?] → 3, 18, 48

b 3, 6, 11 → [+4] → [?] → 21, 30, 45

challenge

Find the two operations for this function.

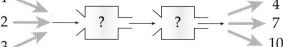

1, 2, 3 → [?] → [?] → 4, 7, 10

16c Using functions

- Use a function machine in a practical situation

Keywords
Function
Mapping

- You can use **function** machines to help you solve a problem.

Connor goes to school on the bus five days each week.
His bus fare costs £2 each day.
He can use a function machine to work out the total cost per week.

number of days → ×£2 → total cost

For five days the total cost is

5 → ×£2 → 20 The total cost is £20.

- You can use double function machines to solve more complex problems.

Asha works in the garden for her Grandad every Saturday.
She is paid £2 per hour worked and £3 per day for lunch.

She can use a function machine to work out her pay.

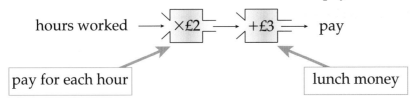

hours worked → ×£2 → +£3 → pay

pay for each hour (×£2) lunch money (+£3)

example

If Asha works for 4 hours one Saturday, how much will she be paid?

Use the function machine above.

4 hours → ×£2 → +£3 → £11

£8 + £3 = £11 Asha will be paid £11.

- You can use a **mapping** to display the calculations from a function machine.

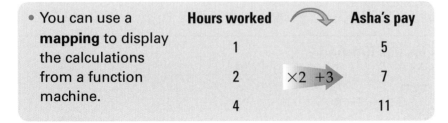

Hours worked	×2 +3	Asha's pay
1		5
2		7
4		11

Exercise 16c

1 Sandeep's bus fare costs £3 each day.

a Draw a function machine to show the total cost for a number of days.

b Use your function machine to work out the total cost for

i 5 days **ii** 10 days **iii** 3 days **iv** 6 days **v** 8 days **vi** 20 days

2 Tracy gets paid £4 per hour and £3 a day for lunch. Use this function machine to calculate Tracy's pay when she has worked these hours.

hours worked → $\times 4$ → $+3$ → pay

a 5 hours **b** 8 hours **c** 12 hours **d** 7 hours **e** 6 hours **f** 1 hour

g Record your answers on a mapping: hours ⟶ pay

3 Mark is going to his school fete.

a Show these prices on a function machine like this.

number of rides → ? → ? → total cost

b Use your function machine to show that Mark would pay a total of £15 if he rode six rides.

c Complete this mapping using your function machine.

rides	?	total cost
6		15
2		☐
10		☐
15		☐
20		☐

Use the mapping to complete this function machine.

input → ? → ? → output

input	?	output
1		4
2		7
3		10
4		13

16d Inverse operations

- Use a function machine in reverse

Keywords
Inverse
Operation

p. 28

- An **inverse operation** takes you back to where you started.

The inverse of turning on the light….. …. is turning off the light.

You can undo a number operation by using the opposite or inverse operation.

- The opposite of + is − and the opposite of − is +.

undo operation

$4 + 2 = 6 \quad 6 - 2 = 4$

- The opposite of × is ÷ and the opposite of ÷ is ×.

undo operation

$3 \times 4 = 12 \quad 12 \div 4 = 3$

You can use function machines to help you.

example

Start with a number and divide it by 4. The output is 6.
Use function machines to show how you find the starting number.

The function machines need to show the operation and the inverse.

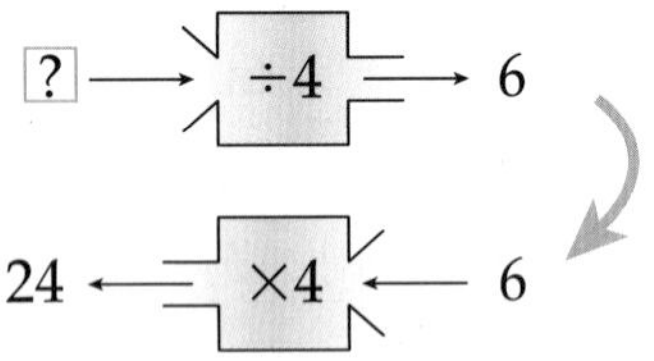

The inverse of ÷ is ×.

The starting number was 24.

Exercise 16d

1 Match each operation with its inverse.

+3   ×12   ÷3   ÷12

−12   −3   +12   ×3

2 Copy and complete these questions by finding the inverse operation.

a $4 + 6 = 10$ ➡ $10 - \square = 4$

b $9 - 5 = 4$ ➡ $4 + \square = 9$

c $13 + 4 = 17$ ➡ $17 - \square = 13$

d $12 - 4 = 8$ ➡ $8 + \square = 12$

e $5 \times 3 = 15$ ➡ $15 \div \square = 5$

f $10 \div 2 = 5$ ➡ $5 \times \square = 10$

g $10 \times 4 = 40$ ➡ $40 \square 4 = 10$

h $12 \div 4 = 3$ ➡ $3 \square 4 = 12$

3 Complete this function machine.
Replace the ? marks with the correct number and operation.

8 → [×4] → 32

? ← [?] ← 32

4 Find each starting number by completing the inverse function machines.

a
? → [×5] → 35
? ← [÷5] ← 35

b
? → [−9] → 22
? ← [?] ← 22

c
? → [+10] → 27
? ← [?] ← 27

d
? → [−7] → 25
? ← [?] ← 25

e
? → [÷2] → 40
? ← [?] ← 40

f
? → [−12] → 18
? ← [?] ← 18

challenge

Draw these statements as function machines.
Use inverse function machines to find the starting numbers.

a Start with a number. Add twelve to the number. The answer is forty.

b Start with a number. Multiply the number three. The answer is twenty seven.

16e Equations

- Find an unknown weight on a balance

Keywords
Balance
Equals
Equation

- An equals sign acts like a **balance**.

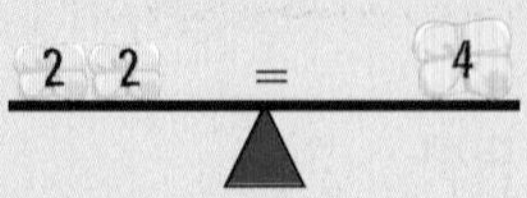

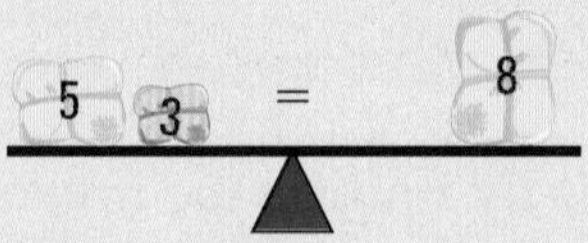

2 + 2 = 4 5 + 3 = 8

The left side **equals** the right side. They are balanced.

- You can use this idea to work out missing values.

There is a weight missing on these scales.
You can write this problem as 20 = ? + 15

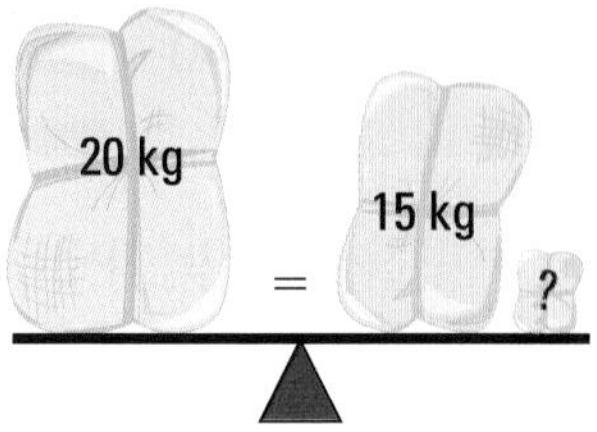

- This is an **equation**.
  It contains an = sign and a missing number.

To find the missing weight you could
count on from 15 to 20, or
subtract 15 from 20 (20 − 15).
The missing weight is 5 kg.
Check: 20 = 5 + 15 ✔

You can also balance using symbols to stand for missing numbers.

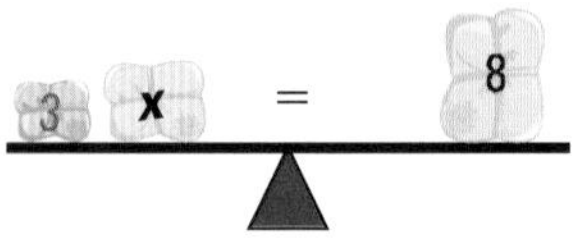

$3 + x = 8$
So, x must be **5**.
Check: $3 + \mathbf{5} = 8$ ✔

example

Find the value that makes the equation balance.

Write the equation: $4 + w = 11$
So, w must be **7**.
Check: $4 + \mathbf{7} = 11$ ✔

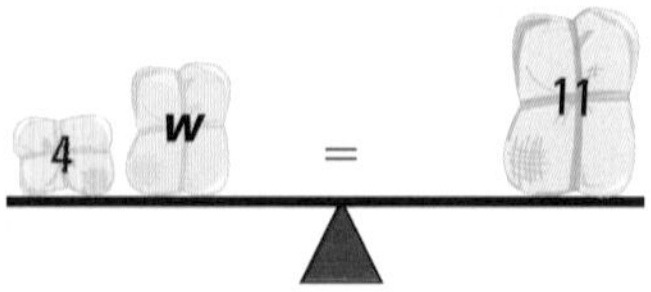

Exercise 16e

1 Write an equation for each drawing.

a

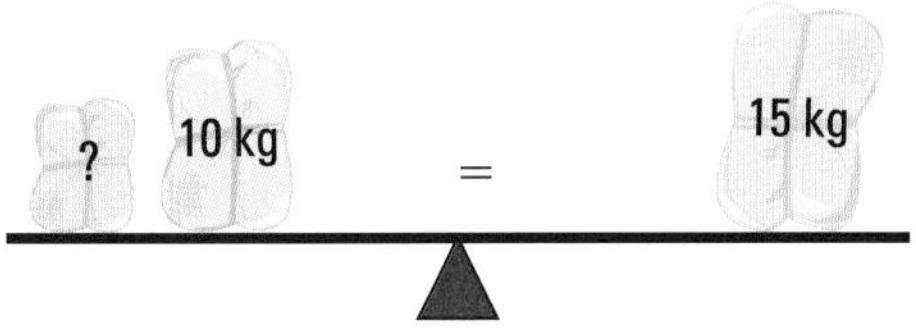

b

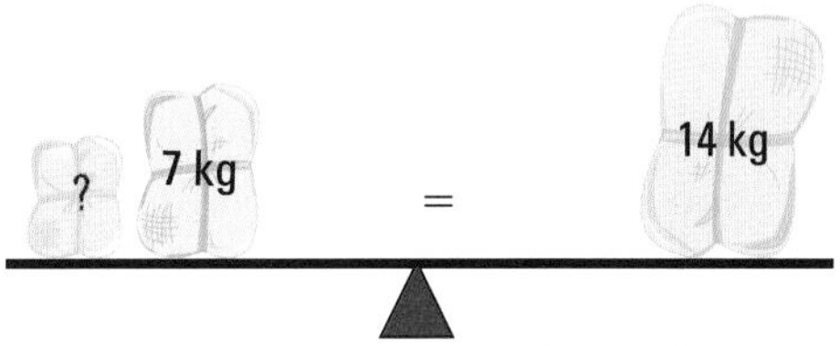

c

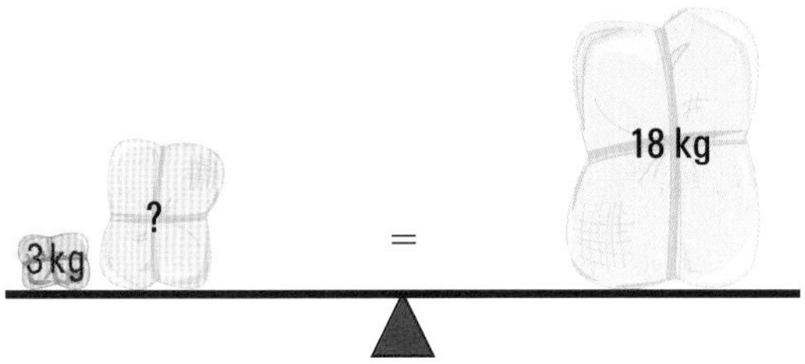

d

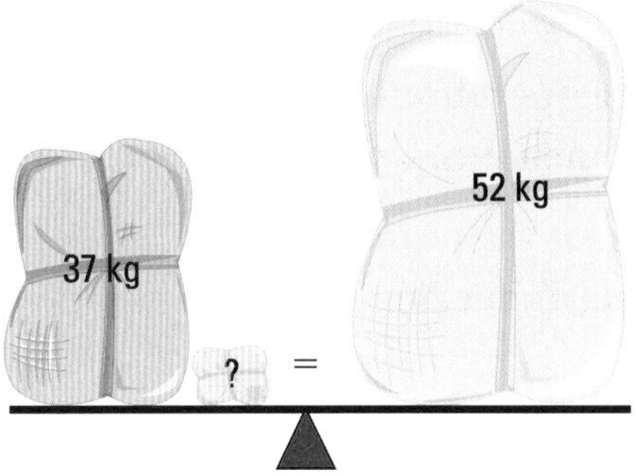

e Find the weight that makes each equation balance.

2 Find the value that makes each equation balance.

a $5 + x = 10$
b $y + 10 = 14$
c $w + 6 = 17$
d $6 + m = 12$
e $15 + z = 20$
f $t + 23 = 30$

3 Find the value that makes each equation balance.

a $4 + 7 = 5 + x$
b $6 + 6 = 10 + y$
c $20 + z = 34$
d $13 = 1 + g$
e $6 \times 2 = 10 + b$
f $3 \times 6 = 12 + p$
g $p - 10 = 10$
h $14 + f = 22$
i $7 + d = 7$
j $q + 17 = 30$
k $24 + b = 28$
l $c + 7 = 18$

challenge

Theo is making muesli.
If he knows the dry ingredients weigh 425g in total, what weight of hazelnuts should he add?

Muesli

200 g porridge oats
25 g wheat germ
[illegible] hazelnuts
50 g almonds
50 g sultanas
25 g dried apricots

Using equations

- Solve simple equations using a function machine

Keywords
Equation
Inverse operations

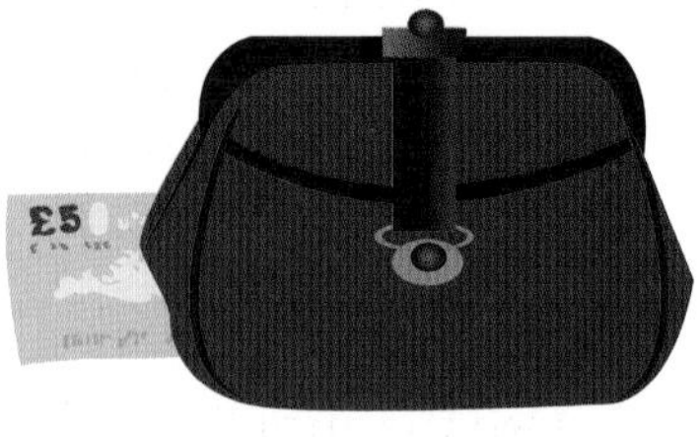

Danielle has a purse full of pound coins and a £5 note.
She knows she has £14 in total.

- You can write this as an equation. $x + 5 = 14$

Use **inverse operations** to work out how many pound coins are in the purse.

The input is x, the number of pound coins in her purse.

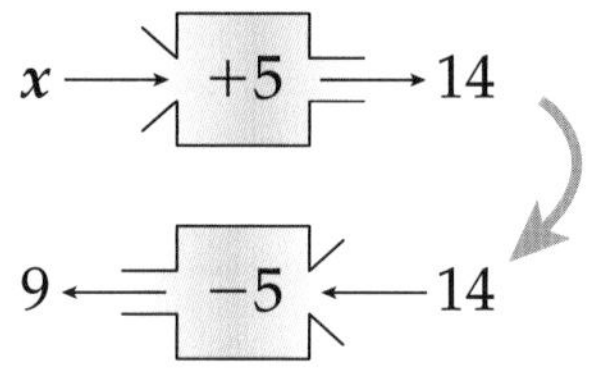

She has £9 in her purse.

example

James had £30 in his wallet.
He spent some of the money and now has £17.

a Draw a function machine to find how much money James spent.
b Check your answer.

---

a Use a letter to stand for the money that James spent.
The money James spent $= x$
The value of x is 13. So James spent £13.

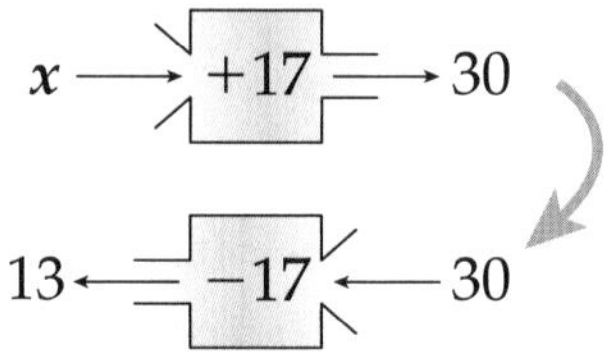

b Check: £17 + £13 = £30 ✓

example

I think of a number. I multiply the number by 4 and get 40.
What number did I start with?

Start with y.

$40 \div 4 = 10$ so $y = 10$

You started with 10.

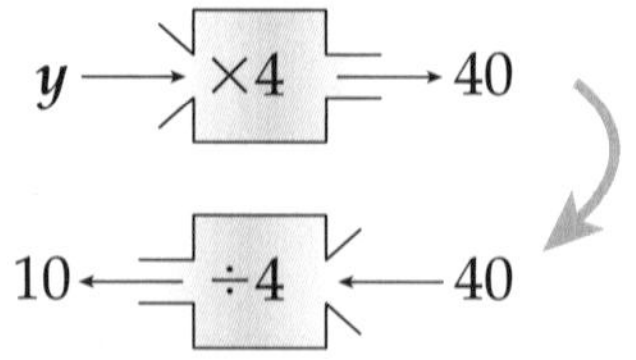

Exercise 16f

1 Find the starting number in each of these puzzles.
You can probably do most of them in your head.

a I think of a number and add 3. Now I have 10.
b I think of a number and add 20. Now I have 30.
c I think of a number and subtract 6. Now I have 5.
d I think of a number and multiply it by 4. Now I have 8.
e I think of a number and divide it by 3. Now I have 10.

2 Use the function machines to find the value of x.
$x + 15 = 32$

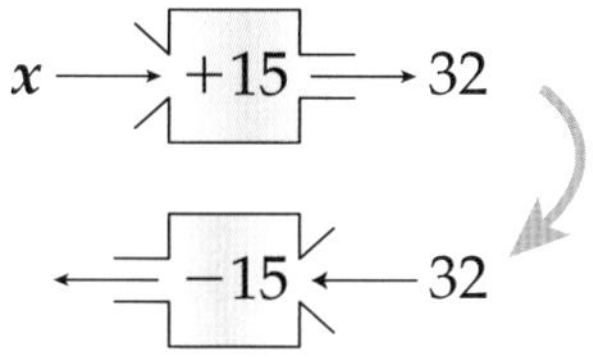

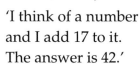

3 Draw a function machine and its inverse to find the value of the letter in each equation.

a $x + 17 = 25$ **b** $m + 20 = 45$
c $d + 23 = 47$ **d** $h + 15 = 15$

4 **a** Write this sentence as an equation.
Use x for the missing number.

'I think of a number
and I add 17 to it.
The answer is 42.'

b Draw a function machine and its inverse to find x.

5 Use function machines to find the value of the letter in each equation.

The inverse of add is subtract.

The inverse of multiply is divide.

a $w + 16 = 17$ **b** $t + 13 = 28$ **c** $b - 20 = 45$ **d** $f - 12 = 11$
e $2 \times t = 24$ **f** $5 \times j = 40$ **g** $e \div 3 = 10$ **h** $d \div 3 = 7$

challenge

Freddy has some sweets in a bag. His sister eats 13 of his sweets.
Now he has 18 sweets left.

a Rewrite the sentence as an equation.
Use ***n*** for the unknown number of sweets.
b Use the inverse operation to find the out how many sweets Freddy had at first.

16 Consolidation

16a

1 A gate is made from five pieces of wood of equal length.

a Write a formula connecting the number of pieces of wood required w, with the number of gates made g.

b Find the number of pieces of wood needed to make

i 4 gates **ii** 8 gates **iii** 15 gates and **iv** 20 gates.

16a²

2 Not every city adds on a whole number of hours. This table shows some more time differences from London. Use the table to calculate the time in each city using the formulas.

time = $g + z$ (going east)

time = $g - z$ (going east)

Time in London 12:00 p.m.

	City	Direction	Number of Zones Difference
a	Tehran, Iran	East	$3\frac{1}{2}$
b	Kabul, Afghanistan	East	$4\frac{1}{2}$
c	Delhi, India	East	$5\frac{1}{2}$
d	Adelaide, Australia	East	$9\frac{1}{2}$
e	St John's, Canada	West	$3\frac{1}{2}$

Use the table on page 249² question **1** to help you.

16b

3 Calculate the input for each of these.

a ? → +9 → 30 **b** ? → −11 → 15

c ? → ×7 → 56 **d** ? → ÷5 → 12

16c

4 For this question draw a function machine, find the output for each input given and show your results on your function machine. Also show your results on a mapping.

Marie heats up some water for a science experiment. When she turns on the heater, the temperature of the water is 8 degrees. If the temperature rises by 2 degrees every minute, find the temperature after

a 2 **b** 4 **c** 5 **d** 10 minutes.

16d

5 Use inverse function machines to find the missing inputs.

a ? → [+5] → 20 **b** ? → [−7] → 11

c ? → [×8] → 40 **d** ? → [÷9] → 8

16e

6 Find the value that makes each equation balance.

a $y - 9 = 15$
b $5t = 75$
c $60 \div v = 12$
d $n \div 6 = 3$
e $p + 11 = 26$
f $50 - r = 39$

16f

7 Use function machines to find the value of the letter in each equation.

a $y + 35 = 60$
b $t - 39 = 15$
c $5 \times m = 90$
d $7 \times p = 224$
e $r \div 12 = 8$

Maths Life

Origami

Origami is an ancient Japanese art using folded paper to create beautiful shapes and figures. Origami uses shapes, angles and lines to build the figures.

Describe the shapes found in these origami figures.
Use the word bank to help you.

square

scalene triangle *trapezium* *congruent*

vertical *centre* *isosceles triangle*

right triangle *kite* *point*

line of symmetry *angle*

quadrilateral *triangle* *pentagon*

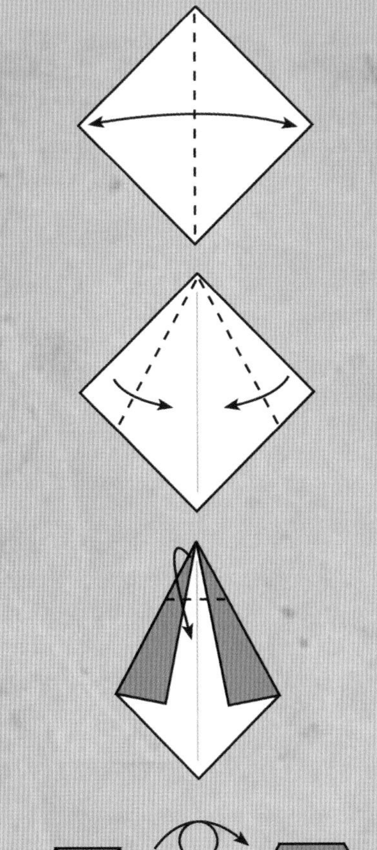

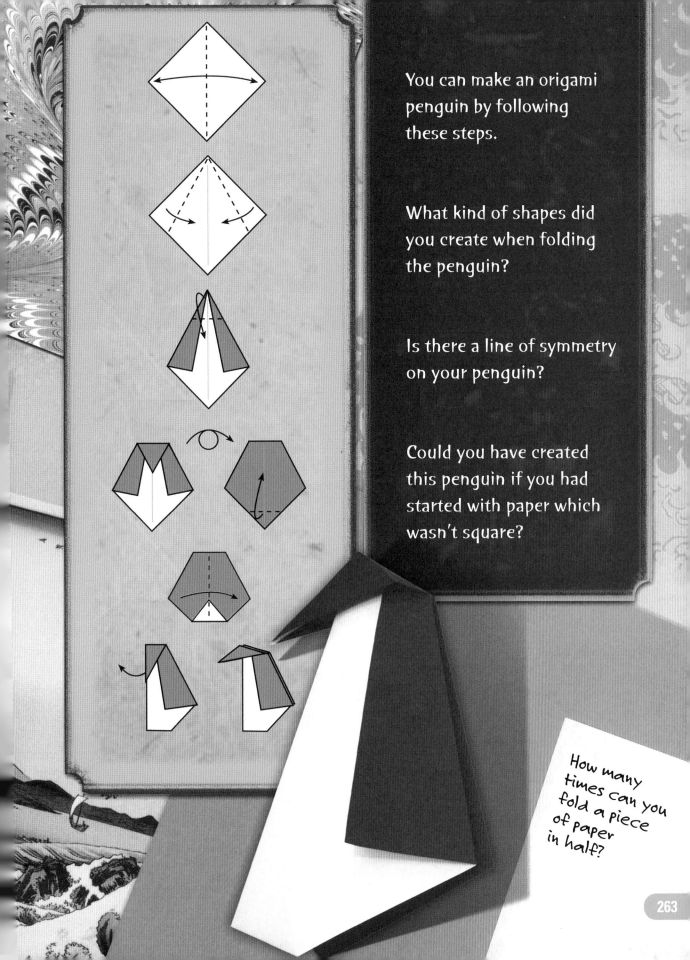

You can make an origami penguin by following these steps.

What kind of shapes did you create when folding the penguin?

Is there a line of symmetry on your penguin?

Could you have created this penguin if you had started with paper which wasn't square?

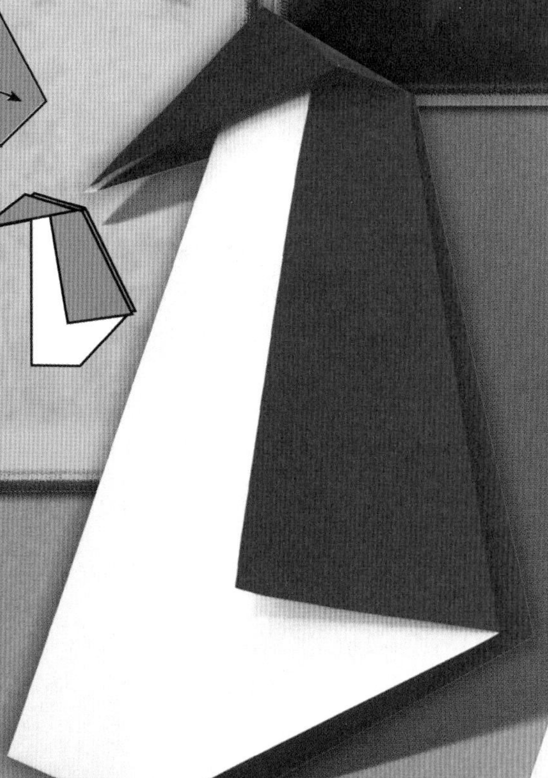

How many times can you fold a piece of paper in half?

16 Summary

Key indicators

- Use letters to represent numbers **Level 3**

Level 4

1 Look at this equation.

$6 + a = b$

a Write down possible values for a and b so that the equation is correct.

b Write down different values for a and b so that the equation is correct.

Courtney's answer ✔

Courtney knows there are many values of *a* and *b* that will make the equation correct.

a $a = 1$ and $b = 7$

b $a = 4$ and $b = 10$

Courtney chooses any value for *a* and adds 6 to get the value of *b*.

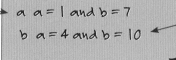

Level 3

2 Fill in the missing numbers.

$68 + \square = 100$

$20 \times \square = 100$

$300 \div \square = 100$

$5 \times \square = 100$

Key Stage 3 2004 3–5 Paper 1

17 Shape

Angles and 3-D shapes

You can use mapping programs on the Internet to see the bird's-eye view of world. This is almost the bird's-eye view of Oxford University Press where this book was made. The inner courtyard is called a quadrangle because four buildings surround the yard.

What's the point? The bird's-eye view of an object is called the plan view. Architects and engineers use plan views.

Check in

Level 3

1 Write the three times each day when the hands of a clock make a right-angle.

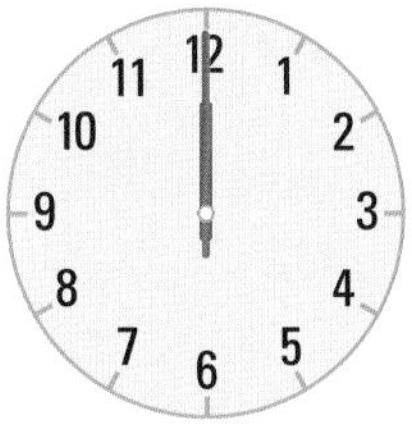

Level 4

2 Copy and complete these sentences.
a There are ____° in half a turn. **b** There are ____° in a full turn.

3 Match each of these angles with one of the diagrams. 110° 50° 90° 315°

a

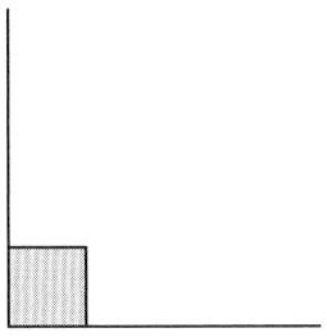

b

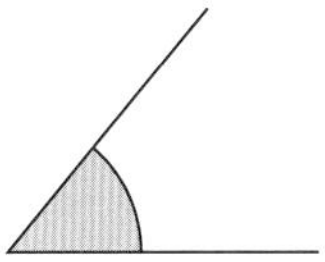

c

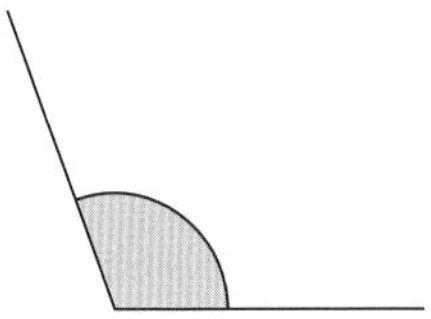

d

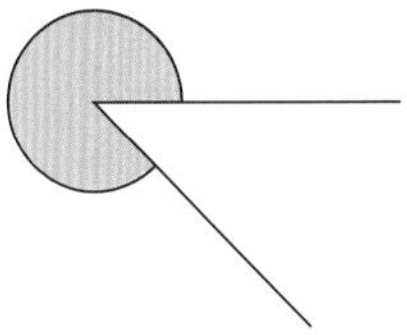

Level 5

4 Find the missing angle in each diagram.

a

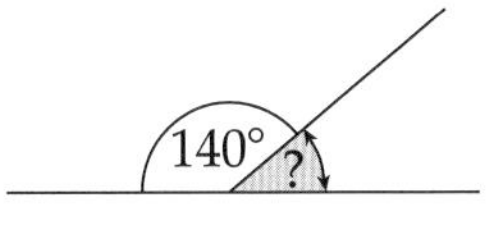

b

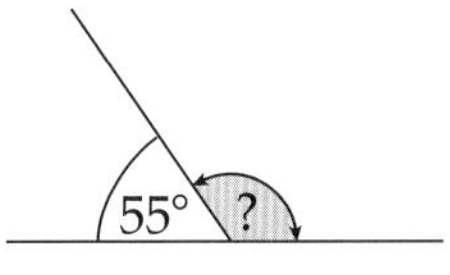

c

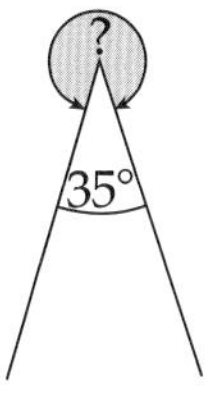

d

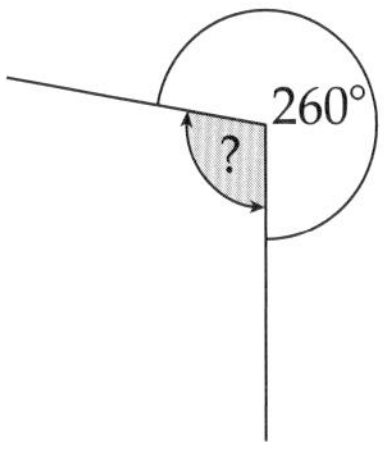

17a Calculating angles

- Calculate angles in a straight line and around a point

Keywords
Acute *Reflex*
Obtuse *Right angle*

Angle facts

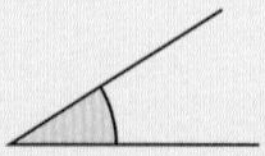

Acute angle
Less than 90°

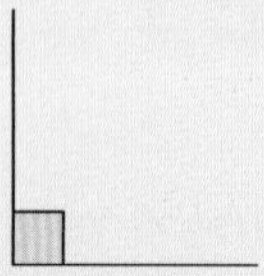

Right angle
Exactly 90°
A quarter turn

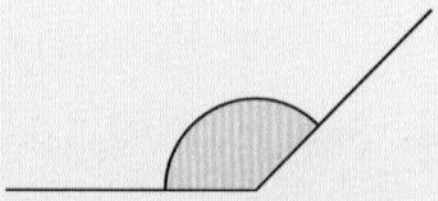

Obtuse angle
More than 90°
less than 180°

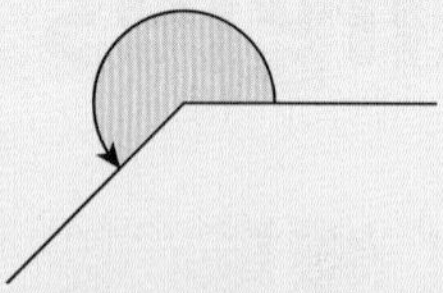

Reflex angle
More than 180°
less than 360°

Angles on a straight line.

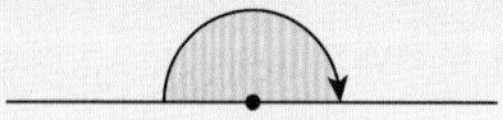

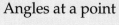

There are 180° in a straight line, or half a turn.

Angles at a point

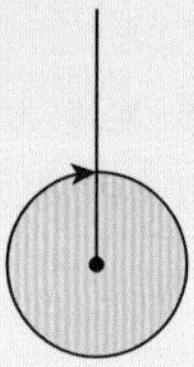

There are 360° in one full turn.

example

p. 138

p. 142

Find the missing angles.

a

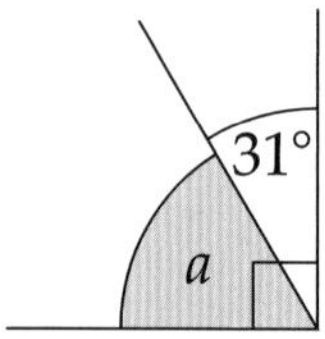

b

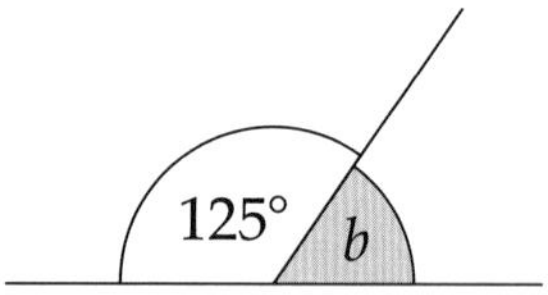

c

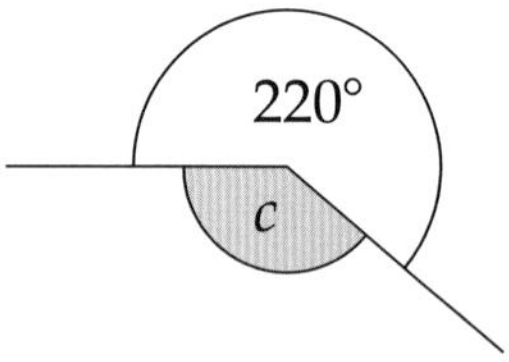

a 90° is a right angle.
The known angle is 31°.
The unknown angle is
$90° - 31° = 59°$

$a = 59°$

b 180° is a straight line.
The known angle is 125°.
The unknown angle is
$180° - 125° = 55°$

$b = 55°$

c 360° is a complete turn.
The known angle is 220°.
The unknown angle is
$360° - 220° = 140°$

$c = 140°$

Exercise 17a

1 Choose the best **estimate** for each angle.

a 50° or 80° b 160° or 110° c 90° or 70° d 155° or 120°

2 Label each angle as an acute angle, right angle or obtuse angle.

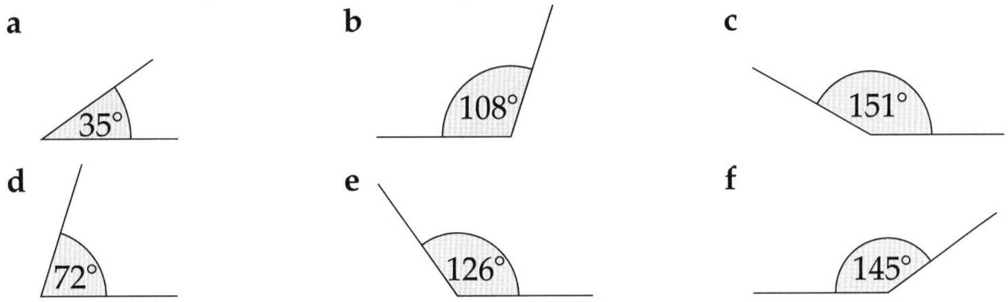

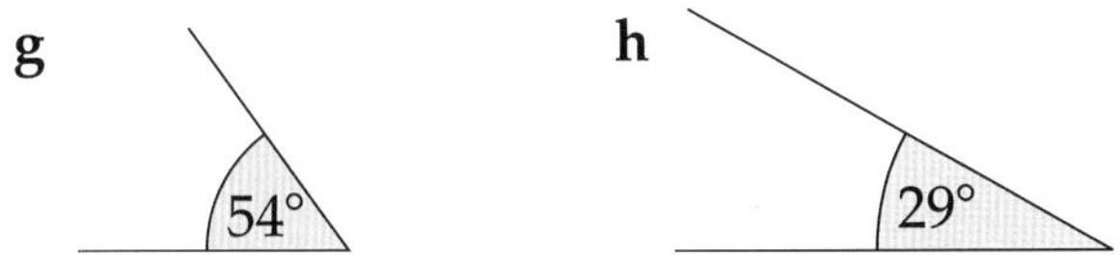

Which pairs of angles fit together to make a straight line?

3 Work out the missing angle in each diagram.

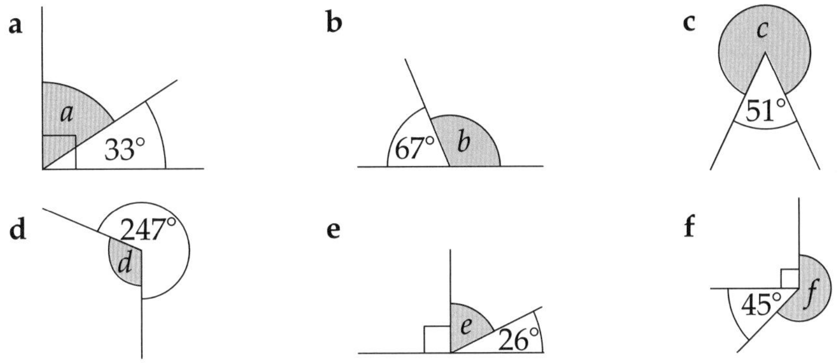

challenge

Here are some wedges of cheese. Each wedge is cut at a different angle.
The pink box has a list of angles which these wedges can combine to make.
Which two wedges are used to make each of these angles? The first is done for you.

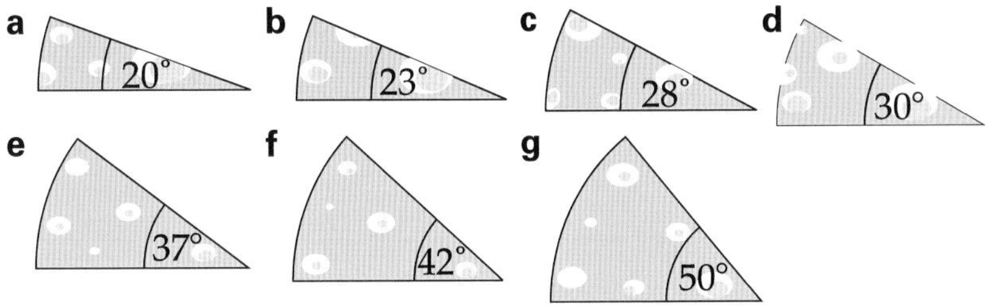

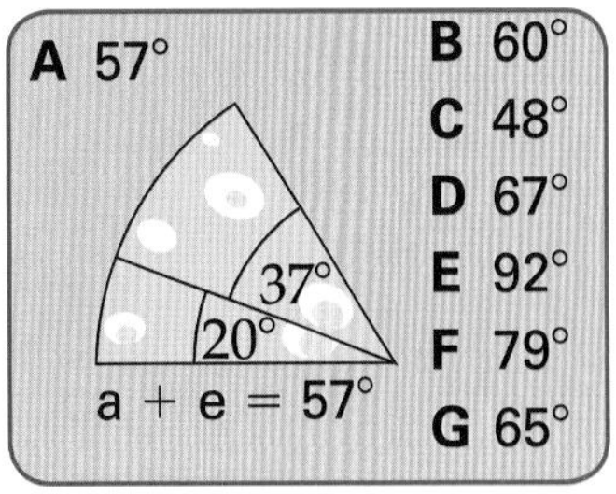

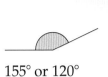

17b Angles in a triangle

- Calculate angles in a triangle

Keywords
TK

- A **triangle** is a three-sided shape with three angles.

p. 144

Isosceles

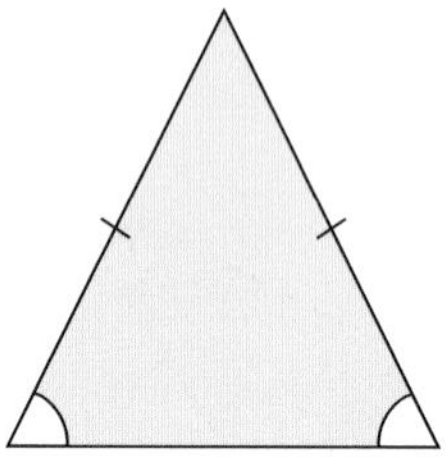

Two sides are equal.
Two angles are equal.

Right angle

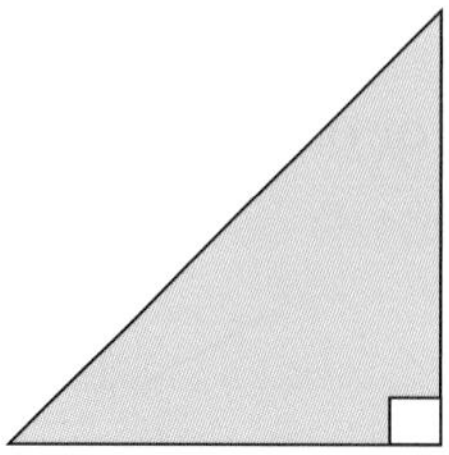

One angle is 90°.

Equilateral

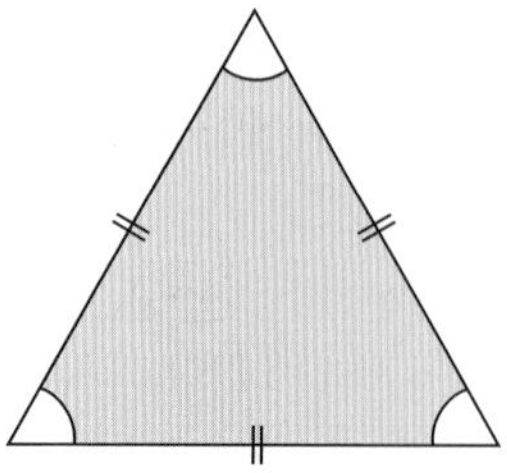

All sides are equal.
All angles are equal.

Scalene

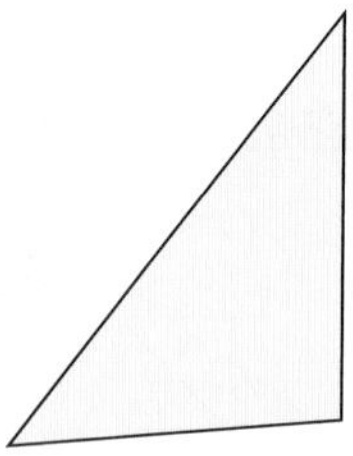

All sides are different.
All angles are different.

- The three angles in a triangle always add up to 180°.

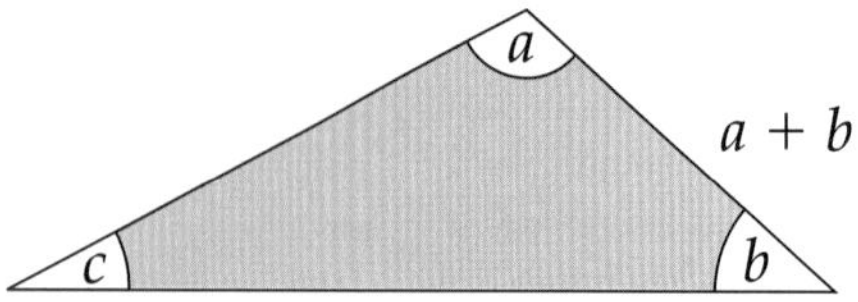

$a + b + c = 180°$

Angles in a triangle = 180° = Angle on a straight line

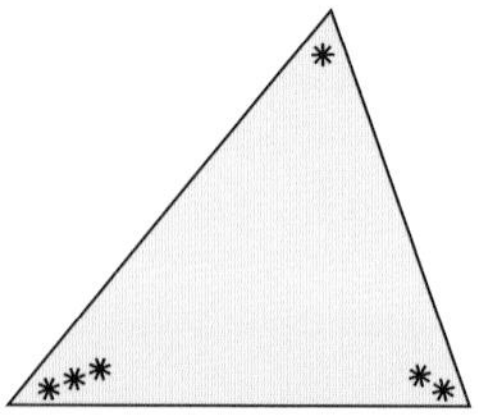

Cut a triangle from card, and mark the three angles with stars.

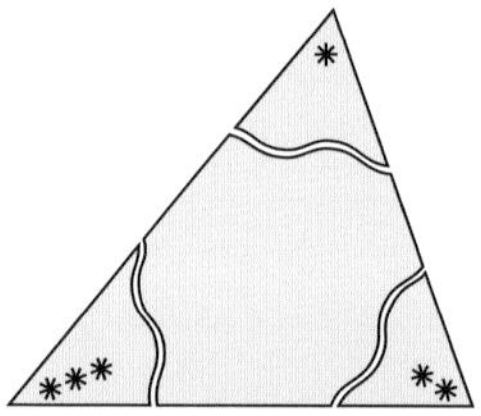

Cut the three angles from the triangle.

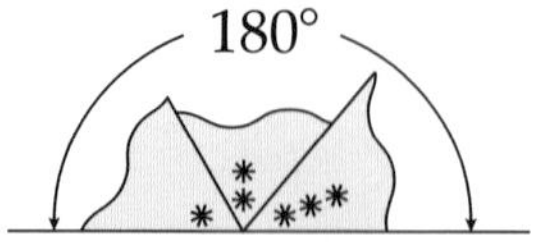

Bring the three angles together on a straight line. The angles add up to 180°, a straight line.

example

Find the missing angle.

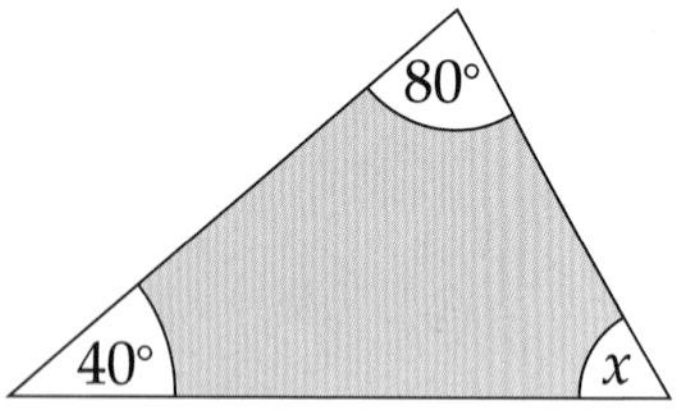

$$40° + 80° + x = 180°$$
$$120° + x = 180°$$
$$x = 180° - 120°$$
$$x = 60°$$

Exercise 17b

1 What is the missing angle in each of these triangles?

a

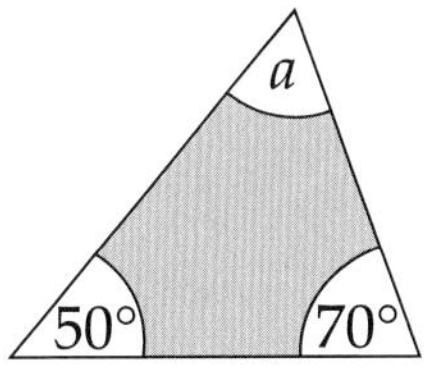

b

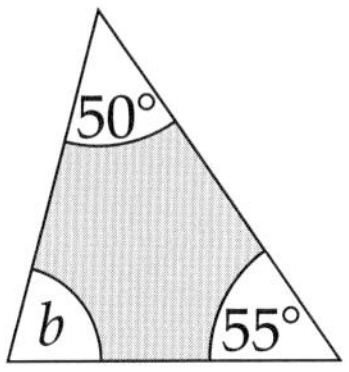

c

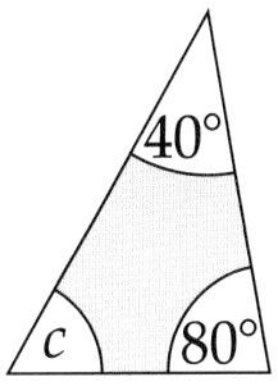

2 Find the missing angles in each triangle.

a

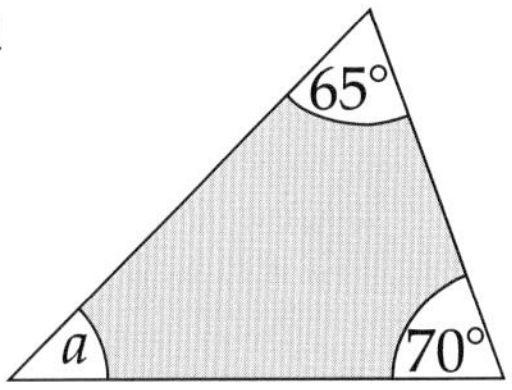

b

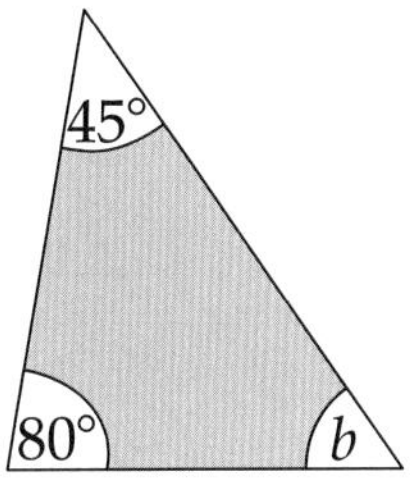

c

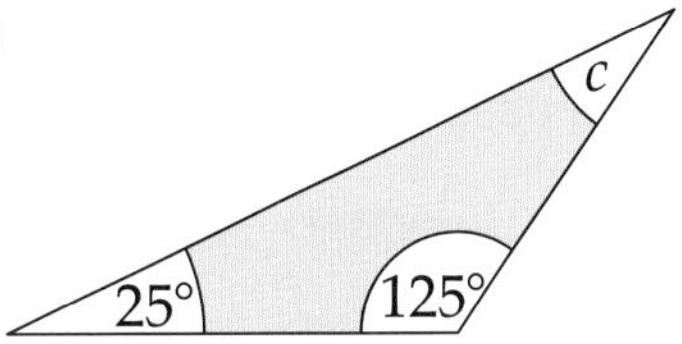

3 Use your knowledge of triangles to find these missing angles.

a

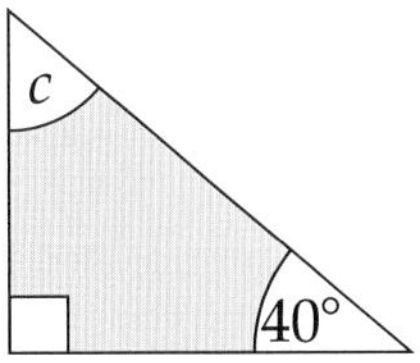

b

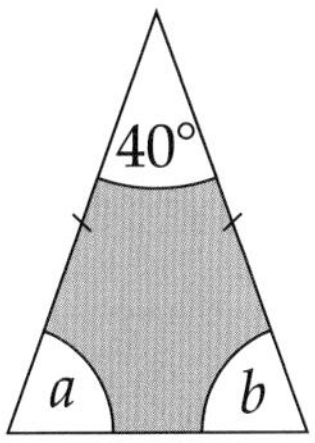

c

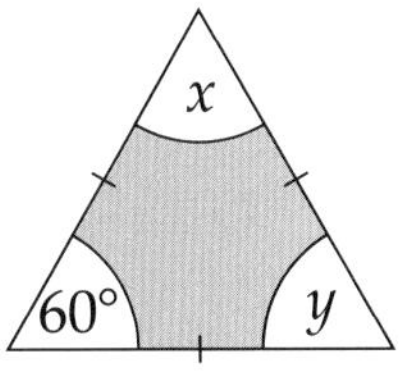

d

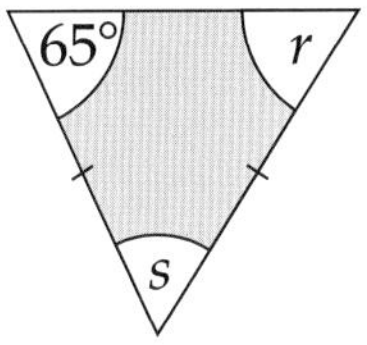

e

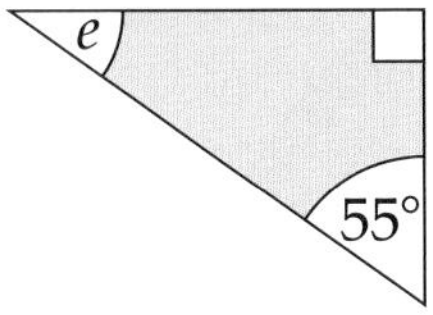

f

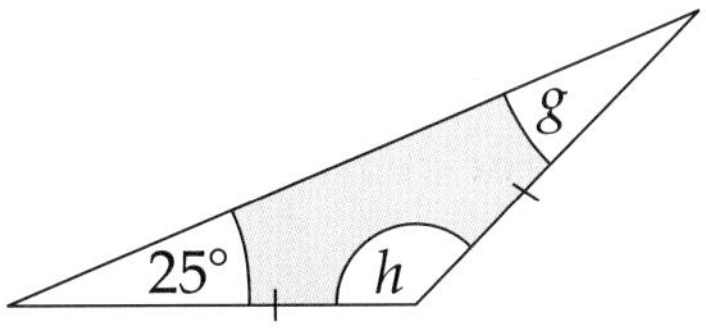

challenge

Use angle facts to find the missing angles.

a

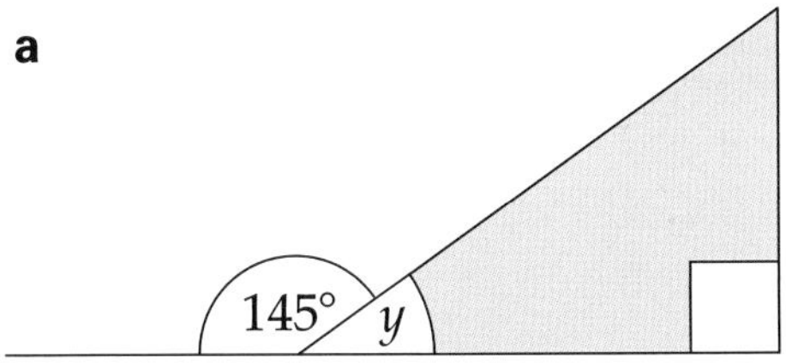

b

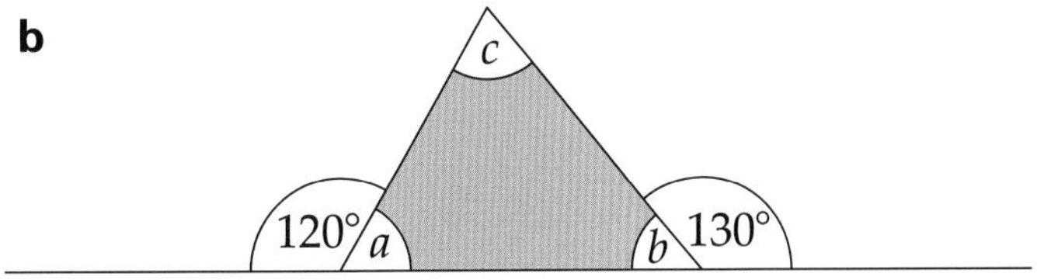

17c Measuring more angles

- Measure angles with a protractor

Keywords
Accurately
Angle
Protractor

p. 140

- A **protractor** is a tool to measure **angles**.

It has two scales

clockwise and **anticlockwise**

Make sure you read the right scale.

This angle uses the anticlockwise scale.

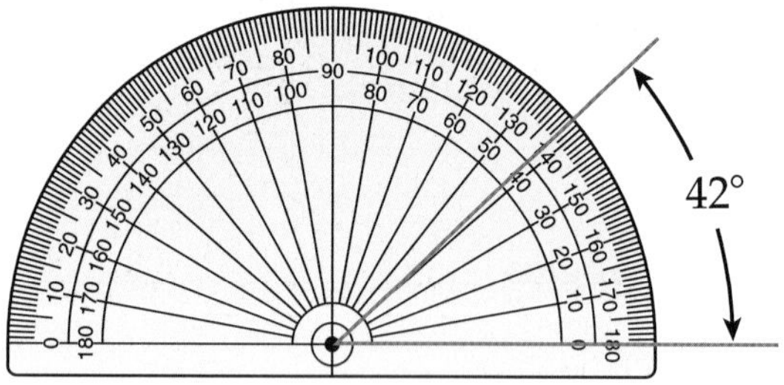

Each mark stands for 1°.

This angle is greater than 40° and less than 45°.

Count the marks to find that the angle is 42°.

Line up the angle very carefully so that you can read the scale **accurately**.

example

a Give the measurements of the angles measured on the **clockwise** scale.

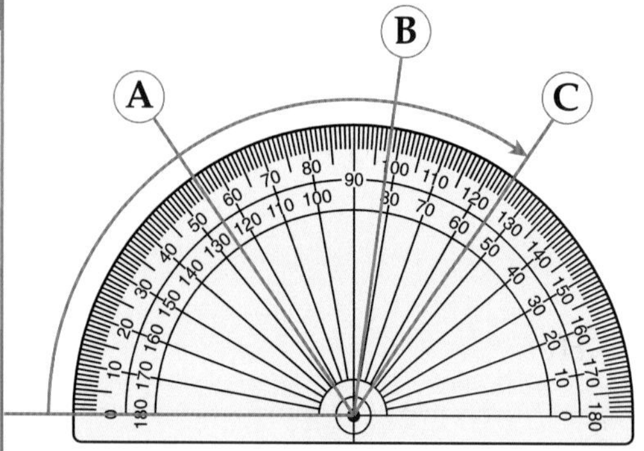

A 55° **B** 98° **C** 125°

b Give the measurements of the angles measured on the **anti-clockwise** scale.

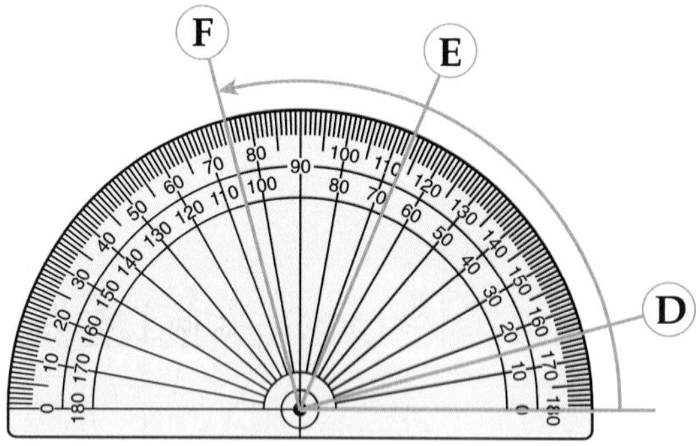

D 15° **E** 67° **F** 105°

Exercise 17c

1 Measure each angle with a protractor.

a

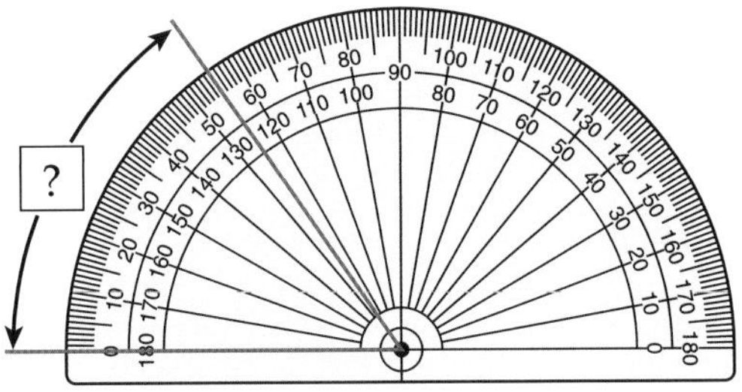

b

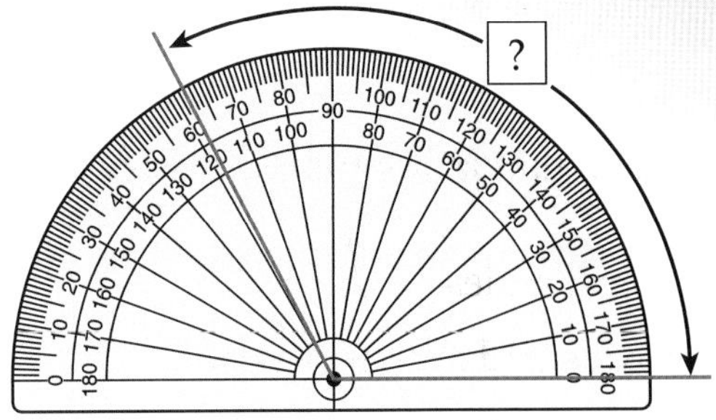

c

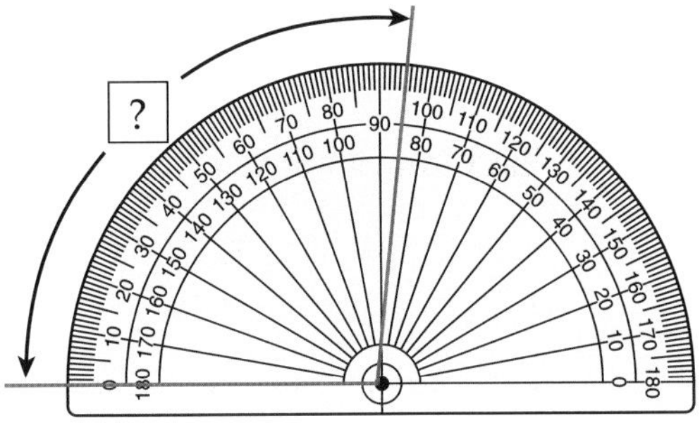

d

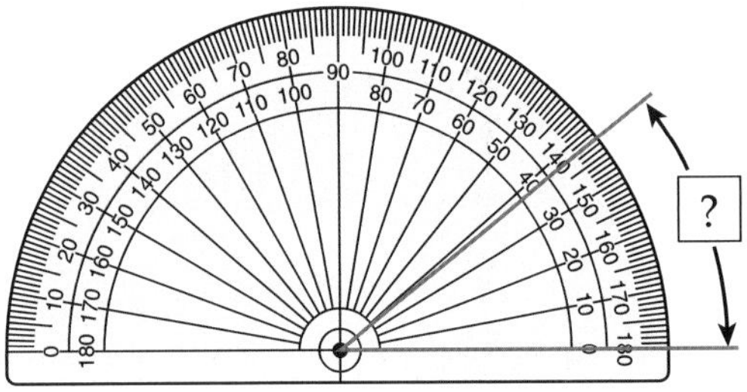

2 Give the measurements of these angles using the clockwise scale.

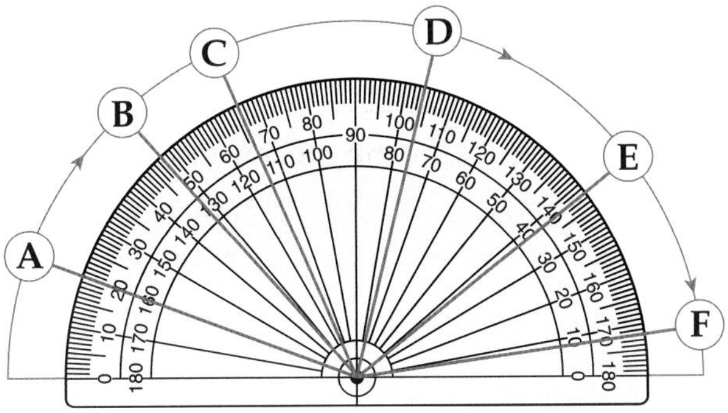

3 Give the measurements of these angles using the anticlockwise scale.

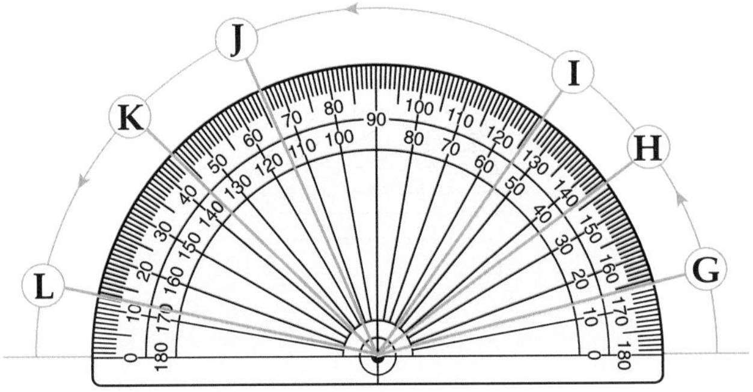

discussion

How would you measure an angle of 220°?

17c² Drawing a triangle

- Use a protractor to measure and draw acute and obtuse angles
- Construct angles to the nearest degree

Keywords
Base line *Ruler*
Construct *Triangle*
Protractor

- You can **construct** this **triangle** using a **ruler** and a **protractor**.

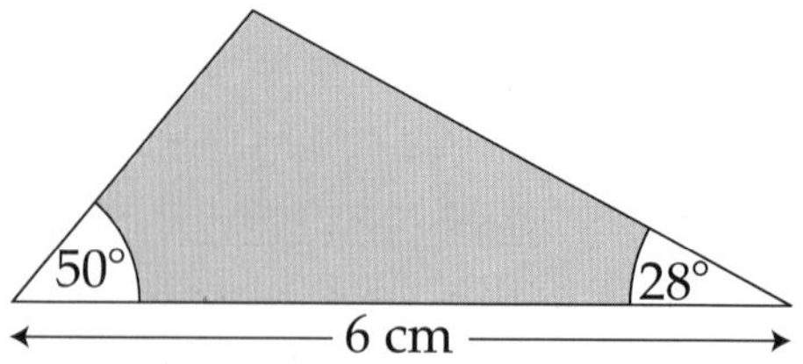

Step 1 Draw a **base line** 6 cm long. Use a ruler and a sharp pencil.

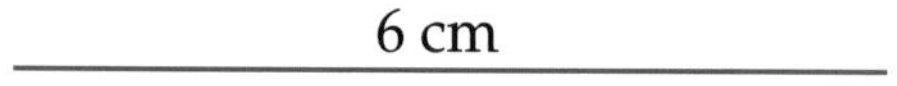

p. 140²

Step 2 Measure the first angle, 28°. Read around the scale from 0, mark 28°, and draw the angle.

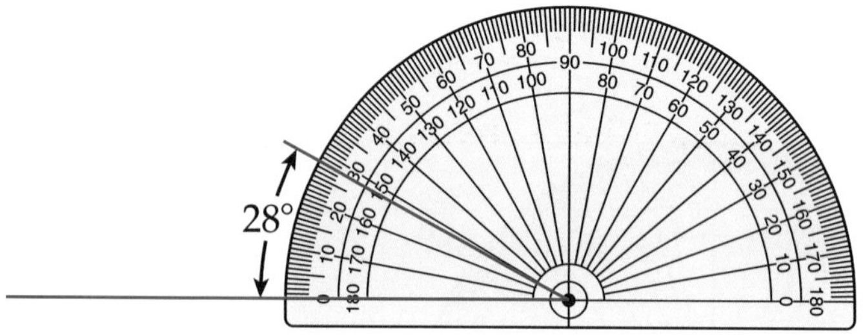

Step 3 Measure the second angle, 50°. Mark 50 and draw the angle.

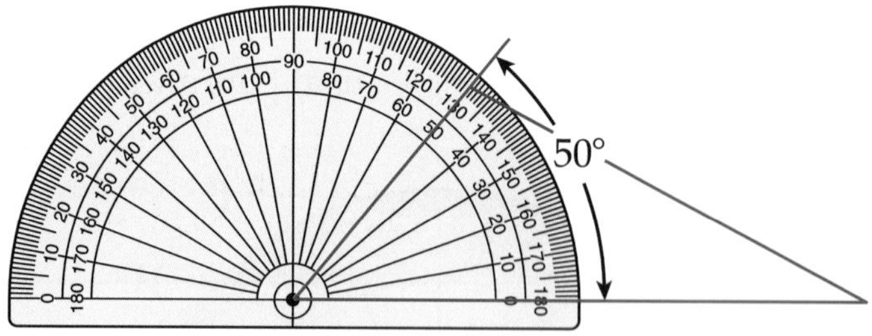

Step 4 The finished triangle.

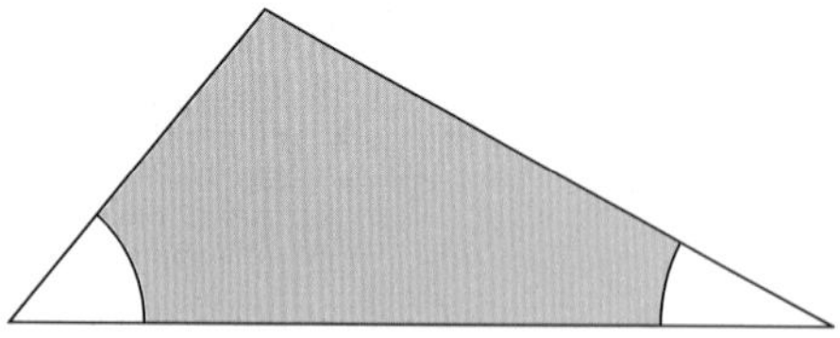

Exercise 17c^2

1 Construct these angles.

a

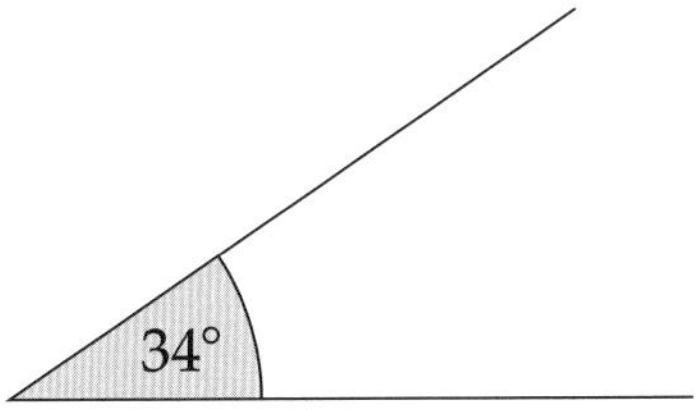

b

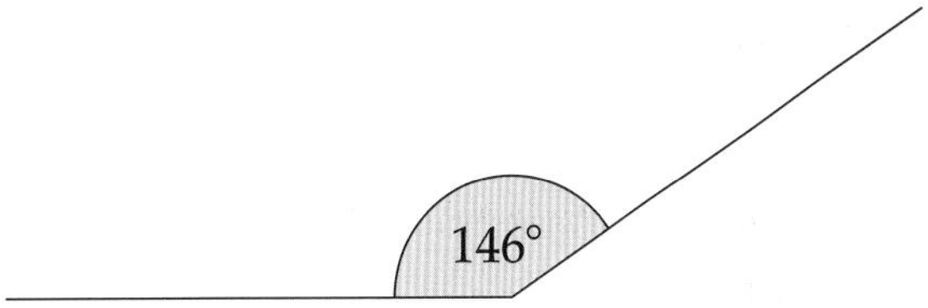

2 Construct each of these triangles accurately.
They are not drawn accurately here.

a What is the missing angle x?

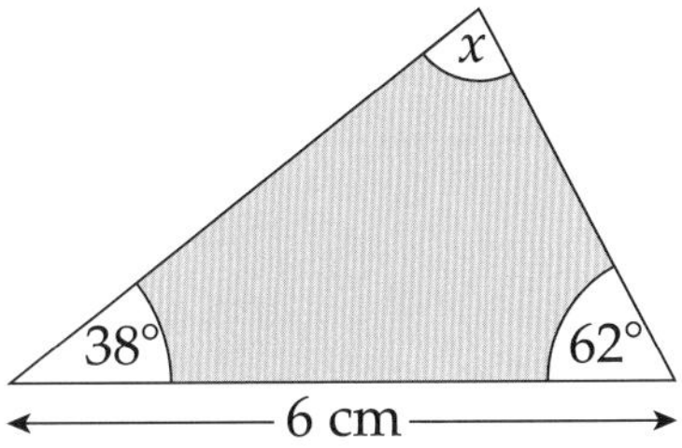

b What is the missing angle y?

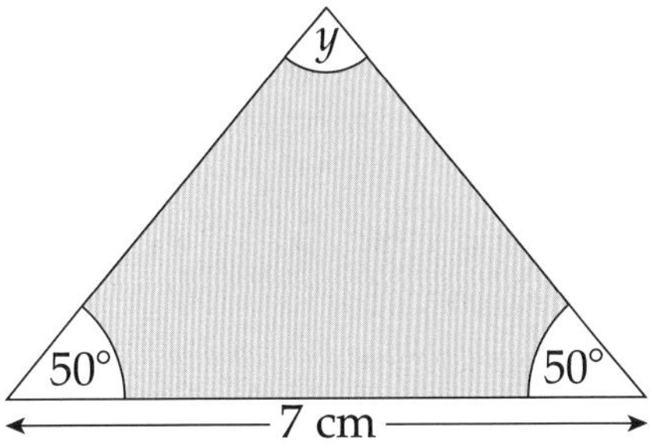

c What is the missing angle r?

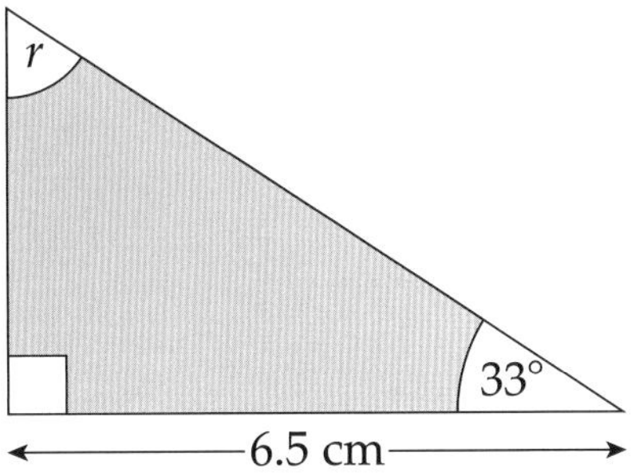

d What is the missing angle s?

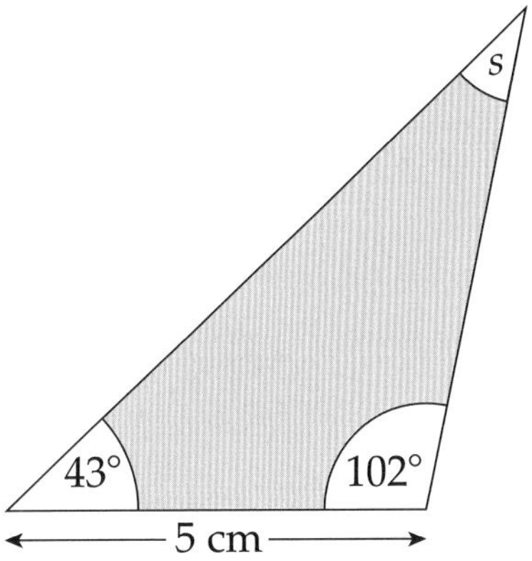

challenge

Del, Claire and Adam are standing in a triangle throwing a Frisbee.
Del throws 60° to Claire.
Claire throws 60° to Adam.
Adam throws 60° to Del.
Are they standing equal distances apart?

Nets of cubes

- Identify nets of a cube

Keywords
Cube
Net

When a 3-D shape is opened out, the flat shape is called its **net**.

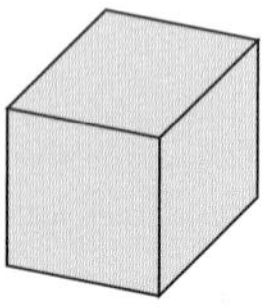

Cube

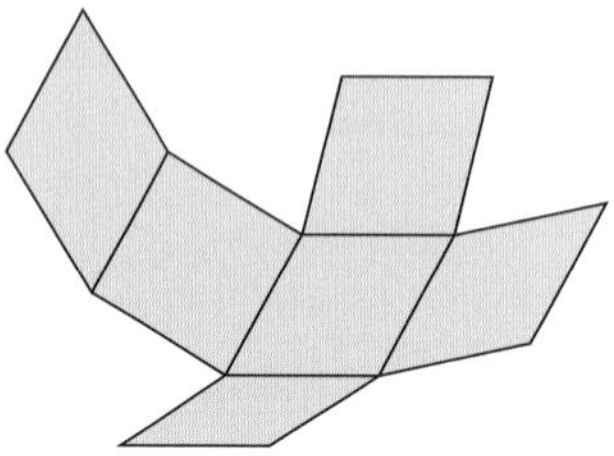

Cube unfolding

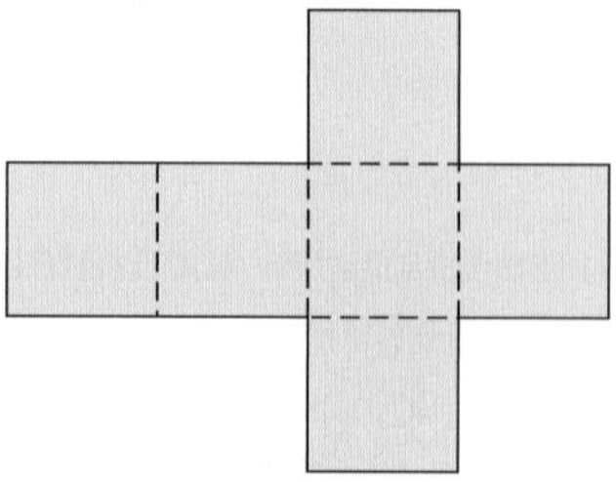

The net of the cube

example

When folded, which of the shapes will this net make?

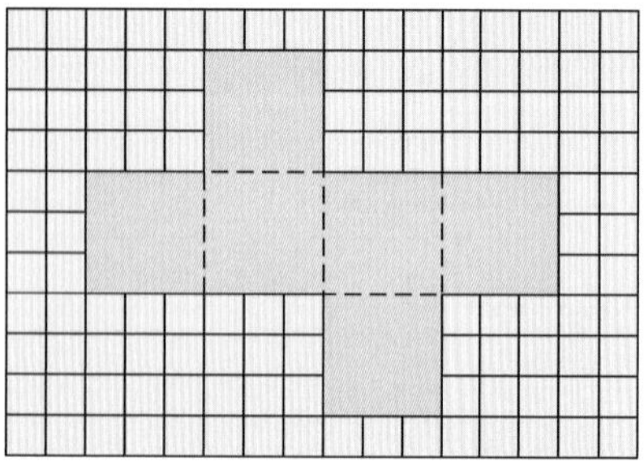

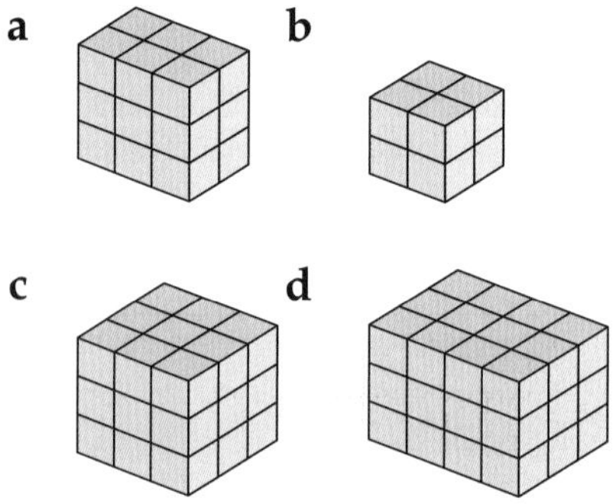

a and **d** are cuboids.
b has only four squares on its face.
c has nine squares on its face.
c matches the net.

Grace is drawing the net of a cube on squared paper.

She carefully draws the outline of the net.

She uses a dotted line to show where the net is to be folded.

She draws 'glue flaps', which will be used to stick the net together.

Finally, she will carefully cut the net out, fold it and glue it.

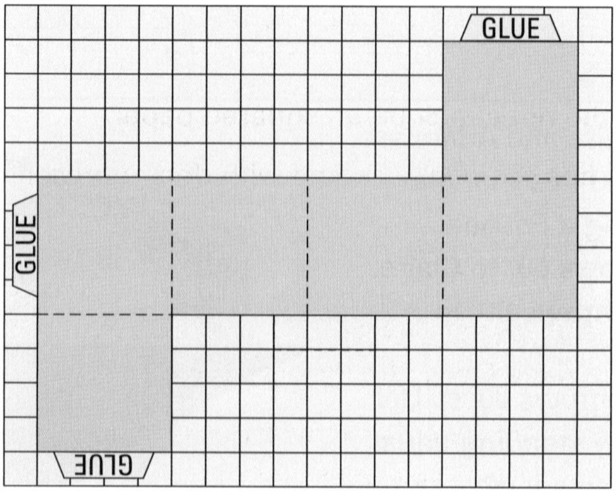

Exercise 17d

1 Two of these nets will **not** fold to make a cube. Which are they?

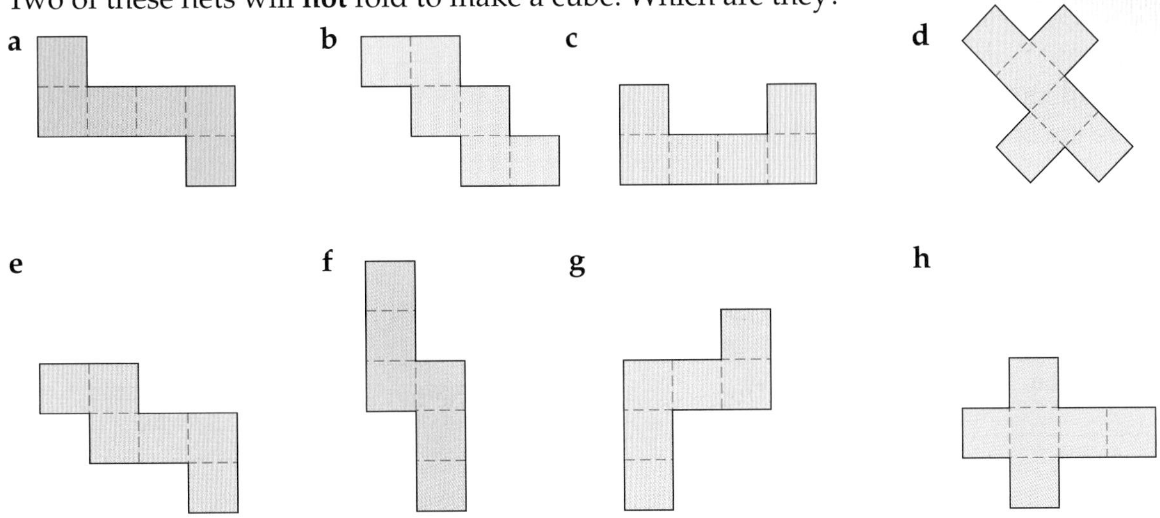

2 Copy this net of a cube onto squared paper.
Draw the 'glue flaps' and the fold-lines.
Cut out, fold and glue your cube.

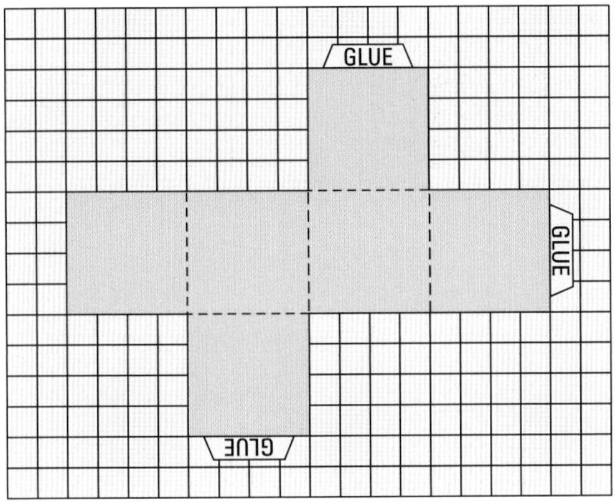

challenge

a Draw the net of a cube on squared paper.

A dice has six faces, marked with dots representing numbers.

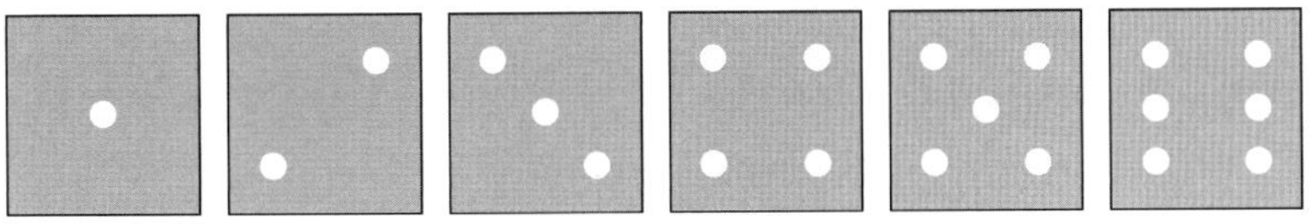

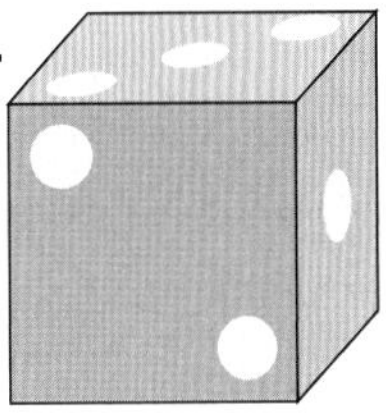

The **opposite** faces of a dice always add up to 7.

b Draw dots on the net of your cube, so that when folded, opposite faces always add up to 7.

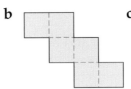

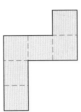

17e Nets of 3-D shapes

- Identify nets of 3-D shapes

Keywords

3-D, Cube, Cuboid, Net, Prism, Pyramid, Solid, Vertices

p. 146

A **solid** shape has three dimensions: length, width and height. Here are some common **3-D** shapes.

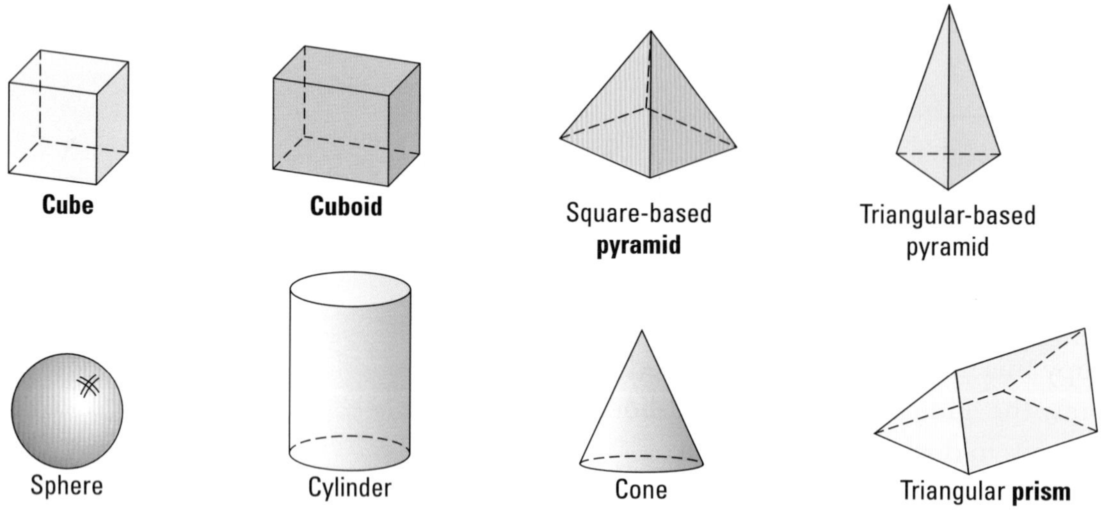

This cuboid has:

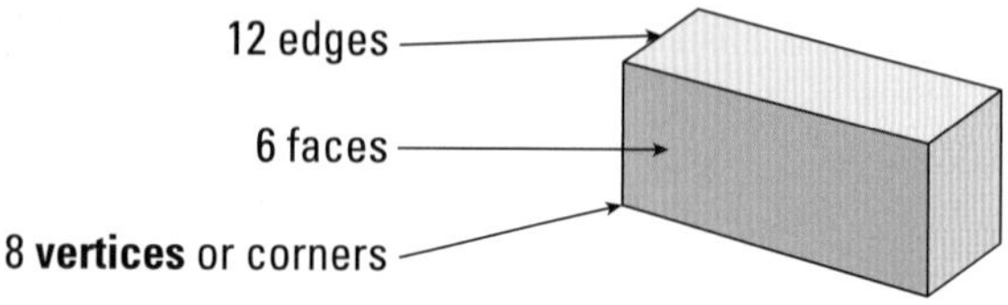

- A **net** is the 'plan' of a solid shape. When cut out and folded it becomes a 3-D shape.

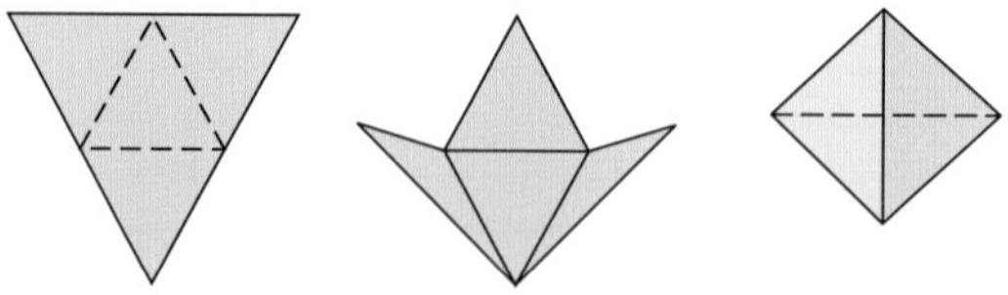

example

Which solid shape will this net make when cut-out and folded?

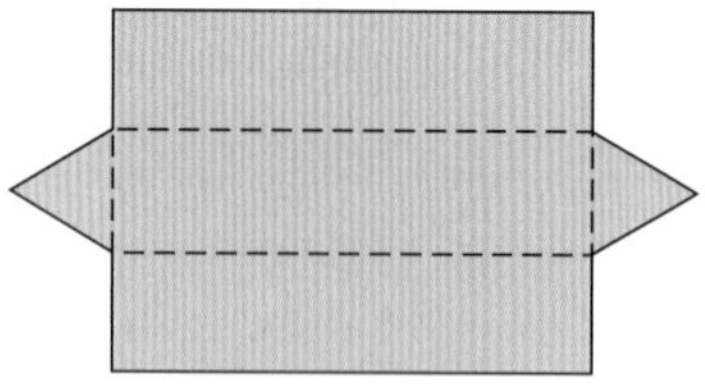

a A cuboid
b A triangular based pyramid
c A triangular prism

c A triangular prism

Exercise 17e

1 Match each solid shape (**a–f**) with its net (1–6).

a **b** **c** **d** **e** **f**

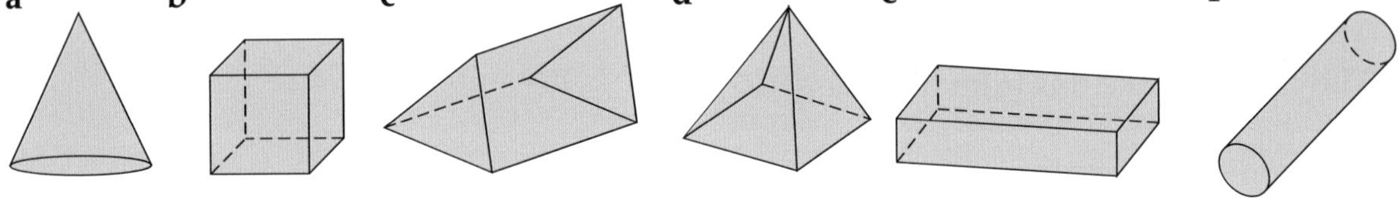

1 2 3

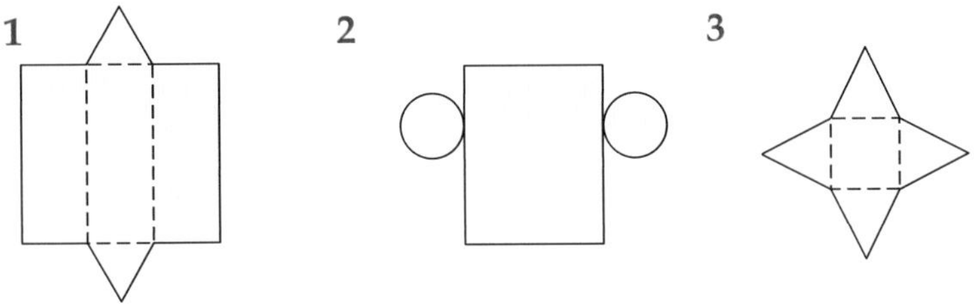

4 5 6

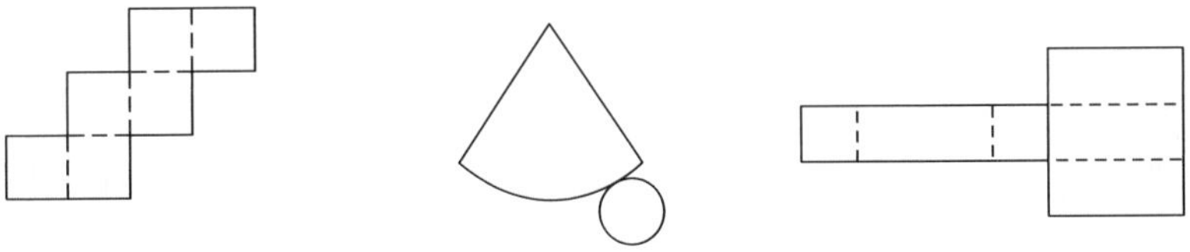

2 Draw the net for this cube on squared paper.

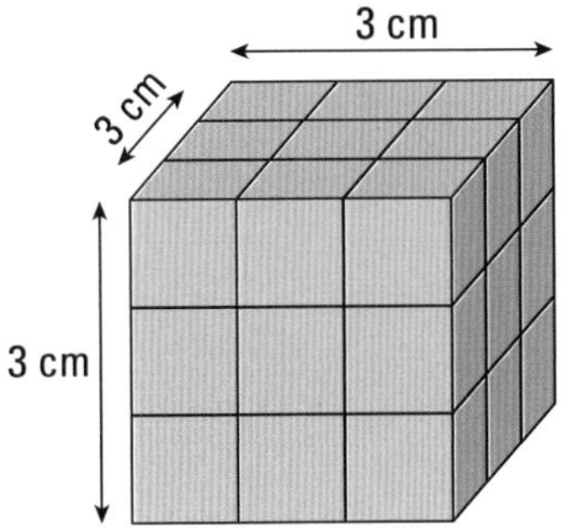

Did you know?

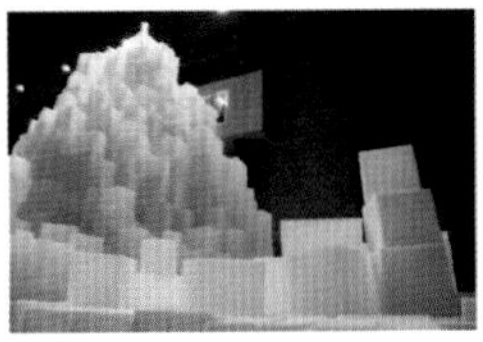

In 2005, the Tate Modern showed an exhibition called *Cube* by Rachel Whiteread.

challenge

Write how many faces, edges and vertices each of these shapes has.

a

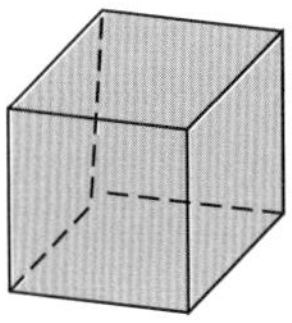

Cube

Faces =?

Edges =?

Vertices =?

b

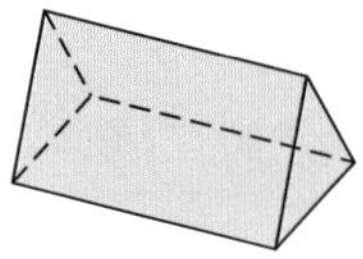

Triangular prism

Faces =?

Edges =?

Vertices =?

c

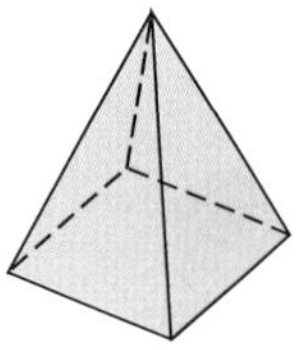

Square based pyramid

Faces =?

Edges =?

Vertices =?

17f 2-D Representations of 3-D shapes

• Visualise 3-D shapes from 2-D drawings

Keywords
2-D/3-D

This car is a 3-D object.
The car looks like this from the side.

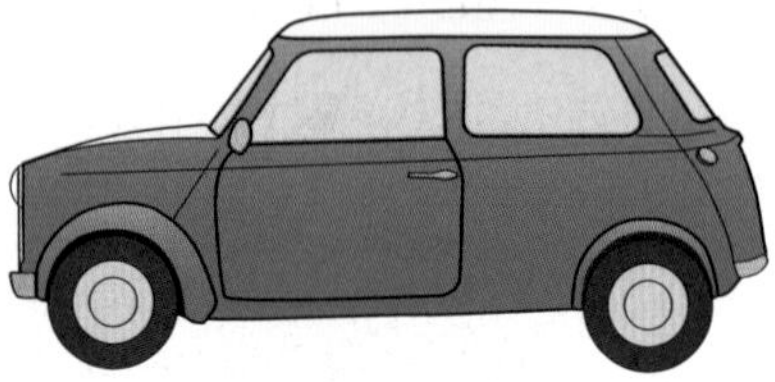

The car looks like this from the top.

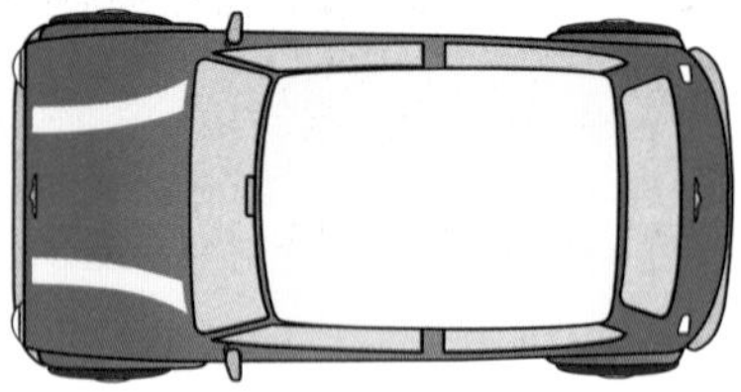

The car looks like this from the front.

example

Draw this can of beans from
a the top **b** the side

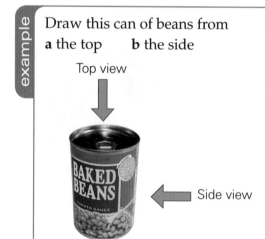

Top view

Side view

3-D view of the can

A can of beans is a cylinder.

The top view of the can is a circle.

The side view of the can is a rectangle.

Exercise 17f

1 **a** Draw this cube from the top.
b Draw this cube from the side.

3-D view of a Rubik's cube

2 **a** Draw this square based pyramid from the top.
b Draw this square based pyramid from the side.

3-D view of pyramid at Giza

3 **a** Draw this cone from the top.
b Draw this cone from the side.

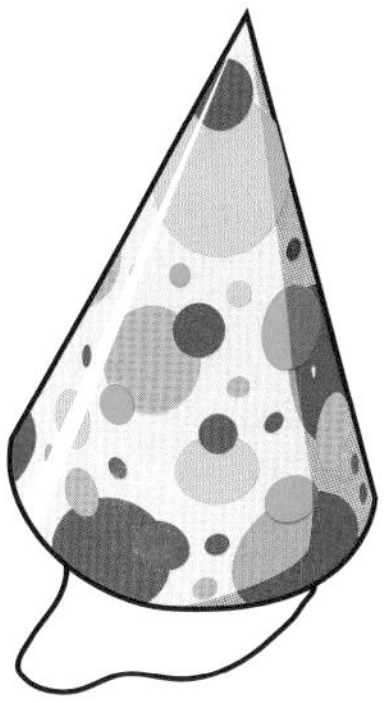

3-D view of a party hat

challenge

Draw the view from the top and side for each of these shapes.

a

b

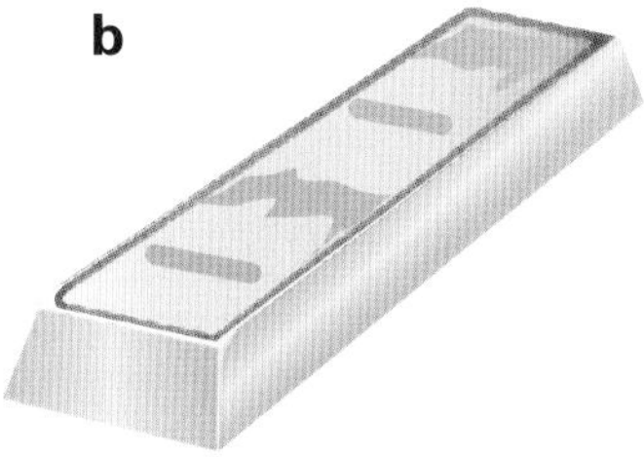

c

17 Consolidation

17a

1 Find the missing angles.

a

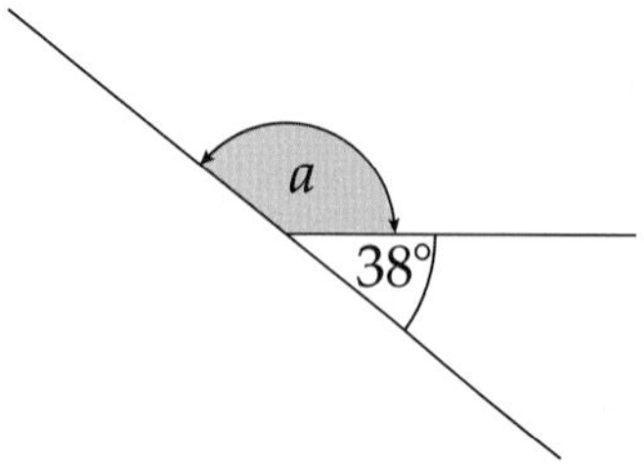

b

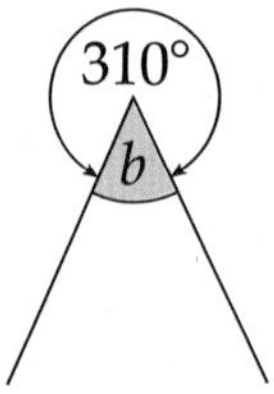

c

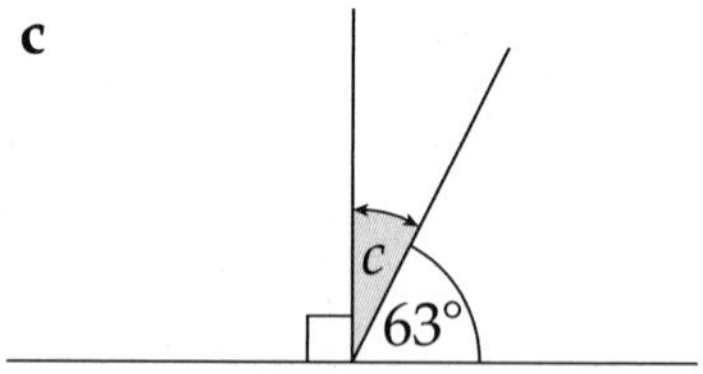

17b

2 Find the missing angles in these triangles.

a

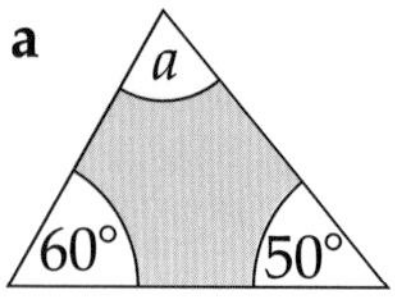

b

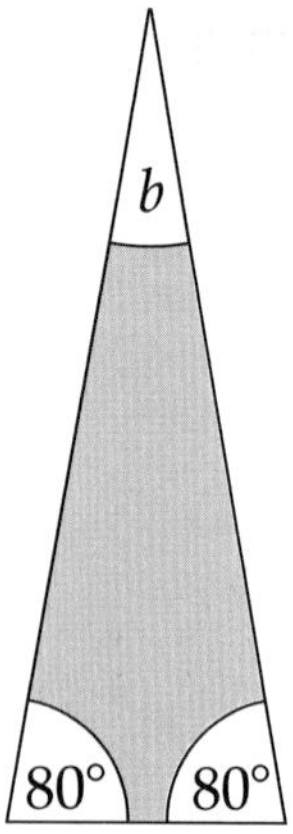

c

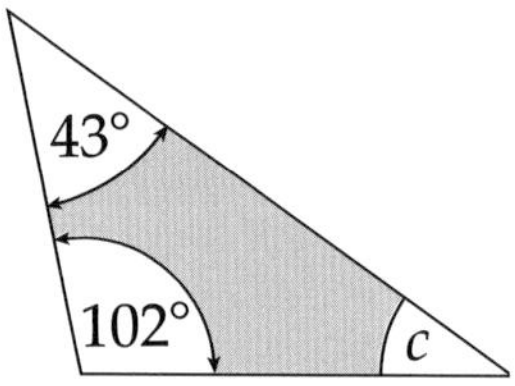

d

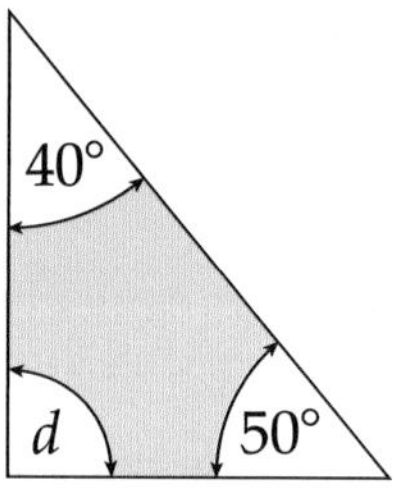

$17c^2$

3 Draw these triangles carefully.

a

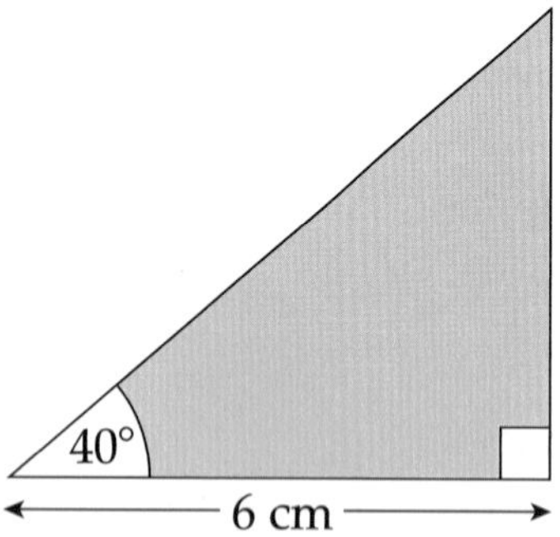

b

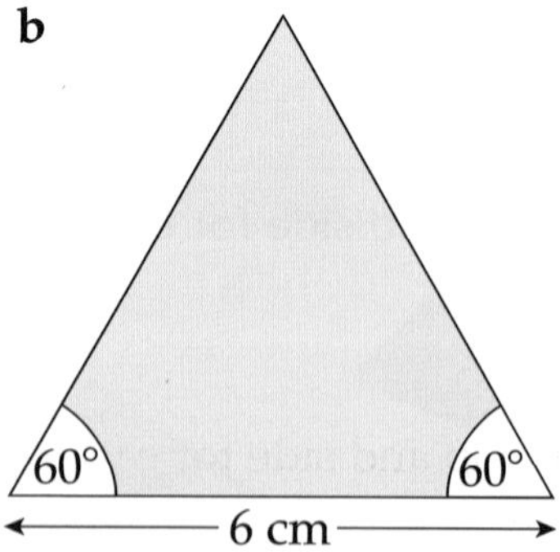

c

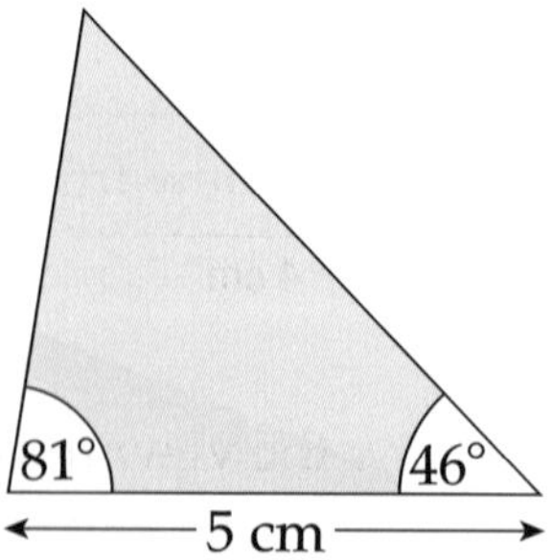

5 Which two nets will fold to make a cube?

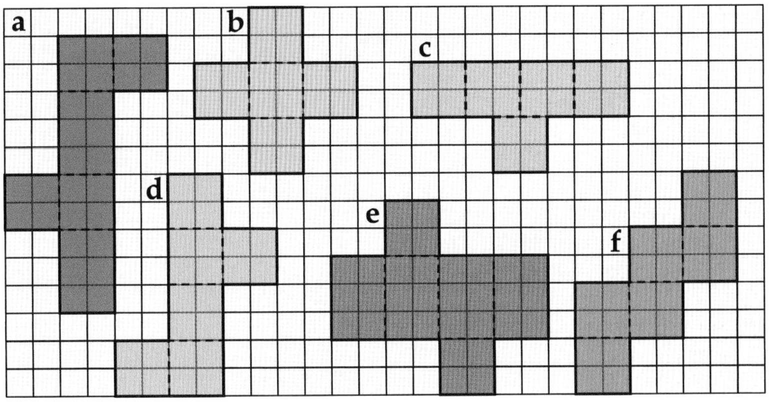

6 Draw a net of each of these solids. Draw your nets accurately.

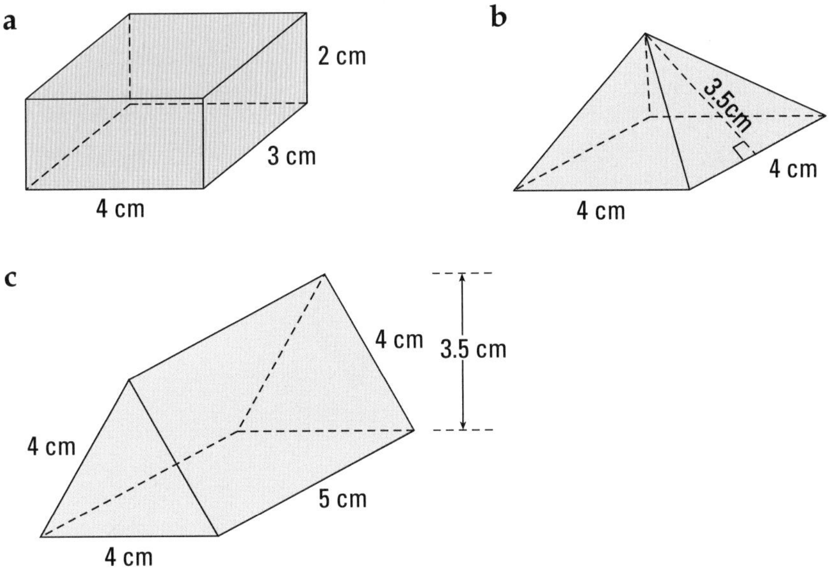

7 Draw the view from the top and side for each of these shapes.

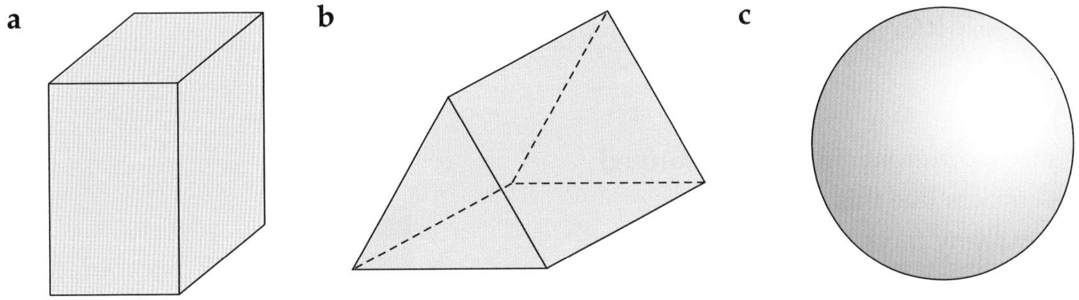

17 Summary

Key Indicators

- Sort 3-D shapes **Level 3**

Level 3

1 **a** Write the name of each shape.

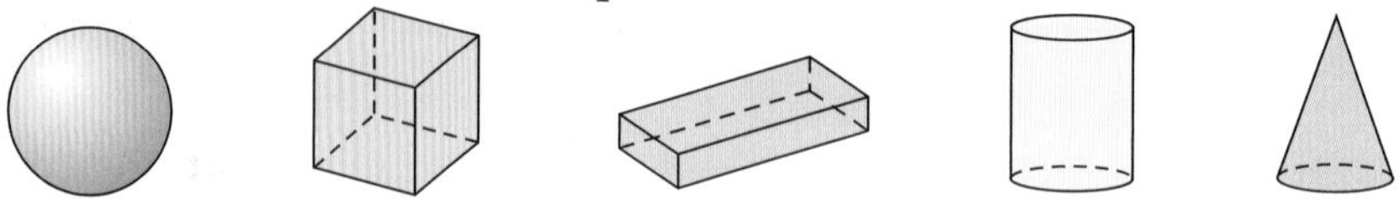

A B C D E

Level 4

b This is the net of one of the shapes.
Which one?

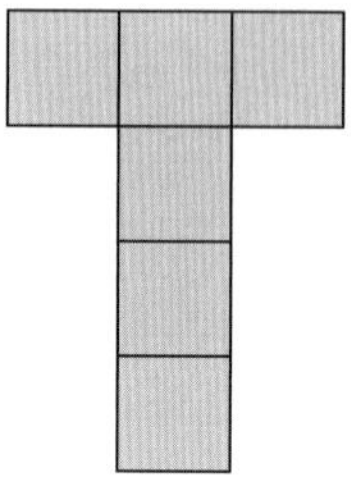

John's answer ✔

a A sphere
B cube
C cuboid
D cylinder
E cone
b The net folds to make a cube (Shape B).

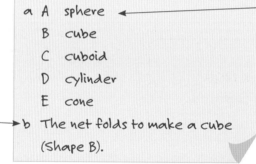

John remembers a ball is called a sphere.

John realises the net is made from 6 squares. The cube is the only shape with 6 square faces.

Level 3

2 **a** I slice a cube in half like this.
How many faces does each piece have?

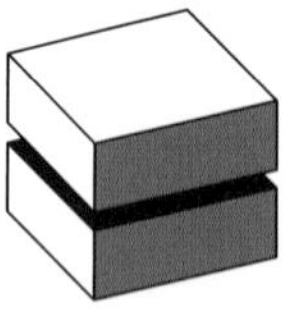

b Then I slice another cube in half like this.
How many faces does each piece have?

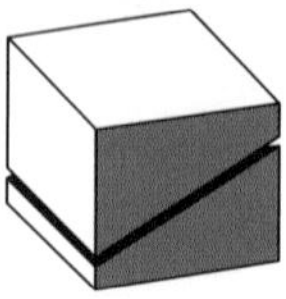

c I slice a different cube in half through its corners like this.
How many faces does each piece have?

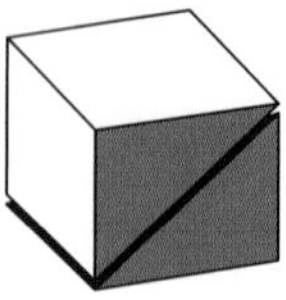

Key Stage 3 2003 3–5 paper 2

Check in and Summary answers

1

Check in

1 a 4, 5, 6, 7, 8 b 10, 11, 12, 13, 14

2 a = 2, b = 6, c = 13, d = 19, e = 25

3 Level 0

Summary

2 a 348 b 843 c 384

2

Check in

1 a 20, 22, 24, 26, 28

b 11, 13, 15, 17, 19

2 a blue circle as on page

b blue diamond as on page

c blue Y as on page

3 a 4 b 15 c 7 d 12

e 3 f 21 g 6 h 24

Summary

2 1, -2, -5

3

Check in

1 a 12:15 b 4:45 c 10:10

2 a anticlockwise b clockwise

c anticlockwise

Summary

2 a 18 cm² b any 1 × 18, 2 × 9 or 3 × 6 rectangle

4

Check in

1 a 4 b 6 c 10

2 a 10 b 2 c 100 d 5

3 a 14 b 20 c 5 d 10

e 2 f 7 g 27 h 5

Summary

2 a £0.20 or 20p b 6

5

Check in

1 a

Shapes with 3 sides	Shapes with 4 sides
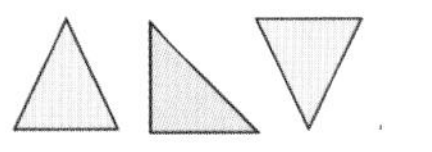	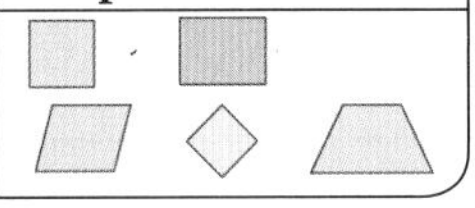

b

Yellow	Pink	Blue
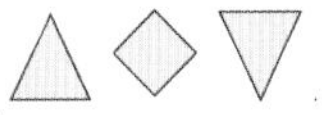		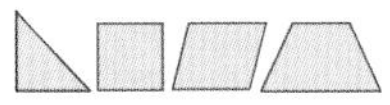

2 a 20 b 29 c 47 d 66

Summary

2 a 3 b Supermarket C

c Supermarket A

6

Check in

1 a 17 b 24 c 0

2 a 2 b 7 c 5 d 4

e 3 f 6 g 8 h 1

3 a 39 b 24 c 5 d 3

Summary

2 a 36, 5, 396

7

Check in

1 a × b − c ÷ d +

e × f − g ÷ h × i ÷

2 a 12 b 20 c 26 d 50 e 100

3 a 4 b 6 c 10 d 14 e 40

4 a

Length	weight	time
metre millimetre kilometre centimetre	gram tonne kilogram	second day year hour century week

Summary

2 a 60

b 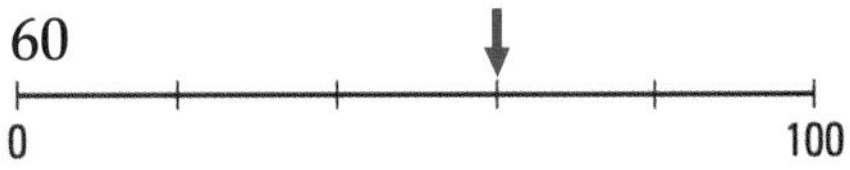

8

Check in

1 a iii b ii

2 a $\frac{1}{4}$ b 20 mins

3 a 0.1 b 0.4 c 0.75 d 0.98

Summary

2 a Write any 3 even numbers and 1 odd number

9

Check in

1 a 120 b 30 c 145 d 90
e 160 f 230 g 175 h 180

2 a cylinder b cube
c cuboid d sphere

3 a 25° b 120° c 90° d 100°

Summary

2 a Angle *d* b It's a right

10

Check in

1 a 10, 18, 20, 26 b 3, 15, 27, 35
c 3, 15, 18, 27, 35 d 10, 15, 20, 35

2 a 12 b 20 c 36 d 40

3 **Input** 4, 8 **Output** 10, 13

Summary

2 a Perhaps 100 or 104
b Any two chosen from 10, 20, 25, 50

11

Check in

1 a $\frac{1}{2}$ b $\frac{1}{4}$ c $\frac{2}{3}$

2 $3\frac{1}{2} = \frac{7}{2}$ $3\frac{2}{3} = \frac{11}{3}$ $1\frac{1}{2} = \frac{3}{2}$
$1\frac{3}{4} = \frac{7}{4}$ $2\frac{2}{5} = \frac{12}{5}$

3 a 50 b 25 c 10 d 3 e 80

Summary

2 a 55% b 5

12

Check in

1 a $x + 4$

2 a $6y$ b $y - 3$

3 a 12 b 3 c 2 d 24 e 4

Summary

2 How many marbles? 10×12
Each bag of marbles weighs? 12×7
Weight of all 10 bags? $10 \times 12 \times 7$

13

Check in

1 a rotate clockwise 90°
b rotate anticlockwise 90°
c rotate either way 180°

2 North

3 a (3, 1) (1, 1) (1, 4)
b (5, 1) (1, 1) (1, 3) (5, 3)
c (4, 0) (4, 4) (2, 5) (2, 1)

Summary

2 West 2, South 1

14

Check in

1 a 2, 3, 4, 5, 6, 9, 12
b 8, 11, 14, 15, 18
c 89, 90, 93, 94, 96, 102

2 a 9 b 3 c 12

3 a 15 b Daily Telegraph c 50

Summary

2 a Claire
b Claire left and Tom joined

15

Check in

1 a 49 b 16 c $56 + 23 = 79$
d $160 + 52 = 212$ e $615 + 342 = 957$

2 $1000 + 50 + 20 = 1070$

3 a $\frac{1}{2}$ b $\frac{1}{4}$ c $\frac{1}{10}$

Summary

2 315

16

Check in

1 a 9 b 6 c 50 d $1\frac{1}{7}$

2 a 3 b 7 c 4 d 6

3 a $p + 5$ b $k - 100$ cm c £$4x$

Summary

2 32, 5, 3, 20

17

Check in

1 Many possible answers like 3 p.m.

2 a 180 b 360

3 a 90° b 50° c 110° d 315°

4 a 40° b 125° c 325° d 100°

Summary

2 a 6 b 6 c 5

Index